Medieval Civilization

Medieval Civilization
400–1500

Jacques Le Goff

Translated by
Julia Barrow

BLACKWELL
Oxford UK & Cambridge USA

English translation Copyright © Basil Blackwell Ltd, 1988
First published in France as
La civilisation de l'Occident médiéval
Copyright © 1964 B. Arthaud, Paris

First published in English 1988
First published in the USA 1989
Reprinted 1989
First published in paperback 1990
Reprinted 1991, 1992

Blackwell Publishers
108 Cowley Road, Oxford, OX4 1JF, UK

Three Cambridge Center
Cambridge, Massachusetts 02142, USA

British Library Cataloguing in Publication Data
A CIP catalogue record for this book is
available from the British Library.

Library of Congress Cataloging in Publication Data
Le Goff, Jacques, 1924–
[Civilisation de l'Occident médiéval. English]
Medieval civilization 400–1500 / Jacques Le Goff:
translated by Julia Barrow.
p.   cm.
Translation of: La civilisation de l'Occident médiéval.
ISBN 0–631–15512–0
0–631–17566–0   (Pbk.)
1. Civilization, Medieval.   2. Europe-Civilization.
3. Middle Ages.   I Title.
CB351.L413   1988
940.1–dc 19

Typeset in 10 on 12 point Plantin
by Dobbie Typesetting Limited, Plymouth, Devon
Printed in Great Britain by
T J Press (Padstow) Ltd

This book is printed on acid-free paper.

Contents

Translator's note

I am deeply grateful to Bob Moore for commenting on my translation of chapters 1 and 2, to my parents for commenting on chapter 3, Gervase Rosser for commenting on chapter 6, Richard Holt for commenting on chapter 7, Chris Wickham for commenting on chapters 7 and 8, and Chris Dyer for advice.

Julia Barrow

Preface

I should like first of all to say how happy I am to see my book *La civilisation de l'Occident médiéval* made available to an English-speaking readership. I have made some additions to the bibliography in the latest French edition, which came out in 1984, and I should also like to add a few words of introduction.

Out of the most significant research developments of the last years, aside from those concerning the contribution of archaeology and, in a general sense, the area of material civilization, including nutrition, the development of the history of *mentalités* and the use of new types of evidence, such as gestures and images, I should like to concentrate on certain fields which extend the ideas which dominated my book. Probably the most important is the interest in the problems of the family and of kinship. Alliance systems, the role of women, and problems of consanguinity have become central themes for the understanding of feudal society. In this perspective feudo-vassalic relations are increasingly posited in terms of artificial kinship. Similarly, the formation of the lordship, a basic unit, like the family, in feudal society, has yielded ground to fertile hypotheses concerning the process of organization of society in microcosms dominated by lords. The notion of *incastellamento*, the creation of concentrated village settlement in the context of castle-building, proposed by Pierre Toubert for Latium, has been given a general application by Robert Fossier under the term *encellulement*. The problems of the growing emergence of the individual in the twelfth and thirteenth centuries, begun by the works of Walter Ullmann and Colin Morris, have been deepened by the researches of, notably, Aaron Gurevitch, Caroline Bynum and myself. The rebirth of political history, which is rather marginal in my book, has stressed the symbolic and anthropological aspects of power and has benefitted from new sociological and anthropological ideas about the forms of power. The important position taken by the body as a new object of attention for historians has been all the more decisive in the field of the middle ages for the fact that this society of warriors and peasants, which saw the birth in courtly circles of modern love, at least in a literary form, lived under the pressure of Christian ideas of contempt for the body – although the prospect of the resurrection of the body at the Last Judgement forced people to look for a salvation also by means of the body.

It seems to me that the development of ideas about the middle ages and the deepening of researches and reflections have reinforced two of the fundamental standpoints of this book. On the one hand, the middle ages, a period of violence, of harsh living conditions, dominated by the natural world, was also a period of exceptional creativity and laid the foundations of the development of western civilization. On the other hand, even more than others, perhaps, the society of the medieval west can only be understood if one shows how its material, social and political realities were penetrated by symbolism and the imaginary world. Only the study of how people represented themselves alongside the study of the way in which they thought and felt can allow us to understand this world which we lost not so very long ago, and which still permeates our minds and our imaginations.

Jacques Le Goff

Plates 1–16 appear between pages 172 and 173.

Plates 17–34 appear between pages 300 and 301.

General maps

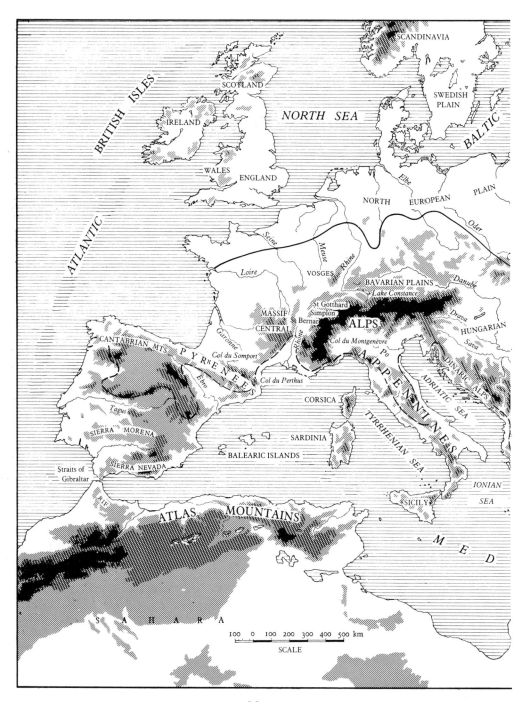

Map 1

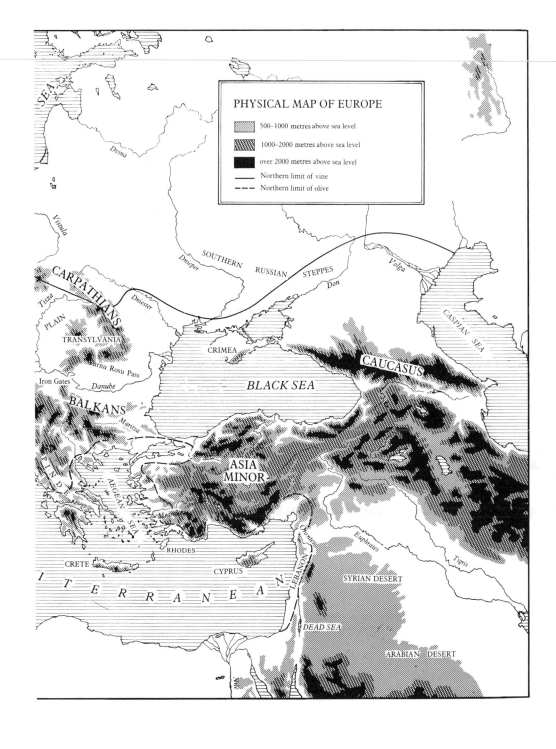

PHYSICAL MAP OF EUROPE

500–1000 metres above sea level

1000–2000 metres above sea level

over 2000 metres above sea level

Northern limit of vine

Northern limit of olive

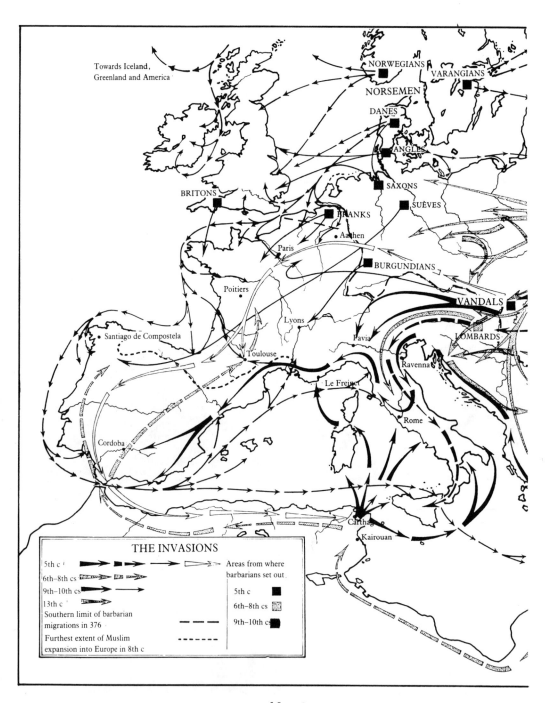

Towards Iceland,
Greenland and America

NORWEGIANS

VARANGIANS

NORSEMEN

DANES

ANGLES

SAXONS

BRITONS

SUÈVES

FRANKS

Aachen

Paris

BURGUNDIANS

Poitiers

VANDALS

Santiago de Compostela

Lyons

LOMBARDS

Toulouse

Pavia

Ravenna

Le Freinet

Rome

Cordoba

Carthage

Kairouan

THE INVASIONS

5th c

Areas from where
barbarians set out

6th–8th cs

9th–10th cs

5th c

13th c

6th–8th cs

Southern limit of barbarian
migrations in 376

9th–10th cs

Furthest extent of Muslim
expansion into Europe in 8th c

Map 2

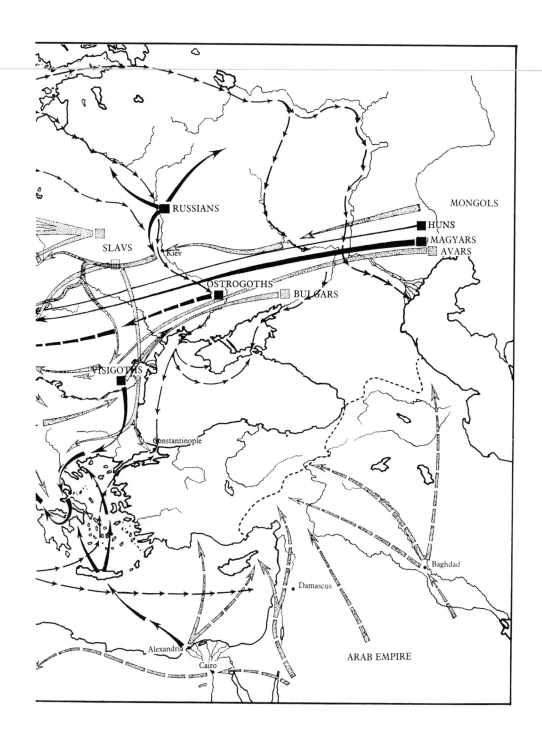

MONGOLS

RUSSIANS

HUNS

MAGYARS

SLAVS

AVARS

Kiev

OSTROGOTHS

BULGARS

VISIGOTHS

Constantinople

Baghdad

Damascus

ARAB EMPIRE

Alexandria

Cairo

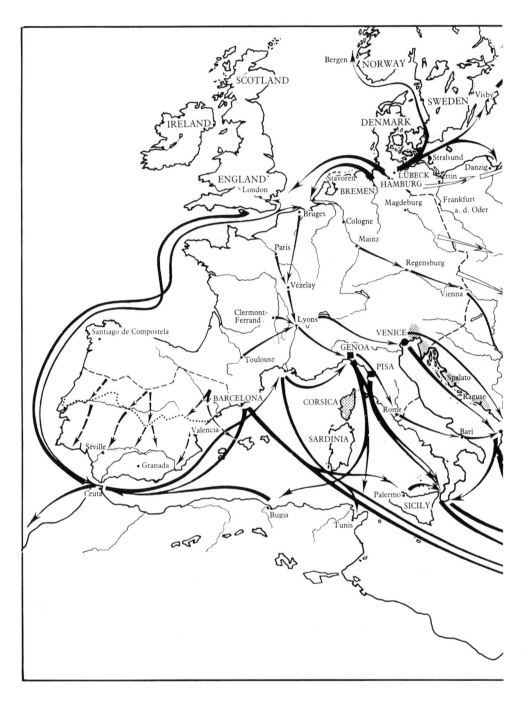

Map 3

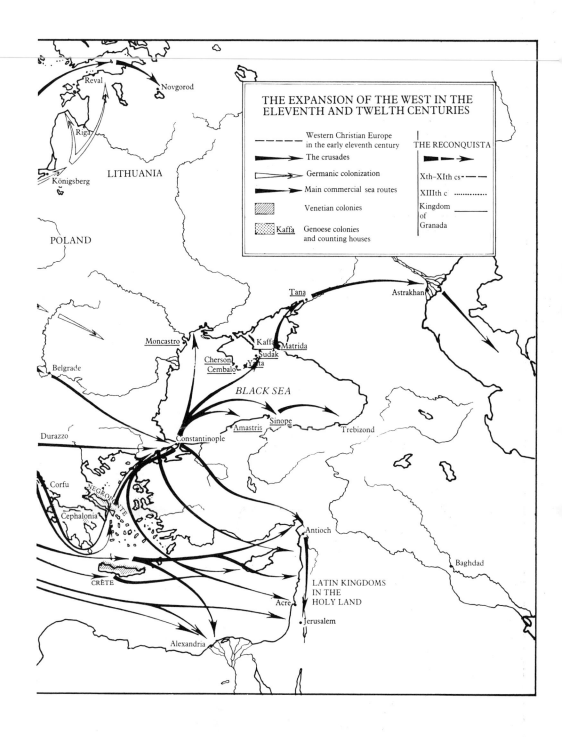

THE EXPANSION OF THE WEST IN THE
ELEVENTH AND TWELTH CENTURIES

- - - - - — Western Christian Europe
in the early eleventh century

▬▬▶ The crusades

▷ Germanic colonization

▬▶ Main commercial sea routes

▨ Venetian colonies

▒ Kaffa Genoese colonies
and counting houses

THE RECONQUISTA

Xth–XIth cs - -

XIIIth c ....

Kingdom _____
of
Granada

Reval
Novgorod
Riga
Königsberg
LITHUANIA
POLAND
Tana
Astrakhan
Moncastro
Kaffa Matrida
Cherson Sudak
Cembalo Yalta
BLACK SEA
Belgrade
Durazzo
Amastris Sinope
Trebizond
Constantinople
Corfu
NEGROPONTE
Cephalonia
Antioch
Baghdad
CRETE
LATIN KINGDOMS
IN THE
Acre HOLY LAND
Jerusalem
Alexandria

ECCLESIASTICAL
ORGANIZATION IN
THE MEDIEVAL WEST

✠ Papal capital
✝ Archbishopric
◉ Site of church council
▲ Place of pilgrimage
● Mother house of religious order
⬤ Centre of monastic reform

0   100   200   300   400   500 km

NORTH SEA

Armagh

Dublin
1040

Cashel
400

York

Hamburg
831–834

Bremen

Canterbury
597

ATLANTIC OCEAN

Brogne

Cologne c. 800

Rouen   Prémontré
Rheims   Mainz
                 Trier   782
          Gorze   c. 800

Sens   Clairvaux   Hirsau

Fontevrault Tours   Citeaux Dijon
                              Besançon

Grandmont   Cluny

            Lyons 1250
            Vienne 1274 Tarentaise
Bordeaux   1311 Gde Chartreuse Milan
                          Fruttuaria
                    Embrun   Genoa
Santiago de   Toulouse Avignon
Compostela   Auch 879   Arles   Pisa 1092
1120   Aix
                   Narbonne
Braga 1104

Alcantara
            Toledo 1088   Tarragona 1091
                                     Sassari
Evora   Calatrava
                                     Oristano

                                     Cagliari

Seville 1248

Map 4

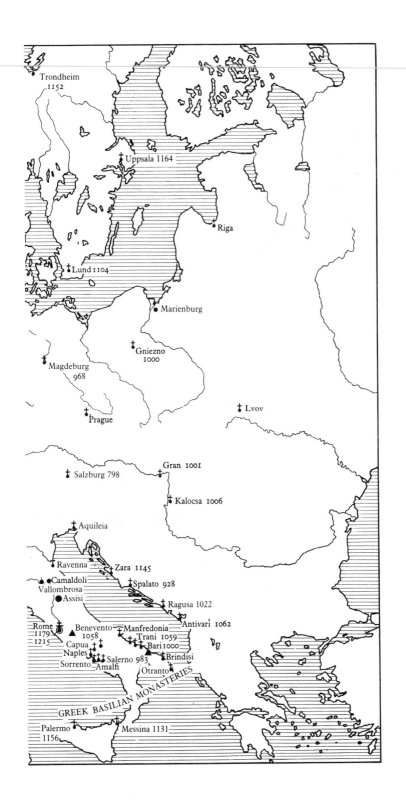

Trondheim
1152

Uppsala 1164

Riga

Lund 1104

Marienburg

Gniezno
1000

Magdeburg
968

Prague

Lvov

Gran 1001

Salzburg 798

Kalocsa 1006

Aquileia

Ravenna

Zara 1145

Camaldoli
Vallombrosa

Spalato 928

Assisi

Ragusa 1022

Rome
1179
1215

Benevento
1058

Manfredonia

Antivari 1062

Trani 1059

Capua

Bari 1000

Naples

Salerno 983

Brindisi

Sorrento

Amalfi

Otranto

GREEK BASILIAN MONASTERIES

Palermo
1156

Messina 1131

NORTH SEA

ATLANTIC
OCEAN

Bergen

Stockholm

Visby

Schonen

Polangen

HERRINGS

Königsberg

WOOL

Bristol

London

Southampton

Emden

Bremen

Lübeck

Stralsund

Danzig

Hamburg

Stettin

Thorn

Minden

Marienburg

CORN

Frankfurt
a.d. Oder

Bruges

Ghent

Cologne

Magdeburg

Breslau

Ypres

Douai

Amiens

Arras

Naumburg

Freiberg

Paris

Lagny

Provins

Troyes

Bar

Cracow

SALT

Oléron

Rochelle

S'.-Bernard

S' Gothard

M' Cenis

Milan

Venice

Montpellier

Genoa

Marseilles

Lucca

Barcelona

Pisa

Florence

Siena

Rome

WOOL

Barletta

Naples

Bari

Seville

Valencia

Palermo

SILK

Bugia

Tunis

Saleh

MEDITERRANEAN

Map 5

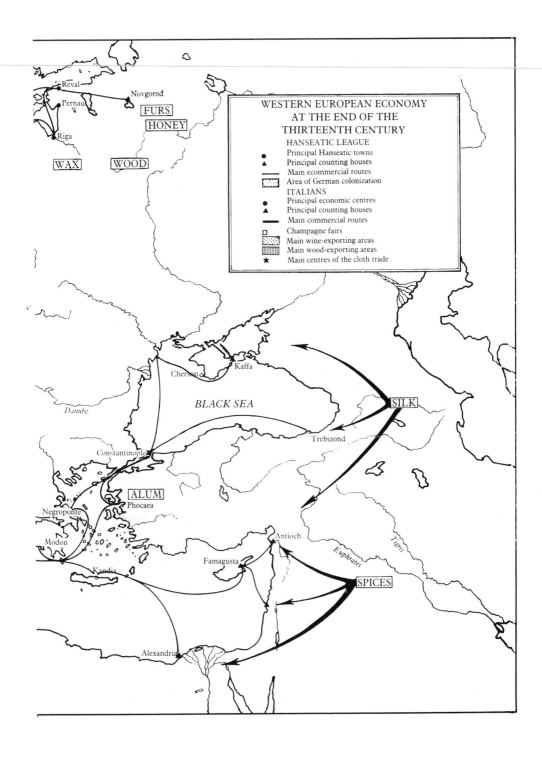

WESTERN EUROPEAN ECONOMY
AT THE END OF THE
THIRTEENTH CENTURY

HANSEATIC LEAGUE
● Principal Hanseatic towns
▲ Principal counting houses
── Main ecommercial routes
▨ Area of German colonization
ITALIANS
● Principal economic centres
▲ Principal counting houses
── Main commercial routes
▢ Champagne fairs
▨ Main wine-exporting areas
▥ Main wood-exporting areas
★ Main centres of the cloth trade

FURS
HONEY
WAX
WOOD

Reval
Novgorod
Pernau
Riga

Danube
BLACK SEA
Cherson
Kaffa
Constantinople
Trebizond
SILK
ALUM
Phocaea
Negroponte
Modon
Kandia
Famagusta
Antioch
Euphrates
Tigris
SPICES
Alexandria

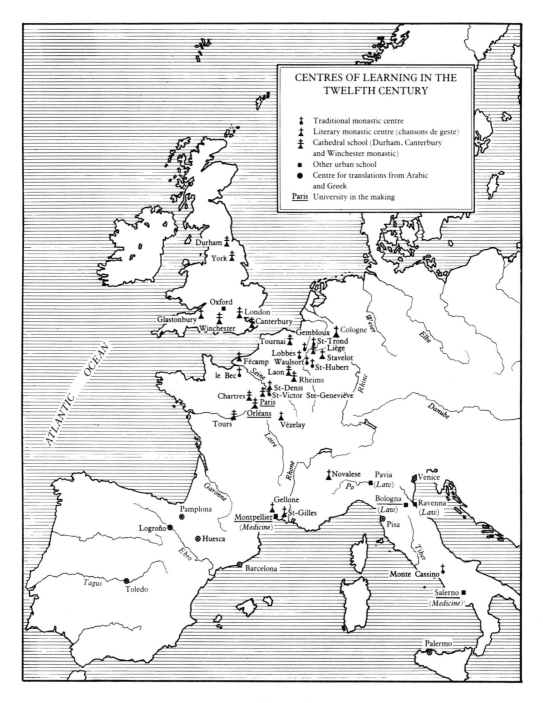

CENTRES OF LEARNING IN THE
TWELFTH CENTURY

✝ Traditional monastic centre
✝ Literary monastic centre (chansons de geste)
✟ Cathedral school (Durham, Canterbury
and Winchester monastic)
■ Other urban school
● Centre for translations from Arabic
and Greek
Paris University in the making

Durham
York

Oxford
Glastonbury London
Winchester Canterbury
Gembloux Cologne
Tournai St-Trond
Liège
Lobbès Stavelot
Fécamp Waulsort St-Hubert
le Bec Laon
Rheims
Chartres St-Denis
St-Victor Ste-Geneviève
Paris
Orléans
Tours Vézelay

ATLANTIC OCEAN

Novalese Pavia
(Law) Venice
Po
Bologna Ravenna
Gellone (Law) (Law)
Pamplona St-Gilles
Montpellier Pisa
Logroño (Medicine)
Huesca

Barcelona Monte Cassino

Tagus Toledo Salerno
(Medicine)

Palermo

Seine
Loire
Rhône
Garonne
Ebro
Weser
Elbe
Rhine
Danube
Tiber

Map 6

PART I

Historical Evolution

1

The Barbarian Settlements
(Fifth to Seventh Centuries)

I

THE MEDIEVAL west was born on the ruins of the Roman world. This was both a help and a hindrance to it; Rome both fed it and paralysed it. And Rome's first bequest was the dramatic choice symbolized by the legend of its origin, in which the enclosed Rome of the *pomerium* and of the *templum* triumphed over the Rome without limits or walls which the unlucky Remus had planned in vain.

Even in its successes, the history of Rome, destined to be enclosed by Romulus, was merely the history of a compound on a grand scale. The Eternal City gathered a territory around itself which it widened by conquests until an optimal perimeter for defence was reached. In the first century, it tried to close off its territory behind the *limes*, the western world's equivalent of the Great Wall of China. Within this boundary Rome exploited its empire, without creating anything. No technical innovation had occurred since the Hellenistic age. Rome's economy was fed by pillage; successful wars provided slave manpower and precious metals drawn from the hoarded treasures of the east. Rome excelled in conservative skills such as warfare, which was always defensive in spite of appearing to be a series of conquests; law, which was founded on a framework of precedents and fended off innovation; a sense of the state which assured the stability of institutions; and architecture, an outstanding example of an art meant to endure.

This masterpiece of ultraconservatism, Roman civilization, was attacked in the second half of the second century by the forces of destruction and renewal. The great crisis of the third century undermined the unity of the Roman world. The heart of the empire, Rome and Italy, seized up, no longer pumping blood to the limbs which were trying to lead their own existence. The provinces freed themselves, and then turned into conquerors. Spaniards, Gauls, and

Orientals invaded the Senate. The emperors Trajan and Hadrian were Spanish by origin, Antoninus Pius Gaulish. In the Severan dynasty the emperors were African, the empresses Syrian. Caracalla's edict of 212 granted the right of Roman citizenship to all the inhabitants of the empire. This ascent of the provinces shows the rise of centrifugal forces as much as the success of Romanization. The medieval west would inherit this struggle: was it to be unity or diversity, Christendom or nation states?

A more serious imbalance was caused by the west losing its substance to the profit of the east. Gold disappeared to the east, to pay for luxury imports produced there, or for which it acted as an entrepôt; Jewish and Syrian merchants monopolized long-distance trade. Western cities bled away while oriental cities prospered. Constantine's foundation (324–30) of the new Rome, Constantinople, was a physical manifestation of this eastward slide of the Roman world. This east–west division was also to be a feature of the medieval world: attempts at union between the two would be unable to resist what from now on was a diverging evolution. The schism was rooted in the realities of the fourth century. Constantinople would enable Rome's continued existence and, while appearing to be prosperous and prestigious, would allow Rome's death agony to drag on within its walls until 1453. The pauperized, barbarized west had once more to climb step by step in a rise which, at the end of the middle ages, would open to it the routes of the entire world.

Even more serious was the fact that the Roman citadel from which the legions departed to capture prisoners and booty was itself besieged and soon captured. The last great victorious war occurred under Trajan, and, after 107, the gold of the Dacians was the last great nourishment for Roman prosperity. The drying-up of supplies from outside was accompanied by internal stagnation, above all the population crisis which made the shortage of slave labour acute. In the second century Marcus Aurelius initiated a barbarian offensive on the Danube, where he died in 180. The third century saw a general assault on the *limes*, which was staved off less by the military successes of the Illyrian emperors at the end of the century and their successors than by the lull produced by welcoming some barbarians as federates or allies into the army or into the frontier lands inside the empire. These were the earliest occurrences of a fusion which would characterize the middle ages.

The emperors thought that they could avert their fate by abandoning the tutelary deities, who had failed, for the new God of the Christians. The renewal under Constantine seemed to justify their hopes: under the aegis of Christ prosperity and peace appeared to return. It was only a short respite. Moreover, Christianity was a false ally for Rome. To the Church, the Roman structures were only a framework on which it could model itself, a foundation on which it could support itself, an instrument for strengthening itself. As a religion with a universal vocation, Christianity was hesitant to shut itself up in the limits of a particular civilization. Of course it was to be the principal agency by which Roman civilization was to be transmitted to the medieval west. Of course it was to inherit from Rome and from its historical origins a tendency to turn in on itself. But against this closed religion the western middle ages were also to know an open religion, and the dialogue between these two faces of Christianity was to dominate this whole period. The medieval west took ten centuries to decide whether it was to be a closed or an open economy, a rural or an urban world, a single citadel or many mansions.

II

Although we can trace the beginnings of the agitation from which the medieval west was to be born to the Roman crisis of the third century, it is right to consider the barbarian invasions of the fifth century as the event which precipitated the changes, gave them a catastrophic turn of speed, and profoundly modified their form. Germanic invasions were not a novelty for the Roman world in the fifth century. Without going back as far as the Cimbrians and the Teutons, who had been beaten by Marius at the start of the second century BC, we should bear in mind that the Germanic menace had been a permanent burden on the empire since the reign of Marcus Aurelius (161–80). The barbarian invasions had been one of the essential elements of the third century crisis. The Gaulish and Illyrian emperors at the end of the third century averted the danger for a time. However – to restrict ourselves to the western part of the empire – the great raid of the Alamans, the Franks, and other Germanic peoples, who ravaged Gaul, Spain, and northern Italy in 276, foreshadowed the great onslaught of the fifth century. It left badly healed scars such as a devastated countryside and ruined towns; it precipitated economic change (agriculture declined and towns shrank); and it encouraged a fall in population and changes in society. Peasants had to put themselves under the increasingly heavy protection of great lords who also became the leaders of military followings. The position of the *colonus* or small tenant farmer grew closer to that of the slave. Sometimes peasant misery was transformed into revolts, such as those of the African Circumcelliones and the Gaulish and Spanish Bagaudae whose revolt was endemic in the fourth and fifth centuries.

Similarly in the east a barbarian people appeared who were to forge ahead and to play a crucial role in the west: the Goths. In 269 they were halted by the emperor Claudius II at Niš. However, they occupied Dacia and won a dramatic victory at Adrianople over the emperor Gratian on 9 August 378.

This was not the decisive event depicted with horror by so many 'romanophile' historians – 'We could stop here,' wrote Victor Duruy, 'for nothing remained of Rome: beliefs, institutions, Senate, military organization, arts, literature, all had disappeared' – but it was nonetheless the thunderclap before the storm that would submerge the medieval west. We are better informed about the Goths than about most other invaders through Jordanes' *History of the Goths*, which is tendentious, it is true, because he himself was of barbarian origin, and late; it was written in the middle of the sixth century. However, it makes use of serious written and oral documentation, in particular Cassiodorus' lost *History of the Goths*. Historians and archaeologists have broadly confirmed what Jordanes tells us about the *Wanderungen* of the Goths, from Scandinavia to the sea of Azov, by way of Mecklenburg, Pomerania and the Pripet marshes. In about 230 they founded a state in southern Russia.

Now from this island of Scandza, as from a hive of races or a womb of nations, the Goths are said to have come forth long ago under their king, Berig by name. . . . Soon they moved from here to the abodes of the Ulmerugi, who then dwelt on the shores of Ocean. . . . But when the number of the people increased greatly and Filimer, son of Gadaric, reigned as king – about the fifth since Berig – he decided that the army of the Goths with their families should move away from that region. In search of suitable homes and pleasant places they came to the land of Scythia, called Oium in their tongue. Here they were delighted with the great richness of the country, and it is said that when half the army had been brought over, the bridge whereby they had crossed the river fell in utter ruin, nor could any thereafter pass to or fro. For the place is said to be surrounded by quaking bogs and an encircling abyss. (Mierow, 1915, p. 57)

The causes of the invasions are of little importance for us. The growth of population and the attraction of more fertile territories, which Jordanes mentions as causes, probably only came into play after an initial impulse which might well have been a change in climate, a cold spell which, from Siberia to Scandinavia, reduced the cultivable land and pasture of the barbarian peoples. This would have set them in motion, with one tribe pushing the next, towards the south and west as far as the western extremities such as Britain (most of which was later to become England), Gaul (which was to be France), Spain (whose southernmost portion was to take the name of the Vandals, Andalusia), and Italy (which was to preserve the name of its late-arriving invaders only in the north, in Lombardy).

Certain aspects of the invasions are of greater importance. First, the invaders were almost always fleeing. They were fugitives driven on by peoples stronger or more cruel than they. Their cruelty was frequently of a desperate nature, especially when the Romans refused them the asylum which they often asked for peacefully. St Ambrose, at the end of the fourth century, saw clearly that these invasions were a set of chain reactions. 'The Huns threw themselves on the Alans, the Alans on the Goths, the Goths on the Taifali and the Sarmatians, and the Goths, driven out of their homeland, have pushed us back in Illyricum. And there is no end!' As for Jordanes, he emphasizes that if the Goths took up arms against the Romans in 378 it was because they had been quartered on a tiny piece of territory without resources, where the Romans sold them the flesh of dogs and of unclean animals at an exorbitant price, making them exchange their sons as slaves for a bit of food. It was famine that armed them against the Romans. The Romans were, traditionally, ambivalent towards the barbarians. Depending on the race involved and the circumstances, they were soon disposed to welcome the people who pressed at their gate, and they respected their laws, their customs and their originality by giving them the status of federates. Thus they disarmed the barbarians' aggressiveness and turned them into soldiers and peasants for their own profit to ease the manpower crisis in the army and the countryside. The emperors who practised such policies were not highly regarded by the traditionalists, for whom the barbarians were closer to beasts than to men: this was the second, and more common Roman attitude to barbarians. The Greek historian Zosimus said 'Constantine opened the door to the barbarians . . . he was the cause of the ruin of the empire'. Ammianus Marcellinus denounced the blindness of Valens, who, in 376, organized the crossing of the Danube by the Goths. 'In this expectation various officials were sent with vehicles to transport the savage horde, and diligent care was taken that no future destroyer of the Roman state should be left behind, even if he were smitten with a fatal disease. . . . With such stormy eagerness on the part of insistent men was the ruin of the Roman world brought in' (Ammianus Marcellinus, 1952, iii, p. 405). Similarly Theodosius, a great friend of the Goths, *amator generis Gothorum* according to Jordanes, came under attack.

Among these barbarians, some acquired a special renown for hideousness and cruelty. Here is Ammianus Marcellinus' famous description of the Huns:

The people of the Huns . . . exceed every degree of savagery. Since there the cheeks of the children are deeply furrowed with the steel from their very birth, in order that the growth of hair, when it appears at the proper time, may be checked by the wrinkled scars, they grow old without beards and without any beauty, like eunuchs. They all have compact, strong limbs and thick necks, and are so monstrously ugly and misshapen, that one might take them for two-legged beasts or for the stumps, rough-hewn into images, that are used in putting sides to bridges . . . they have no need of fire nor of savoury food, but eat the roots of wild plants and the half-raw flesh of any kind of animal whatever, which they put between their thighs and the backs of their horses, and thus warm it a little. They are never protected by any buildings, but they avoid these like the tombs, which are set apart from everyday use. . . . They dress in linen

Map 7   The Roman world at the end of the fourth century

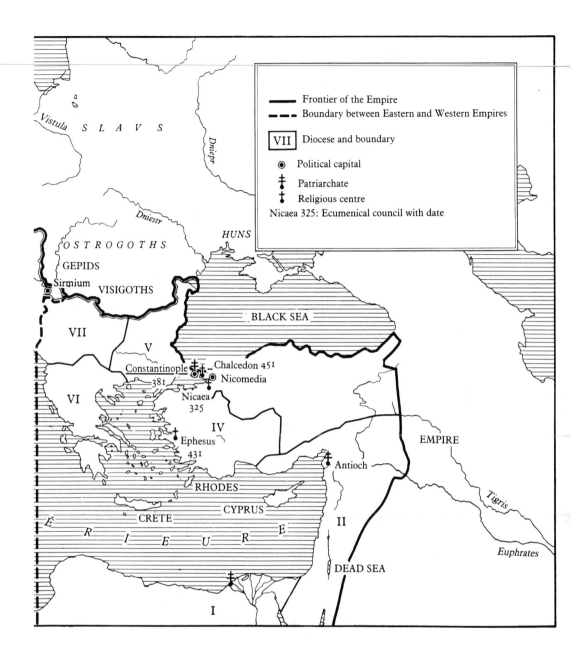

SLAVS

Vistula

Dnieper

Dniestr

HUNS

OSTROGOTHS

GEPIDS

Sirmium

VISIGOTHS

VII

V

BLACK SEA

Constantinople
381

Chalcedon 451

Nicomedia

Nicaea
325

VI

IV

Ephesus
431

EMPIRE

Antioch

RHODES

CYPRUS

CRETE

II

Tigris

M E D I T E R R A N E A N

DEAD SEA

Euphrates

I

Frontier of the Empire

Boundary between Eastern and Western Empires

VII   Diocese and boundary

⊙   Political capital

☦   Patriarchate

✝   Religious centre

Nicaea 325: Ecumenical council with date

cloth or in the skins of field-mice sewn together, and they wear the same clothing indoors and out. But when they have once put their necks into a faded tunic, it is not taken off or changed until by long wear and tear it has been reduced to rags and fallen from them bit by bit. . . . They are almost glued to their horses. . . . From their horses by night or day every one of that nation . . . eats and drinks, and bowed over the narrow neck of the animal relaxes into a sleep so deep as to be accompanied by many dreams. (Rolfe, 1952, iii, pp. 382-3)

And in the sixth century the Lombards were to succeed, after so many atrocities, in distinguishing themselves by their ferocity: 'savages of a worse ferocity than is normally the case with Germanic ferocity'.

Of course the authors of these descriptions were mainly pagans who, as heirs of the Greco-Roman civilization, detested the barbarian who was annihilating this civilization from both without and within, by destroying it or by cheapening it. Yet many Christians for whom the Roman empire was the lucky cradle of Christianity felt the same repulsion for the invaders. St Ambrose saw in the barbarians enemies deprived of humanity, and exhorted the Christians to armed defence of 'the native land against the barbarian invasion'. Bishop Synesius of Cyrene referred to all the invaders as Scythians - a symbol of barbarism - and applied to them Homer's advice in the *Iliad* to 'drive out these cursed dogs which Fate brought'. However, other sources convey a different tone. St Augustine, while grieving over the woes of the Romans, refused to see the sack of Rome by Alaric in 410 as anything other than a piece of random ill-fortune such as many others experienced in Roman history. He stressed the fact that, unlike most conquering Roman generals, who made themselves famous for sacking the towns they had conquered and exterminating their inhabitants, Alaric had agreed to treat the Christian churches as refuges and had respected them.

Everything in the way of devastation, massacre, pillage, arson and ill treatment which was committed in this disaster was done because these are customs of war. But what happened in a new way is that this barbarian savagery, by an amazing change in the face of things, has shown itself mild to the extent of choosing and designating the biggest basilicas to fill them with people. Within them no one was to be touched; no one was to be seized from them, and to them many people were led by compassionate enemies with a view to their liberation. No one was to be led away into captivity from these places, not even by cruel enemies: this must be attributed to the name of Christ and to Christian times. . . .

Yet the most extraordinary source came from a simple monk who was not motivated as were the aristocratic bishops to preserve the Roman social order. In about 440, Salvian, who described himself as 'priest of Marseilles', and who was a monk on the island of Lérins, wrote a treatise called *Concerning the Government of God*, which was an apology for Providence and an attempt to explain the great invasions. The cause of the catastrophe was interior. It was the sins of the Romans – Christians included – which had destroyed the Empire. Their vices had delivered it up to the barbarians. 'Against themselves the Romans were far worse enemies than their enemies outside, for although the barbarians had already broken them, they were being destroyed even more by themselves'. In any case, what could the barbarians be reproached for? They knew nothing of religion; if they sinned it was unconsciously. Their morals and culture were different. Why condemn what was different?

The Saxon race is cruel, the Franks are perfidious, the Gepids inhuman, the Huns unchaste. But are their vices as culpable as our own? Is the unchastity of the Huns as criminal as our own? Is the perfidy of the Franks as blameworthy as our own? Is a drunken Alaman as reprehensible as a drunken Christian? Is a rapacious Alan as much to be condemned as a rapacious Christian? Is deceit in a Hun or a Gepid surprising, since he is not aware that deceit is a fault? Is perjury in a Frank something unheard of, since he thinks that perjury is an ordinary way of talking, and not a crime?

Above all – aside from his personal choice which can be disputed – Salvian gives us the underlying reasons for the success of the barbarians. Of course there was military superiority. The superiority of the barbarian cavalry emphasized the full force of the superiority of their weaponry. The weapon of the invasions was the long, slicing, pointed sword, a slashing weapon whose terrible effectiveness was the origin of the literary exaggerations of the middle ages: helmets cut open, heads and bodies split in two down to, and sometimes including, the horse. Ammianus Marcellinus noted with horror a deed of arms of this type, which was unknown among the Romans. Yet there were barbarians among the Roman armies, and, once the surprise of the first shocks had worn off, military superiority was quickly shared by the other side.

The truth was that the barbarians benefited from the active or passive complicity of the mass of the Roman population. The social structure of the Roman empire, in which the lower levels were increasingly being crushed by a minority of the rich and the powerful, explained the success of the barbarian invasions. Let us listen to Salvian:

The poor are despoiled, the widows groan, the orphans are trodden underfoot, to such an extent that many of them, including people of good birth who have received a superior education, take refuge among the enemies. So as not to perish under public persecution, they go and seek Roman humanity among the barbarians, because they can no longer support barbarian inhumanity among the Romans. They are different from the people among whom they take refuge; they share none of their manners or their speech, and

if I might dare say so, nothing, furthermore, of the foetid odour of the barbarians'
bodies and clothes. Yet they prefer to adapt themselves to this dissimilarity of customs
rather than to put up with injustice and cruelty among the Romans. So they emigrate
among the Goths or the Bagaudae, or among the other barbarians who are powerful
everywhere, and they have absolutely no cause to repent of this exile. For they prefer
to live freely under an appearance of slavery to being slaves under an appearance of
liberty. The title of Roman citizen, once not only greatly esteemed, but bought at a
high price, is nowadays repudiated and avoided, and is not only regarded as being cheap,
but also as being abominable. . . . Hence it comes about that even those who do not
flee to the barbarians are, even so, forced to become barbarians, as has happened to
most Spaniards and to a large proportion of the Gauls, and to all those who, over the
whole extent of the Roman world, are constrained to be no longer Romans by Roman
iniquity. Let us now speak of the Bagaudae who, despoiled by evil and cruel judges,
beaten, and killed, after having lost the right to Roman liberty, have also lost the honour
of the Roman name. And we call them rebels and lost men, when it is we who have
forced them to become criminals.

Everything is said in that passage: the connivance between the barbarians
and the rebels, the Goths and the Bagaudae, and the change in the condition
of the Roman masses, which was barbarizing them before the barbarians had
arrived. André Piganiol, who claimed that 'Roman civilization did not die a
natural death [but that] it was assassinated', uttered three untruths, for Roman
civilization in fact killed itself, there was nothing natural about this suicide,
and yet Roman civilization did not die of it, for civilizations are not mortal,
and Roman civilization survived, beyond the barbarians, throughout the middle
ages and beyond.

To tell the truth, the settlement of many a barbarian on Roman soil was
carried out with general approval. The panegyrist of Constantius Chlorus
declared at the start of the fourth century:

The Chamavian tills for us. He who has ruined us so long by his pillaging is now
busy enriching us; behold him, clad as a peasant, wearing himself out by working;
he visits our markets and brings his beasts there to sell them. Great tracts of uncultivated
land in the territories of Amiens, Beauvais, Troyes and Langres are once more growing
green, thanks to the barbarians.

We hear similar tones from another Gaul, the rhetor Pacatus, who came to
Rome in 389 to declaim the panegyric for Theodosius. He congratulated the
emperor on having made the Goths who had been enemies of Rome into
peasants and soldiers in its service. In the midst of the ordeals, farseeing minds
perceived the solution of the future, the fusion of barbarians and Romans.
At the end of the fourth century the rhetor Themistius predicted, 'For the

moment, the wounds which the Goths have inflicted on us are still fresh, but soon we shall find in them companions at feasts and in war, taking part in public functions'. These predictions were too optimistic, for although in the long run reality was to resemble Themistius' somewhat idyllic picture, it was with this important difference, that the conquering barbarians admitted the conquered Romans to their sides.

Even so, from the very beginning there were certain circumstances which favoured acculturation between the two groups. The barbarians who settled in the empire in the fifth century were not young but savage peoples, barely departed from their forests or their steppes, as they have been depicted by their contemporary detractors or by their modern admirers. Although they were not the relics of a weakened race, as Fustel de Coulanges exaggeratedly claimed, 'torn apart by its long interior struggles, enervated by a series of social revolutions, and which had lost its institutions', they had evolved considerably in the interval since those often century-old developments which had finally cast them upon the Roman world. They had seen and learned much, and retained what they had learned quite well. Their paths had led them into contact with cultures and civilizations from which they had borrowed customs, arts, and skills. Directly or indirectly, most of them had experienced the influence of Asiatic cultures, of the Persian world and of the Greco-Roman world itself, especially within its eastern half which, in the process of becoming Byzantine, remained the richest and the most brilliant. They brought with them refined skills in metal-working such as damascening and goldsmithing, leather-working, and the wonderful art of the steppes with its stylized animal motifs. The barbarians had often been captivated by the culture of neighbouring empires, and they had conceived an admiration for their knowledge and luxury which was doubtless clumsy and superficial but not lacking in respect.

The Huns of Attila were no longer exactly the same as the savages described by Ammianus Marcellinus. Although the picture of Attila's court being open to philosophers is a legend, it is striking that in 448 a celebrated Gaulish physician, Eudoxius, compromised by his relations with the Bagaudae, took refuge with the Huns. In the same year Priscus, a Roman ambassador from Constantinople to Attila, met a Roman from Moesia, a prisoner who had stayed with his new masters and who was married to a barbarian woman. He boasted to Priscus of the social organization of the Huns compared with that of the Roman world. Jordanes, who was admittedly biased, writing in the sixth century said of the Goths,

In their second home, that is, in . . . Dacia, Thrace and Moesia, Zalmoxes reigned, whom many writers of annals mention as a man of remarkable learning in philosophy. Yet even before this they had a learned man Zeuta, and after him Dicineus. . . . Nor did they lack teachers of wisdom. Wherefore the Goths have ever been wiser than other barbarians and were nearly like the Greeks, as Dio relates, who wrote their history and annals with a Greek pen. (Mierow, 1915, p. 61)

The face of the barbarian invaders had been transformed by another crucial fact. Although some of them had remained pagan, another part of them, not the least, had become Christian. But, by a curious chance, which was to have serious consequences, these converted barbarians – the Ostrogoths, Visigoths, Burgundians, Vandals, and later the Lombards – had been converted to Arianism, which had become a heresy after the Council of Nicaea. They had in fact been converted by followers of the 'apostle of the Goths', Ulfilas, the grandson of Christian Cappadocians who had been taken prisoner by the Goths in 264. The 'Gothicized' child had been sent in his youth to Constantinople where he had been won over to Arianism. Returning as a missionary bishop to the Goths, he translated the Bible into Gothic for their edification and turned them into heretics. Thus what should have been a religious bond was, on the contrary, a subject of discord and sparked off bitter conflicts between Arian barbarians and Catholic Romans.

There remained the attraction exercised by Roman civilization upon the barbarians. Not only did the barbarian chiefs appeal to the Romans as counsellors, but they often tried to ape Roman customs and to decorate themselves with Roman titles – Consul, Patrician, and so on. They appeared not as enemies but as admirers of Roman institutions. At the most one could take them for usurpers. They were merely the last generation of those foreigners, Spaniards, Gauls, Africans, Illyrians, and Orientals, who had little by little reached the highest offices and the imperial dignity itself. Furthermore no barbarian ruler dared to make himself an emperor. When Odoacer deposed the western emperor, Romulus Augustulus, in 476, he sent back the imperial insignia to the emperor Zeno in Constantinople, signifying that one single emperor was enough. 'We admire the titles granted by emperors more than our own,' wrote a barbarian king to an emperor. The most powerful of them, Theodoric, took the Roman name of Flavius and wrote to the emperor, '*ego qui sum servus vester et filius* – I who am your slave and your son' – and declared to him that his only ambition was to make his kingdom 'an imitation of your own, a copy of your unrivalled empire'. It was not until 800 and the time of Charlemagne that a barbarian chief dared to make himself emperor. Thus each camp seemed to have yielded ground to the other. The decadent Romans, inwardly barbarized, descended to the level of the barbarians who had outwardly been licked into shape and polished.

It is still far from reality to see the barbarian invasions as a period of peaceful settlement, an outbreak of 'tourist trips' as they have been jokingly called.

These were above all times of confusion, a confusion which arose chiefly out of the very mixture of the invaders. On the course of their journey the tribes and the peoples had fought each other; some had been subjected to others, and they had been mixed together. Some formed ephemeral confederations, such as the Huns whose army swallowed up the remains of conquered Ostrogoths, Alans, and Sarmatians. Rome tried to play off one lot against another, and hurriedly attempted to Romanize the first arrivals and turn them into a tool for use against the following groups which had remained more barbarian. The Vandal Stilicho, guardian of the Emperor Honorius, used an army of Goths, Alans and Caucasians against the usurper Eugenius and his Frankish ally Arbogast.

A unique source, the *Life of St Severinus*, as told by his disciple Eugippius, is full of information about minor but significant events on a key frontier, that of the middle Danube, from Passau to Klosterneuburg, in the second half of the fifth century. Severinus, a Latin who had come from the East, attempted to organize resistance among the remnants of the Roman populations of Ripuarian Noricum, with the help of the Germanic tribe of the Rugii and their kings, against the pressure of other invaders, Alamans, Goths, Heruli and Thuringians, who were ready to force a passage across the river. The hermit-monk went from one fortified place where the Romano-Rugian population had taken refuge to another, and battled against heresy, paganism, and famine. He met the barbarian raids with spiritual weapons, material ones being in short supply. He put the inhabitants on their guard against imprudent behaviour. To leave the camps to go to pick fruit or to take in the harvest was to expose onself to being killed or taken prisoner by the enemy. By his words, by miracles, by the power of saints' relics, he intimidated the barbarians or won them round. He had no illusions. When optimistic or thoughtless men asked him to obtain from the Rugian king the right for them to engage in trade he replied 'What is the use of thinking of merchandise in places where no merchant will be able to go any longer?' Eugippius gives a wonderful description of the confused events in stating that the Danube frontier was permanently involved in trouble and in ambiguous situations: '*utraque Pannonia ceteraque confinia Danuvii rebus turbabantur ambiguis*'. All organization, whether military, administrative or economic, was disintegrating. Famine had settled in. Attitudes and feelings were becoming increasingly rough and superstitious. Gradually the inevitable happened. The fortresses fell one by one into the hands of the barbarians. Finally, after the death of the man of God, who had become the all-purpose leader of these demoralized groups, Odoacer decided to deport those who remained to Italy. The deportees brought Severinus's body with them and ended up installing this relic in a monastery near Naples. Such was and such was to be for many decades the common outcome of the *res ambiguae* or ambiguous events of the invasions.

The confusion was heightened by terror. Even if we allow for exaggerations, the tales of massacres and of devastations which fill the sources of the fifth century leave no doubt about the atrocities and destruction which accompanied the 'outings' of the barbarian peoples. Here is a description by Orens, bishop of Auch of Gaul after the great invasion of 417:

See with what suddenness death weighed on the entire world, how the violence of war has struck the people. Not the rough soil of thick woods or of high mountains, nor the current of rivers with swift whirlpools, nor the shelter formed by the sites of citadels or the ramparts of towns, nor the barrier formed by the sea, nor the sad solitudes of the desert, nor the gorges, nor even the caverns which are overhung by dark crags have been able to escape from the barbarians. Many perished the victims of lies, many of perjury, many were denounced by their fellow-citizens. Ambushes did much evil and so too did popular violence. Whoever was not subdued by force was subdued by famine. The mother succumbed wretchedly with her children and her husband, and the master together with his serfs fell into slavery. Some provided food for dogs; many were killed by their burning houses, which then provided them with a pyre. In the towns, the estates, the countryside, at the crossroads, in all the districts, here and there along all the roads were death, suffering, destruction, arson and mourning. All Gaul was reduced to smoke on a single pyre.

And in Spain Bishop Hydatius wrote:

The barbarians unleashed themselves throughout all Spain; the scourge of plague raged equally. The tyrannical exactors pillaged the wealth and resources hidden in the towns and the soldiery drained them away. There was a famine so atrocious that, under the empire of hunger, men devoured human flesh. Mothers killed their infants, cooked them and fed on their bodies. Animals became accustomed to eating the bodies of those who had died of hunger, by the sword or of sickness, and even killed men in full vigour: not content with feeding off the flesh of corpses, they attacked the human race. Thus the four scourges of the sword, of famine, of plague and of animals raged thoughout the entire world, and the predictions of the Lord through his prophets were realized.

Such is the grisly overture with which the history of the medieval west begins. Through ten centuries it was to continue to set the tone; the sword, famine, plague, and wild beasts were to be the evil protagonists of this history. Of course, it was not the barbarians alone who had brought them. The ancient world had known them and they were ready to return in force at the moment when the barbarians unleashed them. But the barbarians gave unheard-of force to this unleashing of violence. From now on the broadsword, the long sword of the great invasions, later to be that used by the knights, stretched a murderous shadow over the west. Before the work of construction could slowly begin again, the west was gripped for a long period by a frenzy of destruction. The men of the medieval west were indeed the offspring of the barbarians; they resembled the Alans described by Ammianus Marcellinus:

Just as quiet and peaceful men find pleasure in rest, so the Halani [Alans] delight in danger and warfare. There the man is judged happy who has sacrificed his life in battle, whilst those who grow old and depart from the world by a natural death they assail with bitter reproaches, as degenerate and cowardly; and there is nothing in which they take more pride than in killing any man whatever: as glorious spoils of the slain they tear off their heads, then strip off their skins and hang them upon their warhorses as trappings. No temple or sacred place is to be seen in their country, not even a hut thatched with straw can be discerned anywhere, but after the manner of barbarians a naked sword is fixed in the ground and they reverently worship it as their god of war, the presiding deity of those lands over which they range. (Ammianus Marcellinus, 1952, iii, 394-5)

This passion for destruction was expressed by the chronicler Fredegar in the seventh century when he put these words in the mouth of the mother of a barbarian king exhorting her son, 'If you wish to perform an exploit and to make a name for yourself, destroy all that other people have built up and kill the entire people whom you have conquered; for you cannot put up a building better than those constructed by your predecessors and there is no finer exploit with which you can make your name.'

III

Following by turns a rhythm of slow infiltrations and fairly peaceful advances and one of sudden offensives accompanied by battles and massacres, the barbarian invasions profoundly modified the political map of the west (which was nominally under the authority of the Byzantine emperor) between the start of the fifth and the end of the eighth century. From 407 to 429 Italy, Gaul, and Spain were ravaged by a series of raids. The most spectacular episode was the siege, capture and sack of Rome by Alaric and the Visigoths in 410. The fall of the Eternal City stupefied many. 'My voice is choked and sobs interrupt me while I dictate these words,' groaned St Jerome in Palestine. 'The city which conquered the universe is itself conquered.' The pagans accused the Christians of being the cause of the disaster for having driven the tutelary deities out of Rome. St Augustine made a pretext of the event to define the relations between earthly and divine society in *The City of God*. He took the

blame away from the Christians and reduced the event to its true proportions:
a chance, though tragic deed. It was to happen again, this time without
bloodshed (*sine ferro et igne*) in 455 under Genseric and the Vandals. Vandals,
Alans, and Sueves ravaged the Iberian peninsula. The Vandals' settlement
in the south of Spain, though shortlived, gave Andalusia its name. As early
as 429 the Vandals, the only barbarians to possess a fleet, crossed over to North
Africa and conquered the Roman province of Africa, that is to say Tunisia
and eastern Algeria. In 412 after the death of Alaric, the Visigoths flowed
back out of Italy into Gaul, and then into Spain in 414, before doubling back
in 418 to settle in Aquitaine. Moreover, Roman diplomacy was operating
during each of these stages. It was the emperor Honorius who turned the
Visigothic king Athaulf towards Gaul, and on 1 January 414 Athaulf married
a sister of the emperor, Galla Placidia, at Narbonne. Again, it was Honorius
who incited the Visigoths to dispute Spain with the Vandals and the Sueves
after the murder of Athaulf in 415, and then summoned them back to
Aquitaine.

The second half of the fifth century saw decisive changes take place. To
the North, Scandinavian barbarians, Angles, Jutes, and Saxons, started to
occupy Britain between 441 and 443 after a series of raids. Some of the
conquered Britons conquered the sea and came to settle in Armorica, from
then on called Brittany. However, the main event was certainly the formation
of Attila's Hun empire, though ephemeral, for it made everything move.
Firstly, as Genghis Khan was to do eight centuries later, Attila united the
Mongol tribes who had passed into the west in about 434, and then defeated
and absorbed other barbarians. He maintained ambiguous relations with the
Byzantine empire for a while, rubbing shoulders with its civilization while
reconnoitring it as prospective prey (just as Genghis Khan was to do with
China). Finally, after an attempt on the Balkans in 448, he let himself be
persuaded to advance on Gaul. Here the Roman Aetius, thanks chiefly to
Visigothic forces, halted him in 451 on the Catalaunian plain. The Hun empire
fell to pieces and the hordes turned back eastwards after Attila's death in 453;
he was to go down in history, in the phrase of an obscure ninth-century
chronicler, as 'the scourge of God'.

It was a confused period of strange personalities and situations. A sister of
the emperor Valentinian III, Honoria, took her steward as a lover. Angered
by this, her august brother punished her by exiling her to Constantinople.
Acting out of temperament and spite the princess had a ring sent to Attila,
whom women found fascinating. Valentinian hastened to have his sister married
before the Hun claimed his betrothed, and with her half the empire as a dowry.
Attila, returning from Gaul, invaded northern Italy in 452, captured Aquileia
and led away part of the population into captivity. Six years later, the

prisoners, who had been thought dead, returned, and found that their wives had remarried. The patriarch, embarrassed, consulted with Pope Leo the Great, who passed judgement as follows: those returning should have back their wives, slaves, and goods. But the women who had remarried were not to be punished, except if they refused to return to their former spouses, in which case they were to be excommunicated.

The emperor had established a new people in the empire, the Burgundians, who briefly settled at Worms, whence they tried to invade Gaul. However, they suffered a crushing defeat at the hands of Aetius and his Hun mercenaries. The events of 436 in which their king Gunther was killed were to be the starting-point of the epic of the Nibelungen. In 443 the Romans allowed them to occupy Savoy. In 468, the Visigoths once more took up the conquest of Spain, which they completed in ten years. Then Clovis and Theodoric came on the scene. Clovis was the head of the Frankish tribe of the Salians, who had slipped into what is now Belgium and then into the North of Gaul during the fifth century. Clovis gathered around him most of the Frankish tribes, and subjected northern Gaul to him by triumphing over the Roman Syagrius at Soissons, which was to be his capital, in 486. He repulsed an invasion of the Alamans at the battle of Tolbiac and finally in 507 conquered Aquitaine from the Visigoths, whose king, Alaric II, was defeated and killed at Vouillé. When he died in 511, the Franks were masters of the whole of Gaul except Provence.

By now the Ostrogoths too had surged into the empire. Under the leadership of Theodoric they attacked Constantinople in 487 and were turned aside to Italy, which they conquered in 493. Installed at Ravenna, Theodoric reigned there for 30 years and, if the panegyrists do not exaggerate too much, let Italy experience a new golden age, governing it with Roman advisers such as Liberius, Cassiodorus, Symmachus and Boethius. He himself had lived from the age of eight to eighteen at the court in Constantinople as a hostage, and was the most successful and the most attractive of the Romanized barbarians. He restored the *pax romana* in Italy but intervened against Clovis only in 507, forbidding him to add Provence to Aquitaine which he had conquered from the Visigoths. He did not want Clovis to reach the Mediterranean.

At the start of the sixth century, the division of the West seemed assured between the Anglo-Saxons in a Britain cut off from all links with the continent, the Franks who held Gaul, the Burgundians confined to Savoy, the Visigoths masters of Spain, the Vandals settled in Africa, and the Ostrogoths ruling in Italy. In 476 a trivial event had passed practically unnoticed. A Roman from Pannonia, Orestes, who had been Attila's secretary, gathered some of the remains of his army after his master's death – Scyrians, Heruli, Turkilingi, Rugii – and put them at the disposal of the empire in Italy. He became master of the militia and made use of this to depose the emperor Julius Nepos in 475 and have the latter's young son Romulus proclaimed in his place. But in 476 the Scyrian Odoacer, the son of another of Attila's favourites, rose up at the head of another group of barbarians against Orestes. He killed him, deposed the young Romulus and sent the western imperial insignia to the emperor Zeno in Constantinople. The event does not seem to have stirred contemporaries much. However, 50 years later an Illyrian in the service of the Byzantine emperor, the count Marcellinus, wrote in his chronicle, 'Odoacer, king of the Goths, obtained Rome. . . . The Roman empire of the west, which Octavius Augustus, the first of the emperors, had begun to rule in the year 709 AUC, came to an end with the little emperor Romulus.'

The fifth century saw the disappearance of the last great figures in the service of the western emperor: Aetius, 'the last of the Romans', who was killed in 454, Syagrius, who was handed over by the Visigoths to Clovis, who had him beheaded in 486, and the barbarians Stilicho, the Vandal patrician and guardian of the emperor Honorius, executed on the orders of his ward in 408, Ricimer, a Sueve, also with the title of patrician, master of the western empire until his death in 472, and finally Odoacer, who was caught in a trap by Theodoric the Ostrogoth and killed by the latter's own hand in 493.

Until this point the policy of the emperors of the east had been to limit the damage: to prevent the barbarians from taking Constantinople by buying their retreat at a high price, and to divert them to the western part of the empire. They contented themselves with a vague submission from the barbarian kings whom they showered with titles such as Patrician and Consul, and they tried to keep the invaders out of the Mediterranean. The *mare nostrum* was not only the centre of the Roman world, but remained the essential artery of its trade and food supply. In 419 a law issued at Constantinople punished anyone who tried to teach the barbarians 'sea matters' with the death penalty. As we have seen, Theodoric later took up this tradition on his own account and prevented Clovis from reaching the Mediterranean by taking over Provence. However the Vandals had checked these Byzantine pretensions by building the fleet which allowed them to conquer Africa, and to raid Rome in 455.

Byzantine policy changed with the accession of Justinian in 527, a year after the death of Theodoric at Ravenna. Imperial policy abandoned passivity and went over to the offensive. Justinian wanted to reconquer, if not the entire western half of the Roman empire, at least the most important part of its Mediterranean territories. He appeared for a time to have succeeded. Byzantine generals liquidated the Vandal kingdom in Africa (533-4) and Gothic rule in Italy, with more difficulty, between 536 and 555. In 554 they seized Betica from the Spanish Visigoths. These were ephemeral successes which weakened

Byzantium a little more towards the dangers from the east and drained the strength of the west all the more, especially as from the year 542 the ravages of bubonic plague were added to those of war and famine. Most of Italy, with the exception of the Exarchate of Ravenna, Rome and its environs, and the extreme south of the peninsula, was lost between 568 and 572 to new invaders, the Lombards. These had been pushed southwards by yet another Asiatic invasion, that of the Avars. The Visigoths reconquered Betica by the end of the sixth century, and finally the Arabs conquered North Africa after 660.

The great event of the seventh century – even for the west – was the emergence of Islam and the Arab conquests. We shall observe the significance for Christendom of the formation of the Muslim world later on. Here let us examine merely the effect of Islam on the political map of the west. First of all the Arabs snatched the Maghreb from western Christendom; then they overwhelmed Spain, which they conquered with ease from the Visigoths between 711 and 719, apart from the north-east where the Christians remained independent. They briefly dominated Aquitaine, and especially Provence, until Charles Martel halted them in 732 at Poitiers. The Franks drove them back south of the Pyrenees, the Arabs making a complete withdrawal after the fall of Narbonne in 759.

The eighth century was indeed the century of the Franks. Their rise in the west was steady from Clovis' time, in spite of certain setbacks, such as their repulse by Theodoric. Clovis' master-stroke had been to convert himself and his people not to Arianism, like the other barbarian kings, but to Catholicism. Thus he could play the religious card and benefit from the support, if not of the papacy, which was still weak, at any rate of the powerful Catholic hierarchy and the no less powerful monastic foundations. In the sixth century the Franks had already conquered the kingdom of the Burgundians, between 523 and 534, and then Provence in 536. The sharing out of lands and rivalries between Clovis' descendants slowed down the rise of the Franks. In the early eighth century their future even seemed to be compromised by the decadence of the Merovingian dynasty, which has passed into legend with the image of the *rois fainéants*, and by the decadence of the Frankish clergy. By then the Franks were no longer the only orthodox Catholics of western Christian Europe. The Visigoths and the Lombards had abandoned Arianism for Catholicism and Pope Gregory the Great (590–604) had undertaken the conversion of the Anglo-Saxons, which he entrusted to the monk Augustine and his companions. The first half of the eighth century saw Catholicism penetrate into Frisia and Germany thanks to Willibrord and Boniface. Yet at the same time the Franks once more grasped hold of all their opportunities. The clergy reformed themselves under the direction of Boniface and the young, enterprising dynasty of the Carolingians replaced the feeble Merovingian line.

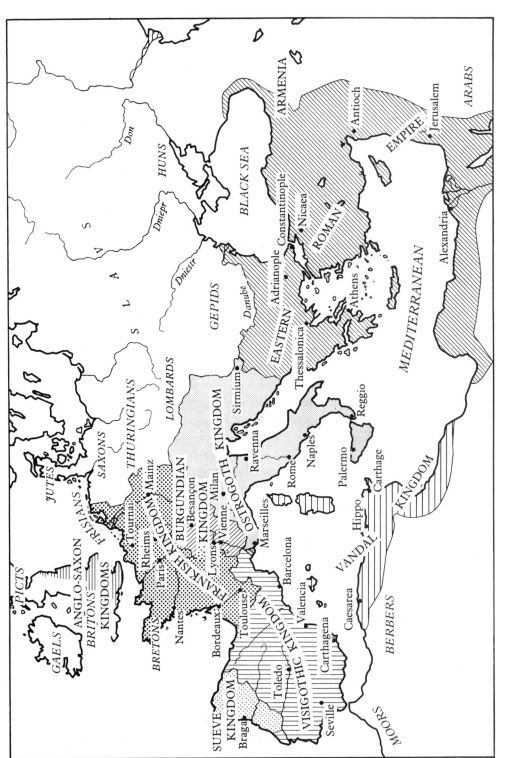

Map 8   The barbarian kingdoms in the sixth century

The Carolingian mayors of the palace had probably really held the reins of Frankish government for decades, but Charles Martel's son, Pippin the Short, took the decisive step of giving the Frankish leadership within the Catholic church its full weight. He concluded an alliance with the pope which was favourable to both sides. He recognized the pope's temporal power over the part of Italy around Rome. Grounded on a document forged by the papal chancery between 756 and 760, the so-called Donation of Constantine, the papal state or Patrimony of St Peter was born and established the temporal power of the papacy, which was to play such a large role in the political and moral history of the medieval west. In return the pope allowed Pippin the title of king in 751 and came north to anoint him in 754, the same year in which the papal state made its appearance. Foundations had been laid which were, half a century later, to permit the Carolingian monarchy to group together the largest part of the Christian west under its rule, and thence to re-establish the western empire for its own benefit. But, during the four centuries which separated the death of Theodosius (395) from the coronation of Charlemagne (800), a new world had been born in the west, which had slowly grown out of the fusion of both the Roman and the barbarian worlds. The western middle ages had taken shape.

IV

The medieval world resulted from the meeting and the fusion of two worlds which were already evolving towards each other. Roman and barbarian structures converged while in the process of being transformed.

Since at least the third century the Roman world had been growing further away from itself. A single edifice, it embarked upon a process of continuous disintegration. In addition to the great divide which was cutting the west off from the east there was growing isolation between the different parts of the west. Trade, which had above all been an interior trade between provinces, declined. The area of diffusion of agricultural or manufactured products destined for export to the rest of the Roman world, such as Mediterranean oil, Rhenish glass, or Gaulish pottery, became restricted. Coins became scarcer and of poorer quality. Cultivated surfaces were abandoned and the number of *agri deserti* (deserted fields) increased. Thus the physiognomy of the medieval west began to be sketched out: a splintering into tiny cells, withdrawn into themselves, separated by 'deserts' - forests, moors and wastes. 'In the middle of the debris of great cities, only scattered groups of wretched peoples, witnesses to past calamities, still attest to us the names of an earlier age,' wrote Orosius at the start of the fifth century. This piece of evidence (among many others), confirmed by aracheologists, underlines an important fact: cities were decaying, hastened by the destruction of the barbarian invasions. Admittedly it is only one aspect of the general consequences of the violence of the invaders, who destroyed, ruined, impoverished, isolated, and reduced. Admittedly the towns were a favourite target because their accumulated riches acted as a provocation and a lure. They were the most severely battered victims. But they were not relieved from their ordeal because their existing population was depleted by an evolutionary process. This disappearance of the townsfolk was only one result of the disppearance of the trade commodities which were no longer arriving to supply the urban market. The urban population was a group of consumers who fed themselves by imports. When the lack of coins left the townspeople without buying power, when the trade routes ceased to feed the urban centres, the citizens were forced to take refuge near places of production. It was the necessity of feeding themselves which above all explains the flight of the rich to the land, and the exodus of the poor on to the estates of the rich. Here too the barbarian invasions, by throwing the economic network into confusion and by dislocating the trade routes, hastened the shift of the population into the countryside without actually causing it.

The shift to the country was not only an economic and demographic phenomenon but was at the same time, and primarily, a social phenomenon, which was shaping the face of medieval society. Contemporaries, and, following them, a number of historians of the Late Empire, were particularly struck by the fiscal aspect of this development. The townspeople are supposed to have fled into the country away from the clutches of the tax-collectors, and, falling from Charybdis to Scylla, the urban poor are supposed to have passed under the control of the great lords and become rural slaves. Salvian wrote:

That is what is most serious and most revolting. . . . When those of whom we speak have lost their houses and their lands following an act of brigandage or when they have been driven out by the tax-collectors they take refuge in estates belonging to the great and become the *coloni* of the rich. Like that all-powerful and also maleficent woman who had the reputation of changing men into beasts, all the people who have settled on the estates of the rich undergo a metamorphosis as though they had drunk from the cup of Circe, for the rich begin to consider those whom they have welcomed as strangers who did not belong to them as their own property. These genuinely free people are transformed into slaves.

What is important to us is that Salvian's explanation, in spite of the small truth it contains, betrays above all an antifiscal obfuscation. This is a way of thinking which is not exclusively the property of medieval minds and which all too often masks the real, more profound causes. The disorganization of the exchanges increased hunger and the hunger pushed the masses into the countryside and subjected them to the servitude of the 'breadgivers', the great lords.

In this ruin of the antique trade network the first victim was the Roman road. The medieval road, which, in material terms, was more of a lane, was to be something different and was to emerge later. In the intervening period only the ways provided by nature, that is to say navigable rivers, existed between the wastes which the land routes no longer managed to cross. Hence the rerouting, along river courses, of the shrunken circulation network of the early middle ages. Simultaneously the urban map was readjusted, as Jan Dhondt has clearly shown. 'From the end of the Roman period, road circulation was giving way to water circulation, bringing with it a correlative shift in urban life. . . . The cities in decline are those which were situated at road junctions, without access to a waterway.' For example, Cassel and Bavai, which had been important land nodal points in the Roman period, went into eclipse, and Tongres dwindled slowly in the fifth century and gave way to Maastricht on the Meuse. But it must be added that not all the navigable rivers, not even all the largest ones, were promoted to the rank of communication routes. The continual invasions to the east and centre of Europe, especially the Avar invasion, the Slav incursions, and the resistance put up by the Saxons and other peoples in Germany to conversion to Christianity, disqualified the Danube, the Vistula, the Oder and the Elbe and even limited the role of the Rhine. The most important route was the one which went up the Rhône, the Saône, and down the Moselle and the Meuse, linking the Mediterranean with the English Channel and the North Sea.

The conversion of England to Christianity in the seventh century, and the diversion westwards of Scandinavian trade impeded by the Avar invasion, turned the coast between the Seine and the Rhine into a preferred place for passenger crossings (notably pilgrims going to Rome) and for the transport of goods. This explains the prosperity of the ports of Quentovic, at the mouth of the Canche, and of Duurstede, at the mouth of the Rhine, from the seventh to the ninth centuries. Marseilles and Arles, which were active in the Merovingian period, declined after 670 because the Alpine land routes experienced a renewal, which was connected with the re-establishment of peace in Northern Italy once the Lombards had settled. This also revived the Po for traffic. The Seine, the Loire, and the Garonne were also much frequented routes, serving Rouen and Paris, Orléans and Tours, Toulouse and Bordeaux, although their mouths into the sea were of less importance, since they opened on to an ocean on which men were increasingly afraid to risk themselves. On the other hand the Arab conquest turned both the Ebro and Douro into frontiers and their depopulated valleys into 'deserts'.

It should not be believed, however, that this movement, chiefly on rivers, bore a sizeable trade. There was traffic in some essential products such as salt. Salt is mentioned being carried on the Moselle between Metz and Trier by a sleeping boatman, thus displaying, according to Gregory of Tours, the miraculous help of St Martin. Salt was also exported by the monks of Noirmoutier to the continent. There were products which had become semi-luxuries, such as wine or oil. St Philibert, abbot of Jumièges at the end of the seventh century, received a cargo of oil from his friends in Bordeaux. Above all there were precious objects, fine stuffs and spices which oriental merchants, called 'Syrians' (chiefly Jews) brought to the west, or, once they had settled in the west, received from their fellow countrymen. The monetary history of this period witnesses to the scarcity and compartmentalization of exchanges. Gold coins barely circulated any longer, and when they were struck by Merovingian rulers, it was chiefly so that they could display their status. It was out of a wish to exercise the prerogative of a sovereign, rather than out of economic need. The increase in the number of mints, far from being connected with active trade, underlined how limited was the diffusion of money. It had to be somehow or other produced locally like the other objects necessary to a fragmented economic life.

The social phenomenon of the shift to the country was only the most spectacular aspect of a development which was to impress a fundamental character on medieval society, one which was to remain fixed in people's attitudes much longer than in material reality. This was a professional and social compartmentalization. The avoidance of certain professions and the mobility of rural labour had led the late Roman emperors to make certain trades hereditary and had encouraged the great landlords to attach tenant farmers to the land, the farmers being destined to replace the slaves who were becoming increasingly scarce. Men who were necessary to an economy which could no longer supply itself from external supplies, and which was becoming fixed on the spot, had to be kept on hand. One of the last emperors of the West, Majorian (457-61), bewailed the 'tricks used by all those men who do not wish to stay in the state of life in which they were born'. Medieval Christian Europe was to turn the desire to escape from one's lot into a major sin. 'Like father, like son' was to be the rule in the western middle ages, inherited from the late Empire. To remain in one place was the opposite of changing, and above all of succeeding. The ideal was a society of *manants* – a French term for villeins, derived from the Latin verb *manere*, to remain. It was a stratified society, boxed off horizontally.

The barbarian invaders managed to slip into these strata or to install themselves by force in them without great difficulty, mainly because they had ceased being nomads long before. They had often halted and only external pressures such as climatic changes or elbowing from other races, perhaps accentuated by internal developments, had made them move once more. The invaders were, to repeat, fugitive sedentaries. They probably retained habits from their nomadic period, which was fairly recent, and an echo of these was to sound effectively throughout the middle ages. To quote Marc Bloch's apt phrase, they had substituted the 'nomadism of the fields' for the 'nomadism of men', that is to say that they practised a seminomadic agriculture, shifting temporary cultivation within a given perimeter by clearing marginal land, or rather by assarting, and by cultivating burnt clearings and by field rotation. However one interprets the famous phrase of Tacitus speaking of the Germans in the first century, '*Arva per annos mutant et superest ager*', it clearly indicates that changing cultivated areas and having a permanent landholding went together.

Probably, too, stockrearing retained a favoured place in the barbarian economy, for it constituted not only a form of property which the farmer could take away if he had to move, but also a visible sign of wealth and, occasionally, a means of exchange. It has been noted that out of 500 cases of theft provided for by the Salic Law at the start of the sixth century, 64 concern domestic animals. When, in the middle ages, land became the basis of wealth, the peasant remained attached to his cow, pig, and goat by ties which went beyond economic utility and manifested a residual way of thinking. In certain regions the cow was for a long time to remain a money of account, a unit by which wealth and exchanges could be valued.

It has even been stressed that attachment to individual rural property was more developed among the barbarians than among the Romans on the morrow of the invasions. Chapter 27 of the Salic Law on theft, *de furtis diversis*, is very detailed and extremely severe towards injuries to this property, such as letting animals wander through someone else's harvest, cutting hay in someone else's meadow, gathering grapes from his vine or ploughing his field. The attachment of the small barbarian peasant to his personal property, his allod, was without doubt all the stronger because he was determined to affirm his independence – a normal attitude on the part of a colonist installed in a conquered territory who wants to show his superiority over the indigenous masses who are subject to the great landlords. Of course, most allods – and some allods were owned by the conquered as well as by the conquerors – were gradually absorbed by the great feudal estates characteristic of the middle ages. But at the level of usufruct if not of property agricultural crimes and misdemeanours are treated as very serious in custumals, penitentials and confessors' manuals throughout the whole of the middle ages. Indeed, the peasant was never more unwilling to put up with the domination of his lord than when the latter heedlessly rode across his serf's or his tenant's land at the head of his pack; the humiliation aggravated the material damage.

As a final point, it is clear that the barbarian groups who settled peacefully or by force on Roman territory were not, or were no longer, if they had ever been, egalitarian societies. The barbarian could try, in the face of the conquered, to avail himself of the status of a free man, which was all the dearer to a small farmer because he *was* a small farmer. In reality social categories, if not classes, had already been created among the invaders by an already advanced process of social differentiation. There were powerful and weak, rich and poor who easily transformed themselves into great and small proprietors or occupants on the conquered land. The legal distinctions of the early medieval law codes could give the illusion of a cleft between the completely free barbarians whose slaves were enslaved foreigners, and the descendants of the Romans in a hierarchy of free and unfree. Social reality was stronger. It quickly separated from each group the *potentiores* or powerful, whether of Roman or barbarian origin, from the *humiliores* or the humble.

Thus the settlement of the barbarians, reinforced by a tradition of coexistence which in some areas went back to the third century, could be fairly quickly followed by a more or less complete fusion. Except in a limited number of cases it is pointless to look for ethnic characteristics in what we can learn of the types of farming practised in the early middle ages. One should chiefly reflect that in the area of farming, which more than any other is one of a permanent state or the *longue durée*, it would be absurd to reduce the causes of diversity to a confrontation of Roman traditions and barbarian customs. Geographical considerations and different trends which had grown up in a past going back to the Neolithic age formed a heritage which was probably more decisive. What was important (and what is obvious) is that the whole of the population was borne along on the same movement: a shift to the countryside and the advance of the great estates.

Place names bear witness to this. Taking French names as an example, we should note first of all that personal names can be deceptive since the fashion quickly spread among Gallo-Romans of giving their children Germanic names out of social one-upmanship. Moreover the invaders, although they influenced vocabulary, and, to a more limited extent, syntax (for example, the word order determinant + determined as in Carlepont, from Caroli Pons, as opposed to the reverse, such as Pontoise from Pons Isarae) adopted Latin instead of imposing their own language. Or rather, they adopted low Latin, then developing and becoming vulgarized just as the economy was becoming ruralized. The significant feature of place names is the increase in names containing '*court*' and '*ville*'. These are indiscriminately preceded by Gallo-Roman or Germanic personal names and betray the advance of the big estate, the *curtis* (chiefly in Lorraine and Artois and Picardy), or *villa* (in the same regions and also in the Ile-de-France and Beauce). In the etymology of Martinville (Martini Villa, Vosges), or of Bouzonville (Bosonis Villa, Moselle, Meurthe-et-Moselle, Loiret), it is not the Gallo-Roman Martin or the Germanic Boso who is important, but the *villa* indicating the big estates to which they both gave their names.

Naturally the intermingling ran into obstacles. For some of the barbarians the most serious of these were probably their small numbers and, until their conversion to Catholicism, their adherence to paganism or above all to Arianism. Of course, according to Marc Bloch, 'the action of one civilization upon another is not necessarily in proportion to the balance of the numbers present'. It is still true that the barbarian peoples, especially after they were divided into small groups settled on Roman territory, had a strong desire not to lose the traditions and customs to which they were attached, and that this wish was particularly reinforced by the fear of being numerically submerged by the older inhabitants. The only people for whom a likely numerical estimate is known are the Vandals under Genseric at the moment of their embarkation for Africa in 429. They numbered 80 000. Neither the Visigoths, nor the Franks, nor any group of invaders is supposed to have exceeded 100 000. The estimate that the total number of barbarians after their settlement in the Roman west formed 5 per cent of the whole population cannot be far from the truth.

Moreover the barbarians had a tendency, at least at the start, to avoid the towns where there was more fear of being absorbed, although the 'capitals' of the barbarian kings, Braga, the capital of the first Catholic barbarian king, the Sueve Rechiarus (448–56); Toulouse, Barcelona, Merida, Toledo, the Visigothic capitals; Tournai, Soissons, Paris, the Frankish capitals; Lyons, the Burgundian capital; Ravenna, the capital of Theodoric the Ostrogoth; and Pavia and Monza, the Lombard capitals, must have had a high proportion of barbarian inhabitants. Moreover, some of the barbarian kings, notably the Franks, preferred to reside on their large estates, in their *villae*, rather than in urban 'palaces'. They too were moving to the country and were adopting the life of the great landholder. In the country it might happen that the new settlers remained gathered in a village whose name preserves their memory, such as Aumenancourt (Marne) which recalls the Alamans, Sermaise (Seine-et-Oise) the Sarmatians, Franconville (Seine-et-Oise) the Franks, Goudourville (Tarn-et-Garonne) or Villegoudou (Tarn) the Goths. Even more interesting, perhaps, are the place names in Flanders, Lorraine, Alsace and Franche-Comté where one finds the collective suffix *-ing* which indicates the following or *familia* of a Frankish, Alaman, or Burgundian chief. Thus we find Racrange (Moselle), derived from Racheringa, the people of Racher. Or above all there are the numerous names in *fère* or *fara* indicating among the Franks, Burgundians, Visigoths and Lombards the Germanic family group which had to settle as a group to ensure its cohesion. Such are La Fère (Aisne), Fère-Champenoise (Marne), Lafavre (Isère), La Fare (Bouches-du-Rhône, Hautes-Alpes, Vaucluse) and the Italian names in '*fara*'.

In the same way the barbarians' desire to preserve their identity can be found in the legislation of the early middle ages where the principle of the 'personality of laws', so foreign to the Roman jurisdictional tradition, appears. In a barbarian kingdom it was not the case that every man was subject to a single law valid for all the inhabitants of a territory: he was judged according to the judicial custom of the ethnic group to which he belonged – the Frank according to Frankish tradition, or rather according to the tradition of his Frankish group, such as the Salian tradition, the Burgundian according to Burgundian custom, and the Roman according to Roman law. Hence there were astonishing disparities. Rape of a virgin was punished by death for a Roman but by a fine for a Burgundian. On the other hand a woman married to a slave was considered by Roman law to be only a concubine and she did not lose her free-born status, whereas Salic law reduced her to servitude. There was such a danger that confusion might result in the new states that an intense effort at legal compilations occurred at the start of the fifth century. The fragments which survive, some of which are later redactions, are very diverse in character. The Edict of Theodoric has the unusual feature of being, in fact, not based on the 'personality' of laws. It wishes to impose the same jurisdiction on all the 'nations', Roman and barbarian, living under its domination. The Ostrogoth Theodoric the Great was indeed the last true heir of the Roman tradition in the west. The Salic law, composed in Latin under Clovis, has only come down to us in a text of the late eighth century which is overloaded with additions and, perhaps, corrections; it codified the customs of the Salian Franks. The celebrated *Lex Gundobada*, written in Latin and promulgated by Gundobad, king of the Burgundians, who died in 516, defined the relations between Burgundians and also between Burgundians and Romans. The customs of the Visigoths were codified first by Euric (466–84) and later by Liuvigild (568–86). Fragments of the code of Euric have been discovered in a palimpsest in the Bibliothèque Nationale in Paris, while parts of the code of Liuvigild have been pieced together using a later code which quoted them as *lex antiqua*. The Edict of Rothari for the Lombards of 643 was enlarged by several of his successors. From the Alamans survives a *Pactus* of the seventh century and a *Lex Alamannorum* of the early eighth century which were influenced by Frankish legislation, just as the *Lex Baiuvariorum* was imposed on the Bavarians in the middle of the eighth century by their Frankish protectors. Although it was the need to codify and write down their own laws which was particularly great for the barbarians, several barbarian kings thought it necessary to provide a new legislation destined for the Romans. This generally involved adaptations and simplifications of the Theodosian Code of 438. Thus we have the Breviary of Alaric (506) among the Visigoths and the *Lex Romana Burgundiorum* among the Burgundians.

The legal diversity was not as great as one might think, firstly because the barbarian laws were very similar to each other, and secondly because in each kingdom one code tended to have precedence over the others, and finally because the Roman influence, fairly strong from the start, as among the Visigoths, tended, given its superiority, to become explicit. The influence of the Church, especially after the conversion of the Arian kings, and the unifying tendencies of the Carolingians in the late eighth and early ninth centuries, contributed to a decline or a disappearance of the personality of laws in favour of their territoriality. As early as the reign of the Visigoth Recceswinth (652-72), for example, the clergy forced the king to publish a new code which would be as much applicable to the Visigoths as to the Romans. However, the particularist legislation of the early middle ages strengthened the tendency to compartmentalization which lasted throughout the middle ages. As we have seen the roots of this lay in the fragmentation of the population, of the occupation and management of the land and of the economy. This reinforced the parochial outlook, the *campanilismo* which were characteristic of the middle ages. Sometimes, indeed, people openly laid claim to the jurisdictional particularism of the early middle ages. As late as the tenth and eleventh centuries the *Lex Gundobada* was invoked in Cluniac charters to justify a personal status which in fact depended on local customs. In the twelfth century we encounter in the acts of Modena opposition between the indigenous people *romana lege viventes*, 'living under Roman law', and a French or Norman colony (probably the one which brought the Arthurian legends portrayed in the sculptures of the Romanesque cathedral) who are defined as *salica lege viventes*, 'living under the Salic law'.

V

Of course the barbarians adopted as far as they could whatever was superior in the legacy of the Roman empire, especially in the cultural field, as we shall see, and in political organization. Yet here as there they hastened, encouraged and exaggerated the decadence which had begun under the late empire. They turned a decline into a regression. They combined a threefold barbarism, their own, that of the decrepit Roman world and that of the old primitive forces, which lay below the Roman varnish and had been freed by the dissolving of the varnish under the impact of the invasions. The regression was chiefly a quantitative one. The barbarians destroyed human lives, great buildings, and equipment necessary for the economy. The population fell sharply; art treasures were lost; the roads, workshops, warehouses, irrigation systems, and cultivated areas fell into decay. The destruction was further prolonged in that the ancient monuments in ruin served as quarries from which people removed stones, columns and ornaments. The barbarian world, incapable of creating or producing, 'redeployed'. In this impoverished, underfed, weakened world a natural calamity succeeded in completing what the barbarians had begun. From 543 bubonic plague from the east ravaged Italy, Spain, and a great part of Gaul for more than half a century. After this came the bottom of the abyss, the sad seventh century, which could well be described by the old expression 'the dark ages'. Two centuries later, with some literary grandiloquence, Paul the Deacon conjured up the horror of the plague in Italy.

Villas or towns hitherto full of crowds of people were plunged in a day into the deepest silence by a general flight. Children fled leaving the bodies of their parents unburied, parents abandoned the steaming entrails of their children. If by chance anyone remained to bury his neighbour he condemned himself to remaining himself unburied . . . . The world was brought back to the silence prior to the creation of man: no voices in the fields, no whistling shepherds . . . . The harvests waited in vain for a reaper and the grapes were still hanging on the vines at the onset of winter. The fields were turned into cemeteries and the houses of men into dens for wild beasts . . . .

There was a decline in skills which was to leave the medieval west deprived for a long time. No one any longer knew how to quarry, transport or work stone, and stoneworking faded into the background to make way for a return to wood as the essential material. The art of glassmaking in the Rhineland disappeared with the natron which was no longer imported from the Mediterranean after the sixth century, or was reduced to coarse products made in huts in the forest in the area around Cologne. Artistic taste, as we shall see, underwent a regression, and so did morals. The penitentials of the early middle ages – lists of the punishments to be applied to each type of sin – surely belong in the 'hells' of libraries. Not only did the old stock of peasant superstitions re-emerge, but all the sexual perversions ran riot and acts of violence turned nastier – blows, wounds, gluttony, drunkenness. Augustin Thierry's *Récits des temps mérovingiens*, faithfully drawn from the best sources, chiefly Gregory of Tours, and adding nothing except a clever literary *mise-en-scène*, has for more than a century familiarized us with the unleashing of barbarian violence. It was all the more savage because the high rank of the perpetrators assured them relative impunity. Only imprisonment and murder put a brake on the excesses of these Frankish kings and queens whose rule Fustel de Coulanges defined as 'despotism tempered by assassination'. 'In that time many crimes were committed . . . each saw justice in his own will', wrote Gregory of Tours.

The refinement of the tortures used was to give inspiration to medieval iconography for a long time to come. The Romans had not submitted the Christian martyrs to the torments to which the Catholic Franks exposed their own martyrs. 'It was common to cut off the hands and the feet and the end of the nose. Eyes were torn out, faces were mutilated with red-hot irons, pointed sticks were jabbed under fingernails and toenails . . . when the wounds began to heal up again after the pus had flowed out, they were reopened. If necessary a physician was summoned so that, once the victim was cured, he could be tortured with a longer agony'. St Leodegarius or Léger, bishop of Autun, fell into the hands of his enemy, Ebroin, mayor of the palace, in 677. His tongue was cut out, his cheeks and lips were slashed, he was forced to walk barefoot across a pool strewn with stones as sharp and piercing as nails, and finally his eyes were put out. Again, there was the death of Brunhild, tortured for three days and finally tied to the tail of an untamed horse which was whipped until it bolted . . . . What is most striking is the unemotional language of the law codes. Here is an extract from the *lex Salica*: 'For tearing off someone else's hand, or a foot, an eye, the nose, 100 solidi, but only 63 if the hand remains attached; for tearing off the thumb 50 solidi, but only 30 if it remains attached; for tearing off the index finger (the finger used to pull the bow with) 35 solidi; any other finger 30 solidi; two fingers together 35 solidi; three fingers together 50 solidi'.

Administration and the majesty of government also regressed. The Frankish king, enthroned by being raised on a shield, bore as his whole insignia a lance in place of a sceptre or a diadem, and as a distinctive sign he had long hair; he was a *rex crinitus*, a Samson-king with long hair who was followed from villa to villa by several scribes, domestic slaves and his bodyguard of *antrustiones* . . . . All of this was adorned with astounding titles borrowed from the vocabulary of the late empire. The chief groom was the count of the stable or constable, the bodyguards were the counts of the palace, and the pack of drunken soldiers and uncouth clerics were 'magnificent' or 'illustrious' men. Since there was no longer any revenue from taxation, the king's wealth was reduced to chests of gold coins, pieces of glass and jewellery which his wives, concubines and legitimate and illegitimate children disputed at his death just as they carved up his lands and even the kingdom.

And what of the Church? In the disorder of the invasions, bishops and monks, such as St Severin, had become the all-capable leaders of a disorganized world. To their religious role they added a political one, that of negotiating with the barbarians; an economic role, that of distributing foodstuffs and alms; a social role, protecting the poor against the rich; and even a military role, organizing the resistance or fighting 'with spiritual weapons' where material weapons no longer existed. By the force of circumstances they had served an apprenticeship in government by clergy, in the confusion of the secular and ecclesiastical powers. Through penitential discipline and the application of canon law (the early sixth century was a period of councils and synods paralleling the codification of civil law) they attempted to fight against violence and to ameliorate people's behaviour. Of the two Manuals of St Martin of Braga, who became the archbishop of the capital city of the Sueve kingdom in 579, the first, *De correctione rusticorum* laid down a programme for correcting the behaviour of peasants, and the second, the *Formula vitae honestae*, dedicated to the king, Mir, laid down the moral ideal of the Christian ruler. Their success was to persist throughout the whole of the middle ages. However, whether they were barbarized themselves or whether they were incapable of fighting against the barbarism of the ruling class and the masses, the ecclesiastical leaders ratified a regression in spirituality and religious practice – God's judgement proclaimed through ordeals, an unheard-of development of the cult of relics, and the strengthening of sexual and food taboos in which the most primitive biblical tradition was linked with barbarian customs. 'Cooked or raw' an Irish penitential declared, 'reject everything which has been contaminated by a leech.'

Above all the Church pursued its own interest, without worrying itself about the *raison d'état* of the barbarian states any more than it had done about the Roman empire. Through the grants which it demanded from the kings and the great men, even the most humble, it accumulated lands, revenues, and exemptions. In a world where hoarding was constantly making economic life yet more sterile, the Church seriously affected production by draining it away. The bishops, who almost all belonged to the aristocracy of the great landowners, were all-powerful in their towns and their dioceses and tried to be so throughout the kingdom. St Avitus, bishop of Vienne, who exercised what amounted to a primacy in the Burgundian kingdom in the early sixth century, favoured the expansionist aims of the Frankish Clovis, who had become a Catholic, over the Arian Burgundian kings. Caesarius of Arles was arrested by Alaric in 505, summoned by Theodoric to Ravenna in 512 to vindicate his behaviour against the Arian king. Whether or not St Remigius said to Clovis at his baptism, 'Bow your head, proud Sicamber' he certainly meant Clovis' head to be bowed, and the heads of Clovis' successors too, to the yoke of the Church, which was easily identified with the yoke of God. St Eligius (Eloi) played on his status and his usefulness as a goldsmith to capture the favour of Dagobert. St Leodegarius, as we have seen, displayed such strong political ambitions that Ebroin martyred him. Above all the bishops, with Gregory of Tours in the lead, preached resistance to taxation, which lessened the wealth of the churches. Thus they removed from the kings the very means of government which on the other hand they wanted to reinforce, to make it serve the interests of religion and the Church.

Finally, wishing to make use of each other, the kings and bishops neutralized and mutually paralysed each other. The Church tried to lead the State and the kings to direct the Church. The bishops set themselves up as counsellors and as critics of the rulers in all areas, forcing them to turn canons of church councils into civil laws, while the kings, even once they had become Catholic, nominated the bishops and presided over these very councils. In the seventh century in Spain, the conciliary assemblies became veritable parliaments of the Visigothic kingdom. They imposed an antisemitic legislation which increased the economic difficulties and the discontent of the inhabitants, who later welcomed the Muslims, if not with open arms, at any rate without hostility. In Gaul the interpenetration of the two powers, in spite of the efforts of the Frankish kings to entrust the offices of their household and their government to laymen, and in spite of Charles Martel's brutal confiscation of part of the huge ecclesiastical estates, was such that the decadence of the Merovingian monarchy and the Frankish clergy went hand in hand. Before starting to evangelize Germany, St Boniface had to reform the Frankish clergy. This was to be the start of the Carolingian renaissance.

Indeed during this period the Church underwent real eclipses, at least in certain regions. Some areas reverted to paganism (as in England in the fifth and sixth centuries), and there were long vacancies in episcopal sees. The episcopal lists for Périgueux have a gap from 675 to the tenth century, for Bordeaux from 675 to 814, for Châlons from 675 to 779, for Geneva from 650 to 833, for Arles from 683 to 794, for Toulon from 679 to 879, for Aix from 596 to 794, for Embrun from 677 to 828, and for Béziers, Nîmes, Uzès, Agde, Maguelonne, Carcassonne and Elne from the end of the seventh century to 788. The return to paganism, the struggle between the priestly class and the warrior class, and the reciprocal paralysis of clerical and royal power also heralded the middle ages. Perhaps the cause above all was the tendency of the Church to set up a government by the clergy which dominated Christendom only to take it away from the things of this world. The pontificate of Gregory the Great (590–604), the most glorious of this period, is also the most significant. Gregory, a former monk who was elected pope during a crisis caused by the plague in Rome, thought that these calamities announced the end of the world. For him the duty of all Christians was to do penance, to detach themselves from this world to prepare themselves for the one which is to come. He only contemplated extending the Christian religion, whether in the case of the Anglo-Saxons or the Lombards, in order better to fulfil his role as the shepherd from whom Christ at the Last Judgement would relentlessly demand an account of his flock. The models he put forward in his works of spiritual edification were St Benedict, who represented monastic renunciation, and Job, who represented a complete stripping away of possessions and resignation. 'Why continue to reap when the reaper cannot survive? Let each consider the course of his life and then he will understand that the little that he has suffices'. The words of the pope, which were to have so much influence on the medieval mind, are themselves a doorway to the middle ages, which were an age of contempt for the world and of rejection of the Earth.

The west had, so to speak, been sliding down a slope since the late Roman empire, to the point where it often seems that continuity was winning over change, in the classic debate between the historians to know whether the early middle ages were the epilogue of the ancient world or the beginning of the new times (but is not every age, or almost every age, one of transition?). But here one senses that the point of arrival was so distant from the point of departure that the people of the middle ages themselves from the eighth century right up to the sixteenth felt the need to return to Rome because they felt that they had indeed left it. In each medieval renaissance the clerics affirmed, even more than a nostalgia for a return to Antiquity, the sense of having become something different. In any case, they never seriously contemplated coming back to Rome. When they dreamed of a return it was of Him who would bring them back to Abraham's bosom, in the earthly paradise, to the house of the Father. In their eyes, to bring back Rome to earth merely meant to restore it, to transfer it: *translatio imperii, translatio studii*. The power and knowledge which at the start of the middle ages had been in Rome had to be transferred to new seats, just as they had once been transferred from Babylon to Athens and then to Rome. To be reborn was to set out again, not to return. The first relaunching occurred in the Carolingian period, at the end of the eighth century.

2

The Germanic Attempt at Organization (Eighth to Tenth Centuries)

I

THIS NEW departure registered itself firstly in a geographic sense. Of course, since they lacked a fleet, the Carolingians could not and did not dream of re-establishing rule from the Continent in Britain, where the kingdom of Mercia had succeeded at the end of the eighth century in swallowing up the other small Anglo-Saxon kingdoms between the Humber and the Channel. King Offa (757-96) dealt with Charlemagne on equal terms, though admittedly this was before the latter had taken the imperial crown; they exchanged gifts as a sign of mutual recognition. Equally the Carolingians made no attempt on Muslim Spain. Finally they had for a time to respect the temporal power of the pope within the new papal state which they had so much helped to create. Within these limits the Carolingians pursued the reconstruction of the unity of the west in three directions, to the south-east in Italy, to the south-west towards Spain, and to the east in Germany. Pippin, an ally of the pope, took Carolingian policy to Italy. The first expedition against the Lombards took place in 754, the second in 756. Charlemagne finally captured King Desiderius in Pavia in 774, depriving him of the Italian crown, which he himself put on. However, he still had to wage war to impose his rule north of the peninsula, while the Lombard duchies of Spoleto and Benevento in fact escaped him. Towards the south-west it was again Pippin who set things in motion by taking Narbonne – still a fairly active port – from the Muslims in 759, although it was Charlemagne who was to have his name attached to the town's reconquest in legend. The *Geste de Guillaume d'Orange* was to make itself the echo of this:

Charles, hearing of this, felt his blood surge: 'Good Sir Naime, what is that city called?' – 'Sire', he said, 'it is called Narbonne. . . . There is no fortress so powerful in this world. The moats are more than forty yards wide and the same in depth. Waves from the sea flow in these moats. A great river, the Aude, runs around the ramparts. It is thence that come the great vessels furnished with iron and the galleys loaded with goods with which the people of the town grow rich . . . ' Charles, hearing of this, started to laugh: 'Oh! God! What a happy juncture!' said the king, put on his mettle. 'Is this Narbonne, of which I have heard so much spoken, the proudest town of Spain? . . . '

In the ballad the young Aimeri who took the town for Charles became Aimeri of Narbonne. Later, in 801, profiting from the internal quarrels of the Muslims, Charlemagne took Barcelona. A Spanish march was set up from Catalonia to Navarre, thanks particularly to Count William of Toulouse who was to become the hero of the sequence of *chansons de geste* about William of Orange. In 806 he withdrew into the abbey of Gellone which he had founded and he was henceforward called Count William of the Desert. This was the subject of the *Moniage Guillaume*. The Carolingians were not always so lucky in their struggle against the Muslims and the inhabitants of the Pyrenees. In 778 Charlemagne took Pamplona, did not dare to attack Saragossa, took Huesca, Barcelona and Gerona, and, abandoning Pamplona, which he razed, turned back northwards. Some Basque mountaineers ambushed the rearguard to lay hold of the Frankish baggage-train. On 15 August 778 the Basques massacred the troops commanded by the seneschal Eggihard, the count of the palace, Anselm, and the Prefect of the March of Brittany, Roland. The Carolingian royal annals do not breathe a word of this misadventure. A chronicler notes for 778 'In this year the lord king Charles went to Spain and there suffered a great disaster'. The vanquished were transformed into martyrs and their names endured. Their revenge was the *Chanson de Roland*.

To the east, it was Charlemagne who inaugurated a tradition of conquest in which massacre and conversion were combined, the forced conversion to Christianity which the middle ages was to practise for a long time. Along the North Sea it was firstly the Saxons who were conquered with difficulty between 772 and 803 in a series of campaigns in which apparent victories alternated with revolts by the allegedly conquered. The most spectacular revolt was the one led from 778 by Widukind, inflicting a disastrous defeat on the Franks at Süntal in 782. Charlemagne responded with savage repression, and had 4500 Saxons decapitated at Verden. Charles ended by reducing the Saxons to submission. He was helped by the missionaries (all injuries done to any one of these and all offences to the Christian religion were punished by death, according to a capitulary issued to aid the conquest). Year after year he led soldiers into the land, and while the missionaries baptised, the troops pillaged, burnt, massacred, and deported people en masse. Bishoprics were founded at Bremen, Münster, Paderborn, Verden and Minden. The German horizon, particularly the Saxon horizon, had attracted Charlemagne eastwards. He abandoned the valley of the Seine, in which the Merovingians had settled at Paris and the surrounding countryside, for the areas of the Meuse, the Moselle and the Rhine. Although he was always on the move, he was happiest visiting the royal villas of Herstal, Thionville, Worms, and above all Nijmegen, Ingelheim and Aachen where he had three palaces built. The palace at Aachen enjoyed precedence by the special character of its architecture, the number of times Charlemagne stayed there, and the importance of the events which took place there.

However, the south of Germany also occupied Charlemagne's attention. He spent almost no summer without fighting (the annalists noted a year with no fighting – *sine hoste*, without an enemy – as an exceptional event). To be more precise he organized and led his troops, for he rarely took part in combat personally. Following his father and grandfather, he had developed the effectiveness of the army, a cavalry force whose strength was founded on the horse, the broadsword, and knowledge of the battle terrain. The basis of Charlemagne's military success was horserearing, recourse to geographers, and the development of metalworking through the exploitation of an increased number of shallow veins (preserved in place names as the numerous '*Ferrières*' dating from the Carolingian period). The conquest of Bavaria was that of a land already Christian and theoretically subordinate to the Franks since the Merovingians. Tassilo, duke of Bavaria since 748, played the Franks off against the Lombards and made Regensburg one of the grandest barbarian capitals. Having conquered the Lombards, and, for the moment, the Saxons, Charlemagne marched on Bavaria in 787, but thanks to the support of the pope, who had excommunicated Tassilo, and thanks to the support of a strong faction among the Bavarian clergy which he had bought over, he obtained Tassilo's submission without striking a blow. Complete submission was assured in 788, when Charlemagne got rid of the Bavarian ducal family by having Tassilo tonsured and shut up at Jumièges and then at Worms, and turning his wife and two daughters into nuns and his two sons into monks. Bishop Arn of Salzburg, who helped Charles integrate Bavaria and its church into the Frankish state and church, became archbishop in 798.

The new province of Bavaria remained exposed to the raids of the Avars, a people of Turkish-Tartar origin who had come from the Asiatic steppes like the Huns. Having absorbed a certain number of Slav tribes they had founded an empire on horseback on the middle Danube from Carinthia to Pannonia. They were professional raiders and had acquired an enormous booty from their raids which they hoarded in their headquarters, the Ring, which preserved the round form of Mongol tents. This wealth was clearly highly attractive

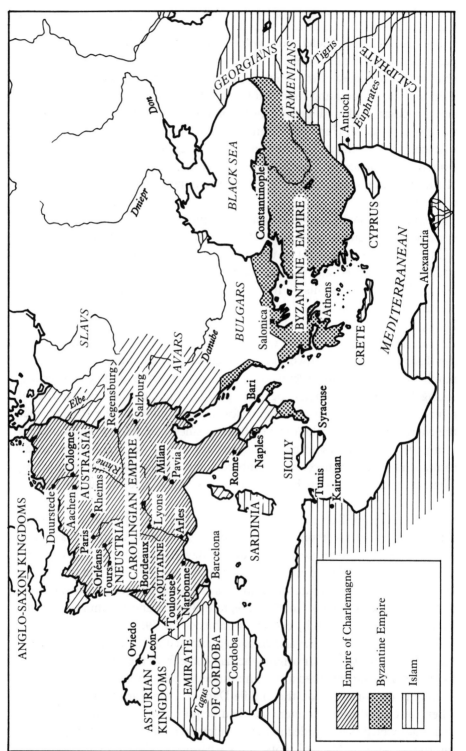

Map 9 The Carolingian Empire, Byzantium and Islam at the start of the ninth century

to the Franks, whose rulers always tried (as the Romans had done) to obtain a sizeable part of their income from conquered treasure. A skilfully planned campaign in 791, which was to make three Frankish armies converge, two coming from the west and progressing along each of the banks of the Danube, and the other brought from Italy by Pippin, Charlemagne's son, was halted by an epidemic which killed a large number of the Franks' horses. In 796 Charlemagne took hold of the Ring, and the principal Avar chief, Tudun, submitted and was converted to Christianity. He was baptized at Aachen with Charlemagne as his godfather. The Frankish ruler annexed the western part of the Avar empire between the Danube and the Drave. The Carolingian empire had barely encroached on the Slav world. Expeditions conducted along the lower course of the Elbe and beyond, after the conquest of Saxony, had repulsed or absorbed certain Slav tribes. The victory over the Avars made Slovenes and Croatians enter the Frankish world. Finally Charlemagne attacked the Greeks, but this conflict was very unusual. Its special significance derived from the fact that, in 800, something had happened which had given Charlemagne's undertakings a new dimension: the Frankish king had been crowned emperor by the pope at Rome.

The re-establishment of the empire in the west seems in fact to have been an idea of the pope's, and not a Carolingian one. Charlemagne was chiefly concerned to preserve the division of the ancient Roman empire into a western half, of which he would be the leader, and an eastern half, which he did not think of disputing with the Byzantine basileus, although he refused to concede to the latter the imperial title which evoked the lost unity. In the *Libri Karolini* of 792, he presented himself as 'king of the Gauls, of Germany, of Italy and the neighbouring provinces', while the basileus was 'the king who dwells in Constantinople'. It seemed all the more necessary to him to indicate this equality and his independence because the iconoclastic upsurge in Byzantium had made the Franks, as in the period of Clovis in the west, the champions of orthodoxy. Charlemagne also wanted to protest against the second council of Nicaea of 787 which had claimed to settle the question of Images for the universal Church.

But Pope Leo III saw a threefold advantage in 799 in giving the imperial crown to Charlemagne. He had been imprisoned and persecuted by his enemies in Rome and needed to see his authority restored *de facto* and *de iure* by someone whose authority would be accepted without dispute by everyone: an emperor. As head of a temporal state, the Patrimony of St Peter, he wanted recognition of this temporal sovereignty to be corroborated by a king superior to all the others in title as well as in reality. Finally, together with a faction among the Roman clergy he contemplated making Charlemagne into an emperor for the whole Christian world, including Byzantium, so as to fight against the iconoclastic heresy and to establish the supremacy of the Roman pontiff over all the Church. Charlemagne went along with this with a certain reluctance. Considering himself to be a 'king crowned by God', *rex a deo coronatus*, he perhaps judged the pope's gesture to be superfluous; nor was the pope considered by all to be the vicar of God. Before all else he was king of the Franks, and he was only moderately beguiled by a ceremony which primarily made him a king of the Romans, and, in a very real sense, king of the inhabitants of the Rome of 800, which certainly lacked the splendour of ancient Rome. In spite of this he let himself be convinced and crowned on 25 December 800. However he only attacked Byzantium to have recognition of his title and his equality with the emperor of Byzantium. Once diplomatic measures, including a project to marry the empress Irene, had failed, he led a series of operations in the north of the Adriatic on the border between the two empires. Here too the lack of ships made him fail against the Greek fleets, but his military superiority on land allowed him to take hold of Friuli, Carniola, Istria, and above all Venice, which had already vainly tried to remain neutral and safeguard its nascent commerce. Finally peace was made in 814, some months before Charlemagne's death. The Franks yielded Venice, kept the lands to the north of the Adriatic, and the basileus recognized Charlemagne's imperial title.

Charlemagne was concerned to administer and govern his vast territory effectively. Although the great officials, the advisers and the secretaries who formed the ruler's court were pretty much the same as they had been under the Merovingians, they were more numerous and above all better educated. Although the acts of government remained chiefly oral, the use of the written word was encouraged, and one of the principal aims of the cultural renaissance (of which more later) was to improve the professional skills of the royal officials. Above all – as is well known – Charlemagne strove to make his authority felt in the whole of the Frankish kingdom by developing administrative and legislative texts and by increasing the number of personal envoys, that is to say the representatives of central power.

The written instruments were the capitularies or ordinances, which could be particular to one region, such as the Saxon capitularies, or general, such as the capitulary of Herstal concerning the reorganization of the state (779), the capitulary *De villis* concerning the administration of the royal estates, and the capitulary *De literis colendis* concerning the reform of education. The human instruments were the *missi dominici*, the great lay or ecclesiastical personages sent out on an annual mission of surveillance over the sovereign's delegates, the counts, and, on the frontiers, the marquises or dukes, or of administrative reorganization. At the top the important figures of the lay and ecclesiastical aristocracy of the kingdom assembled around the ruler each year at the end of winter. This sort of aristocratic parliament (we should not be deceived by the word *populus* which was used to describe it) assured Charlemagne of the obedience of his subjects. On the other hand it was to impose the will of the great on his weak successors. In fact, the grandiose Carolingian structure split up rapidly in the course of the ninth century under blows rained jointly by external enemies (new invaders) and by internal agents of disintegration.

II

The invaders came from every direction, the most dangerous by sea from the north and the south. From the north came the Scandinavians who were called simply the men of the north or Norsemen, or else the Vikings. They came chiefly to plunder. They raided the coastlines, moved up the rivers, attacked the rich abbeys and sometimes laid siege to the towns. Nor should one forget that the Scandinavian expansion took place eastwards as well as westwards. The Swedes or Varangians colonized Russia, certainly economically, by dominating the trade which went across the country, and possibly politically, by inspiring the earliest forms of states there. To the west the Norwegians above all attacked Ireland and the Danes the regions bordering on the North Sea and the Channel. As early as 809 the Channel crossing had ceased to be safe. After 834 the Norse raids, which mainly gunned at the ports of Quentovic and Duurstede, and the commercial outlets of the Scheldt, the Meuse, and the Rhine, became annual occurrences. A settlement phase began, though it was still a question of setting up safer bases closer to hand for plundering raids. In 839 a Norse chief founded a kingdom in Ireland and established his capital at Armagh. In 838 the king of Denmark asked the emperor Louis the Pious to cede the territory of the Frisians to him. In spite of Louis' refusal, the Norse occupied the area round Duurstede. To pick out some of the main events (among others): in 841 Rouen was plundered; in 842 Quentovic was destroyed; in 843 Nantes was sacked; in 844 the Vikings ventured as far as Coruña, Lisbon and even Seville; in 845 the Vikings' targets included Hamburg and Paris which were sacked by fleets of 120 ships commanded by Ragnar, the Ragnar Lodbrok (Leatherbreeches) of the sagas. In 859 they penetrated as far as Italy, up to Pisa; this was to be their furthest-flung raid geographically. One of the victims of their innumerable raids was Aachen where, in 881, they burnt the tomb of Charlemagne. However, like other invaders in other periods they now thought about settling, becoming fixed, and replacing raids with trade.

In 878 through the peace of Wedmore they had their occupation of part of England recognized by Alfred the Great, and they made themselves masters of England in the early eleventh century under Sven and his son Cnut (1019–35). Other Scandinavians settled in the north of Gaul, in a region to which they gave their name (Normandy), which was granted by Charles the Simple to their leader Rollo by the treaty of St-Clair-sur-Epte of 911. The Normans were to swarm throughout western Europe, leaving lasting traces. In 1066 they conquered England; from 1029 onwards they settled in southern Italy and in Sicily, where they founded one of the most innovative states of medieval Europe. They turned up in the Byzantine empire and in the Holy Land at the time of the Crusades.

To the south the attack came from the Muslims of Ifriqiya, after an Arab dynasty, that of the Aghlabids, had made itself effectively independent of the caliphate and had built a fleet. The Ifriqian pirates appeared in Corsica from 806, and after 827 undertook the conquest of Sicily. In less than a century they had completed it, with the exception of a few pockets that remained in the hands of the Byzantines or of the native population. But all the important centres had fallen into their hands – Palermo (831), Messina (843), Enna (859), Syracuse (878), Taormina (902). From Sicily they advanced on to the Italian peninsula, sometimes for pillaging raids, on the most spectacular of which they sacked St Peter's in Rome (846), and sometimes to set up bridgeheads such as Tarentum or Bari, from which the Byzantine emperor Basil I dislodged them in 880. The offensives of the Aghlabids were paralleled in the extreme west of the Mediterranean by new attacks by the Muslims in Spain against Provence, Liguria, and Tuscany. Here too a 'Saracen' bridgehead was set up at Fraxinetum near St Tropez.

Thus, while the Carolingians were establishing their dominion over the continent, the seas seemed to be escaping them. Even on land, they appeared momentarily to be threatened by a new invasion coming from Asia, that of the Hungarians. The Magyar invasion proceeded according to the usual plan. In the seventh century the Magyars settled in the state of the Khazars, Turks converted to Judaism who lived in the Volga basin, where they controlled a very prosperous trade between Scandinavia, Russia, and the Muslim world. But towards the middle of the ninth century, other Turks, the Petchenegs, destroyed the Khazar empire and drove the Magyars westwards. The Magyars reminded the westerners of the Huns: they led the same existence on horseback, they had the same military superiority through their archers, and they were equally fierce. The Magyars advanced towards the plains and steppes of the middle Danube, which had been partly depopulated by Charlemagne's destruction of the Avar empire. From 899 onwards they launched murderous and destructive raids on Venetia, Lombardy, Bavaria, and Swabia. At the start of the tenth century they finished off the state of Moravia and soon penetrated into Alsace, Lotharingia, Burgundy and Languedoc. Among their chief victims were Pavia, which was captured in 924, where they are supposed to have burned '44 churches', and Verdun which they burned in 926. Certain years were particularly disastrous, such as 926 when their ravages stretched from the Ardennes to Rome, 937 when they devastated a large part of Germany, France, and Italy, and 954 when they advanced as far as Cambrai in the west and Lombardy in the south. But in 955 the German king Otto cut them to pieces at the battle of the Lechfeld near Augsburg. Their impetus was shattered, and they went on to complete the historical pattern of the barbarian invaders: they renounced raiding, they settled down, and were converted to Christianity. Hungary came into existence at the end of the tenth century. However, the Magyar invasion helped a new power to emerge in the west, that of the Ottonian dynasty. In 962 it restored the imperial power which the Carolingians, undermined even more by internal decadence than by external assaults, had abandoned.

III

In spite of their efforts to take over the political and administrative inheritance of Rome, the Franks had not acquired a sense of the State. The Frankish kings regarded the kingdom as their property just as they regarded their estates and their treasures. They gave parts of the kingdom away readily. When Chilperic married Galswintha, the daughter of the Visigothic king Athanagild, he offered his young wife five towns in southern Gaul, including Bordeaux, on the morning after the marriage, as a '*Morgengabe*'. The Frankish kings shared out their kingdom among their heirs. From time to time the Frankish states were regrouped under two kings or one single one through chance, infant mortality or mental imbecility. Thus Dagobert pushed his weak-minded cousin Caribert aside and reigned alone from 629 to 639. Similarly the premature death of his brother Carloman, who was the favourite of their father Pippin, left Charlemagne sole master of the Frankish kingdom in 771. The restoration of the empire did not prevent Charlemagne in his turn from sharing out his kingdom between his three sons at the time of the *Ordinatio* of Thionville of 806; he did not, however, say anything about the imperial crown. Here too it was chance that left Louis sole master of the kingdom in 814 after Charlemagne's death, for his other sons, Pippin and Charles, had predeceased him. Bernard, Charlemagne's grandson, who had received the kingdom of Italy from his grandfather, retained it for the time being, but came to Aachen to make an oath of fealty to Louis. As early as 817 Louis the Pious attempted by an *Ordinatio* to regulate the problem of his succession by reconciling the tradition of division with care for imperial unity. He shared out the kingdom between his three sons but assured the imperial pre-eminence to his eldest son Lothar. The late birth of a fourth son, Charles, to whom Louis wanted to give part of his kingdom, put the *Ordinatio* in question once more. Louis the Pious' reign was filled with crises involving the rebellion of his sons against him, the struggle of the sons amongst themselves, and new territorial divisions; he lost all authority. After his death in 840 the divisions and the struggles continued. In 843 came the division of Verdun. Lothar, the eldest son, received a long corridor stretching from the North Sea to the Mediterranean, which contained Aachen, the symbol of the Frankish empire, and Italy, that is to say the protection of Rome. Louis received the lands to the east and became Louis the German, while Charles, nicknamed the Bald, received the lands to the West. In 870 at Meerssen Charles the Bald and Louis the German shared out Lotharingia between themselves, with the exception of Italy, which remained in the possession of Louis II, the son of Lothar I, who was nominally emperor. By an agreement reached at Ribemont (880) Lotharingia shifted eastwards towards eastern Francia. It is true that the unity of the empire seemed for a moment to have been re-established under Charles the Fat, the third son of Louis the German, who was king of Italy (879), emperor (881), sole king of Germany (882), and finally king of western Francia (884). However, after his death (888) Carolingian unity swiftly collapsed. The imperial title was no longer used, except by the Carolingian Arnulf (896–9) and by some petty Italian kings, and it disappeared in 924. In western Francia the kingdom, which had once more become elective, alternated between the Carolingian kings and kings of the family of Odo, count of France, that is to say count of the Ile-de-France, who had been the hero of the resistance of Paris against the Norsemen in 885–6. In Germany the Carolingian dynasty died out with Louis the Child (911), and the royal crown, which here too was granted by the magnates by election, fell to Duke Conrad of Franconia, and then to the duke of Saxony, Henry I (the Fowler). His son was Otto I, the founder of a new imperial line.

Although all these divisions, conflicts, and confusion happened swiftly, they left durable traces on the map and in history. First of all the division created by the 120 experts at Verdun in 843, which seems to defy all ethnic and natural boundaries, suggests, as Roger Dion showed, that economic realities had been taken into consideration. The intention was to assure to each of the three brothers a part of each of the latitudinal botanic and economic bands which make up Europe, 'from the great pastures of the Marschen to the salt-pans and olive-groves of Catalonia, Provence and Istria'. The problem of relations between north and south, Flanders and Italy, the Hanse and the Mediterranean towns, the Alpine routes, the Rhine route, the Rhône route, and the importance of north–south axes was being posed in a Europe in the process of formation,

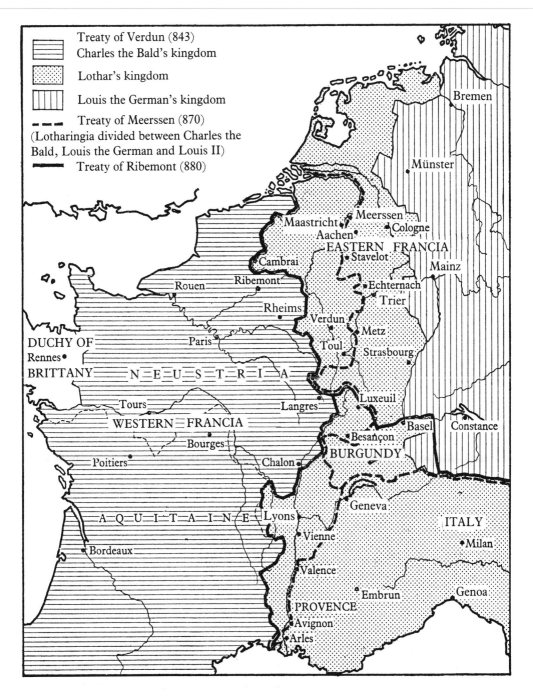

Map 10 Partitions of the Carolingian Empire

which was not centred on the Mediterranean, and where circulation was chiefly aligned 'at right angles to the vegetation zones', which ran across from east to west.

Then, the outlines of future nations were drawn. Western Francia, which was to become France, was beginning to join to itself Aquitaine, which had long been so different and had existed as an individual kingdom. Eastern Francia was to become Germany, and since it had no frontier except to the north it was to be tempted westwards even beyond Lotharingia. For centuries this area was to be an apple of discord between France and Germany, which inherited the rivalry of the grandsons of Charlemagne. The German rulers were tempted southwards; the Italian and imperial mirages were to retain their allure for a long time to come. This *Sehnsucht nach Süden* alternated or combined with the *Drang nach Osten*, which was also beginning on the marches with the Slavs. Throughout these vicissitudes Italy remained a kingdom threatened by the Germanic imperial pretensions and by papal temporal ambitions. In addition there were fragile intermediate political formations, the kingdom of Provence, the kingdom of Burgundy, and Lotharingia, which were destined to be absorbed into larger units, in spite of a few medieval resurgences ending up with the Angevins in Provence and the grand dukes of Burgundy.

Above all, these political crises encouraged, as the invasions had done, a fragmentation of imperial authority and power, which was more revealing and, at least for the immediate future, more important than the political break-up into kingdoms. The magnates gained greater control of economic power, that is of the land and, from this base, of the public powers.

At the end of the reign of Charlemagne the Council of Tours stated 'For various sorts of reasons the property of the poor has been greatly reduced in many places, that is to say the property of those who are known to be freemen, but who are living under the authority of powerful magnates'. Here, increasingly, were the new masters: great churchmen and laymen. The monasteries, whose abbots in any case belonged to the great magnate families, had immense landed estates, of which we know more than the lay estates (royal estates apart) because their administration, better organized by clerics, left written traces. In the early ninth century Irminon, abbot of St-Germain-des Prés, had an inventory or polyptych drawn up of the abbey's estates and of the payments which were due to it from the tenants. It described 24 estates (not the total, as part of the document is missing), of which 19 were situated around Paris, between Mantes and Château-Thierry. These estates often correspond to a modern-day commune, but their surface area could vary (there were 398 hectares of cultivated land on the villa of Palaiseau, but only 76 at Nogent l'Artaud, though it is true that 1000 pigs were reared at Nogent l'Artaud, as opposed to only 50 at Palaiseau).

Economic power on this scale made it possible for the great landowners to monopolize public powers, thanks to a process which had been instituted, or, at least, encouraged, by Charlemagne and his successors in the hope of arriving at quite opposite results. In fact, in order to give the Frankish kingdom a firm foundation, Charlemagne had made many grants of land, or benefices, to the men whose loyalty he wished to make sure of, and he had obliged them to swear an oath to him and enter into his vassalage. He thought that by these personal links he could ensure the solidity of the state. He encouraged the royal vassals to make their dependants enter into their own vassalage, in order that the whole of society, or at least all the people who counted, should be bound to the king or the emperor by the tightest possible network of personal subjection. The invasions strengthened this process because danger drove the weaker to put themselves under the protection of the most powerful, and because the kings demanded military aid from their vassals in exchange for the granting of benefices. From the middle of the ninth century the term *miles*, meaning soldier or knight, often took the place of *vassus* to designate the vassal. In an important simultaneous development benefices started to be made hereditary. The custom was grounded in practice. It was strengthened in 877 by the capitulary of Quierzy-sur-Oise in which Charles the Bald, who was getting ready to leave on an expedition for Italy, gave assurances to his vassals that the right to inherit the paternal benefice would be safeguarded to young or absent sons if their father died. The vassals were formed themselves more solidly into a social class by the operation of the heritability of the benefice.

At the same time, great landowners, especially counts, dukes, and marquises, were allowed or even forced to take initiatives because of economic and political necessities, and these began to transform the lord into a screen between his vassals and the king. As early as 811 Charlemagne was complaining of the fact that certain people were refusing to do military service on the pretext that their lord had not been summoned and that they had to stay with him. Those of the great who, like the counts, were invested with powers arising from their public function, tended to confuse these with the rights which they possessed as lords over their vassals, while the others, following their example, usurped public powers ever increasingly. Of course the Carolingian calculation was not entirely false. If the kings and emperors between the tenth and thirteenth century managed to retain a few sovereign prerogatives, they owed this chiefly to the fact that the great men, once they had become their vassals, could not withdraw themselves from the duties which they had sworn by their oath of fealty. But one is conscious of the development which was taking place in the Carolingian period that was to be decisive for the medieval world. From now on each man was going to depend increasingly on his lord, and this near horizon, this yoke which was all the heavier because it was exercised in a narrower circle, was to be founded in law. The basis of power was more and more to be the possession of land, and the foundation of morality was to be fidelity, the faith which was for centuries to replace the civic Greco-Roman virtues. Ancient man had to be just or righteous, medieval man had to be faithful. From now the wicked were the faithless.

IV

Since the idea of the state had lost its meaning, Otto I, king of Germany, although he had made up his mind to affirm his power, saw no other means of doing this when he ascended the throne in 936 than by attaching the dukes to him by making them all his vassals. 'They gave him their hands and promised him fidelity and help against all enemies,' wrote the chronicler Widukind. This did not prevent them from turning against Otto, who defeated their coalition at Andernach (939). He imposed his rule on Lotharingia (944), arbitrated between the Robertian and the Carolingian candidates for the French throne at the synod of Ingelheim (948), and had himself recognized as king of Italy (951). Finally, flushed with his victories over the Hungarians at the Lechfeld and over the Slavs on the edge of the Recknitz (955), he was crowned emperor in St Peter's, Rome, by Pope John XII on 2 February 962.

Otto I immediately took up the Carolingian policy of Charlemagne and Louis the Pious. As early as 962 relations between the emperor and the pope were renewed in a pact. The emperor once more guaranteed the temporal power of the pope over the Patrimony of St Peter, but in exchange he demanded that no pope would be elected without his consent. For a century he and his successors were to make use of their right and were to push it to the extent of deposing the popes of whom they disapproved. In any case, Otto I, following Charlemagne, viewed his empire as merely the empire of the Franks, limited to the lands which recognized him as king. The campaigns which he undertook against the Byzantines aimed only at obtaining the recognition of his title, which was achieved in 972. The treaty was sealed by the marriage of his elder son with the Byzantine princess Theophanu. Otto I equally respected the independence of the kingdom of western Francia.

The evolution observable under his two successors aimed only at glorifying the imperial title without transforming it into direct domination. Otto II (973-83) replaced the title of Imperator Augustus, which had been habitually borne by his father, with that of 'emperor of the Romans', *Imperator Romanorum*. His son, Otto III, distinguished by the education given to him by his Byzantine mother, installed himself in Rome in 998 and proclaimed the restoration of the Roman empire, the *Renovatio Imperii Romanorum*, on a bull on one side of which was displayed the head of Charlemagne and on the other a woman carrying a lance and a shield, *Aurea Roma*. His dream had a tinge of universalism. A miniature shows him enthroned in majesty and receiving gifts from Rome, Germany, Gaul and Slavia. Yet his attitude towards his eastern neighbours showed that his ideas were flexible. In the year 1000 he recognized the independence of Poland. Gniezno became an archbishopric and the duke Boleslaw the Valiant received the title of 'co-operator' of the empire. Simultaneously he recognized the independence of Hungary whose ruler, Stephen, was baptized and received the royal crown.

For a brief moment of concord the Ottonian dream seemed close to being realized, thanks to the unity of views shared by the young emperor and Pope Silvester II, the learned Gerbert, who favoured this restoration of the empire and of Rome. But the dream soon vanished. The people of Rome rose up against Otto III. Otto died in January 1002, Silvester in May 1003. Henry II was content to return to the *Regnum Francorum*, to the empire based on the Frankish kingdom, which had become Germany. However, the Ottonians had bequeathed to their successors a nostalgia for Rome and a tradition of subordinating the pope to the emperor. From this was to be born the quarrel of Sacerdotium and Imperium, a renewal of the ancient conflict between warriors and priests. The clerical control of administration pursued under the Carolingians (it was bishops such as Jonas of Orléans, Agobard of Lyon and Hincmar of Rheims who governed in the ninth century) and the equilibrium achieved under the Ottonians did not succeed in dispelling this.

V

When the Roman dream of the year 1000 ended, another renewal was about to happen, that of the west as a whole. This sudden blossoming took place in the eleventh century, the age when western Christian Europe really took off. This rise could only occur on economic foundations, and these had doubtless been set in place earlier than is often believed. It may be argued that if there was a Carolingian renaissance, it was first and foremost an economic renaissance. Like the cultural renaissance it was limited, superficial, fragile, and, even more than the other, was almost destroyed by the invasions and plundering of the Norsemen, Hungarians, and Arabs of the ninth and early tenth centuries. These probably delayed the renaissance of the west by one or two centuries, just as the invasions of the fourth and fifth centuries had hastened the decline of the Roman world. It is easier to perceive certain signs of a renewal of commerce in the eighth and ninth centuries. Frisian trade and the port of Duurstede reached their apogee. Charlemagne reformed the

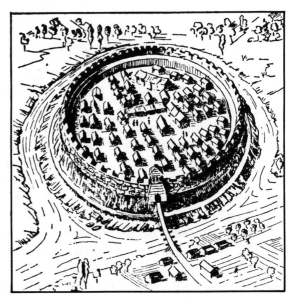

1 Opole
(artist's impression, after
P. Francastel, *Les origines des villes polonaises* [Paris and The Hague, 1960])

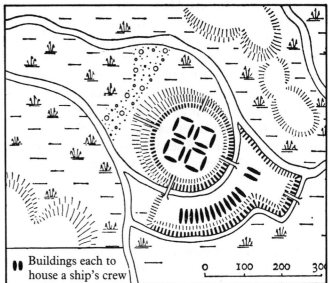

2 Trelleborg
(likely aerial plan, after *Westermanns Atlas zur Weltgeschichte*, ed. H. E. Stier *et al.*, Braunschweig, 1956)

|| Buildings each to house a ship's crew

0   100   200   300

Figures 1, 2, 3 The emergence of towns on the fringes of Christian Europe c.1000: the *grod* and the *wik*.

In Slav and Scandinavian lands, urban centres fulfilled more of a military than an economic function. Opole (1) in Polish Silesia was a Slavonic *grod* built of wood. The island site and fortified enclosure show preoccupation with defence, and the river was a trade route. Trelleborg (2) on the Danish island of Seeland was a Viking camp, one of the Norsemen's departure bases. It was a defensive site, whose inhabitants were moved by a naval, warfaring spirit (it was built at the time when England was being conquered by the Danes) so far as to build boat-shaped houses of wood, each of which probably housed a boat crew. Haithabu (3) on the isthmus of Jutland is, on the other hand, a fortified commercial *wik*, a great transit centre on one of the principal routes joining the Baltic area with the north-west of Europe in about 1000.

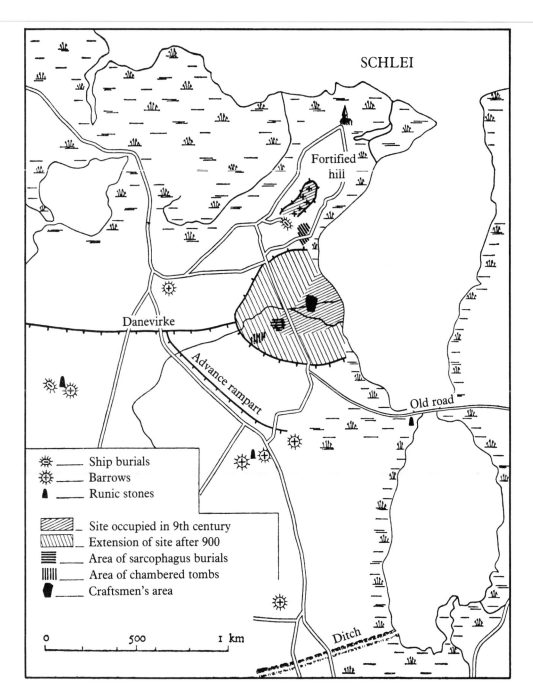

SCHLEI

Fortified hill

Danevirke

Advance rampart

Old road

Ship burials
Barrows
Runic stones

Site occupied in 9th century
Extension of site after 900
Area of sarcophagus burials
Area of chambered tombs
Craftsmen's area

0   500   1 km

Ditch

3 Haithabu
(plan based on the excavations, after *Westermanns Atlas*)

currency (to which we shall return) and cloth was exported which was probably Flemish but which was then called Frisian: Charlemagne sent *pallia fresonica* to the caliph Haroun al Raschid as a present. Yet, in this essentially rural economy, several pointers allow us to conclude that there was an improvement in agricultural production. The basic units, the *mansi*, were often fragmented, doubtless because of clearances. A new harness system appeared which was illustrated for the first time in a Troyes manuscript of about 800. Charlemagne reformed the calendar, giving the months names which are suggestive of progress in farming techniques. The miniatures which show the labours of the months change radically, abandoning the symbols of antiquity for real scenes in which men's technical mastery is displayed: 'Now man and nature are two things, and man is the master.' More certainly, whether the invasions of the ninth century had been responsible or not for a new lapse or for a mere economic standstill, progress is clearly discernible in the tenth century. A congress of American medievalists devoted to this period saw the tenth century as a period of decisive innovations, notably in the field of farming and in the provision of food. According to Lynn White the large-scale introduction of plants which were rich in protein (vegetables such as beans, lentils and peas), and which thus contained a greater energy-giving force, is supposed to have given mankind in the west the strength which was going to make them build cathedrals and clear large areas. 'The tenth century was full of beans' was Lynn White's joking conclusion. For his part, Robert Lopez wondered if one should not think in terms of a new renaissance, that of the tenth century. This was when Scandinavian trade was developing. Trading centres or *wiks* such as Haithabu on the Jutland isthmus replaced military camps such as Trelleborg on the Danish island of Seeland. The Slavonic economy was stimulated both by Norse commerce and Judaeo-Arab trade along the route which linked Cordoba to Kiev by way of central Europe. The lands on the Meuse and the Rhine began their rise. Northern Italy, above all, was already prosperous; the market at Pavia was an international one. Milan, whose rise has been analysed by Cinzio Violante, experienced inflation: 'a symptom of the revival of economic and social life'.

VI

To whom or what can this awakening of the medieval west be attributed? Should we agree with Maurice Lombard that it was a response to the formation of the Muslim world, a world of big cities consuming goods which aroused an increased production in the west of raw materials to export to Cordoba, Kairouan, Cairo, Damascus, Baghdad, such as wood, iron (Frankish swords), tin, honey, and that human commodity, slaves, for which Verdun was a great market in the Carolingian period? This is thus a hypothesis based on an external stimulus, which, furthermore, turns Henri Pirenne's famous theory inside out. Pirenne attributed the closing off of the Mediterranean and the drying up of western trade to the Arab conquest, which now on the contrary becomes the driving force of the economic reawakening of medieval Christian Europe. Or again, should we agree with Lynn White that the rise should be attributed to technical progress developed on the very soil of the west? This explanation is based on agricultural progress, including the wheeled plough with a mould-board, advances in three-yearly rotation, which in particular allowed those famous vegetables rich in proteins to be included, and the spread of the modern system of harness. These allowed an increase in the surface area under cultivation and in yields. Military progress, with the spur, allowed the horse to be mastered and gave birth to a new class of warriors, the knights, who were, moreover, the same as those great landowners who were able to introduce new equipment and techniques on their estates. This is an explanation through internal development, which, in addition, sheds light on the shift in the centre of gravity of western Europe towards the north, which was a land of plains and open spaces where both deep ploughing and breakneck gallops could be deployed.

Probably the truth is that the rise of the great – landed proprietors and knights together – created a class capable of seizing the economic opportunities which were offered to them: improved land management and control of the growing, though still limited, commercial outlets. The lords abandoned some of the profits which Christian Europe drew from these to a few specialists – the first western merchants. It is tempting to consider that the conquests of Charlemagne and his military undertakings in Saxony, Bavaria, and along the Danube, in Northern Italy and towards Venice, and across the Pyrenees, were making contact with the areas of exchange and were trying to absorb the routes of a reviving trade. The Treaty of Verdun could thus have been a sharing out of sections of the trade routes just as it was a sharing out of bands of cultivation. But after the year 1000 things became serious. Medieval Christendom made its real entrance on the scene.

3

The Formation of Christian Europe
(Eleventh to Thirteenth Centuries)

I

THERE IS a well-known passage in the chronicle of the Burgundian Ralph Glaber:

When the third year after the millennium dawned, churches were to be seen being rebuilt over all the earth, but especially in Italy and Gaul; although most of them were very well constructed and had no need of rebuilding, each Christian community was driven by a true rivalry to have a finer church than that of its neighbours. It looked as though the very world was shaking itself to take off its old age and to reclothe itself in all areas in a white cloak of churches. Thus, almost all the churches of episcopal sees, the churches of monasteries dedicated to different saints, and even the little chapels in villages were rebuilt more beautifully by the faithful.

Here we see the most striking outward sign of the rise of western Christian Europe which was becoming apparent around the year 1000. The great wave of building certainly made a major contribution to the advancement of medieval western Europe between the tenth and the fourteenth centuries. Firstly it acted as an economic stimulus. Raw materials such as stone, wood, and iron were produced in bulk, skills were perfected and implements were made to extract, transport, and lift materials of considerable size and weight, labour was recruited and building schemes were financed. Not only cathedrals but also innumerable other churches of all sizes, houses for the rich, and buildings whose purpose was economic, such as bridges, barns, and covered markets were constructed. Building sites were thus the centre of the earliest, and almost the only, medieval industry.

This impetus to build did not spring out of nothing. It was a response to needs, the chief of which was the necessity of accommodating a larger population. Doubtless the size of churches was not always directly related to the numbers of the faithful: the urge to build bigger was motivated just as much by prestige and piety. Even so, an important reason was the desire to enable the whole of the Christian flock, now that it had grown, to be contained within church buildings.

It is difficult to distinguish cause from effect in the evolution of Christian Europe, since most aspects of this process were both of these aspects at once. It is even harder to identify the first, decisive, cause of this process. Reasons can be given for denying this role to all the factors which are often put forward to explain the launch of western civilization; the growth in population, for example, was merely the earliest and most spectacular result of this progress. The same is true of the relative pacification of society which set in in the tenth century. The invasions came to an end and peace associations made some headway. These regulated war by limiting the periods of fighting and by placing certain categories of non-combatants (clergy, women, children, peasants, merchants, and sometimes farm animals) under the protection of guarantees sworn by the warriors. The first organization intended to make people observe the peace of God was established at the synod of Charroux in 989. Declining insecurity was itself only a consequence of the desire of large sectors of Christian society to protect nascent economic progress. 'All were terrified by the calamities of the preceding era, and were affected by the fear of seeing the sweets of plenty being snatched from it in the future,' as Ralph Glaber aptly remarked in explaining the movement of the Peace of God, in which he himself took part, in France at the start of the eleventh century. The protection especially afforded to peasants, merchants, livestock, pack animals and draught animals was typical: the pressure of economic progress made weapons recoil. A limited, controlled disarmament was imposed.

However, the origin of this expansion must be looked for in the land, which was the basis of everything in the middle ages. From the moment when the ruling class established itself in the countryside and became a class of great landowners, the landed aristocracy encouraged progress in agricultural production, especially when the status of the *vassus* changed from inferior to privileged person. From now on vassals were increasingly given benefices, which were almost always pieces of land. Not that the aristocracy took a direct interest in managing its estates, although some ecclessiastical lords and high Carolingian functionaries did so, but the dues and services which it extracted from the peasant masses must have stimulated the latter to improve their methods of cultivation to some extent to pay the dues. Very probably the decisive advances which amounted to what has been called an agrarian revolution between the tenth and the thirteenth centuries had their humble

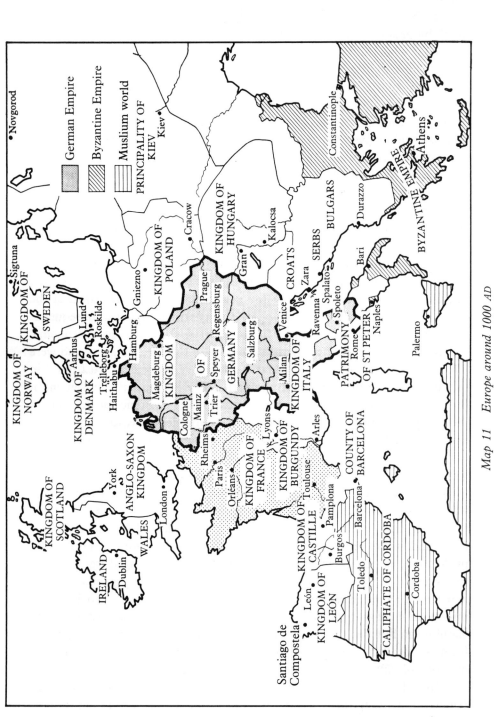

Map 11   Europe around 1000 AD

More fragmented, Europe was by now richer in new Christian kingdoms.

beginnings in the Carolingian era, and developed slowly until the year 1000 when they underwent a great acceleration.

Nor should it be forgotten that once the barbarian tribes had settled the new masters were forced to form a real policy of land development. The history of the earliest dukes of Normandy written by the canon Dudo of St Quentin in the eleventh century shows us how the Normans, during the first century after they had installed themselves in Normandy, turned themselves into cultivators under the leadership of their dukes, who put farming tools made of iron, especially ploughs, under their protection.

The slow diffusion of the practice of three-year rotation meant that the surface area under cultivation could be increased, since only a third, rather than a half, of the land was allowed to rest; also, crops could be varied. Bad weather could be countered by growing spring corn when the autumn corn failed, or vice versa. Adopting the asymmetrical plough with wheels and a mould-board and using a greater quantity of iron in agricultural equipment made it possible to plough deeper and more frequently. With improvements in the amount of land used, in yields and crop variety, came an improvement in nutrition, and one of the first consequences of this was an increase in population; it probably doubled between the tenth and the fourteenth centuries. According to J. C. Russell the population of western Europe went from 14.7 million in *c.*600 to 22.6 in 950 and 54.4 before the Black Death in 1348. According to M. K. Bennett, the population of the whole of Europe rose from 27 million *c.*700 to 42 in 1000 and 73 million in 1300. This population growth in its turn forced Christian Europe to expand. The conditions of feudal production methods were capable of encouraging technical progress to a certain extent, but were more effective in preventing it from rising above a rather low level; they did not allow advances in the standards of agricultural production sufficient to respond to the needs of a growing population. The improvement in yields and in the nutritional value of the yields remained low. Feudal culture – to which we will return – made really intensive cultivation impossible. All that remained was to increase the area under the plough. The chief aspect of the expansion of Christian society between the tenth and the fourteenth centuries was an intensive land-clearance movement. It is hard to establish its chronology; written sources for it are not very numerous before the twelfth century, while agricultural archaeology is not very advanced. It is difficult to undertake, because the medieval countryside has been frequently changed or destroyed by succeeding ages, and it produces results which are hard to interpret. According to Georges Duby, 'the activity of the pioneers, which had remained for two centuries timid, discontinuous, and extremely scattered, became at once more intensive and more co-ordinated around 1150'. In one key area, cereal-growing, the decisive point in the agrarian conquest occurred, as

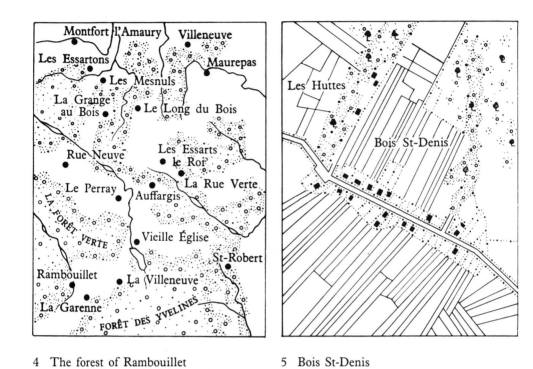

4 The forest of Rambouillet
(after G. Duby and R. Mandrou, *Histoire de la civilisation française*, I [Paris, 1958])

5 Bois St-Denis
(after M. Bloch, *Les caractères originaux de l'histoire rurale française*)

Figures 4, 5, 6, 7 Land-clearance in the Ile-de-France and on the edges of German and Slav territory.

The land clearances pierced holes in the forest cover of western Europe, especially between 1050 and 1250. The plan of the forest of Rambouillet (4) shows the work of medieval land-clearers underlined by place-names. Some of these refer to the labour of clearing, such as Les Essarts and Essartons, some to new human settlement, such as Villeneuve and Rue Neuve, and royal involvement can be detected in the name Les-Essarts-le-Roi. The other plans show how the population was arranged along a road or street and how land was cultivated in thin parallel bands running at right-angles to the axis of the village – the so-called fish-bone pattern. The farmland at Bois St-Denis (Aisne) (5) preserved strips of forest on its fringes which had become coppices. Altheim and Jablonow are two villages built on cleared land which are

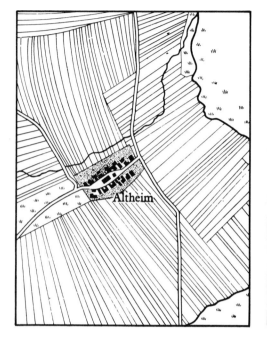

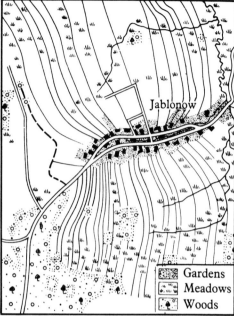

6 Altheim
(after *Westermanns Atlas*)

7 Jablonow
(after *Westermanns Atlas*)

characteristic of German colonization in the east. Altheim (6) near Leipzig, in a completely disafforested region, is a pasture village (*Angerdorf*), where the main street widens in the centre to make room for a village green. Jablonow (7), near Zagan in western Poland, meaning 'apple-tree village', in German Schönbrunn or 'fair well', is a village of wooded *mansi* (*Waldhufendorf*), which is reminiscent of the favourable way in which the settlers were treated in clearance zones. Each received a piece of land called a *Waldhufe* or wooded *mansus*. Here too the forest was preserved as strips on the edge of the village's farmland. In these two cases one can observe the gardens attached to each house and the pasturelands which made up an economy combining cultivation, pasture, and the use of the remaining forest.

palynology has shown, between 1100 and 1150: the proportion of corn pollen in vegetable remains underwent a particularly sharp increase in the first half of the twelfth century.

Most often the new fields were only an extension of lands long-used, 'a progressive enlargement of the clearing', which was wrested from the area bordering the existing clearings and pastures. Assarting land by fire pushed back the area covered by brushwood, but rarely attacked full-grown woodland. This was as much because tools were poor (the broad axe was chiefly used for medieval land clearance) as because the lords were keen to preserve their hunting-grounds. The village communities, too, were keen not to bite too deep into the forest, which provided essential resources for the medieval economy. Land was also won by draining fenland and building polders. In Flanders, which experienced an early, and vigorous, population increase, we can see this movement starting about 1100 with the building of small dikes in many places.

Sometimes, however, completely new lands were won by assarting, and new villages were founded on them. We shall return to this phenomenon whose social aspects assumed particular significance.

Parallel with this internal expansion, Christian Europe resorted to external expansion. Indeed it is likely that to begin with it preferred expanding externally, since military solutions seemed easier than the peaceful solution of land development. Thus a twofold movement of conquest arose which had the result of pushing back the frontiers of Christianity in Europe and of sending out expeditions to distant Muslim lands: the Crusades. The extension of Christianity within Europe, which had enjoyed a strong revival in the eighth century and which had been continued in the ninth and tenth centuries, had become almost entirely a monopoly of the Germans who occupied the marchlands to the north and east where Christian Europe came into contact with the pagans. From the ninth century onwards, the mixture of motives which resulted – piety, demographic and economic expansion, and nationalism – gave this movement very peculiar characteristics. Ultimately it became chiefly a confrontation between the Germans and the Slavs, in which religious motives slid into the background, since the Germans did not hesitate to attack their enemies even after they had been converted to Christianity. Already in the ninth century the Moravian prince Rostislav had summoned the saints Cyril and Methodius into his territory to counteract the influence of German missionaries.

Conversion took place slowly, by fits and starts. Saint Adalbert, archbishop of Prague at the end of the tenth century, estimated that the Czechs had once more become pagan, and, more particularly, polygamous, while after the death of Mieszko II (1034) a violent revolt among the lower classes in Poland was accompanied by a return to paganism. In 1060, Stenkil, king of Sweden, refused to destroy the old pagan sanctuary at Uppsala even though he was a Christian, and at the end of the eleventh century King Sven encouraged a brief return to blood sacrifices which earned him the nickname Blot-Sven. Lithuania reverted to idolatry after the death of Mindaugas (1263), who had been baptized in 1251.

In about the year 1000, however, a new group of Christian states grew up, enlarging the area of Christian Europe to the north and east – Poland under Mieszko in 966, Hungary in 986 under Vâik, who became Stephen (St Stephen) and a king in 1001, Denmark under Harald Bluetooth (950–86), Norway under Olaf Tryggvason (995–1000), and Sweden under Olaf Skötkonung. At the same time, however, Vladimir, prince of Kiev, received baptism from Byzantium (988), just as the Bulgarian Boris and the Serbs had a century earlier. The schism in 1054 was to separate all of the Balkans and the extreme east of Europe from Roman Christianity.

The Prussians were only converted in the thirteenth century and their conversion was to be the basis for the formation of the German state of the Teutonic Knights who were imprudently summoned into the area in 1226 by the Polish duke Conrad of Mazovia and Cujavia. The Lithuanians were only reconverted in 1385 after the union of Poland and Lithuania and the marriage of Jadwiga of Poland with Jogailo, who thenceforth became the Christian king Wladislaw of Poland and Lithuania and was baptized on 15 February 1386 at Cracow.

Not only were lands annexed to the *Respublica Christiana* by the conversion of pagan peoples, but the map of western Europe was profoundly altered by large-scale migrations, of which the most important was unquestionably German colonization to the east. It helped to put new regions under cultivation, and it transformed the urban network by making it much denser. We shall return to this later. German expansion was also political in character. Viewed from this aspect, the most spectacular successes were those of Albert the Bear, who became margrave of the new March of Brandenburg in 1150, and those of the Teutonic Knights, who conquered Prussia between 1226 and 1283.

Scandinavian expansion was no less impressive. In the tenth century it stretched towards Iceland, Greenland, and possibly America, where 'Northmen' are supposed to have landed in *c.*1000. The Scandinavians had great success in England, primarily at the end of the tenth century under King Svein. After his death (1014) Cnut the Great ruled over England, Denmark, Norway and Sweden, but after he died in 1035 the Anglo-Saxon Edward the Confessor removed England from Danish control. In 1066 it was once more conquered from another Scandinavian base, this time Normandy, whose duke, William, won control of most of England in a single battle, at Hastings. However, other Normans went further, outside northern Europe, and established themselves in the Mediterranean. Norman principalities emerged in southern Italy from the start of the eleventh century. Robert Guiscard seized Campania, defeated the papal troops and had himself recognized by Pope Nicholas II in 1059, took Sicily from the Muslims in 1060-1, and drove the Byzantines out of Italy by capturing their last strongholds, Reggio in 1060 and finally Bari in 1071. In 1081-3 he even sent his son Bohemund to ravage Epirus and Thessaly. Thus was founded the Norman kingdom of Sicily, one of the most original political creations of the middle ages. In the second half of the twelfth century the Muslim traveller Ibn Jobaïr was amazed by the court of Palermo where Normans, Sicilians, Byzantines, and Muslims were to be found side by side. Indeed, the royal chancery had three official languages, Latin, Greek, and Arabic. The Norman kingdom was a political model (it was a clear example of how a feudal monarchy could be run on modern lines) and also a cultural one for the rest of Christian Europe. It was a centre for translations from Greek and Arabic and for the fusion of different styles of art; we can still see the traces of the latter in the magnificent churches of Cefalù, Palermo, and Monreale, which combine Romanesque and Gothic ideas with Byzantine and Muslim traditions in a novel synthesis. It was in this milieu that the character of the Emperor Frederick II, the most unusual and the most fascinating personality of the middle ages, was formed.

French expansion was just as vigorous. Here the impetus came from northern France; the rise in population reached its peak in the flat open country where the agricultural revolution produced its most effectual results. Northern French colonized southern France by means of the Albigensian Crusade, which was brought to an end by the Treaty of Paris in 1229, and which led to the reunion of Languedoc and Capetian France which took place after the death of Alphonse of Poitiers, brother of Louis IX, in 1271. The French launched themselves, under another of Louis IX's brothers, Charles of Anjou, into the conquest of the Kingdom of Sicily, which had been seized from the descendants of Frederick II, his illegitimate son Manfred who was defeated and killed at Benevento in 1266 and his grandson Conradin who was defeated and killed at Tagliacozzo in 1268. Yet Sicily fell from Charles' grasp after the Sicilian Vespers in 1282 and passed to Aragon.

French emigration into Spain was particularly important. One of the great successes of Christian expansion between the tenth and the fourteenth centuries was the reconquest of almost the whole of Spain from the Muslims, which was effected by the Spanish Christian kings, assisted by mercenaries and knights from the other side of the Pyrenees, the majority of them French. Amongst these auxiliary forces of the Reconquista, French Cluniac monks played a prominent part.

The Reconquista was not a series of uninterrupted successes. It experienced reverses, such as the destruction of the basilica of San Diego of Compostela in 997 by the famous Al-Mansour, the Almanzor of the *chansons de geste*, or the defeat inflicted by another Al-Mansour in 1195 on the king of Castile at Alarcos. There were also successes which led to nothing, such as the brief capture of Valencia by Ferdinand I in 1065, which had to be begun again by Rodriguez Diaz de Vivar in 1094, and there were long periods of standstill. However, decisive steps were taken with the capture of Toledo by Alfonso VI of Castile and with the conquest of all the country between the Douro and the Tagus in 1093, when Santarem, Cintra, and Lisbon were captured. They were lost and then reconquered in 1147. The most important date was 16 July 1212. On that day the kings of Castile, Aragon, and Navarre won a startling victory over the Caliph of Cordoba at Las Navas de Tolosa. However, the benefits of the victory at Las Navas, which broke the Muslim resistance, were enjoyed only later. In 1229 James I of Aragon conquered Majorca, in 1238 Valencia and in 1265 Murcia. From now on the Aragonese and the Catalans had a maritime vocation before them, which was confirmed in 1282 by the capture of Sicily. In 1248 the Castilians seized Seville. At the end of the thirteenth century the Spanish Muslims were confined to the tiny kingdom of Granada, though this was to display outstanding splendour in the fourteenth century with the adornments of the Alhambra. The Spanish Reconquista was accompanied by a systematic undertaking to repopulate the devastated countryside and make it productive. Each stage in the conquest was accompanied by *población*, which offered land particularly suited to settlement to the northern Spaniards and Christian foreigners, especially the French.

From the mid-eleventh century the Spanish Reconquista had taken on the tone of a religious war, which it had in fact lacked hitherto, and this opened the way to the military and spiritual reality of the crusades. Later, French colonization in southern France and in the Kingdom of Sicily, and German colonization in Prussia officially acquired the name crusades, yet the fact that the idea of the crusade could be broadened and degenerated, which allows us to place apparently isolated and completely different undertakings in the context of western expansion as a whole, should not disguise the fact that the crusading movement *par excellence* was that in the Holy Land. Although its end results were feeble, and, as far as the west was concerned, unsuccessful, it was none the less, because of its psychological effects, the spearhead of the expansion movement in medieval Christian Europe. Thus while we should not forget that material causes (chiefly the growth in population, rather than directly economic causes) played an essential role in triggering off the crusades, we must pay special attention to the intellectual and emotional background

of the crusades, basing our survey on the fine analyses of Paul Alphandéry
and Alphonse Dupront.

To the knights and peasants of the eleventh century the crusade probably
seemed to be an outlet for the excess population of the west, even if this impulse
was neither clearly formulated nor felt by the crusaders. Furthermore, the
desire for lands, wealth, and knights' fees overseas was a major attraction.
However, the crusades, even before they came to an end in complete failure,
did not satisfy the westerners' hunger for land. They soon had to look for
the solution, which the mirage of Outremer had failed to give them, in Europe,
chiefly in the expansion of agriculture. The Holy Land was a battle front,
not the centre of cultural borrowing, good or bad, which historians (whether
deceived, or, often enough, deceiving) have happily made it out to be. The
crusades brought western Europe neither commercial growth, which had arisen
out of earlier links with the Muslim world and out of the internal development
of the western economy, nor skills and products, which came by other routes;
nor intellectual equipment, which was provided by translation centres and
libraries in Greece, Italy (above all in Sicily), and Spain, where contacts were
close and productive, quite unlike Palestine. The crusades did not even bring
a taste for luxury and soft habits, thought by gloomy western moralists to
be a prerogative of the east, the poisoned gift of the infidels to the ingenuous
crusaders who were defenceless before eastern charms and charmers. Probably
a few Italian towns, notably Genoa and Venice, were able to enrich themselves
from the benefits which accrued not from trade, but from hiring out ships
and lending money to the crusaders, but no serious historian any longer believes
that the crusades stimulated the awakening and growth of commerce in medieval
western Europe. On the contrary, they helped to impoverish the west,
especially the knightly class. Far from creating a unity of mind throughout
western Christianity they actually encouraged awakening national hostilities
to become poisoned; although there are several sources which show this one
only needs to read the account of the Second Crusade by Odo of Deuil, monk
of St Denis and a chaplain of the Capetian king Louis VII. Here hatred between
the Germans and the French was provoked at every turn. Again, we might
think about what relations in the Holy Land were like between, for example,
Richard I of England and Philip Augustus, or between Richard and the duke of
Austria, who was quick to imprison him on his way home. Furthermore, the
crusades built a decisive barrier between the westerners and the Byzantines.
Hostility between Latins and Greeks grew sharper from crusade to crusade,
and culminated in the Fourth Crusade and the sack of Constantinople by the
crusaders in 1204. Far from softening manners, the fanaticism of holy war
led the Crusaders on to the worst excesses, from the pogroms perpetrated on
their journeys to the massacres and sackings such as those of Jerusalem in

1099 and Constantinople in 1204, which we can read about not only in
the accounts of Muslim or Byzantine chroniclers but also in the accounts
of Latin chroniclers. Financing the crusades was a motive or a pretext for
heavier papal taxation and for the ill-considered practice of selling indulgences.
Finally the military orders, which were powerless to defend and guard the
Holy Land, fell back on the west, where they took to all sorts of financial
and military exactions. This was the debit side of the expeditions. Probably
the apricot was the only benefit brought back from the crusades by the
Christians.

It is true that the ephemeral crusading stages in Palestine were the earliest
example of European colonialism, and that, as a precedent, they are full of
lessons for the historian. Doubtless Fulk of Chartres somewhat exaggerated
the scope of the colonization movement overseas in his chronicle, but the
description which he gives of the psychology and of the behaviour of Christian
settlers may nonetheless serve as a sample:

Consider, I pray, and reflect how in our time God has transformed the Occident into
the Orient. For we who were Occidentals have now become Orientals. He who was
a Roman or a Frank has in this land been made into a Galilean or a Palestinian. He
who was of Rheims or Chartres has now become a citizen of Tyre of Antioch. We
have already forgotten the places of our birth; already these are unknown to many of
us or not mentioned any more. Some already possess homes or households by inheritance.
Some have taken wives not only of their people but Syrians or Armenians or even
Saracens who have obtained the grace of baptism. One has his own father-in-law as
well as his daughter-in-law living with him, or his own child if not his own stepson
or stepfather. Out here there are grandchildren and great-grandchildren. Some tend
vineyards, others till fields. People use the eloquence and idioms of diverse languages
in conversing back and forth. Words of different languages have become common
property known to each nationality, and mutual faith unites those who are ignorant
of their descent. Indeed it is written, 'The lion and the ox shall eat straw together'
[Isaiah, 62.25]. He who was born a stranger is now as one born here; he who was
born an alien has become as a native. Our relatives and parents join us from time to
time, sacrificing, even though reluctantly, all that they formerly possessed. Those who
were poor in the Occident, God makes rich in this land. Those who had little money
there have countless bezants here, and those who did not have a villa possess here by
the gift of God a city. Therefore why should one return to the Occident who has found
the Orient like this? God does not wish those to suffer want who with their crosses
dedicated themselves to Him, nay even to the end. You see therefore that this is a
great miracle and one which the whole world ought to admire. Who has heard anything
like it? God wishes to enrich us all and to draw us to Himself as His dearest friends.
And because He wishes it we also freely desire it, and what is pleasing to Him we
do with a loving and submissive heart in order that we may reign with him throughout
eternity. (Fulk of Chartres, 1973 edn, pp. 271-2)

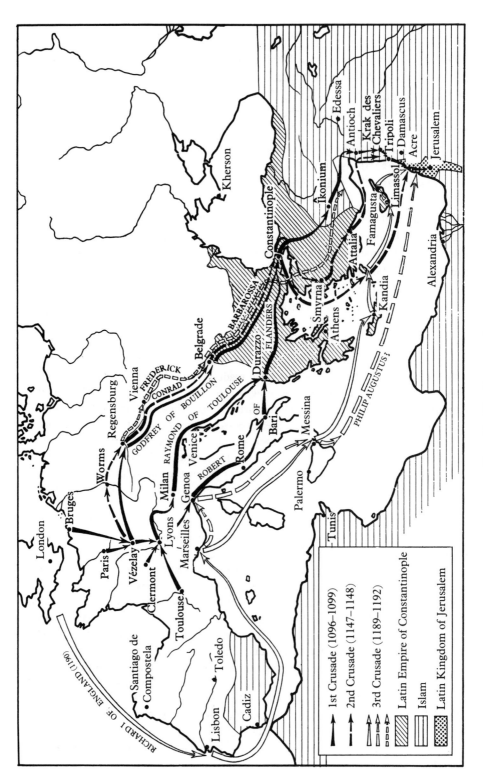

Map 12 The first crusades

When Urban II first aroused enthusiasm for the crusade at Clermont in 1095, and when St Bernard revived this enthusiasm in 1146 at Vézelay, they hoped to transform the warfare which was endemic in the west into a just cause, the fight against the infidel. They wanted to purge Christianity of the scandal of battles between coreligionists, and to provide a praiseworthy outlet for the passion for fighting that characterized the feudal world. They wanted to show Christendom the great goal, the great scheme which was necessary to forge the unity of thought and deed which it lacked. And, of course, the Church and the Papacy reckoned that, thanks to the crusades whose spiritual leadership they assumed, they could give themselves the means of controlling in western Europe itself this *Respublica Christiana* which was victorious yet turbulent, divided against itself and incapable of containing its vitality within itself.

This great scheme failed. Yet the Church had been able to come up to expectations, and it succeeded in making the crusading spirit into a means of giving shape to the vague desires and muffled anxieties of the West. A lengthy preparation of feelings and attitudes had moulded men's hearts for the quest of the heavenly Jerusalem. The Church showed Christians that this ideal vision had been made a physical reality and that one could embrace it by way of the earthly Jerusalem. The thirst for wandering which gripped those Christians who were not to be tied to the land by earthly realities could suddenly be quenched by a pilgrimage which could supply all one's desires: adventure, wealth, and eternal salvation. The Cross was once more a sign of triumph in the west, not one of suffering, and in pinning it on the breasts of the crusaders the Church finally endowed this emblem with its true meaning and gave it back the role it had performed at the time of Constantine and the early Christians.

Social divisions could be found on the crusades too, but here they aroused enthusiasms which ran parallel with each other or converged. The army of knights was matched by the army of the poor. At the time of the First Crusade, the People's Crusade, which was the more eager, set out first, massacred many Jews on the way, dispersed bit by bit and perished under the blows of famine, epidemics, and the Turks before it had reached the Holy City which was its goal. Later on the crusading spirit was still preserved among the lowest classes which were the most deeply affected by its spirituality and its mythology. At the start of the thirteenth century the Children's Crusade - an army of young peasants - movingly showed how enduring the appeal was.

Successive defeats, and the rapid degeneration of the crusading mystique into politics, and before long into scandal, were for a long time insufficient to stifle this great yearning. For the whole of the twelfth century and beyond, the call of Outremer, of the 'crossing', stirred the imaginations and the feelings of westerners who could not manage to find a sense of their individual and collective destiny at home. In 1099 Jerusalem was captured and a Latin kingdom was formed in the Holy Land, but it was quickly threatened. Louis VII and Conrad III were powerless to help it in 1148, and from then on the Christian territory in Palestine was a *peau de chagrin* which shrank without cease. Saladin recaptured Jerusalem in 1187. Richard I performed many acts of valour in the Third Crusade (1189-92) while Philip Augustus hastened to get back to his kingdom; the Fourth Crusade was diverted by the Venetians to Constantinople, and created another shortlived Latin kingdom (1204-61) in Constantinople and Greece; Frederick II, who had been excommunicated by the Pope, obtained the restitution of Jerusalem by negotiations in 1229 only for it to be reconquered by the Muslims in 1244. By then only a few idealists retained the crusading spirit. Louis IX of France was one of these. To the consternation of most of the members of his family, beginning with his mother, Blanche of Castile, and of his advisers, he succeeded in leading off an army of crusaders, most of whom followed him more for love of him than for love of Christ, first of all in 1248 (until 1254), but only to be taken prisoner by the infidels in Egypt, and secondly in 1270, but only to die in front of Tunis.

Until the end of the fifteenth century and beyond people still often talked of leaving on crusade. No one actually did so again.

II

At the very time when Jerusalem was capturing the imaginations of men in western Europe, other towns which were more real and had a more important earthly future ahead of them were evolving in the west itself. Most of these towns existed before the year 1000 and went back to antiquity or even further. Even in barbarian lands which were converted late to Christianity, among the Scandinavians, the Germans, or the Slavs, medieval towns were a continuation of the primitive Slavonic *grods* or Nordic *wiks*. Urban foundations *ex nihilo* were rare in the middle ages. Even Lübeck existed before the foundation charters of Adolf von Schauenburg in 1143 and Henry the Lion in 1158. And yet, even in these cases of continuity, which were the most common, it is surely impossible to say that the medieval towns were the same as their ancestors. In the Roman world the towns had been primarily political, administrative, and military centres, and then economic ones. During the early middle ages they were shrivelled up into a corner of their ancient walls, which had now grown too big, and their functions were reduced almost exclusively to those of government and administration, though these too had atrophied. The least

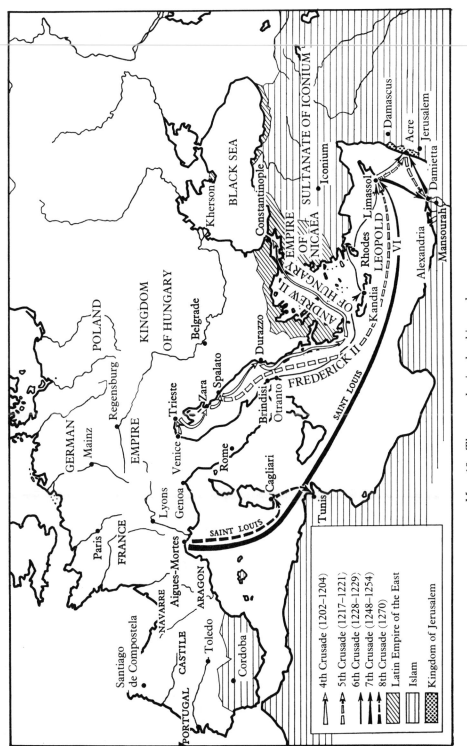

Map 13   *The crusades in the thirteenth century*

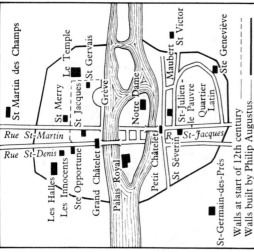

9 Paris

(after G. Duby and R. Mandron, *Histoire de la civilisation française*, vol. 1 [Paris, 1958])

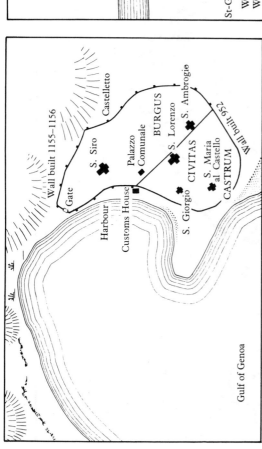

8 Genoa

(after Y. Renouard, *Les villes d'Italie de la fin du Xe siècle au début du XIVe siècle*, 2nd edn, 2 vols [Paris, 1969])

Figures 8, 9 The towns at the peak of the thirteenth century: an Italian port and a national capital

Genoa (8) was transformed between the mid-tenth and the mid-twelfth centuries. The tenth-century walls were built in a defensive period at the time of the Saracen raids. It encompassed the feudal *castrum*, or castle, and the episcopal city, the *civitas* with the cathedral of San Lorenzo, and excluded a *burgus* with the other cathedral, San Siro. In the eleventh and twelfth centuries Genoa went over to the offensive and its sailors became first pirates making lucrative raids and then merchants who grew rich from the crusades. A second wall built after 1155–56 surrounded the *burgus*, the economic centre which stretched northwards along the sea and the political centre around the Palazzo Comunale. Since 1122 the commune was in fact identifiable with the *compagna* which included all the citizens, noble or non-noble, who were engaged in maritime trade. The importance of this trade can still be seen in the Customs House. Philip Augustus (1179–1223) built a new wall around Paris (9). Like all the important towns of the west, Paris had grown considerably in the course of the twelfth century. But this growth was only partly due to the development of economic activity, which was sited on the right bank of the Seine (Halles and Place de Grève, which was both a place for hiring workers and a port for unloading goods, and the Templars' keep, where the Templars, acting as bankers, kept the royal treasure). It was also caused by the emergence of a university town on the left bank, the Latin quarter. Finally, the ancient heart of the city, the Ile de la Cité, contained the episcopal centre around the newly rebuilt cathedral of Notre-Dame, together with the political capital around the Palais-Royal. The abbeys of St Martin-des-Champs, St Germain-des-Prés, Ste Geneviève, and St Victor, which had originally been situated well outside the town nexus, were surrounded or threatened by the new walls.

humble of them generally owed what importance they had less to the presence of a king (kings enjoyed travelling and living in the country) or of a high functionary (there were few of these and they lacked a large entourage outside the royal palaces) than to that of the bishop. Christianity had originally been an urban religion and it maintained urban continuity in the west. And if the bishop's town retained something of an economic function it was the very simplified one played by the episcopal or the monastic granaries. These were built in towns to stock foodstuffs brought in from the surrounding countryside, which were distributed to most of the tiny group of town inhabitants in return for services rather than for money; in times of scarcity they were given away.

Henri Pirenne demonstrated that the medieval town was born and evolved as a result of its economic role. It was created by the rebirth of trade; it was made by merchants. That the continuity of the urban entity from the first millennium AD into the middle ages is misleading is very often revealed by the fact that the medieval town set itself up next door to the nucleus of the ancient one. It was a town in a suburb, known as a *podgrozie* in Slav lands and a *portus* in the West. Moreover, even where there was continuity, the big medieval towns were usually the successors of what had been small towns in the ancient world or the early middle ages. Venice, Florence, Genoa, Pisa, even Milan (which was of limited importance until the fourth century and overshadowed by Pavia from the seventh to the eleventh centuries), Paris, Bruges, Ghent, and London, let alone Hamburg or Lübeck, were essentially creations of the middle ages. With the exception of the Rhineland cities such as Cologne or Mainz, and above all with the exception of Rome (which, however, was almost nothing but a great religious centre in the middle ages, a San Diego de Compostela with a rather larger permanent population), the most important Roman cities disappeared or became second class in the middle ages.

The towns were born not only out of the reawakening of trade, but also out of the growth of agriculture in the west, which was beginning to supply urban centres with a better supply of food and manpower. We have to resign ourselves to attributing the birth and growth of medieval towns to a combination of various factors. Above all, a variety of social groups was involved. According to Pirenne, Lucien Febvre organized a famous debate around the question *'Nouveaux riches ou fils de riches'* - 'Upstarts or rich men's sons?' Of course the towns attracted *homines novi*, new men who had escaped from the land or from monastic *familiae*, who were free of prejudices and ready to undertake tasks and to earn. Yet they were joined or supported by members of the ruling classes, who helped notably by lending money which they alone had at the outset. The landed aristocracy and the clergy played a decisive role. Then, too, the category of the *ministeriales*, seigneurial agents who had usually had their origins in slavery and serfdom, but who rose fairly quickly towards the upper levels of the feudal hierarchy, certainly played an important part in urban growth. The strongly urbanized regions of the medieval west, if one sets aside those where Greco-Roman, Byzantine, or Muslim tradition had left more solid bases, such as southern Italy, Provence, Languedoc, or Spain, were the regions at the ends of the great trade routes. Northern Italy lay at the end of the end of the Alpine passes and the Mediterranean sea routes, north Germany and Flanders were the points of arrival for trade from the north-east, and north-eastern France was where merchants and produce from the north and south met at the Champagne Fairs, especially in the twelfth and thirteenth centuries.

Yet these regions were also those with a flat, open countryside, the most fertile in Europe, and they were the areas where progress in using three-year rotation was surest and use of the wheeled plough and of horses for ploughing was most widespread. Here again it is admittedly difficult to distinguish cause from effect, given the close relations between town and country in the middle ages. In order to come into existence, towns needed a favourable rural environment, but gradually as they developed they exercised an ever-larger attraction over a surrounding area extending in proportion to their demands. The urban population was a group of consumers who only took part in farming as a sideline and who needed to be fed. There were no fields, strictly speaking, inside medieval towns, but there were gardens and vineyards which played a significant role in feeding the townsfolk. Around the towns more land was cleared and yields rose, the more so since towns not only drew food from their surrounding areas but also took away people. Emigration from the countryside to the town between the tenth and fourteenth centuries was one of the most important events which took place in Christian Europe. What is certain in any case is that towns forged a new society out of the varied human elements which they took in. Of course this society also belonged to feudal society, which is too often pictured as exclusively rural.

The town as a whole turned itself into a lordship: the rural *banlieue* which it provided for itself by putting it under its feudal jurisdiction or 'ban' was contemporary with the evolution of the lordship towards what is known as *seigneurie banale*, which was itself founded on a highly developed exercise of the 'ban'. The towns were influenced by feudal lords who sometimes, as in Italy, lived in them. The town notables imitated the nobleman's way of life, built stone houses for themselves, and towers which, while they were used for defence and storing food, were also and indeed chiefly status symbols. Of course town society accounted for only a tiny minority of the population in a world that remained primarily rural. Daniel Thorner reckoned in his model of the peasant economy, which can be applied to the medieval west, that at least 5 per cent of the population has to consist of towndwellers if more than

50 per cent of the total working population is engaged in farming. Yet little by little this urban society succeeded in substituting its own impulses for the catchwords of the countryside, and the Church did not fail to notice this. In the twelfth century it was still monks such as the Cluniac Peter the Venerable or above all the Cistercian St Bernard who pointed the way to Christianity. For all that, St Bernard had to come and preach the crusade at Vézelay, a hybrid settlement with a new town built around its monastery, and he had to try – in vain – to tear away the student population from Paris and the seductions of the town because he wanted to bring them back to the desert and the school of the cloister. In the thirteenth century the spiritual leaders, the Dominicans and the Franciscans, established themselves in the towns and governed souls from their pulpits and their university chairs.

From now on the towns took over the role of directing, inspiring, and developing ideas; at first this manifested itself in the economy. Even if the town had originally been a trading centre, a commercial nexus, a market, its basic function in economic terms was production. Towns were workshops; more importantly, it was in these workshops that the division of labour originated. In the countryside in the early middle ages all forms of production were concentrated within the manor, even if some skilled craftsmanship did find a home there too. Perhaps an intermediate stage is to be seen in the Slav lands, notably Poland and Bohemia, where one can observe how the great landowners apportioned specialists, such as ostlers, blacksmiths, potters, and cartwrights, among particular villages, whose place names preserve the memory of this to this day, for example Szewce (*sutores* or shoemakers) in Poland. Aleksander Gieysztor defined them thus: 'we are dealing with villages under the authority of the ducal castellan, inhabited by craftsmen who, while they owed their basic subsistence to farming, were obliged to pay dues in the form of specialized craft products'. However, in the towns such specialization was carried to its limits. The craftsman had ceased to be primarily, or even additionally, a peasant, and the burgess had ceased to be primarily or additionally a landowner.

The dynamism and the autonomy of the new professions should not be exaggerated. Feudal lords controlled economic activity by restricting it in various ways: economically, for most raw materials came from manors; and institutionally, since lords restricted milking production and trade, by feudal privileges, notably taxes, in spite of the freedoms obtained by the towns. The guilds which formed the framework for the new professions were, as Gunnar Mickwitz has described them, primarily cartels that eliminated competition and put a brake on production. Extreme specialization was, if not a cause, at least a sign of the weakness of the new economy. We need only open the *Livre des métiers* of Etienne Boileau, which regulated the Parisian guilds at

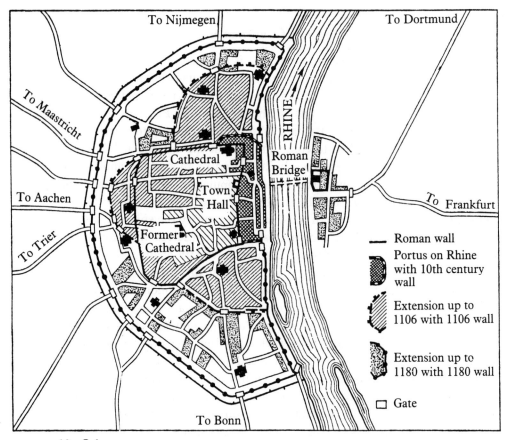

10 Cologne
(after *Westermanns Atlas*)

Legend:
— Roman wall
Portus on Rhine with 10th century wall
Extension up to 1106 with 1106 wall
Extension up to 1180 with 1180 wall
□ Gate

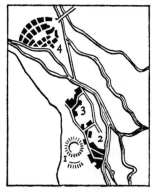

1 Original Polish *grod*.

2 Portus

3 Old Polish town

4 Old German town

11 Kalisz
(after P. Francastel, *Les origines des villes polonaises* [Paris and The Hague, 1960])

Figures 10, 11, 12, 13 Towns of central Europe at their peak (thirteenth and early fourteenth centuries)

The economic role in the development of these three cities of central Europe (Cologne, Lübeck and Kalisz) can be seen clearly in these plans. At Cologne (10) economic activity awakened early. As early as the tenth century a wall was built around a new part of the town centred on a market lying to the east of the Roman town on the Rhine. In 1106 new walls protected two new areas to the north and south, on the bank of the Rhine. Finally in 1180 the town reached its furthest medieval expansion, taking in the churches of St Severin (founded 348), St Pantaleon (866) and St Gereon (fourth century). Lübeck (12) was a new foundation arranged by Henry the Lion, duke of Saxony, who, in 1159, wanted to attract merchants from the Baltic and Slav lands thither. He made use of the *wik* founded in 1143 by Count Adolf von Schauenburg around the cathedral and also the castle put up by Count Adolf on the site of a Slav *grod*. As early as 1230 city walls were built within the area of land separating the rivers Trave and Wakenitz, on which the busy quays and

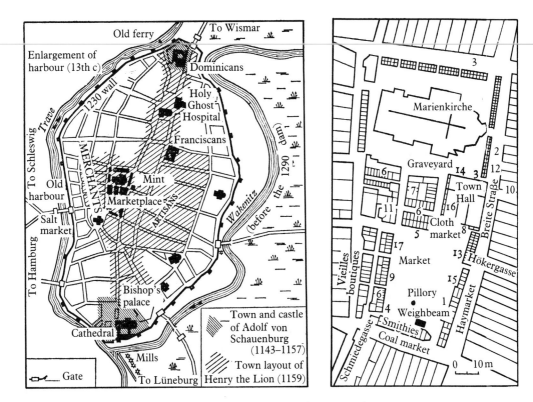

12 Lübeck
(after *Westermanns Atlas*)

13 Lübeck marketplace

1 Armourers 2 Butchers 3 Bakers
4 Beltmakers 5 Monkey-changers 6 Shoemakers 7 Spice merchants 8 Needle-makers
9 Felters 10 Herring merchants 11 Grocers
12 Minters 13 Goldsmiths 14 Cookshops
15 Saddlers 16 Tailors 17 Tanners

mills were set up. The centre of the city was the market (13), which was completely in the hands of the merchants, with shops and streets of specialized traders and craftsmen, the town hall and the Marienkirche – the Kaufmannskirche or merchants' church characteristic of Hanseatic towns. Lübeck was open to long-distance trade and swiftly took the lead within the Hanse. Since ancient monastic foundations were lacking, Dominicans and Franciscans installed themselves in force early on (1225 and 1227). The case of Kalisz (11) in Poland was more complex. Four settlements can be distinguished in it. There was the old defensive Slav *grod* (ninth to twelfth centuries) with a collegiate church, which was soon doubled in size to the East by a suburb (*podgrodzie*) on the river with an economic function. Then appeared first, to the north, an old town (*stare miastro*) of the twelfth century, and finally in the thirteenth century a *locatio* town given German law, whose position, at a meeting point of roads and river routes, and whose institutions allowed economic activity to develop fully.

the end of the reign of Louis IX, between 1260 and 1270, to be amazed by
the number of occupations involved in iron-working: 22 out of a total of 130.
This economy was above all limited to satisfying local needs. Towns which
manufactured for export were rare: the only trade which reached dimensions
that were almost those of an industry was the textile trade in north-western
Europe, especially in Flanders, and in northern Italy. It produced luxury and
semi-luxury items such as broadcloth and silk and stimulated associated forms
of production, such as the growing of dye plants, among which woad or pastel,
from the thirteenth century, was particularly prized. In addition there was
building, which was a special case.

III

Yet towns were also the nodes in the network of long-distance trade. Traditional
historiography, especially since Pirenne, has rightly recognized this, even though
it has somewhat exaggerated their importance in this regard. For a long time
this trade was only sustained by luxury products, such as cloth, woad, and
spices, or those of prime necessity, such as salt. Heavy goods such as grain
or timber were only gradually drawn into long-distance trade. A few centres
sufficed to cope with the sale of these items and with the rudimentary
commercial practices, in particular changing currency, which accompanied
them. The most important of these centres, in the twelfth and thirteenth
centuries, were the Fairs of Champagne. Ports and other towns in Italy and
northern Germany emerged into prominence. Italian traders – Venetians,
Genoese, Pisans, Amalfitani, men of Asti, Milanese, Sienese, and, soon,
Florentines – acted more or less in isolation, within the framework of their
towns, as did the inhabitants of Amiens or Arras, but to the north long-distance
trade was dominated by a huge commercial confederation, which quickly
acquired political power as well. This was the Hanse, whose origin can be
fixed in the peace which was concluded in 1161 under the aegis of Henry the
Lion between the Germans and the inhabitants of Gotland, in which we find
mentioned the community of German merchants who visited Gotland seasonally
(*'universi mercatores imperii Romani Gotlandiam frequentantes'*). At the end of
the thirteenth century the Hanse extended its grasp from Flanders and England
to northern Russia. To quote a recent historian of the Hanse, Philippe Dollinger,
on the organization as it was in about 1300, 'Everywhere Germans were ousting
their competitors, particularly in the Baltic but also in the North Sea. They
went so far as to stop the Gotlanders passing westwards through the Danish
straits, and the Frisians, Flemings and English eastwards. They even got hold
of the trade between Norway and England' (Dollinger, 1970, pp. 42–3).

At the same period the relations between the two groups which dominated long-distance trade, the Italians and the Germans, underwent a change. Instead of meeting each other along the land routes which led to the Champagne Fairs, which were long, expensive, and always under threat, they established a direct, regular contact by sea. Merchant fleets went directly from Genoa and Venice to London and Bruges and thence to the area of the Baltic and its hinterland. From modest beginnings, medieval trade, which in the early middle ages had been limited to rivers, had developed gradually along land routes between the tenth and the fourteenth centuries. Now, by venturing out on to the sea, going from Alexandria to Riga by way of the Mediterranean, the Atlantic, the Channel, the North Sea, and the Baltic, it opened the way to the commercial expansion of modern Europe.

This emerging long-distance trade, which was supported by the towns, encouraged two other important developments. With the establishment of counting houses in distant places, the expansion of medieval Christian Europe was completed. In the Mediterranean, Genoese and Venetian expansion went beyond the limits of commercial colonization. The Venetians, who had obtained a series of increasingly exorbitant privileges from the emperors of Constantinople (992 and 1082), founded what was effectively a colonial empire on the shores of the Adriatic, in Crete and in the Ionian and Aegean islands (notably at Negroponte, that is to say Euboea) after the Fourth Crusade in 1204. In the fourteenth and fifteenth centuries they went on to take over Corfu and Cyprus. The Genoese formed establishments on the coast of Asia Minor (Phocaea, which was a great producer of alum which was essential as a mordant for the textile industry) and on the northern shore of the Black Sea (Kaffa) which they turned into solid bases from which they could drain the hinterland of commodities and human beings (domestic slaves of both sexes).

To the north, the Hanse established its merchants on Latin Christian territory, at Bruges, London, Bergen, Stockholm (founded in 1251) and also further to the east in lands which were pagan (they had a base in Riga from 1201) or Orthodox (Novgorod). Mercantile colonization ran parallel to German urban and rural colonization, and sometimes peacefully and sometimes by violence the merchants obtained privileges which, over and above a financial profit, established a real racial superiority. In a commercial treaty agreed by the Prince of Smolensk and the German merchants in 1229 we read: 'If a Russian buys on credit from a German visitor when he is also in debt to another Russian, the German shall receive the money owed to him first'. If a Russian and a German should arrive simultaneously at a point where goods had to be reloaded on to another form of transport, where there was a break in the portage (*volok*) of merchandise, the German was to go ahead of the Russian, unless the latter was from Smolensk, in which case the two drew lots to decide which should go first. The commercial form of colonization itself made westerners used to a colonialism which brought them both successes and later rebuffs as we know.

Long-distance trade did not only impel geographical expansion, but furthermore was instrumental in bringing about development which was also rooted in the towns, the expansion of the monetary economy. As centres of consumption and trade, towns increasingly had to rely on money to regulate their transactions. The thirteenth century was the decisive period. In order to respond to these needs, Florence, Genoa, Venice, and Spanish, French, German, and English rulers had to strike firstly silver coins of higher value than the penny (*grossi* or groats), and then gold coins. The Florentine florin dates from 1252, the *écu* of St Louis from between 1263 and 1265, and the Venetian ducat from 1284. Roberto Lopez described the thirteenth century as 'the century of the return to gold'.

We shall see later on the consequences of this growing predominance of the monetary over the natural economy. When it emerged in the countryside and altered the form of ground rents it decisively helped to transform the medieval west. The monetary reforms of Charlemagne had been carried out in the face of general indifference and ignorance, save for a small group of royal counsellors, but the monetary changes made by Philip the Fair at the end of the thirteenth century and in the first years of the fourteenth century – the first serious devaluations in the west – aroused an outcry among almost all the social classes and inspired popular emotions and riots. The peasant masses probably barely saw gold coins as yet, and even silver groats only rarely, but they handled small coins more and more frequently. They took part, though only distantly as yet, in the important change that caused money to enter daily life in western Europe.

IV

The towns scored equally highly in both intellectual and artistic fields. The monastic world doubtless remained the most favourable milieu for the development of learning and art in the eleventh and to a lesser extent in the twelfth century. Mystic spirituality and Romanesque art blossomed in the monasteries. Cluny with its great church built by Abbot Hugh (1049–1109) symbolized the way in which the monks dominated the dawn of the new era; Citeaux and her daughter-houses and grandaughter-houses continued this pre-eminence by other means. However, the cultural *translatio* which made the monasteries lose the first place to the towns occurred chiefly in the fields of teaching and architecture. In the course of the twelfth century the town schools, which grew out of episcopal schools, decisively overtook the monastic ones. The new centres of learning freed themselves from controls by being able to recruit their masters and their pupils, and by choosing their teaching programmes and methods. Scholasticism was a child of the towns, and reigned in the new institutions, the universities or intellectual guilds. Study and teaching became a profession, one of the many activities which were becoming specialized in the urban workplace; the name itself is significant, for *universitas* means a corporation. The universities were merely *universitates magistrorum et scolarium*, or corporations of masters and students, though they varied to a greater or lesser extent from each other, from Bologna where the students were in control to Paris which was ruled by the masters. Books became tools rather than objects of worship, and like any tool they came to be mass-produced, objects for manufacture and retail.

Romanesque art, a product and an expression of the expansion of Christianity from 1000, transformed itself in the course of the twelfth century. Its new outward appearance, Gothic art, was an art of the towns. The cathedrals springing up out of the huddle of town buildings dominated and purified the landscape. The iconography of the cathedrals expressed urban culture. Within it, the active and contemplative lives sought an uneasy balance, and while the guilds paid to decorate the church with stained glass scholastic knowledge was deployed in its design. In the surrounding countryside the churches copied the plan of the cathedral of the town as their model, or one or two of its most distinctive elements such as the belfry, the tower, or the tympanum, though with less success artistically and much more limited physical resources. The cathedral, built to shelter a new people which was more numerous, more humane, and more realistic, did not neglect to remind them of rural life which was so near and of so much benefit to them. The theme of the months of the year which formed the framework for agricultural labours remained one of the traditional decorations in city churches.

V

The Church was well to the fore in the expansion of Christian Europe, although its role in economic development was not the direct, essential one which has often, rather exaggeratedly, been ascribed to it, especially in the wake of Montalembert. Georges Duby has stressed that the monks were hardly involved at all in land clearance because 'the Cluniacs and the Benedictines of the old observance led a manorial, and thus an inactive, life', while the new orders in the twelfth century 'established themselves on lands which had already been at least partially cleared and made ready for use'. They were particularly keen on stock rearing, 'and thus did not bother very much about enlarging the amount of land under the plough', and finally, 'through the care which the abbeys of the new orders took to protect their "desert" and to keep peasants at a distance, they actually helped to protect several pockets of forest from attempts at land-clearance which, without the abbeys, would have reduced them considerably'.

However, at the actual economic level, the Church was efficacious. During the period when the economy was getting under way it invested resources which it alone possessed. It had amassed far more wealth than anyone else during the period when economic activity was restricted to treasure hoarding. After the year 1000, at a time when economic growth, in particular the increase in building, demanded ready money which could not be provided by the normal operation of production, it 'unhoarded', so to speak, and put the treasure it had accumulated into circulation. Naturally this took place in a climate of miracles, but this thaumaturgical disguise should not blind us to economic realities. If a bishop or abbot wished to enlarge or rebuild his cathedral or monastery he was immediately enabled by a miracle to discover a buried treasure which allowed him, if not to complete his undertaking, at least to start it off. Here, some years before 1000 AD, is Arnulf, bishop of Orléans, who is contemplating rebuilding the church of Holy Cross 'in a magnificent manner', as described by Ralph Glaber:

> A clear piece of divine encouragement was shown to him. It happened one day, when the masons were testing the firmness of the ground, so that they could choose sites for the foundations of the basilica, that they discovered a great quantity of gold. They judged it to be certainly enough to cover all the costs for rebuilding the whole basilica, even though this was to be a large structure. They took the gold which they had discovered and carried it in its entirety to the bishop. The latter gave thanks to almighty God for the gift which He had bestowed on him, took the money and entrusted it to the men supervising the work, ordering them to spend it faithfully on the building of the church. It is said that this gold owed its existence to the foresight of St Evurtius, a former bishop of the same see, who is supposed to have buried it there for the purpose of this restoration.

During the period of the eleventh and twelfth centuries, when the Jews were no longer numerous enough to fill the role of creditors which they had hitherto assumed, and before the Christian merchants had taken it over from them, the monasteries, as Robert Génestal has shown, acted as 'credit establishments'. Throughout the whole of this period, the Church protected the merchant and helped him to conquer the prejudice which made the inactive seigneurial class despise him. The Church undertook to rehabilitate the work by which economic growth was achieved. It turned the punishment of work laid down by Genesis (that fallen man must earn his bread by the sweat of his brow, as a penance) into a means of salvation. Above all it adapted to the evolution

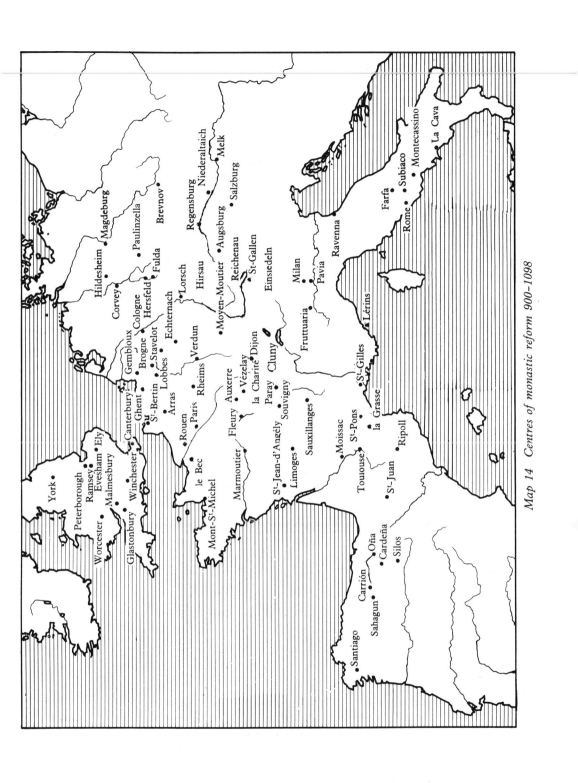

Map 14 Centres of monastic reform 900–1098

of society and provided it with the spiritual watchwords which it needed, as we have seen in the case of the crusades. The Church offered the dreams which were a necessary counterweight to harsh realities. During the whole of this period, when prosperity was slowly increasing, when the use of money was becoming more widespread, and when wealth was becoming more and more enticingly attractive, it provided an ideological safety valve, the justification of poverty, for those who were successful but were anxious about their success (for the Gospel expressed serious doubt about the possibility of the rich man entering the Kingdom of Heaven) and for those who remained crushed.

The movement began to emerge in the eleventh century, when reforms and many various approaches to a return to apostolic simplicity (*vita vere apostolica*) began to take shape. It inspired a reform of the clergy, encouraging them to live in communities. This was the movement of the canons regular, which revived canonical life by making the canons live according to a rule known as the Augustinian Rule. The search for apostolic poverty became more widespread at the end of the eleventh and the start of the twelfth century. It gave birth to new religious orders which declared that it was necessary to go out into the 'desert' and rediscover in solitude the true values from which the western world seemed ceaselessly to be distancing itself. However, these new orders continued the Benedictine tradition, though at the same time they transformed it. They also continued its economic example, because they extolled manual labour, and they organized new forms of economic activity, combining new methods of cultivation, such as three-year rotation, with the more intensive practice of stock rearing, which produced wool and fed the textile industry, and with the adoption of technical innovations such as mills and ironworks.

Reformed monasticism had its origins in Italy, and probably derived from the great source of Byzantine and oriental monasticism by way of the Greek Basilian monks of Latium, Calabria, and Sicily. St Nilus, who founded Grottaferrata as early as the tenth century, St Romuald, who founded Camaldoli in 1012, and finally St John Gualberti, founder of Vallombrosa in Tuscany in about 1020, were the men who inspired the great founders of the new orders around 1100, the men who created the 'white' monks, who set themselves up in opposition to the traditional 'black' monks or Benedictines. Etienne de Muret founded the order of Grandmont in 1074, St Bruno founded the Grande Chartreuse in 1084, Robert of Molesme founded Cîteaux in 1098, Robert of Arbrissel founded Fontevraúlt in 1101 and St Norbert founded Prémontré in 1120. The opposition between the old and the new forms of monasticism was symbolized by the strongly worded debate between the Cluniac Peter the Venerable, abbot of Cluny from 1122 to 1156, and the Cistercian St Bernard,

Map 15 *The Cistercian order in the twelfth and thirteenth centuries*

abbot of Clairvaux from 1115 to 1153. On the one side there were men practising a spirituality whose essence was the divine service, the *Opus Dei*, which they had plenty of time for because of their large flock of serfs, while on the other there were fervent adherents of a mysticism which united prayer and manual labour, which was carried out by monks shoulder to shoulder with the *conversi* or lay-brothers. On the one side were monks inspired by religious feelings which were nourished by splended church buildings, the glory of the liturgy and the pomp of services, while on the other there were monks who were passionately attached to simplicity and pure, unadorned lines. Against the almost Baroque Romanesque art which took pleasure in sumptuous trappings and the quirks of a perverted ornamentation – the idea that Romanesque art was simple is a charming, but anachronistic, fiction of the nineteenth century – Citeaux welcomed Gothic architecture, then in its infancy, which was more rigorous and better ordered, and which neglected details in its search for the essentials.

Throughout this period it was above all the anarchic characters on the fringes of religious life who fostered the aspirations of the masses towards purity. These were the hermits, who have as yet been little studied. They multiplied throughout Christian Europe, living in clearings tucked away in the forests, where they were beset by visitors, or else as suitable points for helping travellers to find their way or to cross a ford or a bridge. They were considered to be models of behaviour who had not been corrupted by the politics of the organized clergy and they acted as directors of conscience to rich and poor, souls in torment and lovers alike. They swarm over art and literature with their staffs, the symbols of magic power and of wandering, with their bare feet and their clothing made out of animal skins. They were the embodiment of a society which, faced with economic growth and its contradictions, sought the refuge of a solitude which yet was alert to the world and its problems.

However, the development and the success of the towns pushed monastic communities and hermits, who were linked to a rural and feudal society, into the background. Whether old or new, they were anachronisms. The Church adapted yet again by putting forth religious orders of a new sort, the Mendicant Orders, though this did not happen without difficulties or, indeed, crises. In about 1170 Peter Waldes, a merchant of Lyons, and his followers, the Poor Men of Lyons, who were called Waldensians, took their criticism of the Church so far that they ended up by leaving it. In 1206 the son of a rich merchant of Assisi, Francis, seemed to be heading in the same direction. The one ambition of the group surrounding him, originally twelve 'little brothers' or minor brothers (friars minor) was to be the leaven of purity in a corrupt world, by practising humility and absolute poverty. They lived by begging. The Church was disturbed by such extremism. The popes (Innocent III,

Honorius III, and Gregory IX), the Roman Curia and the bishops wished to impose a rule on Francis and his companions and turn them into an order which could be fitted into the great order of the Church. The heartbreak of Francis of Assisi, caught between his unnatural ideal and his passionate attachment to the Church and to orthodoxy, was dramatic. He gave way, but went into retirement. Shortly before his death he received the stigmata in the solitude of La Verna as the culmination, the ransom, and the reward of his anguish. After him, his order was for a long time torn by the struggle between those who adhered to absolute poverty and those who supported coming to terms with the world. The papacy supported the moderates against the extremists, the Fraticelli and the Spirituals, who themselves ended up by leaving the Church. At the same time that St Francis was unwillingly giving the initiative for the birth of the order of the Friars Minor, who were called Franciscans, a Spanish canon of noble birth, Dominic Guzman, was more willingly agreeing that the papacy should give a rule to the small group of preachers which he had gathered together to bring the heretics back into the paths of orthodoxy by preaching and also by practising poverty. The orders of the Friars Minor and the Preaching Friars (who acquired the name of Dominicans) were founded at about the same time. They were the most important of the mendicant orders, who were the Church's new militia in the thirteenth century. What was particularly new and useful about them was that they deliberately addressed themselves to the people in the towns. They tried to supply answers to the new problems of this new society by their preaching, their confession and their example. They brought the desert communities to the mob. A map of the Franciscan and Dominican houses at the end of the thirteenth century is a map of urban Christian Europe. Although they had some difficulty in doing so, they acquired university chairs in addition to the pulpits in their conventual churches where they installed themselves and shone with an incomparable brilliance. Thomas Aquinas and Bonaventure, both masters of the University of Paris, were the most celebrated Dominican and the second most celebrated Franciscan respectively.

However, in spite of these adaptations and successes, the Church followed the evolution of Christian Europe rather than leading it as it had done in the early middle ages. Already at the end of the twelfth century the 'new' orders, the Cistercians and the Premonstratensians, had fallen away from their ideals and been overtaken. Even the mendicants did not rally a united body of support; in an age when work had become the basic value of the new society, it was difficult to make people accept that one could live by begging. Academics and writers, who without doubt were voicing the feelings of a wider public, criticized the friars severely for this. William de St-Amour, who was a Parisian master, and Jean de Meung, in the second part of the *Roman de la Rose*, made vehement accusations against the new orders. Thomas Aquinas and Bonaventure had to make use of all their resources to reply to them. In the eyes of part of the populace, Dominicans and Franciscans became the symbol of hypocrisy, and the former excited even more hatred because of the way in which they had taken the lead in repressing heresy through their part in the Inquisition. The first Dominican martyr, Peter Martyr from Verona, was murdered on the road between Milan and Como in 1252, and the order had dozens of pictures made of his skull with a knife stuck in it as propaganda.

The synods of the early middle ages had set the fashion for Christian society. The councils of the twelfth and thirteenth centuries followed its evolution. The most famous and most important of them, the Fourth Lateran Council, which organized education and made Easter communion compulsory, was already an *aggiornamento*: it was catching up after a pause. Even more than being a century of cathedrals and theological *summae*, the thirteenth century was a century of laicization. In 1277 the bishop of Paris, Etienne Tempier, tried to put a brake on intellectual evolution in a syllabus in which he condemned 217 propositions; the archbishop of Canterbury, the Dominican Robert Kilwardby, issued a similar document. They condemned courtly love and the relaxation of morals, the immoderate use of reason in theology, and the beginnings of an experimental and rational science. This counterthrust was effective in so far as it aimed at avant-garde tendencies lacking a firm enough base, but it certainly showed that the Church had become not just old-fashioned but reactionary, even if these condemnations were not approved by all clerics.

It is true that its ideological monopoly had been seriously threatened. From the first signs of the expansion of western Europe around the year 1000, people had openly started to dispute the leadership of the Church. These outbreaks of heresy were of limited importance. The peasant Leutard from Champagne, who preached a not very orthodox gospel to the inhabitants of Vertus and its surroundings, the Italian heretics of Monforte, and even those of Milan who formed the Pataria, which was closely linked with the rise of the towns, and many other outbreaks, only agitated a town or a district for a time. Similarly the learned heresies of Roscelin, of Abelard (if he was a heretic), and of his pupil Arnold of Brescia, who brought heresy out of the schools to project it in the streets of Rome, where he gathered together the people against the pope, disturbed only restricted circles. In any case, the Church, which was often supported by secular monarchs who willingly gave it the support of their 'secular arm', acted quickly and firmly. At Orléans in 1022 the first heretics were burnt at the stake.

Soon, however, a much larger and more dangerous movement formed and spread. Inspired by oriental heresies and linked to the Bogomils in the Balkans, it made its way along the routes from Italy to France and central Europe. It joined together heterogeneous coalitions of social groups, in which sections of the nobility, of the new burgess class, and of the artisan class, combined to make movements which were connected with each other fairly closely, though they had different names. The movement which enjoyed the greatest success was that of the Cathars. The Cathars were Manichaeans, and for them, there were two first principles of equal power, Good and Evil, the good god being powerless in the face of the evil one, whether the latter were, in their view, a god equal to him, or a devil who was inferior but who had revolted successfully. Creation and the matter of which it was composed had been made by the evil god. The Catholic Church was a church of evil. Faced with the world, with its social organization (feudal society), and with its guide, the Church of Rome, men could only display an attitude of complete rejection. Catharism soon formed itself into a church, with its bishops and its clergy (the *perfecti*), and it imposed special rites on its adherents. It was an anti-church, an anti-catholicism. It had certain similarities, indeed, certain links, with the other heretical movements of the thirteenth century, the Waldensians and the Spiritual Franciscans, and above all with that vaguer movement which existed on the fringes of orthodoxy and heterodoxy, which was called Joachimism after the name of the man who had inspired it, the Calabrian monk Joachim of Fiore. The Joachimites believed in three ages: that of the Law or of the Old Testament, which had been succeeded by the age of Justice, and of the New Testament, still corrupted and led by the present-day church, which was to disappear to make way for the rule of Love and the Eternal Gospel. This millenarianism even expressed itself in the anticipation of a date which was supposed to mark the end of society and of a corrupt church and the arrival of the new order: 1260. After this year had passed, many thought that the Joachimite era had arrived when a pope was elected who shared their views, Peter Morone or Celestine V, in 1294. Celestine's pontificate was brief. He had to abdicate after a few months, and was shut up in a monastery where he soon died. His successor, Boniface VIII, was suspected of having a hand in his death. The death of the man who, in the words of Dante, made 'the great refusal', symbolized a turning-point in the history of Christianity just as the year 1277 had done.

At the end of the thirteenth century the Church had prevailed. Since traditional peaceful means had failed against Catharism and similar heresies, it turned to force, firstly to war, in the form of the Albigensian Crusade, which culminated in the victory of the church aided by the nobility of northern France, and finally, after much reluctance, by the king of France in the Treaty of Paris of 1229. Second, the Church relied on repression organized by a new institution, the Inquisition. In material terms, in spite of great difficulties, the Church had almost won the day by the start of the fourteenth century. It had lost it according to the judgment of posterity.

VI

The great heresies of the twelfth and thirteenth centuries have sometimes been defined as 'anti-feudal' heresies, and although this term can be disputed in a detailed historical analysis it is valid within the framework of a general explanation. In calling the very structure of society into question, these heresies attacked its basic component: the feudal system. The feudal system and urban evolution have often been contrasted. The political side of urban evolution, the communal movement, was indeed often directed against lords, especially against ecclesiastical lords; several bishops were the victims of communal revolts, for example the bishop of Laon in 1112 who was killed in a riot of which we have a gripping account by Guibert de Nogent. Town life supported itself by craft and trade, while feudalism lived off the manor, that is to say off the soil. The attitudes of townsmen, at least at the start, were egalitarian, since they sprang from fellowships which cut across society horizontally and united equals to each other by an oath. By contrast the feudal concept of society rested on a sense of hierarchy which expressed itself in vertical bonds held together by the oath of fidelity sworn by inferiors to superiors. Yet feudalism and the evolution of towns were two aspects of a single development which simultaneously shaped society and the environment in which it existed. To use the terminology of Daniel Thorner, the society of the medieval west was a peasant society, which, like every peasant society, had a certain percentage of town-dwellers (a minority), and which, in the particular case of western Christian Europe, was dominated by a superstructure which can be defined by the term feudalism.

As we have seen feudalism existed in an embryonic form in the Carolingian period, but it blossomed around the year 1000, appearing in different varieties according to the region. The length of time taken over the phases in its evolution varied from country to country. It was more advanced in France and Germany, and was never completely achieved in Italy, where its development was checked by the persistence of traditions from the ancient world, and by the unusually early involvement of the landowners in city life. It was even further from being complete in Spain, where the special conditions of the Reconquista gave the kings, who were its leaders, powers which limited those of the magnates; moreover, franchises preserving liberties were granted to those who fought and to the settlers in the *repoblación* (as we may learn from the work of Claudio Sanchez Albornoz). In England, in the Norman kingdom of Sicily, and in the Holy Land, the feudal system was 'imported'. It was more rigorous and sometimes closer to certain theoretical models than elsewhere, but it was also more fragile. In the Slav lands particular traditions produced other subtle differences in the feudal pattern, and Scandinavia lacked a feudal system almost entirely.

Since we are only aiming in this outline to set the feudal system in the context of the development of western Europe between the tenth and the fourteenth centuries, let us content ourselves with summarizing François Ganshof's description of how it installed itself, Georges Duby's account of how it evolved in one particular region, the Mâconnais, and Marc Bloch's view of its periodization.

Essentially the feudal system was composed of the whole group of personal ties which between them united the members of the ruling classes of society in a hierarchy. These ties were supported by a material foundation. This was the benefice, which was granted by the lord to his vassal in exchange for a certain number of services and an oath of fealty. The feudal system in the strict sense meant homage and the fief. The lord and his vassal were joined to each other by a feudal contract: the vassal did homage to his lord. The earliest sources where this word appears concern the county of Barcelona in 1020, the county of Cerdagne in 1035, eastern Languedoc in 1033 and Anjou in 1037. It became widespread in France in the second half of the eleventh century, and appeared for the first time in Germany in 1077. The vassal placed his hands, joined together, between those of his lord, who closed his hands over those of his vassal; the vassal then declared his wish to give himself to his lord following the customary formula: 'Sir, I become your man' (the phrase used in thirteenth-century France). Next he pronounced an oath of fealty, he gave the lord his faith and he could add a kiss, as was usual in France, which made him a 'man by mouth and hands'. As a result of the feudal contract, the vassal owed his lord *consilium* or counsel, which consisted in a general way of the obligation to take part in gatherings summoned together by his lord and in particular of rendering justice in the lord's name. The vassal also owed *auxilium* or aid, which was essentially military in character but which came to be financial. Thus the vassal had to make a contribution to seigneurial administration, justice, and warfare, while in return the lord owed his vassal protection. The lord, usually with the advice of his counsellors, could pronounce sanctions against a faithless or 'felonious' vassal, the chief of which was the confiscation of the fief. Conversely, the vassal could issue his 'defiance', that is to say withdraw his faith from a lord who failed to fulfil his promise. Theoretically the act of defiance, which first emerged in Lotharingia at the end of the eleventh century, was supposed to be accompanied by a solemn proclamation and the renunciation of the fief.

Obviously the fief was the key to the system. The word appeared in the west of Germany at the start of the eleventh century and, with its technical meaning, became widespread at the end of the eleventh century, although it was not always, or everywhere, used in this precise sense. It is more a term used by modern legal scholars and historians than a word in frequent use at the time. The most important thing is that the fief was most often a piece of land, a fact which established the feudal system on its rural basis and showed that it was chiefly a system for owning and cultivating land.

The grant of the fief by the lord to the vassal occurred during a ceremony known as an investiture which consisted of a symbolic act, in the handing over of an object such as a standard, a sceptre, rod, ring, knife, glove, or a scrap of straw. Usually it came after the oath of fealty and homage. It was only rarely recorded in a written document before the thirteenth century; the feudal system was a world of gesture and not of the written word. The fief underwent a major transformation. Whereas at the beginning the lord had rights over it which were similar to the bare ownership of Roman law, and the vassal a right similar to usufruct, from the eleventh century onwards the vassal's right over it became considerably stronger than that of a usufructuary. It came close to being a proprietary right without actually reaching it, although the word *proprietas* was used in the twelfth and thirteenth centuries, while the lord's right dwindled and was defined by the term *dominium*. Thus the feudal system more or less excluded the notion of property defined as the right to use and abuse. From this point of view the monetary economy and, generally speaking, the system of ownership in towns, were in opposition to the feudal system, especially as far as movable property, which tended to push immovable property into the background, was concerned. However, for as long as land remained the basis of the medieval economy, the burgess who tried to acquire lordships found himself in a false position, up to the point when the lordship dissociated itself from the fief, at the end of the middle ages.

What ensured the vassal's growing control over the fief was clearly the fact that it could be inherited, which was an essential part of the feudal system. This evolution came about early on in France, in the tenth and at the start of the eleventh century. It was slower in Germany and northern Italy, where it was precipitated by Conrad II in 1037. It only became general in England in the twelfth century.

In addition to cases where the feudal contract was broken, political activity in the feudal system was engendered by the fact that a vassal could have many different loyalties. Almost every vassal was the man of several lords, which sometimes put him in an awkward position, but also gave him the opportunity to give a preferential fealty to the lord who was the highest bidder. In order to protect themselves against the anarchy which could result from this, the most powerful lords tried, not always successfully, to make their vassals do a pre-eminent homage, 'liege' homage, to them, superior to that done to other lords. Kings in particular claimed the right to obtain this from all the vassals of their kingdoms. But here we are dealing with a different system from the feudal one, the monarchical system, to which we shall return.

The advantage of a concise study of the development of feudalism in a particular region, such as the feudalism studied by Georges Duby in the Mâconnais, is that it shows in concrete terms how the feudal system, as we have just described it theoretically and schematically, based itself on the cultivation of the land through the intervening control of the feudal hierarchy of lords and vassals over the peasants, and how it went beyond the terms of the feudal contract to ensure to each lord, great or small, a combination of extremely wide-ranging rights over his lordship or fief. The management of land through the manor formed the foundation of a social and political organization, the lordship or honour. Duby lays stress on an important fact, one which is not peculiar to the Mâconnais, namely that the castle was the centre of feudal organization. One of the most noticeable features of the history of the west from the tenth to the thirteenth century was the springing up of castles. Their military aspect should not blind us to their much wider significance.

At the end of the tenth century the social structure of the Mâconnais was still, on the surface, that of the Carolingian period. The main dividing line was the one which separated the free men from the serfs, and many peasants were still free. The power of the counts, in whom public power resided, still seemed to be respected. Rapidly, however, matters altered and the feudal system was established: the fief did not become very common in the region, but castles became centres of lordships which gradually took over all powers, whether economic, judicial, or political. In 971 the title of knight made its first appearance, and in 986 the first private court, that of the abbot of Cluny; in 988 a lord, the count of Chalon, levied exactions for the first time on free men as well as on serfs. The last mention of a vicarial court (a public court dealing with minor cases) which was independent from a lord is in 1004, and the last sentence passed against a castellan by the court of the count (the public court which dealt with higher justice) was in 1019. From 1030 onwards the feudal contract was introduced into the region, and in 1032 the term *nobilis* disappeared, giving way to the term *miles*. Whereas the whole peasant community, with a few exceptions such as allod-holders and *ministeriales*, saw its status become more uniform, with everyone sinking into a huge class of villeins or *manants*, a hierarchy sprang up in the ruling class. In about 1075 the knightly class, 'originally a class formed by fortune and way of life', became 'a hereditary caste, a true nobility'. However, it was composed of two levels according to the way in which 'powers over the weak were divided': the higher stratum was that of the lords of castles (*domini, castellani*), who exercised all the old public powers (the old royal ban) over a territory of some size, while the lower stratum was that of the simple knights 'who had only a small number of personal dependants behind them'. From his castle the lord was master of a territory in which he exercised all public and private powers mixed together; this was the so-called 'bannal' lordship (though the term *bannus* was fairly uncommon at the time).

In about 1160 further changes occurred and between 1230 and 1250 another feudal society was formed. 'The castellany ceased to be the crucial factor in the organisation of jurisdiction.' To begin with it more or less disintegrated in a levelling of the nobility which enabled the small village knights to build fortified houses on mottes. The number of castles which had existed in the eleventh and twelfth centuries had doubled by the start of the thirteenth century. The castellany was attacked from above and below. It was threatened from below by a gradual slackening of the lords' control over their villeins, and from above because the castellans gave up some of their powers in favour of a tiny minority of the new power-holders: the magnates, the princes, and above all the kings. In 1239 the Mâconnais was annexed to the royal domain, and the classic feudal system came to an end.

Marc Bloch distinguished two ages of feudalism. The first, which lasted until the middle of the eleventh century, corresponded to the organization of a fairly stable rural territory where trade was insignificant and uncommon, coins were rare, and a wage-earning class almost non-existent. The second was the result of the great land clearances, the revival of trade, the diffusion of a monetary economy, and the growing superiority of the merchant over the producer. Duby found this division into two periods occurring in the Mâconnais, but he placed the turning-point a century later, about 1160, at the point when 'the age of fiefs, land tenures owing a money payment or *census*, and feudal principalities succeeded the age of independent castellanies'.

Historians have described the evolution and the chronology of the medieval feudal system. Duby, who considers that 'from the middle of the eleventh century, the evolution of society and the evolution of the economy are going in opposite directions: the former, which is slowing down, is tending to tighten up the class structure into closed groups, while the other, which is accelerating, is leading to freedom and the relaxation of all restrictions', is basically of the same mind as Bloch. However it is more likely that the two processes may have gone on for rather longer in the same direction. The feudal lordship organized production and passed the produce on to the group of townsfolk, merchants, and burgesses who, willynilly, remained dependent on it for a long time. Of course in the long run the growth of the urban bourgeoisie undermined the feudal system, but at the end of the thirteenth century it was far from dominating it, even at the economic level. It took a long time before the growing distance between the economic power and the social and political weakness of the upper classes in the towns produced the middle-class revolutions of the seventeenth and eighteenth centuries.

It remains the case that economic evolution helped a large section of the peasant class to improve its lot. The peasant *hospites* or settlers obtained exemptions and freedoms on the newly cleared land which are particularly noticeable in place names of an urban or semi-urban character such as the many French '*villeneuves*', '*villefranches*', or '*bastides*'. A process of liberation occurred over all the landed estates of western Europe which improved the legal condition of peasants if not their material welfare. Seigneurial exactions were restricted by replacing labour services with a due or *census* which was often fixed, and a fixed total (a quit-rent or *taille abonnée*) of the principal payments was determined by a charter. The written word which thrust aside the gesture assisted social liberation, at least to begin with. These processes symbolized and brought about a certain advancement for the peasant classes, especially for the highest class of peasants, the *laboureurs* or ploughmen who owned their own teams and gear as opposed to the less skilled farm-workers.

It is also true that the evolution of the economy, especially after the thirteenth century, did not favour the poorer and middling members of the knightly class who got into debt faster than they could get out of it and had to sell some of their lands. In the Mâconnais, the last sum of money granted by knights to military subordinates dates from 1206, and from 1230 the lesser knights who held allods turned to doing homage and changing their allods into fiefs. They sold off their inheritances bit by bit, though they usually retained the core of their estates. The men who benefited from this were the most powerful lords, who, even if they did not have much ready money, could borrow easily, the churches, especially the town churches, which were the first to drain off a proportion of the coin in circulation through alms, and finally men of non-noble birth who had grown rich. A few of these were peasants, but most of them were burgesses. The crisis which was beginning to affect the landlords' income, 'the feudal revenue', turned into a general crisis in the fourteenth century, which in fact was, essentially, a crisis of the feudal system.

VII

At the political level of historical evolution (if one can call it that) the pattern often seems to be complex. It is easy to lose the thread in the details of men, events, and the writings of historians who have been willingly seduced by these superficial appearances and apparitions. The political history of the medieval west is especially complicated because it is a survey of numberless tiny areas which owed their existence to the fragmentation of the economy and society and to the fact that public powers were monopolized by the leaders of these relatively isolated groups. This, as we have seen, was one of the consequences of the feudal system. Yet the reality for the west in the middle ages was not only the fact that government was split up into small particles but also the fact that vertical and horizontal powers were entangled. People in the middle ages did not always know to which of the many lords, the Church and individual churches, the towns, princes, and kings, they were subordinate. We can observe this complexity even at the administrative and judicial level in the jurisdictional conflicts with which medieval history is filled.

Since we know the historical outcome, we may take the development of nation states as a guiding thread in this area.

In the period which immediately followed the year 1000 two figures appeared to be leading Christendom, the pope and the emperor. Antagonism between the two was to occupy the front stage for the whole of our period, but it was a mere shadow play behind which the serious events took place. Even so, the papacy did not cut a splendid figure on the death of Silvester II in 1003. It fell under the influence of the nobility in Latium, and then, after 1046, under the influence of the German emperors. However, it swiftly disengaged itself, and, furthermore, freed not only itself but the whole Church from the grip of lay lords. This is known as the Gregorian Reform, which takes its name from Gregory VII (1073-85). It was merely the outermost aspect of the great movement which was leading the Church back to its roots. It was a question of restoring the autonomy and the power of the priestly class in the face of the military class. The clergy had to renew and define itself: hence the battle against simony and the slow imposition of clerical celibacy. Hence, too, the attempt to establish the independence of the papacy by restricting the election of the pope to the cardinals (as decreed by Nicholas II in 1059), and, above all, the efforts to remove the clergy from the hands of the lay aristocracy. The aim was to deprive the emperor and, thus, other lords of the right to nominate and invest bishops, and by the same stroke to make the temporal power subject to the spiritual one, by making the temporal sword bow to the spiritual one or even by committing both swords to the pope.

Gregory VII appeared to have succeeded when the emperor Henry IV was humiliated at Canossa in 1077, but the penitent emperor soon took his revenge. Urban II, more prudent than Gregory, carried on with the task at a deeper level, sidestepping to use the crusade to gather Christian Europe together under his authority. A compromise was reached in Worms in 1122, by which the emperor abandoned investiture 'by ring and staff' to the pope, and promised to respect the freedom of elections and consecrations, but kept for himself the right to invest bishops with the temporalities of their sees 'by sceptre'.

The struggle broke out again in a slightly different form under Frederick Barbarossa (1152-90). After he too had had to humble himself at Venice before Alexander III in 1177, a hundred years after Canossa, he recovered what was essential, his domination over Italy and hence one of his chief means of putting pressure on the papacy. The conflict between Sacerdotium and Imperium reached a climax with Frederick II in the first half of the thirteenth century. The popes Innocent III (1198-1216), Gregory IX (1227-41), and above all Innocent IV (1243-54) attacked the emperor with varying degrees of success. Finally the papacy appeared to have won definitively. Frederick II, excommunicated and deposed at the Council of Lyons in 1245, his authority contested by almost everyone in Germany and Italy, died in 1250, leaving the Empire a prey to the anarchy of the Great Interregnum (1250-73). Yet in persistently attacking the emperor, who was merely an idol with clay feet, an anachronistic power, the papacy failed to observe, and sometimes even encouraged, the rise of a new power, that of the kings.

The conflict between the most powerful of these, the French king Philip the Fair and the pope Boniface VIII, ended with the humiliation of the pope at Anagni in 1303, and with the exile or 'captivity' of the papacy at Avignon between 1305 and 1376. The confrontation in the first half of the fourteenth century between the pope John XXII and the emperor Ludwig the Bavarian was merely a relic of the earlier struggle. It gave Ludwig's supporters, notably Marsilio of Padua in his *Defensor Pacis* of 1324, the opportunity to define a new Christendom in which temporal and spiritual power were clearly separated. With Marsilio, secularization attained the status of political ideology. The last great proponent of the fusion of the two powers had been Dante, the last great man of the middle ages, which he summed up in his masterpiece, the *Divine Comedy*, who had died, his gaze still turned towards the past, in 1321.

VIII

Among the monarchies and the states which inherited political power and which consolidated themselves between the eleventh and the fourteenth century, even the strongest had neither a secure dynasty nor clearly delimited frontiers. To take only one example, the whole of the west of modern France lay in the balance between France and England and remained so until the fifteenth century. Yet the future was being outlined by the formation of groupings of territories. By way of advances, retreats, and metamorphoses, these were tending to put together the little cells of the early middle ages. Monarchs were the wanderers of medieval Christendom.

Three success-stories occupy the foreground. England, after the Norman Conquest of 1066, was the first country to present the image of a centralized monarchy, under Henry I (1100-35) and especially under the Plantagenet

Henry II (1154-89). As early as 1086, royal possessions and rights were listed in Domesday Book (the Book of the Last Judgement) which provided an incomparable foundation for royal authority. This administrative achievement was completed by a solidly based financial institution (the Court of Exchequer) and by functionaries who were closely subordinated to the throne (justiciars and sheriffs). A serious crisis arose at the start of the thirteenth century and lasted for decades. King John had to agree to the limitation of royal power by the Great Charter or Magna Carta in 1215, and after a revolt of the nobility conducted by Simon de Montfort the monarchy was watched even more closely by means of the Provisions of Oxford. However, Edward I (1272-1307) and even Edward II (1307-27) were able to restore royal power by agreeing to some supervision by a parliament in which nobles, ecclesiastical lords and burgesses participated in government. In successful wars against the Welsh and unsuccessful wars against the Scots the English learnt new weaponry and tactics and made some of the common people take part in military activity as well as in local and central government. At the start of the fourteenth century England was the most modern and the most stable Christian state. This allowed a relatively small nation of four million inhabitants to win brilliant victories at the start of the Hundred Years War over the French Colossus with its fourteen million inhabitants.

Even so, France at the start of the fourteenth century was not unprepossessing. Under the Capetian kings its progress had been slower, but perhaps surer. Between the election of Hugh Capet in 987 and the accession of Louis VII in 1137 the weak Capetian monarchs saw their strength used up in obscure, endlessly recurring struggles against petty lords of the Ile-de-France who engaged in pillage and barricaded themselves inside their keeps. The kings looked wretched beside their great vassals, the most powerful of whom, the duke of Normandy, added the throne of England to his duchy in 1066 and then the vast estates of the Plantagenets in the middle of the twelfth century. Even so, as early as 1124, France showed that it could stick together behind its king when faced with the threat of the German emperor, and the latter had to retreat. The Capetians based their growing power on the enlargement of the royal domain, cleansed of its feudal troublemakers. Progress, already appreciable under Louis VII (1137-80), was dazzling under Philip Augustus (1180-1223). Control was extended and made firmer under Louis VIII (1223-6), Louis IX (Saint Louis, 1226-70), Philip the Bold (1270-85), and Philip IV, the Fair (1285-1314). The financial base of French royal power remained weak, and the king continued to draw his basic resources from his domain, to 'live of his own'. However, he had control over the administration once *baillis*, *sénéchaux*, and *prévôts* had been instituted by Philip Augustus, and this control was tightened with the enlargement of the king's *Conseil en*

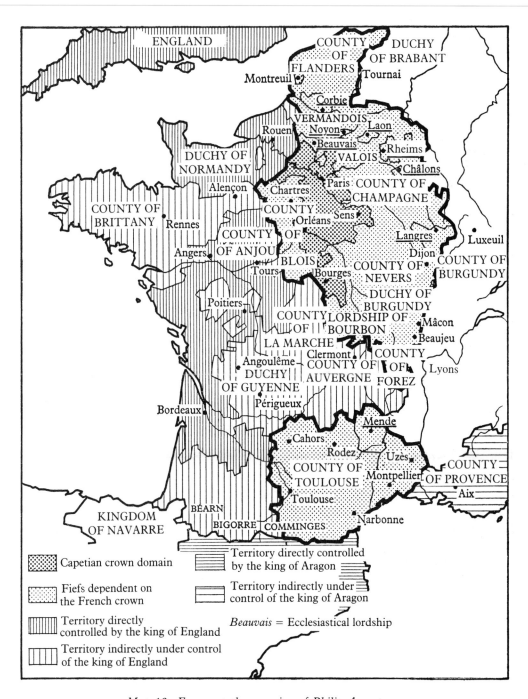

ENGLAND

COUNTY OF FLANDERS

DUCHY OF BRABANT

Montreuil

Tournai

Corbie

VERMANDOIS

Rouen

Noyon

Laon

Beauvais

Rheims

DUCHY OF NORMANDY

VALOIS

Châlons

Alençon

Chartres

Paris

COUNTY OF CHAMPAGNE

COUNTY OF BRITTANY

Rennes

COUNTY OF

Sens

Orléans

Langres

Luxeuil

Angers

OF ANJOU

Dijon

COUNTY OF BURGUNDY

Tours

BLOIS

Bourges

COUNTY OF NEVERS

Poitiers

DUCHY OF BURGUNDY

COUNTY OF BOURBON

Mâcon

LORDSHIP OF

Beaujeu

LA MARCHE

Clermont

COUNTY OF

Angoulême

COUNTY OF

FOREZ

Lyons

DUCHY OF GUYENNE

AUVERGNE

Périgueux

Bordeaux

Mende

Cahors

Rodez

Uzès

COUNTY OF PROVENCE

KINGDOM OF NAVARRE

BÉARN

COUNTY OF

Montpellier

Aix

BIGORRE

COMMINGES

TOULOUSE

Narbonne

Toulouse

Capetian crown domain

Territory directly controlled by the king of Aragon

Fiefs dependent on the French crown

Territory indirectly under control of the king of Aragon

Territory directly controlled by the king of England

Beauvais = Ecclesiastical lordship

Territory indirectly under control of the king of England

Map 16   France at the accession of Philip Augustus

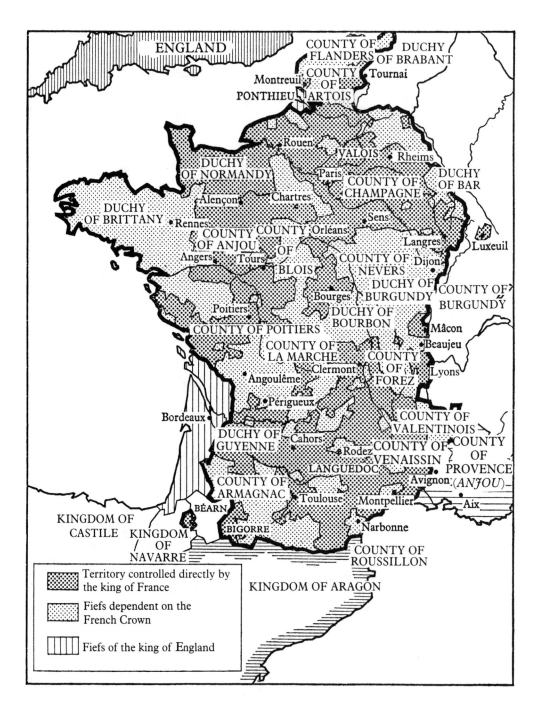

Map 17 *France at the accession of Philip VI of Valois*

Labels on map:

ENGLAND

COUNTY OF FLANDERS

DUCHY OF BRABANT

Tournai

COUNTY OF PONTHIEU

Montreuil

COUNTY OF ARTOIS

Rouen

VALOIS

Rheims

DUCHY OF NORMANDY

Paris

COUNTY OF CHAMPAGNE

DUCHY OF BAR

Alençon

Chartres

DUCHY OF BRITTANY

Rennes

COUNTY OF ANJOU

Orléans

Sens

Langres

Luxeuil

Angers

Tours

COUNTY OF BLOIS

COUNTY OF NEVERS

Dijon

COUNTY OF BURGUNDY

Bourges

DUCHY OF BURGUNDY

Poitiers

DUCHY OF BOURBON

Mâcon

COUNTY OF POITIERS

Beaujeu

COUNTY OF LA MARCHE

COUNTY OF FOREZ

Lyons

Clermont

Angoulême

Périgueux

COUNTY OF VALENTINOIS

COUNTY OF VENAISSIN

COUNTY OF PROVENCE (ANJOU)

Bordeaux

DUCHY OF GUYENNE

Cahors

Rodez

LANGUEDOC

Avignon

Aix

COUNTY OF ARMAGNAC

Toulouse

Montpellier

BÉARN

KINGDOM OF CASTILE

KINGDOM OF NAVARRE

BIGORRE

Narbonne

COUNTY OF ROUSSILLON

KINGDOM OF ARAGON

Legend:

Territory controlled directly by the king of France

Fiefs dependent on the French Crown

Fiefs of the king of England

Cour and its growing specialization in the field of finance. Above all the king had control of justice through the *Parlement* organized by Philip the Fair in 1303, which attracted a growing number of cases with the continuing success of appeals to the king. As in England, the Estates General, composed of prelates, barons and the rich burgesses from chartered towns, summoned by Philip the Fair, were more of an assistance to the king and his counsellors than a limitation of their power. The king's counsellors were civil lawyers who had been educated in the universities and who were imbued with Roman Law which they devoted to the service of their sovereign or 'emperor in his own kingdom'. A feudal reaction set in in 1315 after the death of Philip the Fair, but a change of dynasty in 1328, when the Capetians were replaced by the Valois, went ahead without difficulty. At the most the new dynasty seemed to be more open to the influence of the feudatories who were still very powerful at the Parisian court.

The third success-story of a centralized monarchy was achieved by the papacy. This success owed little to the pope's temporal power, the territorial base provided for him by the limited Patrimony of St Peter. It was by making sure of its powers over the bishops, and above all by tapping the Church's financial resources (not without arousing vigorous protests in England and France, to name but a few), and by taking the lead in the codification of canon law, that the papacy turned itself into an effective supranational monarchy in the twelfth and especially in the thirteenth century. Not only did it resist the Avignonese exile, it actually strengthened its power over the Church, and Yves Renouard has rightly maintained that Avignon was a better geographical centre for this monarchy than the more remote Rome.

Unification under a king had less success in the Iberian peninsula, where, in spite of temporary unions, the kingdoms remained distinct. Portugal, which was a kingdom from 1140, Navarre, Castile, which took in León after 1230, and Aragon, not to mention the persistence of the two entities of Aragon and Catalonia even after the political union of 1137, seemed to be durable formations. Yet each kingdom achieved remarkable progress towards centralization within its frontiers, although they changed according to the progress of the Reconquista and according to dynastic combinations. In Castile the reign of Alfonso X, the Wise (1252-84) was the period of the compilation of the great code called the *Siete Partidas*, and, thanks to royal favour, of the growth of the university of Salamanca. Aragon, spurred on by the Catalans, passionately wanted its own Mediterranean horizon; it was a great power under James the Conqueror (1213-76). After it was divided in 1262 the kingdom of Majorca flourished, with its capital at Perpignan and the favoured royal residences, the towns of Majorca and Montpellier. The special conditions of the Reconquista and the repopulation of the Iberian peninsula were above all responsible for allowing the people a large say in government in very lively local assemblies and in the Cortes which functioned in all the kingdoms from the thirteenth century.

The failure to achieve centralized monarchy was most striking in Italy and Germany. In Italy the temporal power of the popes in the centre of the peninsula and imperial authority in the north prevented a joining up of territories, while factions and parties within each town or between towns mostly organized themselves along the lines of that long-running soap opera, the Guelf-Ghibelline dispute. In the south, in spite of the efforts of Norman kings, German ones such as Frederick II who founded the first state university at Naples in 1224 and who kept a tight hand on the feudal system with the Constitutions of Melfi in 1231, and Angevin kings, the kingdom of Naples (or Sicily) saw too many forms of foreign domination to arrive at a solid administration.

In Germany the emperors were distracted from the realities of the German situation by the Italian mirage. Frederick Barbarossa appeared to have imposed royal authority over the feudal lords, especially after he had defeated the most powerful German magnate, Henry the Lion, duke of Saxony and Bavaria. Yet dynastic quarrels, wars between pretenders to the crown, and the growing interest in an Italy which was, however, ever yet more rebellious, led to the defeat of monarchic centralization with the Great Interregnum of 1250-73. The active political forces in Germany at the end of the thirteenth century were the towns of the Hanse and the old or new princely houses on the edges of the colonized areas to the north and the east. In 1273, a minor Alsatian prince, Rudolf of Habsburg, donned the imperial crown, and took advantage of his accession to the throne chiefly to found the future fortunes of his dynasty to the south-east, in Austria, Styria, and Carinthia.

To the east and the north, dynastic quarrels, feudal fragmentation, and uncertain frontiers operated against centralized authority, which in addition was undermined by Germanic colonization.

In Denmark the crown survived ups and downs and seemed to have won the day over the magnates at the start of the fourteenth century, but the king was so poor that in 1319 he had to pawn his kingdom to his creditor, the count of Holstein. In Sweden the crown became elective in the thirteenth century, but the family of the Folkungar succeeded for a time in imposing themselves under Magnus Laduslas (Barnlock) (1274-90) and more especially under Magnus Eriksen (1319-63). Norway seemed the luckiest; Haakon V (1299-1319) broke the power of the lay and ecclesiastical aristocracy and made the monarchy hereditary.

In Poland there was no king following Boleslaw the Bold, who was crowned at Gniezno on Christmas day 1076; however, the Piast dynasty continued with dukes, several of whom did not forget the anxiety for unification, such as Boleslaw III Wry-mouth (1102-38) and Mieszko the Old after 1173. Here too, revolts by lay and ecclesiastical magnates, who were helped directly or indirectly not only by Germans but also by Czechs and Hungarians, turned Poland into a group of independent duchies whose number increased during the thirteenth century. In 1295 Przemyslaw II of Great Poland restored the Polish kingdom for his own profit, but after him two kings of Bohemia took the title of king of Poland. It was necessary to wait for 1320 and the coronation, this time in Cracow, of a minor lord of Cujavia, Wladyslaw the Dwarf, for the *Corona regni Poloniae* to assert itself. Wladyslaw's son was Casimir the Great (1333-70). Meanwhile, however, Conrad of Mazovia had called in the Teutonic Knights against the Prussians, and the Teutonic Order, basing itself on the new diocese of Thorn (Torun), Kulm (Chelmno) and Marienwerder, founded a German state. After conquering Prussia, they invaded Pomerania and captured Danzig (Gdansk) in 1308, turning their fortress at Marienburg (Malbork) into what was effectively a capital from 1309.

The case of Bohemia is more complicated. At the end of the twelfth century, Otakar I (1192-1230) had himself crowned king in 1198 and made the throne hereditary under the dynasty of the Przemyslids, but the kings of Bohemia also acted as princes within the Empire and played a dangerous game in Germany. Otakar II (1253-78), who was nicknamed 'the king of gold' because of the splendour of his court, was not content with being an imperial elector, and tried to win support for his own election to the imperial crown. He added Austria, Styria, Carinthia, and Carniola by conquest to Bohemia and Moravia, but he collided with Rudolf of Habsburg, who was elected emperor instead of Otakar and who crushed him at the battle of Dürnkrut in 1278. The dream of a Great Bohemia was at an end, but not the German dream, which was realized by a king from a new foreign dynasty, Charles of Luxembourg, the emperor Charles IV, though the most significant fact was the growing colonization of Bohemia by German immigrants.

In Hungary, numerous succession disputes had weakened the Árpáds, the descendants of King Stephen, in the eleventh and twelfth centuries, but they had been able to enlarge their kingdom in Transylvania, Slovenia, and Croatia, in spite of the Germans and especially the Byzantines, who were briefly tempted to annex Hungary. Béla III (1173-96), who was married to a sister of Philip Augustus, appeared to have put the monarchy on a firm footing, but the rising class of the magnates forced his son Andrew II to issue a Golden Bull in 1222. This has been wrongly described as the Magna Carta of Hungary, for rather than establish national liberties it ensured the supremacy of the nobles which quickly led the country into anarchy. To make things worse, the death of the last of the Árpáds in 1301 led to a crisis which was to bring rulers of foreign origin into Hungary.

On 1 August 1291 the men of the valley of Uri, the free community of the valley of Schwyz and the association of the men of the lower valley of Nidwalden swore a perpetual league against the Habsburg menace. This oath resembled numerous other leagues between town communities or groups of mountain-dwellers; it would have been difficult to predict that this was the kernel of a new form of political organization, the Helvetic Confederation. On 15 November 1315 the league won a startling victory over Leopold of Habsburg at Morgarten. The military success of the Swiss and their political future announced themselves simultaneously.

IX

Now that we have reached the moment when western Christian Europe had reached its apogee, but was preparing to confront a crisis and undergo a deep transformation, we might pause to wonder which institutions and forces would take over from the feudal system, which was in decline politically, although it was still strong economically and socially. One might think of the towns, whose prosperity grew ceaselessly, whose cultural influence was unrivalled, and which enjoyed military triumphs in addition to their economic, artistic, intellectual, and political success. As early as 1176 the most precocious of them, the cities of northern Italy, had inflicted a disastrous blow on Frederick Barbarossa at Legnano which stunned the feudal world, and in 1302 at Courtrai the infantry of the Flemish towns cut to pieces the flower of French chivalry who left behind the 500 golden spurs which gave the battle its name. The future seemed to belong to Genoa, Florence, Milan, Siena, Venice, Barcelona, Bruges, Ghent, Ypres, Bremen, Hamburg, and Lübeck. And yet modern Europe was not built around towns but out of nation states. The economic base of the towns was never to be large enough either to establish a first-class political power or even to found a large-scale economic force. Gradually as long-distance trade ceased to concentrate overwhelmingly on luxury merchandise and came to rely on traffic in bulk materials (chiefly grain) as well, the urban centre was no longer big enough. Already at the end of the thirteenth century the towns only made a mark for themselves within the framework of confederations of towns, which was the Hanseatic solution, or by forming a large rural area around them, an ever-widening territory, which was the solution in Flanders (Bruges and Ghent drew as much of their power from their 'Francs' as from long-distance trade), and above all in Italy: the towns of Liguria, Lombardy, Tuscany, Venetia, and Umbria padded themselves out with *contados* which they found essential. Perhaps the most urbanized of them all, Siena (its bank already had its most glorious moments behind it in the thirteenth century), gave clear artistic expression to the need which the town had of the country. In the frescos which Ambrogio Lorenzetti painted to the glory of the citizens in the Palazzo Municipale between 1337 and 1339, portraying Good and Bad Government, the town, although enclosed by walls and bristling with towers and important buildings, was not separated from its countryside, from its indispensable *contado*. Venice only survived by means of its *Terra Ferma*. Perhaps it is hard to discern this trend as early as 1300, and yet the age when humanity had been scattered in islets, outposts and small cells was passing away at the same time as the feudal system. Another way of organizing the space in between had begun to make itself felt, that of territorial states. Observant men of the period perceived the truth of this in terms of population: Pierre Dubois considered that the king of France was the most powerful king in Christian Europe because he had the largest number of subjects, and Marsilio of Padua made population into one of the principal forces of the modern state. But a large population could only exist on a large surface area, and progress began to demand the unification, not just of small territories, but of large ones.

4

The Crisis of Christian Europe
(Fourteenth to Fifteenth Centuries)

I

LTHOUGH MOST of the Christian nations at the start of the fourteenth
century were still floating within shifting frontiers, Christian Europe
as a whole had stabilized. As A. Lewis has said, it was the 'edge
of the frontier'. Medieval expansion was complete. When it took off again
at the end of the fifteenth century it was a different phenomenon. On the
other hand, the period of the great invasions appeared to have ended. The
Mongol incursions of 1241–3 had left terrible traces in Poland and Hungary,
especially the latter. Here the invasion of the Cumans, driven on by the
Mongols, had increased the anarchy and had given the Hungarians a king
who was half Cuman and half pagan, Ladislaus IV (1272-90), against whom
Pope Nicholas IV preached a crusade. Yet these were only raids and the
scars healed up quickly afterwards. Little Poland and Silesia experienced a
new wave of clearances and agricultural and urban growth after the Tartars
had gone away.

However, Christian Europe at the turn of the thirteenth and fourteenth
centuries not only halted, but shrank. There were no more clearances or
conquest of new ground, and even the marginal lands, which had been put
under the plough under the pressure of a growing population and out of
enthusiasm for the expansion, were abandoned because their yields were in
fact too small. Deforestation threatened in many places. The desertion of fields
and even of villages - the Wüstungen studied by Wilhelm Abel and his pupils -
began. The building of the great cathedrals, still unfinished, was interrupted.
The population graph stopped climbing and began to come down. Inflation
stopped and a depression set in.

II

Besides these large-scale general phenomena, certain events announced that Christian Europe was entering a crisis. Some of these were noticed by contemporaries while others only acquired significance in the eyes of modern historians. A series of strikes, urban uprisings and revolts broke out in the last third of the thirteenth century, especially in Flanders. Bruges, Douai, Tournai, Provins, Rouen, Caen, Orléans, Béziers in 1280, Toulouse in 1288, Rheims in 1292, and Paris in 1306 were all affected. The culmination was an almost general insurrection in 1302 in the regions which now make up Belgium. According to the chronicler Hocsem, 'In this year, the popular party rose up almost everywhere against the great. In Brabant this uprising was snuffed out, but in Flanders and Liège the masses prevailed for a long time.'

In 1284 the vaults of Beauvais Cathedral, which had been built up to a height of 48 metres, collapsed. The Gothic dream was never to rise higher. Building on cathedrals stopped, at Narbonne in 1286, and Cologne in 1322. Siena reached the limit of its possibilities in 1366. The devaluation of the coinage and currency alterations began. France experienced several under Philip the Fair, the first serious ones of the middle ages. The Italian banks, especially the Florentine ones, suffered catastrophic bankruptcies in 1343. The Bardi, Peruzzi, Acciaiuoli, Bonaccorsi, Cocchi, Antellesi, Corsini, da Uzzano and Perendoli, and, according to the Florentine chronicler Giovanni Villani 'many other small companies and private craftsmen' were dragged down in the fall.

Of course these crisis symptoms appeared in the most vulnerable sectors of the economy: in the towns, where the textile trade had undergone a boom which put it at risk when the rich clientèle for whom it produced and exported cloth declined; in the building trade, where the huge plans to be executed cost more and more because the manpower, the raw materials and the financial resources found employment in other, more lucrative areas. In the area of the monetary economy the difficulties inherent in a type of economy with which even the specialists were unfamiliar were increased by the lack of skill in managing bimetallism, now that gold coins were once more being struck, and by imprudent bankers, who were asked for money by princes who were increasingly both greedy for loans and in debt. 'In currencies things are very obscure; they go high and low, one knows not what to do: When one thinks to gain, one finds the reverse,' wrote Gilles Li Muisit, abbot of St Martin of Tournai, in the early fourteenth century.

The crisis was revealed in its full extent when it reached the basic level of the rural economy. In 1315–17 a run of bad weather brought bad harvests, a rise in prices, and the return of general famine which had almost disappeared from the west, at least from the extreme west, in the thirteenth century. At Bruges two thousand people out of thirty-five thousand died of hunger. The lowering of physical resistance resulting from the new outbreak of malnutrition must have played a part in the ravages which the Black Death finally exercised after 1348. The Black Death made the population curve, which was already dipping, fall violently. It turned the crisis into a catastrophe. But it is clear that the crisis predated the plague, which merely exaggerated it. The causes of the crisis are to be sought in the very foundations of the economic and social framework of Christian Europe. The lessening of the feudal income and the upheavals owing to the growing proportion of money in peasant dues called the basis of the power of the great into question.

III

Although it went to the foundations, the crisis did not bring with it a depression in the entire western economy. It did not affect either all classes or all individuals equally. One geographical or economic sector might be hit while alongside it a new growth area was emerging to replace and compensate for the losses next door. The traditional luxury cloth trade, the 'old cloth trade', was seriously affected by the crisis and the centres where it had been dominant declined, but next door new centres were rising up which were dedicated to making less expensive cloth destined for a less rich, less exacting market. This was the triumph of the 'new cloth trade' based on Flanders serge and fustians with a cotton base. One family might go bankrupt but another, next door, would go on in its place.

After a brief moment's disarray, the seigneurial class adapted itself, replacing cultivation to a large extent by stockrearing, which was more remunerative, and thus they transformed the rural landscape by increasing the number of enclosures. The lords modified the peasants' contracts, the nature of the dues and of their method of payment, and learned how to control real money and money of account, a skilled use of which allowed them to cope with changes in the value of the coinage. But, of course, only the most powerful, the most skilled or the luckiest benefited; others were hit. Again, the fall in population, aggravated by the plague, cut down the number of the workforce and the consumers, but salaries were rising and the survivors were generally richer. Finally, the feudal system, which was affected by the crisis, resorted to the easy solution of the ruling classes when under threat – war. The most remarkable example of this is the Hundred Years War, demanded indiscriminately by the English and French nobles as an answer to their difficulties. But, as always, war accelerated the process and brought to birth

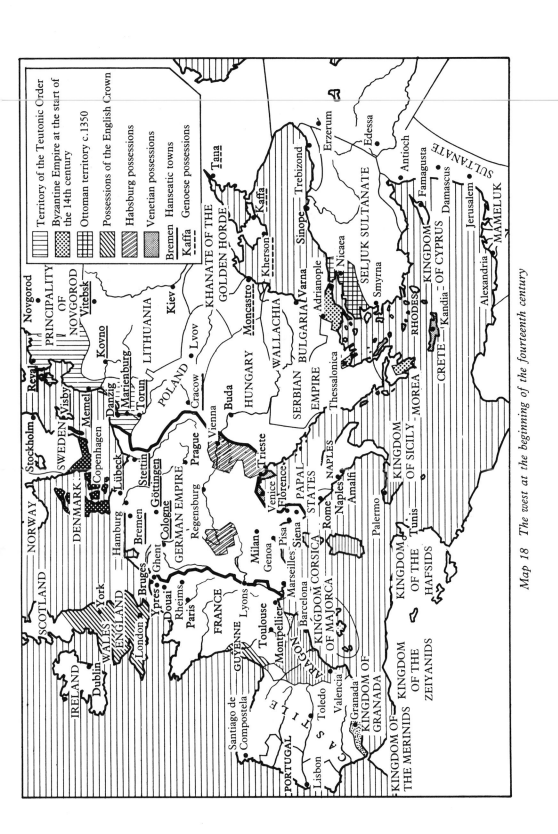

Map 18 The west at the beginning of the fourteenth century

Territory of the Teutonic Order
Byzantine Empire at the start of the 14th century
Ottoman territory c.1350
Possessions of the English Crown
Habsburg possessions
Venetian possessions
Genoese possessions
Bremen Hanseatic towns
Kaffa

NORWAY
SCOTLAND
IRELAND
Dublin
WALES
ENGLAND
York
London
Bruges
Ghent
Ypres
Douai
Rheims
Paris
FRANCE
GUYENNE
Lyons
Toulouse
Montpellier
Marseilles
ARAGON
Barcelona
KINGDOM OF MAJORCA
CORSICA
PORTUGAL
Lisbon
CASTILE
Santiago de Compostela
Toledo
Valencia
Granada
KINGDOM OF GRANADA
KINGDOM OF THE MERINIDS
KINGDOM OF THE ZEIYANIDS
KINGDOM OF THE HAFSIDS
Tunis
KINGDOM OF SICILY

Novgorod
Reval
Stockholm
SWEDEN
Visby
DENMARK
Copenhagen
Lübeck
Hamburg
Bremen
Stettin
Cologne
Göttingen
GERMAN EMPIRE
Regensburg
Prague
Vienna
Milan
Genoa
Pisa
Siena
Florence
Venice
Trieste
PAPAL STATES
Rome
Naples
Amalfi
NAPLES
Palermo
MOREA

PRINCIPALITY OF NOVGOROD
Vitebsk
Kovno
Marienburg
Danzig
Torun
Memel
LITHUANIA
POLAND
Cracow
Lvov
Kiev
HUNGARY
Buda
WALLACHIA
SERBIAN EMPIRE
Thessalonica
BULGARIA
Varna
Adrianople
Moncastro
KHANATE OF THE GOLDEN HORDE
Tana
Kaffa
Kherson
Sinope
Trebizond
Erzerum
Nicaea
Smyrna
SELJUK SULTANATE
RHODES
KINGDOM OF CYPRUS
Famagusta
CRETE
Kandia
Edessa
Antioch
Damascus
Jerusalem
Alexandria
MAMELUK SULTANATE

a new economy and society by way of deaths and ruins – although one should not exaggerate these in the circumstances. The crisis of the fourteenth century quickly ended up in a redrafting of the economic and social map of Christian Europe. It encouraged and accentuated the already existing development in the direction of centralized states. It prepared the way for the French monarchy of Charles VII and Louis XI, the English Tudor dynasty, Spanish unity under the Catholic kings, and the arrival of the 'prince', particularly in Italy and to some extent everywhere else. It created new clientèles, mainly of the middle class, for products and for an art which perhaps tended in the direction of mass-production. Printing was to permit this too in the intellectual domain. However, these products were on a level of quality which was still fairly high on average. They also corresponded to a rise in the standard of living of the middle classes, and to an increase in comfort and taste. The crisis gave birth to the society of the Renaissance and modern times which were more open and, for many, happier than the stifling feudal society.

PART II

Medieval Civilization

5

Genesis

I

IN THE history of civilizations, as in that of individuals, childhood is
decisive. Much, if not everything, is then at stake. Between the fifth
and the tenth century habits of thinking and feeling were born and ideas
and works came into being which formed, and informed, the future structures
of the way medieval men thought and felt. First we should look at the way
in which the new structures were organized. Obviously there are different
levels of culture in each civilization according to social groups on the one hand
and the contributions of the past on the other. Alongside this stratification
new syntheses are created by combining, bringing together and mixing. This
is particularly noticeable in the early western middle ages. The thing that was
most obviously new about the culture was the relations which were being
established between the pagan inheritance and the Christian contribution, if
we suppose (although this is far from the truth, as is well known) that each
of these formed a coherent whole on its own. Yet, at the level of the educated
classes, each of them had reached a sufficient level of homogeneity for us to
be able to consider them as two partners – or perhaps two adversaries?

Early Christian writings, followed by those of the middle ages and, since
then, a number of modern works devoted to the history of medieval civilization,
are filled with the debate, or perhaps the conflict, between pagan culture and
the Christian spirit. The two ways of thinking and feeling were, admittedly,
opposed to each other, as nowadays Marxist ideology and bourgeois ideology
are. Pagan literature as a body posed a problem to the Christian middle ages,
but in the fifth century the question had in fact already been settled. Until
the fourteenth century there were to be fanatical supporters of each of the
two opposed tendencies, those who forbade the use and even the reading of
ancient authors, and those who made use of them, though in a rather artless
way. Circumstances favoured the one side or the other alternately. However,

the basic attitude had been fixed by the Fathers of the Church and defined once and for all by St Augustine, who had declared that Christians ought to use ancient culture as the Jews had used the spoils of the Egyptians. 'If the philosophers [pagan philosophers, understood] chanced to utter truths useful to our faith, as the Platonists above all did, not only should we not fear these truths but also we must remove them from these unlawful usurpers for our own uses'. Thus the Israelites had carried out of Egypt the golden and silver vessels and precious objects with which they were later to construct the Tabernacle. This message of the *De Doctrina Christiana*, which was to be a medieval commonplace, in fact opened the door to a whole gamut of uses of Graeco-Roman culture. Often medieval men were to adhere to Augustine's text literally, that is to say only using isolated fragments, such as the stones of demolished temples, but sometimes materials which were entire pieces, such as the columns of temples which became the pillars of cathedrals. Sometimes the temple itself, like the Pantheon in Rome, which was turned into a church in the early seventh century, became a Christian building at the cost of slight changes and a thin disguise. It is very difficult to appreciate to what extent the intellectual equipment (vocabulary, notions, and methods) of antiquity was transferred into the middle ages. The degree of assimilation, metamorphosis, and denaturation varied from one author to another and often the same author swayed between the two extremes which marked the limits of medieval culture – flight in terror before pagan literature and passionate admiration leading him to make large-scale borrowings. Already St Jerome had set an example for these variations of attitude. He usually indulged in long quotations from pagan authors on which he had been fed as much as on the Bible, but he one day heard himself being called on in a dream by God, who said to him severely, '*Ciceronianus es, non christianus*', 'You are a Ciceronian, not a Christian'. Alcuin was to have the same dream on Virgil. Yet Jerome himself settled on the same compromise which had been pronounced by St Augustine, that the Christian author should use his pagan authorities as the Jews of Deuteronomy had dealt with their female war captives, by shaving their heads, cutting their nails and giving them new clothes before marrying them. In practice, medieval clerics were to find plenty of ways of using 'pagan' books while still keeping their consciences happy without much effort. Thus in the library at Cluny a monk who wanted to consult a manuscript by an ancient author had to scratch his ear with a finger in the style of a dog scratching itself with its paw, 'for the pagan is justly compared with this animal'.

Yet, although this compromise safeguarded some continuity of ancient tradition, it betrayed this tradition sufficiently for the intellectual elite to feel the need of a true return to the ancient sources on several occasions. These were the renaissances which punctuated the middle ages: in the Carolingian period, in the twelfth century, and finally at the dawn of the great Renaissance. Admittedly the fact that the authors of the early western middle ages needed to use the irreplaceable intellectual equipment of the Graeco-Roman world but at the same time make it conform to Christian thinking encouraged, if it did not create, very tiresome intellectual habits: the systematic deformation of the authors' thoughts, perpetual anachronism, and thinking through quotations taken out of context. Ancient thought only survived in the middle ages in a fragmented form. It was pushed out of shape and humiliated by Christian thought. Forced to have recourse to the services of its conquered enemy, Christianity saw itself forced to deprive its enslaved prisoner of his memory and to make him work for it by forgetting his traditions. But concomitantly with this Christianity was dragged into a system of thinking which was atemporal. All truths could only be eternal. In the thirteenth century Thomas Aquinas was still saying that what the authors intended mattered little, since the essential thing was what they had said and what one could use to please oneself. Rome was no longer in Rome. The *translatio* or transfer of civilization inaugured the great confusion of the middle ages, but this confusion was the precondition for a new order.

II

Here too, antiquity in decline had facilitated the work of the Christian clerics of the first centuries of the middle ages. What the middle ages knew of ancient culture had been bequeathed to it by the Late Empire, which had rechewed, impoverished and dissected Graeco-Roman literature, thought, and art in such a way that the barbarized early middle ages could assimilate it more easily. The clerics of the early middle ages did not borrow their scheme of knowledge and education from Cicero or Quintilian, but from a Carthaginian lawyer, Martianus Capella. He had defined the seven liberal arts in the second half of the fifth century in a poem called *The Marriage of Mercury and Philology*. Medieval clerics did not look so much to Pliny and Strabo (who anyway were themselves inferior to Ptolemy) for their knowledge of geography as to a mediocre compiler of the third century (when the decay began), Julianus Solinus, who bequeathed to the middle ages a world of prodigies and monsters: the Wonders of the East. Through this, admittedly, imagination and arts were to gain where science had lost. Medieval zoology was to be that of the *Physiologus*, a second-century Alexandrian work translated into Latin in the fifth century of all periods. It watered science down into verse full of legends and moralizing lessons. The animals were changed into symbols. But the middle ages was to draw its bestiaries from them, and here again medieval feeling for animals was to be fed on scientific ignorance. The main point is that these rhetors and compilers provided medieval men with learning broken down into crumbs. The Late Empire transmitted an elementary mental and intellectual equipment to the middle ages, composed of word-lists, mnemonic verses, etymologies (false ones), and florilegia. It was a culture consisting of quotations, choice morsels and digests.

Nor were things different for the Christian sector of medieval culture. The *doctrina christiana* was above all and essentially Holy Scripture, and the *sacra pagina* (Scriptures) was to be the basis of the whole of medieval culture. However a double screen was interposed between the text and the reader. The text was deemed difficult, and above all it was so rich and so mysterious that it had to be explained at different levels according to the meanings which it contained. Hence there grew up a great series of keys, commentaries and glosses behind which the original began to disappear. The Bible succumbed under exegesis. The Reformation in the sixteenth century had the justifiable feeling that it had rediscovered it. Then, the Bible was very long, and it had to be put within everyone's reach in extracts, whether in the form of citations or paraphrases. The Bible turned into a collection of maxims and anecdotes. The Fathers themselves became a raw material from which the substance was extracted somehow or other. The true sources of medieval Christian thought were the treatises and poems of the third or fourth century such as the *Historiae contra Paganos* by Orosius, a disciple and friend of Augustine, who turned history into a vulgar apologia, the *Psychomachia* of Prudentius who reduced moral life to a combat between vices and virtues, and Julianus Pomerius' *Treatise on the Contemplative Life*, which taught contempt for the world and for secular activities.

III

It is not enough merely to observe this intellectual regression. The most important thing is to see clearly that it was a necessary adaptation to the conditions of the period. A few pagan or Christian aristocrats, such as Sidonius Apollinaris, might be free to take pleasure in the games of a culture that might be refined but was restricted to a dying social class. The barbarized writers wrote for a new public. As R. R. Bolgar rightly said concerning the educational systems of Augustine, Martianus Capella, and Cassiodorus,

But the greatest virtue of the new theories was perhaps their providing a reasoned alternative to the system of Quintilian. For the world in which oratory had flourished was dying; and the new civilization destined to replace it was to have no knowledge of popular assemblies or forensic triumphs. The men of the centuries to come, whose lives were to be centred on the manor and the monastery, would have found it a definite disadvantage if the education on which they depended had put before them an ideal whose significance they could not grasp, if Capella and Augustine had not replaced Quintilian (Bolgar, 1954, pp. 36-7).

It is striking to see the most cultivated and the most eminent representatives of the new Christian elite, conscious of their cultural unworthiness compared with the last purists, renounce what they yet possessed or could acquire in the form of intellectual refinement so that they could make themselves accessible to their flocks. They chose to grow stupid in order to conquer. If this leaves us dissatisfied it is none the less impressive. This farewell to antique literature, often uttered by men fully aware of the circumstances, is by no means the least moving aspect of the abnegation of the great Christian leaders of the early middle ages. Avitus, bishop of Vienne, announced to his brother in the preface to a new edition of his poetic works in the early sixth century that he was giving up this genre, 'for too few understand the measure of syllables'. In the same period Eugippius was hesitating to publish his *Life of Saint Severinus*, for he feared that 'the obscurity of his speech might prevent the multitude from understanding these admirable facts' that he was relating. Caesarius of Arles took this point of view further:

I humbly beg that the ears of the educated may be content to bear rustic expressions without complaint, so that all the Saviour's flock can receive heavenly food in a simple and down-to-earth language. Since the ignorant and the simple cannot raise themselves to the height of the educated, let the educated deign to lower themselves to their ignorance. Educated men can understand what has been said to the simple, whereas the simple are not able to profit from what would have been said to the learned.

And he quoted the saying of Jerome, 'The preacher must arouse groans more than applause'. Of course the preachers in both cases were trying to subjugate and dominate. Yet the ways and means had changed, and this shift of sensibility and propaganda between the ancient world and the middle ages defined a new society.

The shift was also an intellectual one. By way of barbarization, it attained or tried to attain values which were no less important than those of the Graeco-Roman world. When Augustine stated that it was better 'to see oneself reproved by the grammarians rather than not understood by the people', and that things and realities should be preferred to words, *res* to *verba*, he was giving voice to a medieval utilitarianism, indeed a materialism, which was to free people, not without benefit, from a certain antique logomachia. Medieval men declared themselves not very fussy about the state of the roads, provided that they reached the goal. Thus, in spite of dust and mud, the medieval lane, by way of its windings, led to the port. The work to be accomplished was enormous. When one reads the canon law texts, the canons of synods and councils, and the articles of the penitentials of the early middle ages, one is struck by the size of the task which presented itself to the leaders of Christian society. Material life was precarious, morals were barbarous, and all goods were scarce, and this great deprivation demanded strong souls, contemptuous of subtleties and of refinements, who wanted to succeed.

This age was also, as we too often tend to forget, that of the great heresies, or rather of the great hesitations over doctrine, for orthodoxy, which appears fixed to us only by retrospective illusion, was far from being defined. It is not possible here to say what consequences would have been produced by a triumph of the great currents of Arianism, Manichaeanism, Pelagianism, or Pricillianism, to mention only the best known of the religious movements which stirred up the west in the fifth and sixth centuries. One can say very roughly that the success of orthodoxy was the success of a *via media* between Arian or Manichaean simplisticism and Pelagian or Pricillianist subtlety. Everything appears to be summed up in the attitude towards free will and grace. If Christianity had inclined towards the strict doctrines of predestination as the Manichaeans wished, the weight of divine determinism would have weighed heavily on western Europe. It would have been handed over without any counterweight to the ruling classes, which would not have failed to proclaim themselves the interpreters of this divine omnipotence. Had Pelagianism triumphed and installed the supremacy of human, individual choice, the west, which was under so much threat, would probably have been submerged in anarchy. Yet one senses clearly that the west did not have a choice. The numbers of slaves were drying up, but it was necessary to set the masses to work. The technical equipment was limited but capable of improvement. Man was to sense that he could have a certain hold over nature, modest though it might be. The monastic institution, which expresses this period so well, linked flight from the world with the organization of economic and spiritual life. The balance between nature and grace which was being established betrays the limits of the power and of the powerlessness of men in the early middle ages. Above all, it left the door open to future developments. Built to await the end of the world, early medieval society had, without being aware of it, provided itself with the framework necessary to welcome the rise of mankind in the west, when the moment came.

IV

The setting of civilization did not change violently with the Great Invasions. In spite of the pillaging and the destruction, the traditional cultural centres rarely ceased to exist or to sparkle overnight. Even that great victim of the new age, the town, survived for a fairly long time with some success. The towns which preserved some vitality owed it in some cases to the maintenance of a certain economic role, ancient or new, linked especially to the importation of luxury products and the presence of eastern merchants who were called Syrians but who were chiefly Jews. Sometimes towns owed their survival to visits by groups of pilgrims. In this way Rome, Marseilles, Arles, Narbonne, and Orléans remained ports for the east. Yet the most important urban centres were those used by the new barbarian kings as residences, or above all were bishops' sees or the focus of famous pilgrim cults.

The barbarian courts attracted workshops for luxury crafts, such as stone-working, clothweaving, and especially goldsmithery, although most of the royal and episcopal treasure-hoards were chiefly accumulated out of imported objects, primarily Byzantine ones. However one senses the attraction for artists of Pavia under Liutprand (712–44), of Monza at the time of Queen Theodelinda at the turn of the sixth and seventh century, of Toledo from the reign of Recared (586–601) to the Muslim conquest (711), and of Paris and Soissons under the Merovingians. Even so, the falling-off of skills, economic resources, and taste is discernible everywhere. Everything was shrinking. Buildings were most often built of wood. Those which were built in stone, which was often borrowed from ruined ancient monuments, were of small dimensions. The main thrust of aesthetic effort concentrated on decoration, which masked the lack of building skills. The art of cutting stone, freestanding sculpture, and the representation of the human figure died out almost entirely. Mosaics, ivories, cloth and especially gold objects shone, satisfying the barbarian taste for tinsel. Art was often hoarded in the treasure-piles of palaces and churches and was even buried away in tombs. It was a period when the lesser arts triumphed. They produced true masterpieces which displayed the skill of barbarian artists and craftsmen at metalwork and the fascinating stylized art of the steppes. These were fragile pieces and few have come down to us, but we possess precious and marvellous evidence such as pins, belt-buckles, and sword pommels. The crowns of the Visigothic kings, the copper crown of Agilulf, and the Merovingian tombs at Jouarre are some of the rare treasures still surviving from these centuries.

Yet the rulers, especially the Merovingians, increasingly took pleasure in their villas in the country, where most of their diplomas are dated. Many towns, if one can believe the episcopal lists, remained, as we have seen, deprived of bishops for a fairly long time. Sixth-century Gaul appears to have been still strongly urbanized, if we read Gregory of Tours, and dominated by the rich episcopal cities such as Soissons, Paris, Sens, Tours, Orléans, Clermont, Poitiers, Bordeaux, Toulouse, Lyons, Vienne, and Arles. In Visigothic Spain, Seville was a lively cultural centre during the pontificates of the brothers Leander (579-600) and Isidore (600-36). But the great focal point of civilization in the early middle ages was the monastery, and increasingly the isolated monastery in the countryside. With its workshops it was a conservatory for crafts and artistic skills; with its scriptorium and library it maintained intellectual culture. Thanks to its estates and its tools and workforce of monks and dependants of all sorts it was a centre of production and an economic model, and of course it was a focus of spiritual life, often based on the relics of a saint.

It would be absurd to deny the attraction and influence of these monastic centres. At the same time, the new urban Christian society was being organized around the bishop, and increasingly around the parishes which were being set up slowly within the dioceses (the two words parish and diocese were for a time synonymous). Religious life was also establishing itself in the villas of the landowning and military aristocrats, who were founding its private chapels from which the feudal *Eigenkirchen* were to grow. Yet it should be stressed that it was the monasteries which made Christianity and the values it conveyed penetrate slowly into the countryside, which hitherto had been little affected by the new religion. This rural world of long traditions, where little changed, became the basic world of medieval society. Hagiography and iconography (often later in date) do not allow us to be deceived. In the period of urban evangelizing the main action of a missionary saint was the destruction of idols, that is to say statues in temples. From the fifth to the ninth centuries it was the destruction of natural idols in a rural milieu – the cutting down of a holy tree, the baptism of a well, placing a cross on a rustic altar. But one also senses that the pre-eminence of the monastery shows that the civilization of the medieval western world was precarious. It was a civilization of isolated points, of oases of culture in the middle of 'deserts', of forests and of fields returned to waste, or of countryside barely brushed by monastic culture. The disorganization of the networks of communication and relations of the ancient world had returned most of the west to the primitive world of traditional rural civilizations anchored in prehistory, barely touched by the Christian gloss. The old customs and old skills of the Iberians, Celts and Ligurians resurfaced. Where the monks thought they had conquered Graeco-Roman paganism, they encouraged the reappearance of a much older subsoil of craftier demons, submissive merely in outward appearance to Christian law. The west had been returned to savagery, which was to recur and erupt from time to time throughout the whole of the middle ages. The limits of monastic action have to be noted; but it is essential to evoke its force and effectiveness.

Let us consider a few examples out of the huge number of names made illustrious by hagiography and history. In the period of conversion in the cities, Lérins; when conversion launched out deep into the countryside, Montecassino and the great Benedictine adventure. To illustrate the routes taken by Christianity in the early middle ages, the epic of Irish monasticism. Finally for the time when the conversion movement started up again on the frontiers, the role of the monasteries in missionary work in the eighth and ninth centuries; this in fact is a continuation of the Irish movement.

Lérins was closely linked to the development of Provence as a great centre of Christianization in the fifth and sixth centuries. Pierre Riché has recently reminded us that Lérins was first and foremost a school for asceticism and not for intellectual formation. The eminent churchmen who went there on fairly long visits did perhaps demand biblical learning from the place, but principally a 'spiritual meditation on the Bible more than a learned exegesis'. The first abbot, Honoratus, who had come to Lérins by way of a detour in the east, shaped the milieu of Lérins in close connection with Cassian, also from the east, who was the founder of St Victor of Marseilles. Indeed, between 430 and 500, almost all the great names of the Provençal church passed through Lérins: Salvian, Eucher of Lyons, Caesarius of Arles, and Faustus of Riez, who inspired the great Provençal synods whose canons made a deep impression on western Christianity.

The activity of Benedict of Nursia, which radiated from Montecassino from about 529 onwards, was even more profound. This was first because the very personality of Benedict became well known to the people of the middle ages, due particularly to Gregory the Great, who devoted an entire book of his Dialogues to the saint's miracles. Benedict's miracles, narrated by Gregory, enjoyed an extraordinary popularity throughout the whole of the middle ages. The humble miracles of the active life, of the daily life, of the spiritual life which make up the story of Benedict were to put the supernatural within everyone's reach. Benedict's influence was also and chiefly due to the fact that he was the true founder of western monasticism. This was thanks to the rule that he probably wrote, almost certainly inspired, and which, as early as the seventh century, was attributed to his name. Without being unaware of, still more without condemning, the eastern monastic tradition, he did not retain its ascetic extremes. His rule and the behaviour and spirituality and sensibility which it helped to form were miracles of moderation and balance. St Benedict divided up the use of the monks' time harmoniously into manual work, intellectual work, and more properly spiritual activity. Thus

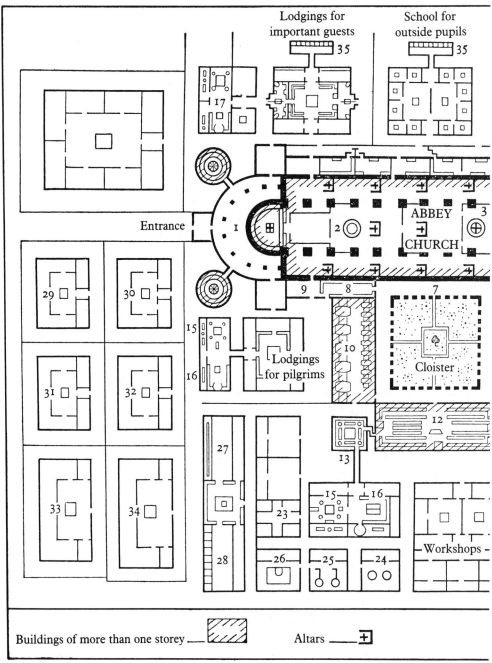

Lodgings for
important guests

School for
outside pupils

Entrance

ABBEY
CHURCH

Lodgings
for pilgrims

Cloister

Workshops

Buildings of more than one storey ___ Altars ___

14 St Gall
(after *Westermanns Atlas*)

Figures 14, 15 16 Monasteries: St Gall, Fontenay, Cluny

Medieval monasteries had to supply all the needs of the monks and their dependants.

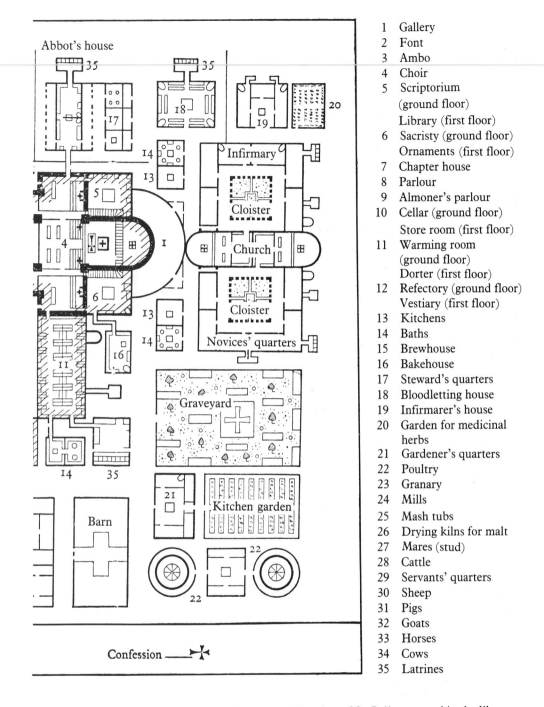

Abbot's house

Infirmary
Cloister
Church
Cloister
Novices' quarters
Graveyard
Kitchen garden
Barn

Confession ———

1	Gallery
2	Font
3	Ambo
4	Choir
5	Scriptorium (ground floor) Library (first floor)
6	Sacristy (ground floor) Ornaments (first floor)
7	Chapter house
8	Parlour
9	Almoner's parlour
10	Cellar (ground floor) Store room (first floor)
11	Warming room (ground floor) Dorter (first floor)
12	Refectory (ground floor) Vestiary (first floor)
13	Kitchens
14	Baths
15	Brewhouse
16	Bakehouse
17	Steward's quarters
18	Bloodletting house
19	Infirmarer's house
20	Garden for medicinal herbs
21	Gardener's quarters
22	Poultry
23	Granary
24	Mills
25	Mash tubs
26	Drying kilns for malt
27	Mares (stud)
28	Cattle
29	Servants' quarters
30	Sheep
31	Pigs
32	Goats
33	Horses
34	Cows
35	Latrines

In all periods they were independent microcosms. The plan of St Gall preserved in the library there is probably a project presented to abbot Gozbert in 820, so its interest from a theoretical view is great. Around a church with two apses (a plan which enjoyed great popularity after the Carolingian period in western Germany, though only a single apse was in fact built at

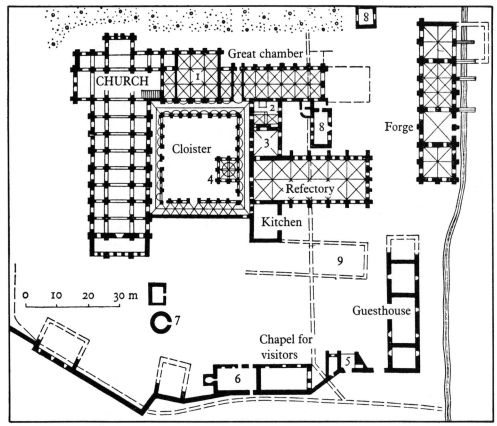

15   Fontenay (after L. Bégule)   16   Cluny (after Kenneth Conant in *Speculum*, 1964)

St Gall) stretches a big *villa* similar in type to Carolingian palaces. A school for outsiders was provided for in spite of the edict of the synod of Aachen of 817 ordering that such schools should be shut down. The well-organized plan of Fontenay (14) shows an equal balance between buildings with a religious use and buildings with an economic use (note especially the forge to the right on the edge of the river). The simplicity of the church, with its plain, square East end, is clear even from the plan. Finally we have Cluny at the end of the Romanesque period as reconstructed by the American archaeologist and historian Kenneth Conant (16). The plan shows the monastery with the immense church built by Abbot Hugh (1049–1109), begun in 1088, in which we can see the traces of the earlier church (Cluny II, consecrated in 991, and enlarged by St Odilo between 994 and 1048, which itself replaced the modest church of Cluny I which was built between 915 and 927). It measured 187 metres in length. The plan indicates the predominance of religious buildings in a monastic house which was preoccupied more with the *opus dei* than with manual work. The integration of the abbots and monks into feudal society is clear from the great stables well provided with horses. A rich abbey, Cluny was protected by a stout wall.

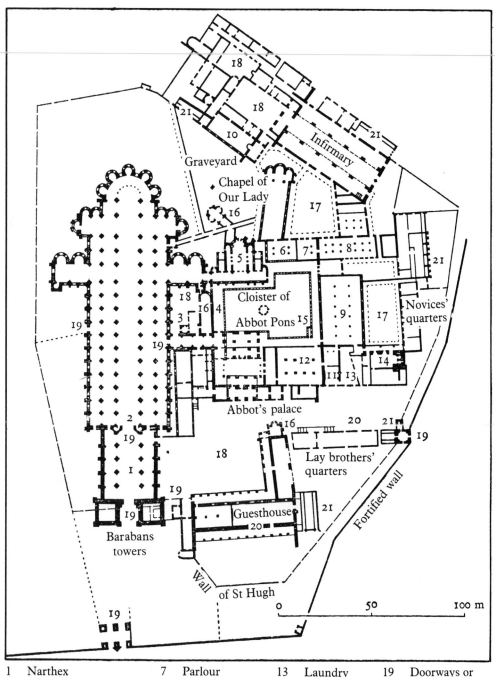

1	Narthex	7	Parlour	13	Laundry	19 Doorways or
2	Chapel of St Michael	8	Dorter	14	Bakehouse	formal entrances
3	Sacristy	9	Refectory	15	Lavatorium	20 Stables
4	Scriptorium	10	Old infirmary	16	Chapels	21 Latrines
5	East end of Cluny II	11	Kitchen	17	Cloisters	
6	Chapter house	12	Cellar	18	Courtyards	

Labels within the plan: 18, 18, 21, 10, Infirmary, 21, Graveyard, Chapel of Our Lady, 16, 17, 5, 6, 7, 8, 21, 18, 16, 4, Cloister of Abbot Pons, 15, 9, 17, Novices' quarters, 3, 19, 19, 12, 11, 13, 14, 21, Abbot's palace, 16, 20, 21, 19, Lay brothers' quarters, 2, 19, 18, Fortified wall, I, 19, Guesthouse, 21, 20, Barabans towers, Wall of St Hugh, 0 50 100 m, 19 he introduced the threefold way of economic management, intellectual and artistic activity, and spiritual asceticism to Benedictine monasticism, which experienced an immense success in the west from the sixth to the eleventh century, and then coexisted with other monastic congregations. Following him, monasteries were to be centres of economic production, places where manuscripts could be copied and illuminated, and where religious fervour could glow. He reconciled the need for abbatial authority with the mildness and brotherhood which made obedience easier. He demanded simplicity, but without exaggeration, either in asceticism or in poverty.

If it should happen that something hard or impossible be laid on any brother, let him receive the command of his superior with all docility and obedience. But if he see that the weight of the burden altogether exceeds the measure of his strength, let him explain the reasons of his incapacity to his superior calmly and in due season, without pride, obstinacy, or contentiousness . . . . Let us follow the Scripture: *Distribution was made to every man according as he had need* (Acts, 4.35). By this we do not mean that there should be respect of persons (God forbid), but consideration for infirmities. He that needeth less, let him thank God and not be discontented; he that needeth more, let him be humbled for his infirmity and not made proud by the mercy shown to him: so will all the members be at peace (McCann, 1976, pp. 75 and 41).

Moreover Benedict recommended above everything 'discretion, that mother of the virtues'. Moderation, temperance to the ancients, took on a Christian form with St Benedict. Moreover, this was being said in the sixth century. When we think of all the violence which was still to be unleashed during the savage middle ages, we are inclined to think that Benedict's teaching was barely heard, but we should ask to what extremes medieval people might not have been carried if that great gentle voice had not spoken at the outset of this period.

The spirit of Irish monasticism was quite different. Since St Patrick had been taken in his youth in the early years of the fifth century to Ireland by pirates and sold as a slave, had converted himself to Christianity while looking after the sheep, and had preached the gospel to the country, Ireland had become the island of saints. Monasteries sprouted there in large numbers. They followed the pattern of eastern cenobitism; they were monastic strongholds with a group of huts for hermits around the abbot's hut. These monasteries propagated missionaries. Between the fifth and the ninth century they spread into neighbouring England and Scotland, and then on to the continent, bringing with them their usages and their own rites, such as a special type of tonsure and an unusual Easter calendar which the papacy had some difficulty in replacing with the Roman computation. They also brought an inexhaustible passion for founding monasteries. From them they rushed out to attack idols and pagan customs and convert the countryside. Some, like St Brendan, went to look for a desert in the ocean, and Irish hermits inhabited deserted islets and skerries, which swarmed with saints 'in peril of the sea'. The legendary odyssey of Brendan was to haunt the imagination of the whole of the medieval west. In the sixth and seventh centuries, Ireland is supposed to have exported 115 saints to Germany, 44 to England, 36 to Belgium, 25 to Scotland, and thirteen to Italy. That most of them were legendary and that their memory was closely linked with folklore only shows the better, as Bernard Guillemain has pointed out, how deep was the trace left on minds and hearts by this brand of monasticism which was near to the primitive heritage.

The most famous of these saints was Columbanus, who was to found Luxeuil and Bobbio. His disciple, Gall, gave his name to another monastery (St Gallen) which was to enjoy a great influence. To these foundations, and to others, Columbanus gave his own rule, which, for a time, seemed to be a successful rival to that of St Benedict. The Irish spirit had no trace of Benedictine moderation. Encouraged in its excesses by northern rigours, it easily equalled the extravagances of eastern asceticism. Admittedly Columbanus' rule remained basically one of prayer, manual work, and study, but fasting and ascetic practices were added unsparingly. Those which most impressed the men of the period were the *crosfigill*, or prolonged prayer with the arms stretched out in a cross (St Kevin of Glendalough is supposed to have stayed for seven years leaning against a plank in this position, without shutting his eyes day or night, and so immobile that the birds built their nests in his hands), immersion in an almost frozen river or pond while reciting psalms, and going without food (Columbanian monasteries had a single meal every day which never included meat).

The same eccentricity and tortured harshness occur in the penitentials, which, according to Gabriel Le Bras, 'testify to the social and moral state of a people as yet half-pagan and for whom the missionary monks envisaged an ascetic ideal'. They made the biblical taboos, close to old Celtic prohibitions, come to life again in all their strength. In the same way, before it was adulterated, Irish art, with its stone crosses and miniatures, displayed what Françoise Henry has called 'a prehistoric taste for covering the surface, a rejection of all realism, and a rigorously abstract treatment of the human or animal form'. It was to be one of the sources of Romanesque art, and of the latter's eccentricities. Its interlacing was to inspire one of the most persistent tendencies of medieval aesthetics and taste. Finally, some Irish monks took part in the great movement of conversion in Germany and its borders in the seventh and eighth centuries. This was often based on monastic foundations. Thus St Gallen (founded by Gall *c.*610), opened the way to St Bavo's at Ghent (founded by St Amandus *c.*630), St Emmeram in Regensburg (founded by Emmeram *c.*650), Echternach (founded by Willibrord *c.*700), Reichenau (founded by Pirmin in 724), Fulda (founded by Sturmi at the instigation of St Boniface in 744), and Corvey (the new Corbie), founded in 822. On all the mission fronts, from the fifth to the eleventh century, in towns and in the countryside, away from the borders of Christian Europe, the monasteries played a crucial role.

V

In addition, there were a few brilliantly learned men between the fifth and eighth century, who were for centuries to illumine the medieval night. K. Rand has called them the 'founders of the middle ages'. The role of all of them, or almost all, was to rescue the essential part of ancient civilization, to collect it in a form in which it could be assimilated by medieval minds and to give it the necessary Christian clothing. Four of them stand head and shoulders above the others: Boethius (*c.*480–524), Cassiodorus (*c.*480–573), Isidore of Seville (*c.*560–636), and Bede (*c.*673–735). The middle ages owed all that it was to know of Aristotle before the mid-twelfth century to Boethius. This was the *Logica vetus* or old logic, and, 'in assimilable doses, the conceptual and verbal categories which were to be the earliest stock-in-trade of scholasticism'. Hence came the definition of nature: *natura est unamquamque rem informans specifica differentia*', 'nature is what informs each thing by a specific difference', and the definition of the person: '*reperta personae est definito: natura rationabilis individua substantia*', 'the individualized substance of rational nature'. Abelard was to say of Boethius, 'He built up our faith and his own impregnably'. The middle ages was also indebted to Boethius for giving an exceptional place in his culture to music, by which he attached himself to the Greek ideal of $\mu o \upsilon \sigma \iota \varkappa o \varsigma \ \alpha \nu \eta \varrho$ (musical man).

To Cassiodorus the men of the middle ages owed the literary schemas of the Latin rhetors, which he introduced into Christian literature and pedagogy in his *Institutiones divinarum et saecularium litterarum*. He imposed a task on the monks of his monastery of Vivarium which the middle ages were not to neglect: that of copying ancient manuscripts. This essential labour of conserving and handing down was to inspire the monastic scriptoria. The legacy of Isidore of Seville, 'the most famous pedagogue of the middle ages', was passed on through his *Etymologiae*. It consisted of the teaching programme of the seven liberal arts, the vocabulary of knowledge, the belief that names are the key to the nature of things, and the repeated affirmation that secular culture was necessary for a good understanding of the Scriptures. Isidore's passion for encyclopaedias was widely shared by medieval clerics. Finally Bede gave voice to the most complete expression of the multiplicity of meaning in the Scriptures, and to the theory of the four meanings on which the whole of medieval biblical exegesis was to be based, as Henri de Lubac has shown. He also gave learning a new orientation towards astronomy and cosmography by way of the needs of biblical exegesis and ecclesiastical computation. However, Bede, like most learned Anglo-Saxons of the early middle ages, turned his back yet more resolutely on classical culture. He set the middle ages off on an independent route.

VI

Pierre Riché has shown that the Carolingian renaissance was only the culmination of a series of little renaissances, which, after 680, had manifested themselves at Corbie, St Martin de Tours, St Gallen, Fulda, Bobbio, York, Pavia and Rome. He has helped us to reduce this overrated renaissance to its true dimensions. For a start, it was not innovative. Its educational programme was that of the earlier church schools: 'Psalms, *notae* (shorthand), singing, computation and grammar must be taught in every diocese and in every monastery, and people must have carefully corrected books'. The culture of the Carolingian court was that of the barbarian kings, for example Theodoric or Sisebut. It was often reduced to childish games which fascinated the barbarians. With its verbal displays, riddles, and 'posers', it was close to our quizzes and the puzzle pages in magazines. This royal academy did not go beyond being a social amusement. It was a provincial coterie around the ruler whose followers amused themselves by calling him David or Homer. The emperor, who knew how to read, which was quite a lot for a layman, but not how to write, took a childish pleasure in having an alphabet of big letters made for him which he tried to decipher at night by feeling them with his fingers under the pillow. Enthusiasm for antiquity was often limited to discovering it in the works of Cassiodorus and Isidore of Seville. As Aleksander Gieysztor has shown, the limits of the Carolingian renaissance were caused principally by the fact that it answered the needs of a small social group. It had to assure a minimum of culture to a few high functionaries. In spite of the intention of Carolingian legislation to open a school in every diocese and every monastery, Louis the Pious put up no resistance to Benedict of Aniane, who wanted to close external schools attached to monasteries to protect the monks from corruption from outside, or in other words to maintain the cultural monopoly of the clergy. Moreover, to this little group culture meant, besides being an amusement, more an object of aesthetic delectation and above all more a means of displaying status, than an instrument for instructing oneself and for administration. If culture was useful for government it was by impressing the vulgar, not by instructing them. Manuscripts increasingly became luxury objects diverted from any utilitarian use, including any intellectual use. They were looked at rather than read. The reform of handwriting which established Carolingian minuscule was directed towards calligraphy, an unintellectual, indeed uncultivated, preoccupation. Carolingian culture was a luxury, like a taste for fine cloth and spices.

It is still true that the Carolingian Renaissance marked a stage in the formation of the intellectual and artistic equipment of the medieval west. Several of its works came to enlarge the cultural equipment of men in the middle ages. The corrected and emended manuscripts of ancient authors were able later to serve a new diffusion of texts from antiquity. Some original works came to form a new layer of learning, following that of the early middle ages, which was put at the disposal of clerics in future centuries. Alcuin provided a relay-station in the perfection of the programme of the liberal arts. Rabanus Maurus, Alcuin's spiritual son, who was abbot of Fulda and then archbishop of Mainz, 'the preceptor of Germany', gave the middle ages an encyclopaedia, *De universo*, and a pedagogical treatise, *De institutione clericorum*. The latter was a plagiarized version of Augustine's *De doctrina christiana*, and replaced it for many readers. Both Rabanus' works were to figure in the basic library of clergy in the middle ages, next to Cassiodorus and Isidore. Then there was the brilliant and obscure John the Scot Eriugena, who was rediscovered in the twelfth century. Haloed with the prestige of Charlemagne, the most popular great man in the eyes of the middle ages, the Carolingian authors were to provide one of the layers of intellectual 'authorities', just as certain buildings of the period, of which the most famous was the chapel of the palace at Aachen, were to be oft-imitated models.

Although its achievements were very far from its aspirations and pretensions, the Carolingian renaissance, through its superficial slogans, communicated healthy passions to the men of the middle ages, such as a taste for quality, for textual correction, for humanistic culture, even if unpolished, and the idea that instruction is one of the essential duties and principal strengths of states and princes. And how can we fail to recognize that the Carolingian Renaissance also produced authentic masterpieces: those miniatures in which realism, a taste for the concrete, liberty of handling, and brilliant colour all reappear? Looking at them, we understand that although people have been too indulgent towards the Carolingian renaissance, it does not do to be too severe towards it. Just like the economic growth of the eighth and ninth centuries, it was admittedly an aborted launch, which ended or was broken off prematurely. But it was in fact the first manifestation of a longer and more profound Renaissance, one which asserted itself from the tenth to the fourteenth century.

6

The Framework of Time and Space
(Tenth to Thirteenth Centuries)

I

WHEN THE young Tristan had escaped from the piratical Norse traders and landed on the Cornish coast, 'with a great effort he climbed the cliff and saw that beyond wild and undulating moorland there stretched a forest without end'. However, a hunt was pouring out of the forest and the child attached himself to the troop. 'So they set off, talking, until they at last discovered a fine castle. It was surrounded by meadows, orchards, running water, fishponds and ploughed fields'. King Mark's country was not a legendary land dreamed up by the troubadour. It was the physical reality of the medieval west. The face of Christian Europe was a great cloak of forests and moorlands perforated by relatively fertile cultivated clearings. It was rather like a photographic negative of the Muslim east which was a world of oases in the midst of deserts. In the near east timber was rare, in the west it was plentiful; in the east trees meant civilization, in the west barbarism. A religion born in the east under the shelter of palms made a way for itself in the west at the cost of trees, for these were a refuge of pagan spirits and were pitilessly attacked by monks, saints, and missionaries. Any progress in medieval western Europe meant clearings, struggle and victory over brushwood and bushes, or, if it was necessary and if tools and skill permitted, over standing trees, the virgin forest, the 'gaste forêt' of Percival, or Dante's *selva oscura*. What in fact was striking about the medieval topography was that it was a collection of greater or smaller clearings. It was made up of economic, social, and cultural cells. For long the medieval west remained a collection, juxtaposed, of manors, castles, and towns arising out of the midst of stretches of land which were uncultivated and deserted. Moreover the word 'desert' at this time meant forest. It was there that the practitioners of *fuga mundi*, willing or unwilling, took refuge: hermits, lovers, knights-errant, brigands and outlaws. Thus we find St Bruno and his companions in the 'desert' of the Grande Chartreuse and Robert of Molesme and his disciples in the 'desert' of Cîteaux, and Tristan and Iseult in the forest of Morois (' "We return to the forest which protects and guards us. Come, Iseult, my love!" ... they went into the tall grass and the bracken, the trees closed their branches over them and they disappeared behind the foliage'). Similarly the adventurer Eustache le Moine, the precursor of and perhaps the model for Robin Hood, took refuge in the woods of the Boulonnais at the start of the thirteenth century. As a place of refuge, the forest had attractions. To the knight it was a world of hunting and adventure. There Percival discovered 'the fairest things that there are' and a lord advised Aucassin, when he was lovesick for Nicolette, 'Get on a horse and go and disport yourself in the forest yonder. You will see all the flowers and greenery and hear the birds singing. For aught one knows you may hear something to your advantage' (Matarasso, 1971, p. 42). For the peasants and a mass of poor working people it was a source of profit. Herds and flocks went there to feed. Above all pigs were fattened there in the autumn. They were a source of wealth to the poor peasant; after the acorns had fallen he would kill his pig, which was a promise of subsistence if not of plenty for the winter. In the forest wood could be cut which was indispensable to an economy that for a long time was short of stone, iron, and coal. Houses, tools, hearths, ovens, and forges could not exist or operate without wood or charcoal. Wild berries could be picked in the forest; they were an essential contribution to the limited diet of the peasant, and were the main chance of survival in times of dearth. Oak bark could be stripped off for tanning and potash could be made for bleaching and dyeing. Above all, resinous products could be collected for torches and candles, and honey, so sought-after in a world for long deprived of sugar, could be taken from wild swarms. At the start of the twelfth century the anonymous French chronicler – Gallus Anonymus – who had settled in Poland, listed the advantages of that country, mentioning its *silva melliflua* or forests rich in honey immediately after the healthy air and the fertile soil. Thus a whole army of shepherds, wood-cutters, charcoal-burners (Eustache le Moine, the 'forest bandit', accomplished one of his most successful pieces of brigandage disguised as a charcoal-burner), and gatherers of wild honey lived off the forest and provided for the sustenance of others. These poor people liked poaching too, but game was first and foremost a product of the chase, which was reserved for the lords. Thus, from the smallest to the greatest, the lords jealously defended their rights over the riches of the forest. The forest bailiffs were always on the look out for scrounging villeins. Kings were the greatest lords of forests in their realms and energetically endeavoured to remain so. For this reason the rebellious English barons imposed a special Forest Charter on King John in 1215 in addition to the political Great Charter. When, in 1382, Philip VI of France had an inventory drawn up of the rights and resources with which he wanted to constitute a dowry in the Gâtinais for Queen Jeanne of Burgundy, he had a valuation of the forests drawn up separately. Their profits made up a third of the whole of the income from this lordship.

Yet the forest was also full of menace and imaginary or real dangers. It formed the disquieting horizon of the medieval world. The forest encircled the medieval world, isolated it, and restricted it. It was a frontier, the no man's land par excellence between countries and lordships. Hungry wolves, brigands, and robber-knights could suddenly spring out of its notorious dark depths. In Silesia in the early thirteenth century two brothers controlled the forest of Sadlno for years, emerging from it periodically to hold the poor peasants of the neighbourhood to ransom, and prevented Duke Henry the Bearded from establishing any village there. In 1114 it was necessary for the synod of San Diego de Compostela to issue an edict organizing wolf-hunts. Every Saturday, except Holy Saturday and the eve of Pentecost, priests, knights and peasants who were not working were called on for the destruction of wandering wolves and the setting of traps. Those who refused to take part were fined.

It was easy for the medieval imagination, drawing on an immemorial folklore, to turn these devouring wolves into monsters. In how many hagiographies do we encounter the miracle of the wolf tamed by the saint, such as Francis of Assisi subjugating the savage beast of Gubbio. From every forest emerged wolfmen or werewolves in which the beast and the half-wild man were merged by the savagery of the middle ages. Sometimes the forest harboured even more bloodthirsty monsters, which had been bequeathed to the middle ages by paganism, such as the Provençal *tarasque* subdued by St Martha. Thus, because they harboured terrors that were only too real, the forests became a world of marvellous and frightening legends. There was the Forest of Arden (the Ardennes) with the monstrous boar, the refuge of the Four Sons of Aymo, where St Hubert the hunter became a hermit, and the knight St Theobald of Provins became a hermit and charcoal-burner. The forest of Broceliande was the scene of the sorceries of Merlin and Vivien. There was the forest of Oberon where Huon of Bordeaux succumbed to the enchantments of the dwarf; Odenwald where Siegfried ended his tragic hunt under the blows of Hagen; and Le Mans where Bertha of the big foot wandered piteously and where Charles VI of France went mad.

II

And yet, even if the horizon of most men in the medieval west, sometimes for the whole of their lives, was the edge of a forest, we must not imagine medieval society as a world of stay-at-homes and stick-in-the-muds who were attached to their patch of ground surrounded by wood. The mobility of men in the middle ages was extreme, even disconcerting, but it is easily explained. Property, whether as a fact or as a concept, was almost unknown in the middle ages. From the peasant to the lord, each individual and each family had only relatively extensive rights of provisional possession or usufruct. Not only did each have above him a master or someone with a more powerful right, who could deprive him by force of his land, whether it was a peasant holding or a seigneurial fief, but the law itself recognized that the lord had the legal power to take away a landholding from his serf or vassal on condition that he gave him an equivalent holding, which might sometimes be far away from the first. The Norman lords who went to England; the German knights settling in the East; the feudal lords of the Ile-de-France who conquered a fief in the Midi with the help of the Albigensian Crusade, or in Spain during the course of the Reconquista; and the crusaders of all sorts who carved out lordships for themselves in the Morea or in the Holy Land – all emigrated easily, because they barely had a homeland to leave. The peasant's fields were only a concession on the part of the lord, who could revoke it fairly easily. The fields were often redistributed by the village community according to crop and field rotation. Thus the peasant was not bound to his land except by the will of his lord, from which he was eager to escape by flight in the early period, and later on by legal emancipation. Individual or collective peasant emigration was one of the great phenomena of medieval society and population. On the road, the knights and peasants encountered clerics on journeys authorized by their superiors or on the run from their community (wandering monks or *gyrovagi* against whom the councils and synods of the church legislated in vain), students on their way to the schools or the famous universities (did not a twelfth-century poem say that exile or *terra aliena* was the obligatory lot of the scholar?), pilgrims, and vagabonds of all sorts.

In most cases, not only was there no material benefit to keep men at home, but the very spirit of the Christian religion drove them out on to the road. 'In his exile on earth man is only a perpetual pilgrim' was the teaching of the Church, which barely needed to repeat the words of Christ: 'Leave everything and follow me'. Those who had little or nothing were numerous; they could set out easily. Their skimpy baggage could be contained in the double sack carried by the pilgrim. The less badly off had a few coins in their pocket – at this time money was for a long time uncommon. The richest travellers had boxes in which they locked up the best part of their wealth, a small number of precious objects. When, later on, travellers and pilgrims encumbered themselves with baggage – Joinville and his companion the count of Saarbrücken left for the crusade in 1248 laden with chests which were carried

on carts to Auxonne and by boats down the Saône and the Rhône to Arles –
not only the crusading spirit, but also the taste for travel, was dying. Medieval
society became a society of settled people, and the middle ages, the era of long
journeys on foot or on horseback, were almost at an end. It was not that
wandering was unknown in the late middle ages, but, from the fourteenth
century onwards only vagabonds and wretches wandered. To begin with,
wanderers had been the normal people, whereas later on normal people were
the stay-at-homes.

However, before this weariness became widespread, the middle ages were
full of itinerants who constantly occur in pictures. The implement used by
the wanderers, which swiftly became symbolic, was the staff, a T-shaped stick.
Bowed over their staffs the hermit, the pilgrim, the beggar, and the sick man
made their way, a restless people still symbolized by the blind like the ones
in this *fabliau*: 'One day it happened that three blind men were wandering
along a road near Compiègne, without anyone to guide them and show them
their way. All three of them had begging-bowls; all three of them were poorly
clad. In this way they were following the road to Senlis'. They were a
disquieting people mistrusted by both the Church and moralists. Pilgrimage
itself, which often was a cover for mere vagabondage or vain curiosity (the
medieval form of tourism), was easily suspect. As early as the twelfth century,
Honorius of Autun was inclined to condemn it and advise against it. 'Is there
any merit,' asked the pupil in the *Elucidarium*, 'in going to Jerusalem or visiting
other holy places?' and in response the master said, 'It is better to give to
the poor the money required for the journey.' The only pilgrimage that he
accepted was one with penance as its cause and object. In fact, from early
on – and this is significant – pilgrimage was not what men wished to do, but
more an act of penance. It was the penalty for any serious sin; it was a
punishment, not a reward. As for those who undertook a pilgrimage 'out of
curiosity or in order to show off', to quote the master of the *Elucidarium* once
more, 'the only profit which they draw from it is that of having seen pleasant
places or fine buildings, or of winning the fine name which they desired'.
Wanderers were wretches and tourism a vanity.

The pitiable reality of pilgrimage, even if it was less extreme than the tragic
cases of the crusaders who perished of hunger on the way or who were
massacred by the Infidels, was often like the story of this poor man which
is told in the *Golden Legend*.

In about the year 1100, a Frenchman went off to St James of Compostela with his
wife and children, partly to escape the epidemic which was laying waste their land
and partly to see the saint's tomb. In the town of Pamplona his wife died and their
innkeeper stripped the man of all his money, even taking away the mare on which

he carried his children. So the poor father took two of his children on his shoulders, and led the others by the hand. A man who was passing by with a donkey took pity on him and gave him his donkey, so that he could put his children on the beast's back. When he arrived at San Diego de Compostela, the Frenchman saw the saint, who asked him if he recognized him and who told him: 'I am the apostle James. It was I who gave you a donkey so that you could come here and who will give it to you again to return with'.

But how many pilgrims were left without even the help of a miraculous donkey. . . .

Indeed, ordeals or obstacles to movement were certainly not lacking. Probably rivers were used everywhere where it was possible, but there were still a lot of land-masses to cross. Here, however, the fine network of Roman roads had almost disappeared. It had been ruined by the invasions, it had not been kept up, and anyway was not well suited to the needs of medieval society. For this race of walkers and riders, whose freight was carried on the backs of pack animals or on archaic carts, and who were unhurried (they would willingly make a detour to avoid the castle of a robber knight, or, on the other hand, to visit a shrine) the straight, paved, Roman road, designed for soldiers and civil servants, had no advantages. Medieval people travelled along paths and lanes, through a network of diverse routes which rambled about between certain fixed points: towns where fairs were held, places of pilgrimage, bridges, fords, and mountain passes. As for the obstacles to overcome, there was the forest with its dangers and terrors, although it was crisscrossed by tracks. Nicolette, 'Down a leafy woodland ride / Trod by folk in ancient times; / At a cross-roads she arrived / Where seven paths on seven sides / Stretched as far as eye could see' (Matarasso, 1971, p. 41). Then there were bandits of the knightly or the peasant class, lurking in ambush in the corner of a wood or on the summit of a crag. When he was going down the Rhône, Joinville noticed 'the ruins of a castle called Roche-de-Glun, which the king had pulled down because Roger, the lord of the castle, had been found guilty of robbing merchants and pilgrims' (Joinville, 1971, p. 196). Then there were the innumerable duties imposed on merchandise, and sometimes even on the travellers themselves, at bridges, on mountain passes, and on rivers. Finally there was the bad state of the roads, where people got bogged down so easily that driving an oxcart required professional skill. A hero of a *chanson de geste*, such as Bertrand in the *Charroi de Nîmes*, the nephew of William of Orange, made a fool of himself when he tried to disguise himself as a carter.

The medieval road was hopelessly long and slow. If we look at some of the travellers most pressed for time, the merchants, we notice that the stages of their journeys varied from 25 to 60 kilometres per day according to the nature of the ground. It took two weeks to go from Bologna to Avignon, 22 days from the Fairs of Champagne to Nîmes, eleven to twelve days to go from Florence to Naples. And yet medieval society moved constantly according to 'that sort of continuous yet irregular "Brownian movement" ', as Marc Bloch said. Almost all medieval men moved contradictorily between two sets of horizons: the limited horizons of the clearing in which they lived, and the distant horizons of the whole of Christendom, within which anyone could all of a sudden go away from England to San Diego de Compostela or Toledo, like those twelfth-century English clerics who were eager for Arab culture. Gerbert of Aurillac, as early as the end of the tenth century, went from Aurillac to Rheims, to Vich in Catalonia and to Ravenna and Rome. One could go from Flanders to Acre, as did so many crusaders, or from the banks of the Rhine to those of the Oder or the Vistula, as did so many German settlers. In the eyes of medieval Christians, the only true adventurers were those who went outside the borders of Christian Europe, the missionaries and merchants who landed in Africa or the Crimea or who went deep into Asia.

Sea routes were the most rapid. When the winds were favourable, a ship could go as far as 300 kilometres in 24 hours. However, the dangers at sea were even greater than those on land. Occasional speed could be counterbalanced by hopeless calms, or contrary winds and currents. Let us embark for Egypt with Joinville.

We ourselves had a very strange experience while we were at sea. On evening, round about vesper time, as we were sailing along by the Barbary coast, we came to a mountain shaped exactly like a bowl. We sailed all night, and reckoned we had covered well over 50 miles; but when morning came we found ourselves back alongside that very same mountain. Precisely the same thing happened another two or three times. . . .

These delays pale into insignificance if one considers pirates and storms. Joinville soon discovered that 'merchant venturers' were insanely rash:

I give you these details so that you may appreciate the temerity of the man who dares, with other people's property in his possession, or in a state of mortal sin himself, to place himself in such a precarious position. For what voyager can tell, when he goes to sleep at night, whether or not he may be lying at the bottom of the sea the next morning. (Joinville, 1971, p. 196)

Of all medieval clichés (which were, however, full of a vividly felt reality) few were so popular as that of the ship in the storm. Few episodes occur more frequently in saints' lives than that of a crossing, real or symbolic, and we see voyages portrayed in many miniatures and stained glass windows. No miracle was more widespread than that of an intervention by a saint to calm a tempest or bring a castaway back to life. Thus we have this story of St Nicholas in Jacopo da Voragine's *Golden Legend*:

One day some sailors, finding themselves in peril on the sea, prayed thus in tears: 'Nicholas, servant of God, if what we have been told of you is true, let us experience it now'. Immediately someone appeared before them, who had the form of the saint, and said to them, 'You have summoned me, and here I am', and he began to help them, with the sails and the ropes and the other rigging of the ship, and immediately the storm ceased.

But now we must grasp how the forest, the road, and the sea stirred the feelings of men in the middle ages. Their potency lay less in their real characteristics or their real dangers than in their symbolic significance. The forest was the twilight or, as in the 'song of childhood' of the wandering Minnesänger Alexander ('*der wilde Alexander*') this age with its illusions, the sea was the world and its temptations, and the road was the quest and the pilgrimage.

III

Medieval people thus came into contact with physical reality by way of mystical and pseudoscientific abstractions. To them, nature was composed of the four elements which made up the universe and man who was a microcosm or miniature universe. As the *Elucidarium* explains, corporeal man is made up of four elements, 'that is why he is called a microcosm, that is to say a world in reduced form. Indeed he is made of earth (the flesh), water (blood), air (breath) and fire (heat).' A single vision of the universe was shared by all, from the most learned down (in a degraded form) to the most ignorant. It was a fairly elaborate Christianization of old symbols and pagan myths which personified the forces of nature in a strange cosmography: the four rivers of Paradise, the four winds of the innumerable points of the compass in manuscripts on the model of the four elements, interpose their image between the natural realities and human perception. As we shall see, medieval people had a long way to go before they could penetrate the screen of symbolism and encounter the physical reality of the world in which they lived.

The extent of these movements, migrations, shakings-up, and journeyings was in fact very restricted. The geographical horizon was a spiritual one, that of Christian Europe. What is striking, even more than the imprecise knowledge shown by the learned on the subject of cosmography (generally the world was believed to be round, immobile and in the centre of the universe, and following Aristotle people pictured a system of concentric spheres, or, increasingly from the thirteenth century, a more complicated system following Ptolemy which was nearer to the reality of the movement of the planets) is the fantasy of medieval geography away from Europe and the Mediterranean basin. Even more remarkable is the theological plan which was to inspire Christian geography and cartography until the thirteenth century. As a general rule, the way in which the Earth was arranged was determined by the belief that the navel or umbilicus of the Earth was Jerusalem, and that the east, which maps usually placed at the top, where we put the north, came to an end in a mountain, recently identified as the Takt-i-Sulayman in Azerbaijan, where was situated the earthly Paradise and from which flowed the four rivers of Paradise: the Tigris, the Euphrates, the Pison (generally reckoned to be the Ganges), and the Gehon which was the Nile. The vague scraps of knowledge available to Christians about these rivers posed certain difficulties, it is true, but these were easily evaded. It was explained that the known sources of the Tigris and the Euphrates were not the original ones situated on the side of the mountain of Eden. Their waters ran hidden for a long way under the desert sands before resurfacing. As for the Nile, Joinville, in his description of the Seventh Crusade in Egypt, attested that the Muslims had been stopped by the cataracts and had been unable to trace its source, a marvellous but true story.

Before I go any further I must tell you about the river that flows through Egypt, and also about the earthly paradise. I do this so that you may understand certain things connected with my story. . . . Before this river enters Egypt, the people who usually do such work cast their nets of an evening into the water and let them lie outspread. When morning comes they find in their nets such things as are sold by weight and imported into Egypt, as for instance ginger, rhubarb, aloes and cinnamon. It is said that these things come from the earthly paradise; for in that heavenly place the wind blows down trees just as it does the dry wood in the forests of our own land . . . . The people of this country said that the Sultan of Cairo had often tried to discover the source of this river. With this object in view he had sent out people . . . . They reported that after they had gone a considerable distance up the river they had come to a great mass of rocks, so high and sheer that no one could get by. From these rocks the river fell streaming down, and up above, on the top of the mountain, there seemed to be a marvellous profusion of trees. (Joinville, 1971, pp. 211–12)

The Indian Ocean, which was believed to be enclosed, was a storehouse of dreams in which the unsatisfied desires of penniless, repressed Christian Europe worked off their inhibitions. These were dreams of wealth connected with islands: islands of precious metals, of rare woods, and of spices (Marco Polo saw there was a naked king covered with precious stones). Or they were fantastic dreams peopled with mythical men, and animals, and monsters, or dreams of abundance and extravagance invented by a poor and limited world. They were dreams of a different life where taboos were destroyed and where there was liberty in opposition to the strict morality imposed by the Church. It was a fascinating world of alimentary aberrations such as coprophagy and cannibalism, of nudism, polygamy, sexual liberty, and debauchery. The most curious thing was that when, exceptionally, a Christian took risks and managed to get as far as the Indian Ocean, he did find wonders. Marco Polo encountered there men who had tails 'as big as those of dogs', and unicorns (perhaps rhinoceroses), which disappointed him: 'It is a very ugly beast to see, and disgusting. It is not at all as we say and describe when we claim that it lets a virgin catch it by its breast'.

Of course the men of the middle ages, accepting the tradition they had received from the geographers of antiquity, viewed the world as being divided into three parts, Europe, Asia, and Africa. However each of these parts tended to be identified with a religious area, and the English pilgrim who wrote the *Itinerary of the Third Crusade* observed: 'Thus two parts of the world assail the third, and Europe, which however does not in its entirety recognize the name of Christ, has to fight against the other two'. The idea of Europe, which could not be identified with Christianity because of the Muslim presence in Spain, remained an awkward, pedantic, abstract notion for westerners.

IV

It was Christendom which was the reality. It was in terms of Christendom that the medieval Christian defined the rest of humanity and placed himself in relation to others, beginning with the Byzantine Empire. The Byzantines had been schismatic since 1054. Yet, although the grievance over separation and secession was a fundamental one, westerners did not succeed in defining it properly. At any rate they did not succeed in putting the right name to it. The Byzantines were Christians too, in spite of theological differences, in particular the question of the 'Filioque' clause, for the Byzantines rejected the double procession of the Holy Spirit, who according to them proceeded only from the Father and not from the Son, in addition to, and above all in spite of the institutional conflict. From as early as the mid-twelfth century, at the time of the Second Crusade, we can see a western fanatic, the bishop of Langres, already dreaming of the capture of Constantinople and encouraging the French king Louis VII in this direction. He declared 'that Constantinople is Christian only in name, not in fact' (Odo of Deuil, 1948, p. 69). A large part of the crusading army believed that 'they [i.e. the Greeks] were judged not to be

Christians, and the Franks considered killing them a matter of no importance'
(Odo of Deuil, 1948, p. 57). This antagonism was the result of a growing
distancing which had become a rift since the fourth century. The two sides
did not understand each other; this incomprehension was most marked among
the westerners, who, even the most learned among them, did not know Greek:
'*graecum est, non legitur*'.

Little by little this incomprehension turned into hatred, the daughter of
ignorance. Towards the Greeks, the Latins felt a mixture of covetousness and
contempt which derived from a feeling (largely repressed) of their own
inferiority. The Latins accused the Greeks of being affected, cowardly, and
deceitful and, above all, of being rich. It was the natural reaction of the poor
barbarian warrior faced with men of wealth and civilization. As early as 968
the Lombard Liutprand, bishop of Cremona, who was an ambassador of the
German emperor Otto I at Constantinople, came home with hatred in his heart
born of the small respect which he had been shown. Had not the basileus
Nicephorus demanded of him, 'Surely you are not Romans, but Lombards?',
to which he had replied,

Romulus was a fratricide as history shows, and it says that he created an asylum where
he took in insolvent debtors, fugitive serfs, murderers and men condemned to death,
and that he surrounded himself with a crowd of people of this sort whom he called
Romans; we, the Lombards, Saxons, Franks, Lotharingians, Bavarians, Swabians, and
Burgundians, despise these people so much that when we are angry we have no other
insult for our enemies than the word, 'Roman!', comprehending in this single name
'Roman' all baseness, cowardice, cupidity, debauchery, lying and yet worse - an epitome
of all the vices.

And even before the schism there was a religious grievance: 'All the heresies
had their origins with you and succeeded with you whereas we, the westerners,
have throttled and killed them'. To complete his humiliation, Liutprand was,
on his departure, stripped by Byzantine customs men of five purple cloaks
whose export was forbidden. It was a system incomprehensible to a barbarian
who lived in a society with a rudimentary economic organization. Hence his
final insult: 'These soft, effeminate men with large sleeves who wear tiaras
and turbans, who are liars, eunuchs, and lazybones, go about clad in purple,
and heroes, men full of energy, experienced in war, full of faith and charity,
submissive to God, and full of virtues, do not!'

When the western army on the Fourth Crusade was preparing itself to capture
Constantinople in 1203, the official pretext was that the emperor Alexis III
was a usurper, but the ecclesiastics removed the religious scruples felt by some
laymen by emphasizing the schismatic nature of the Byzantines. 'The bishops

and clerks talked together,' wrote the chronicler Robert de Clari, 'and judged that battle was legitimate, and that the Byzantines could be attacked, since formerly they obeyed the law of Rome and now they no longer obeyed it. Thus, said the bishops, to attack them was not a sin but on the contrary a great work of piety.'

The union of the churches, that is to say the reconciliation of Byzantium with Rome, probably remained on the agenda almost continuously. Negotiations took place under Alexis I in 1089, John II in 1141, Alexis III in 1197, and under almost every emperor from the mid-thirteenth century to 1453. Union even seemed to have been achieved at the Council of Lyons in 1274 and finally at the council of Florence in 1439.

However, the attacks directed against the Byzantine Empire by the Normans under Robert Guiscard and Bohemund in the early 1080s, the capture of Constantinople by the westerners in 1204, and the failure of the union of the churches all arose out of a fundamental hostility between those who called each other, abusively, Latins (and not Christians) and Greeks (and not Romans). The unpolished barbarians stood in incomprehension contrasting their simplicity with the sophistication of this civilization of ceremony and worldly politeness with its rigid system of etiquette. In 1097, when the Lotharingian crusaders were being received by Alexis I, one of them, irritated by this etiquette, sat down on the throne of the basileus, 'finding that it was not fitting that only one man could sit down when so many valiant warriors remained standing'. The French on the second crusade reacted similarly. Louis VII and his counsellors were impatient faced with the manners of the Byzantine envoys and the inflated language of their addresses. The bishop of Langres 'taking pity on the king and not able to endure the delays caused by the speaker and interpreter, said, "Brothers, do not repeat 'glory', 'majesty', 'wisdom', and 'piety' so often in reference to the king. He knows himself and we know him well. Just indicate your wishes more briefly and freely"' (Odo of Deuil, 1948, p. 27).

Furthermore, political traditions were opposed. The westerners, for whom the chief political virtue was the faithfulness – the good faith – of the vassal, accused Byzantine methods, which were completely permeated with *raison d'Etat*, of hypocrisy. 'In general they really have the opinion that anything which is done for the holy empire cannot be considered perjury' wrote Odo of Deuil (1948, p. 57).

The hatred felt by the Latins found its response in the detestation felt by the Greeks. Anna Comnena, daughter of the emperor Alexis, who saw the westerners on the First Crusade, depicted them as coarse, garrulous, vain, and fickle barbarians. They were warriors, and the Greeks, who preferred negotiation, felt revulsion for war. They were opposed to the idea of a holy war, and were, like Anna, horrified by all the churchmen, bishops, and priests, who engaged personally in combat. How could one be at once a man of God and 'a man of blood who breathed murder'? Worst of all, the cupidity of the westerners 'ready to sell their wives and children for a halfpenny' also shocked the Byzantines. In short, the wealth of Byzantium was what the Latins most criticized and at the same time most coveted. The awe felt by the chroniclers of the first crusades which went through Constantinople inspired them to overblown descriptions. To these barbarians who lived wretchedly in primitive fortresses or slummy villages (for western towns only ran to a few thousand inhabitants and urbanism was unknown), Constantinople, with probably about a million inhabitants and its wealth of shops and fine buildings, was a revelation of what a town was. It is touching to observe the crusaders. Odo of Deuil shows them changing their money or receiving Greek merchants actually in their tents:

In front of the palace and even in the tents we had a rate of exchange which would have been adequate if it had lasted; namely, less than two denarii for one stamina and a mark for 30 staminae (three solidi). (Odo of Deuil, 1948, p. 67)

Fulk of Chartres' eyes were popping too in 1097:

Oh what a noble and beautiful city is Constantinople! How many monasteries and palaces it contains, constructed with wonderful skill! How many remarkable things may be seen in the principal avenues and even in the lesser streets! It would be very tedious to enumerate the wealth that is there of every kind, of gold, of silver, or robes of many kinds, and of holy relics. Merchants constantly bring to the city by frequent voyages all the necessities of man. (Fulk of Chartres, 1973, p. 79)

Above all there was the attraction of relics. Here is the inventory, made by Robert de Clari, of those found by the crusaders in 1204 in the church of Our Lady of Pharos alone:

There were found two pieces of the Holy Cross as thick as the leg of a man and a yard long. And there were found also the iron from the spear with which Our Lord's side was pierced, and the two nails which he had fixed in his hands and feet. And there was also found in a phial a large part of his blood; and there was also found the tunic which he had worn and which had been stripped from him when he had been taken to the hill of Calvary; and there was also found the blessed crown with which he had been crowned, which was made of whins as sharp as the iron parts of awls. And there were found also the garment of Our Lady and the head of our lord Saint John the Baptist and so many other rich relics that I could not describe them.

It was a choice booty for the pious thieves who were going to keep their spoils and for the greedy pillagers who were going to sell it dear.

Byzantium was the source of all wealth in the middle ages, even for the westerners who had not contemplated its marvels, for the most precious imports into western Europe came from Byzantium, whether they were produced there or distributed from there. From there came precious textiles (silk, the secret of making which the Byzantines had stolen from the Chinese in the sixth century, remained for a long time a secret from the west) and gold coins, unaltered up to the end of the eleventh century, which the westerners simply called bezants (Byzantines) – the medieval equivalent of the dollar. How many temptations there were in the face of these riches! In the spiritual domain men could still be content with borrowing, sometimes with awe and gratitude. The western theologians of the twelfth century discovered or rediscovered Greek theology, and some saluted this light from the east or *orientale lumen*. Alain of Lille even added, humbly, '*Quia latinitas penuriosa est* . . . ' 'For Latin is poor . . ..'

One could still try to compete with Byzantium, and one of the most curious attitudes shown by the medieval west in its attempt to free itself from the reality and the myth of Byzantium was the imaginary humiliation expressed in the second half of the eleventh century in the astonishing *chanson de geste* entitled *Pèlerinage de Charlemagne*. Charlemagne, returning from Jerusalem with the twelve peers, passed through Constantinople where he was ceremoniously welcomed by the King Hugo. After a copious banquet, the emperor and his companions, somewhat the worse for drink, amused themselves in their bedroom in '*gaber*', or vaunting, that is to say vying with each other in making up imaginary stories in which each strained his ingenuity in boasting of extraordinary prowess, the 'gab' being the coarse side of chivalric humour. As one might suppose, the 'gabs' of the Franks ridiculed King Hugo and his Greeks. In particular, Roland undertook to sound his horn so powerfully that Hugo's moustaches would be singed. There would have been nothing in this but inconsequential pleasantry if a Byzantine spy hidden behind a pillar had not heard everything and hastened to tell King Hugo about it. Furious, the latter challenged his guests to fulfil their boasts. Divine intervention allowed the Franks actually to achieve what they had boasted, and King Hugo, vanquished, declared himself to be the man, the vassal, of Charlemagne, and ordained a great feast where the two emperors each wore a golden crown. Yet this poetic elaboration could not manage to appease so much accumulated envy and rancour. Latin jealousy of the Byzantines culminated in the assault of 13 April 1204, an atrocious massacre of men, women, and children, and a pillage in which envy and hatred were finally sated. 'So much booty had never been gained in any city since the creation of the world' (Joinville, 1971, p. 92).

The Byzantine chronicler Nicetas Choniates wrote: 'The Saracens themselves are good and compassionate compared with these people who wear Christ's cross on their shoulders.'

IV

The medieval Christians who found themselves face to face with the Byzantines could not continue to feel hostility towards them without a crisis of conscience. There appears to have been no problem face to face with the Muslims. The Muslim was the infidel, the enemy-elect with whom there could be no question of coming to terms. The antithesis between Christians and Muslims was total. Pope Urban II defined it thus when he preached to the First Crusade at Clermont in 1095:

What a dishonour it would be for us if this infidel race, so justly scorned, which has sunk from the dignity of man and is a vile slave of the devil, should defeat the chosen people of Almighty God . . . . On the one side there will be wretches deprived of true good, on the other men overwhelmed with true riches; on the one hand the enemies of the Saviour will be fighting, on the other his friends.

As the pope said, the Christians saw the Muslims as subhuman. In the *chanson de geste*, *Aliscans* the poet, speaking of the dying Vivien, exclaimed: 'He has fifteen wounds gaping all over his body / A Saracen would die of the smallest of them'.

Mahomet was one of the worst scourges of medieval Christendom. He haunted Christian imaginations in an apocalyptic vision. He was only ever mentioned with reference to Antichrist. For Peter the Venerable, abbot of Cluny in the middle of the twelfth century, he was situated in the hierarchy of the enemies of Christ between Arius and Antichrist; for Joachim of Fiore at the end of the twelfth century he 'prepared the way for Antichrist just as Moses prepared the way for Jesus'. In the margin of a manuscript copied in 1162 – a Latin translation of the Koran – Mahomet was represented in a caricature as a monster.

Even so, the history of the attitudes of medieval Christians towards the Muslims was a history with variations and nuances. As early as the ninth century, of course, Alvar of Cordoba saw Mahomet as the Beast of the Apocalypse. Paschasius Radbertus, however, while he noted the fundamental antagonism, which he rightly perceived as a geographical confrontation, between Christianity which was supposed to spread over the entire world and Islam which had snatched a vast tract of the Earth from it, carefully distinguished between the Muslims, who had received knowledge of God, and the Gentiles who were completely unaware of him. As late as the eleventh century Christian pilgrimages in Palestine, which had been conquered by the Muslims, took place peacefully, and it was only among certain theologians that Islam was portrayed in an apocalyptic form. All this changed in the course of the eleventh century, when the crusaders were softened up, and then organized, by an outpouring of propaganda which brought the followers of Mahomet into the forefront of Christian hatreds. The *chansons de geste* bear witness to the moment when the memories of an Islamic–Christian symbiosis on the borders of the two domains met the declaration that henceforth there would be merciless confrontation. In *Mainet*, the *geste* of the little Magne, that is to say of Charlemagne when a child, we see the hero serve the Saracen king of Toledo and receive from him the title of knight, an echo of historico-legendary realities in Spain personified by El Cid. But at the same time, Charlemagne and almost all the heroes of the *chansons de geste* are presented as animated by a single desire: to fight and defeat the Saracen. A great mythology held sway from now on which was summed up in the duel of the Christian knight and the Muslim. The struggle against the Infidel became the ultimate goal of the chivalric ideal. The Infidel, moreover, was from now on regarded as a hardened pagan, who had definitively rejected truth and conversion. In the bull convoking the Fourth Lateran Council in 1215, Innocent III summoned the Christians to the crusade against the Saracens whom he considered to be pagans, and Joinville constantly called the Muslim world '*la païennie*' or 'pagandom'.

Although there was a curtain lowered between Christians and Muslims who appeared to raise it only to fight each other, peaceful currents and exchanges continued and even increased across this military front. Chiefly there were commercial exchanges. The papacy might well put an embargo on Christian goods destined for the Muslim world, but such prohibitions were defeated by contraband. Christians suffered more than Muslims from the embargo. The popes ended up by admitting loopholes and breaches in the blockade and even issued licences. The Venetians were past masters in this game. In 1198, for example, they made the pope recognize that they could only live by commerce, since they were deprived of agricultural income, and they obtained from Innocent III an authorization to trade 'with the Sultan of Alexandria'. Products of strategic importance were, admittedly, excepted; the papacy put them on a blacklist which it imposed on all of Christian Europe: iron, weapons, pitch, tar, wood for building and ships.

Then there were the intellectual exchanges, not that many Christian intellectuals had the temptation to cross over to the other side. Only Abelard, apparently, downcast at the witch-hunt directed against him by persistent adversaries, dreamed of it momentarily. 'I fell into such a state of despair that I thought of quitting the realm of Christendom and going over to the heathen, there to live a quiet Christian life amongst the enemies of Christ at the cost of what tribute was asked' (Abelard, 1974, p. 94). But in the thick of the crusades, Arab science broke over Christian Europe and if it did not arouse it at any rate it nourished what has been called the twelfth-century Renaissance. What the Arabs provided Christian scholars with above all was, in fact, Greek science which had been hoarded in oriental libraries. Muslim scholars had put it back into circulation, carrying it to the farthest western limits of Islam, in Spain, where Christian clerks eagerly came to absorb it as the Reconquista progressed. Toledo, which was recaptured by the Christians in 1085, became a magnet for these enthusiasts, who at the beginning were chiefly translators. The fashion for Muslim science indeed became so great in Christian Europe that one Christian scholar, Adelard of Bath, declared that in order to have his own ideas accepted he had often attributed them to the Arabs.

Furthermore, relations of peaceful coexistence were quickly established in the Holy Land, which was the chief area of military confrontation between Christians and Muslims. It was a Muslim chronicler, the Spaniard Ibn Jobair, who observed this with, it must be noted, scandalized astonishment, on a trip to Palestine in 1184:

The Christians exact a tax from the Muslims on their territory which is applied in good faith. In their turn, Christian merchants pay dues on their goods in Muslim territory; understanding between them is complete and fairness is observed in all circumstances. The military men are occupied with their war and the people remain in peace . . . . The situation of the land in this respect is so extraordinary that it would be impossible to exhaust the subject by talking about it. May God through his favour exalt the word of Islam!

VI

In addition to the Muslims or 'special' pagans, towards whom the only official Christian response was one of Holy War, there were other pagans who were regarded quite differently. These still worshipped idols and were available as potential Christians. Until the end of the thirteenth century, when Catholic Christianity had more or less definitively been established to the West of Russia, the Ukraine, and the Balkans, the Christian world was enlarged by an almost ceaseless missionary labour. Once the Arian invaders, notably the Visigoths and the Lombards, and then, at the start of the seventh century, the pagan Anglo-Saxons, had been converted to Christianity, this missionary front, as we have seen, set itself up in eastern and northern Europe and tended to merge into Germanic expansion. Western Germany was converted fairly peacefully by Anglo-Saxon missionaries, the most famous of whom was Saint Boniface or Winfrith. Then from Charlemagne onwards the Carolingians inaugurated a tradition of military, enforced conversion typified by Charlemagne's conduct towards the Saxons. These rulers retained a defensive attitude towards pagans up to 955, the year of Otto I's double victory over the Magyars and the eastern Slavs, following which the Germans began a longlasting aggressive policy, proceeding to convert the pagans by force. In the early eleventh century Bruno of Querfurt criticized Henry II, king of the Germans and not yet crowned emperor, for waging war on Christians, the Poles, and for neglecting the pagan Liutizians. In accordance with the command of the Gospel it was right to force the latter to enter the Christian religion by arms. From now on the phrase *compelle intrare* became the watchword against the pagans. Moreover, people were keen to describe these pagans as barbarians. The chronicler Gallus Anonymus in the twelfth century, describing the geographical situation of Poland, wrote, 'Towards the northern sea she has as neighbours three very ferocious barbarian nations, Seleucia (the land of the Liutizians) Pomerania and Prussia, against which the duke of Poland fights without cease to convert them to the faith. But he has not succeeded in snatching their hearts away from perfidy by the sword of preaching nor in extirpating this viper race by the sword of massacre.'

Indeed resistance was strong and pagan revivals were numerous and violent in the face of this conquering proselytism. In 973 a great Slav insurrection wiped out ecclesiastical organization between the Elbe and the Oder among the Veleti and the Obodrites; in 1038 there was a popular uprising in Poland in favour of paganism, and in 1040 it was Hungary's turn to apostasize. Gallus Anonymus noted, 'The princes of these barbarian nations conquered in battle by the duke of Poland often take refuge in baptism, but as soon as they have built up their forces again they abjure the Christian faith and start to wage war on Christians again.' Christian preaching was almost always unsuccessful when it tried to address pagan peoples and to win over the masses. Generally it was only successful when it won over the leaders and the dominant social groups. For the Byzantines and the Muslims, integration into Roman Christianity would have been a derogation, a lowering into an inferior civilization. On the contrary, the pagans' conversion to Christianity was social advancement. The Frankish Clovis in the early sixth century, the Norman Rollo in 911, the Pole Mieszko in 966, the Hungarian Vaïk (St Stephen) in 985, the Dane Harald Blue-Tooth (950–86) and the Norwegian Olaf Tryggvason understood this clearly.

Moreover, the pagan revolts were usually simultaneously social insurrections, the masses reverting to paganism out of hostility to their Christian lords, who generally had large enough forces at their disposal to crush these rebellions quickly. Thus the 'new Christendom' of the middle ages, in contrast to early Christianity, which for centuries had been composed mainly of lesser people who ended up by imposing their faith on the emperor and on a section of the ruling classes, was a Christendom converted from the top and by constraint. We should never lose sight of this shift in the Christian religion in the middle ages. In this violent world the chief form of violence was conversion. For those prudent leaders who recognized the power which Christianity possessed to advance them, there was no hesitation, except sometimes that between Rome and Constantinople. Whereas Poles and Hungarians, directly or indirectly, were in favour of Rome, the Russians, Bulgarians, and Serbs inclined towards Byzantium. A curious struggle for influence took place in Greater Moravia in the ninth century: this was the episode of Cyril and Methodius and the unprecedented attempt to set up Roman Catholicism with a Slav liturgy. It was an ephemeral attempt, like the empire of Greater Moravia itself. Roman Catholicism triumphed in Moravia and Bohemia with the feudal state of the Przemyslids.

Western Christianity succeeded in forcing the Byzantine empire and Islam out of Sicily, southern Italy, and Spain but failed in Greece and Palestine in the thirteenth century. Stabilized on the northern side of the western basin of the Mediterranean it thus became fixed in the thirteenth century from Lithuania to Croatia.

VII

It was then that the Christians caught sight of a third type of pagan different from the Muslims and the barbarians: the Mongols. The Mongol myth is one of the strangest of medieval Christian Europe. The Christians of central Europe, in Little Poland, Silesia, and Hungary, who had been battered by them three times in destructive raids, could not hesitate to recognize these people, whom they called the Tartars, as pagans pure and simple. Indeed, they were among the cruellest which the oriental invasions had ever pushed towards the west; turning himself into an echo of their terror, Matthew Paris wrote, 'They are inhuman beings resembling beasts, whom one should call monsters rather than men, who are thirsty for blood and drink it, who seek out and devour the flesh of dogs and even human flesh.' In the rest of Christian Europe, on the other hand, the Mongols inspired strange dreams among princes, clerks, and merchants. They were believed to be not only ready to be converted to Christianity, but already converted in secret by Prester John, that mysterious Christian sovereign placed in Asia in the thirteenth century (before being placed in Ethiopia in the fifteenth), and only waiting for an opportunity to declare themselves. A myth around Prester John had been formed in medieval imaginations out of vague pieces of information gathered concerning the small groups of Nestorian Christians who had survived in Asia, and it became attached to the Mongols. Out of this illusion developed a great dream. It pictured an alliance between Christians and Mongols who by locking Islam within their grip would destroy or convert it and would in the end make the true faith reign over all the world. Hence the missions sent in the middle of the century to the Mongols: two Dominican and two Franciscan missions sent by Pope Innocent IV in 1245, an embassy sent by Louis IX of France, and in 1253 yet another Dominican mission and one led by the Flemish Franciscan William of Ruysbroek. Two valuable travellers' accounts survive to us from these adventures, that written by William of Ruysbroek and one written by another Franciscan, the Italian John of Piano Carpino. These embassies began with high hopes but ended up in great disappointment. Joinville tells us about the disillusionment felt by Louis IX: 'His Majesty, I can assure you, bitterly regretted that he had ever sent his envoys to the great King of the Tartars' (Joinville, 1971, p. 288). Disappointment was also felt by Marco Polo, who tried at the end of the century to justify the hopes placed in the conversion of the Mongols and to explain their failure: 'If men clever in preaching our faith to him had been sent by the pope, the Great Khan would have become a Christian, because it is known for certain that he had a very great desire to be one.' This explanation, based on the limitations of individuals, allowed the dream to survive, but it could not deceive. On the same page Marco Polo even put into the mouth of Kublai Khan a speech in which the ruler neatly explained how the Tartars' social and political systems were incompatible with Christianity.

The Mongol myth gave rise to a number of expeditions around 1300. A series of missions, of which the most important were those led by John of Monte Corvino and by the Franciscan Odoric of Pordenone, even resulted in the formation of small, ephemeral Asiatic Christian states. Medieval Christianity remained European, but it had ventured to the end of the world.

The Tartars [wrote Joinville] had originally come from a vast plain of sand, where no good thing would grow. At the farthest limit of this plain were certain huge and awe-inspiring rocks, right on the edge of the world, towards the East. No man, so the Tartars affirmed, had ever managed to get past them. They said that within these rocks are enclosed the giant race of Gog and Magog, who are to appear at the end of the world, when Antichrist will come to destroy all things. (Joinville, 1971, p. 283)

Thus, while Christianity failed in Asia and Africa (where the first Franciscan missionaries were killed by the Muslims), it rediscovered through its experiences the frontiers of an imaginary world whose geography remained that of the Bible.

VIII

Christianity in the thirteenth century looked as though it wanted to emerge from its frontiers; it had begun to replace the idea of the crusade with the idea of mission and it had appeared to open itself to the world. However, it remained a closed world, a society which could join new members to itself by force (*compelle intrare*), but which excluded others and defined itself by what amounted to religious racism. Whether or not one belonged to the Christian flock was the criterion of its values and its behaviour. War, which was an evil between Christians, was a duty against non-Christians. Usury, which was forbidden among Christians, was permissible to unbelievers, in other words the Jews. For the non-Christians, all those pagans confused together, whom Christianity rejected or kept outside its frontiers, existed in its bosom and were affected by exclusions which we shall examine later.

Here we merely wish to define medieval Christianity within its spatial horizons. Faced with the two tendencies in the Christian religion, one springing from the Old Testament, towards a closed religion belonging to the chosen people, and one towards an open religion with a universal vocation outlined by the Gospels, Christianity shut itself up in particularism. In that breviary of the average Christian of the twelfth century, the *Elucidarium*, a pupil poses the problem of whether Christianity is an open or closed religion working from two texts of St Paul: 'Since it is written, "Christ died for the ungodly" (Romans 5.6) and "he by the grace of God should taste death for every man" (Hebrews 2.9), was his death of benefit to the ungodly?' And in response the master says 'Christ died for the elect alone' and piles up quotations which exclude the possibility that Christ died 'for every man'.

The tendency of Christianity to shut itself off is clearly apparent in its behaviour towards the pagans. Already, before Gregory the Great, the Irish monks had refused to preach the gospel to their hated Anglo-Saxon neighbours whom they wished to consign to hell. They did not want to run the risk of meeting them in heaven. For a long time the pagan world was a great reservoir of slaves for Christian trade, whether it was conducted by Christian merchants or by Jewish merchants in Christian territory. Conversion, which dried up this fruitful market, was not carried out without hesitation. Anglo-Saxons, Saxons, and Slavs (the last-mentioned gave their name to the human cattle of medieval Christian Europe) supplied the medieval slave-trade before being integrated into the Christian world and thus protected from slavery. One of the great criticisms which Adalbert bishop of Prague made in the late tenth century of his flock, whom he accused of having returned to paganism, was selling Christians to Jewish slave-merchants. A non-Christian was not really human; only a Christian could enjoy the rights of a man, among them protection from slavery. The Christian attitude towards slavery was a manifestation of Christian particularism, the primitive solidarity of the group and the policy of apartheid with regard to outside groups. A thirteenth-century catechism, faithful to the Jewish concept of the God of the tribe (Exodus 20), indicated as the first precept: 'Your God is one God; you shall not take the name of your God in vain.' Medieval Christianity was jealous of its God and far from ecumenism.

And yet, this closed society, opaque and hostile to others, was, in spite of itself, a sponge, a field fertilized by foreign infiltrations. At the technical level it was transformed by borrowings such as the mill, windmill or watermill, which came from the east; at the economic level it was for a long time passive with regard to Byzantium and Islam, receiving from Constantinople or Alexandria, for its food or clothing, everything that was not a basic necessity (precious fabrics and spices). It woke up to the idea of a monetary economy through the stimulus of Byzantine gold, the bezant, and of Muslim coins such as the gold dinar and the silver dirhem. Its art, from the motifs of the steppes which inspired all barbarian goldsmiths' work up to the domes and pointed arches of Armenia, Byzantium, and Cordoba, and its science, drawn from Greek sources through the intermediary of the Arabs, were fed by borrowings. Although it was able to find in itself the resources which allowed it to become a creative force, then a model and a guide, it had been to begin with a pupil, a tributary of the whole of the world which it scorned and condemned, the paganism of antiquity and the paganism of other worlds which nourished and instructed it during the long period when it was poor and barbarous and thought that it could enclose itself in its arrogant certainties.

IX

Although the world of Christianity was enclosed and shut off on this earth below, it was wide open to heaven above. Materially and spiritually there were no watertight barriers between the terrestrial world and that beyond. Of course there were stages in between which represented ditches to cross or leaps to make, but both cosmography and mystical asceticism made it clear that there was an itinerary (to use St Bonaventure's term) which, step by step, along the great route which the soul took on its pilgrimage, led to God.

That the universe was a system of concentric spheres was a generally held view, though opinions divided over the number and nature of these spheres. Bede, in the eighth century, considered that the earth was surrounded by seven heavens (we still speak of being transported to the seventh heaven) – the air, the ether, Olympus, the fiery space, the firmament of the stars, the heaven of the angels and the heaven of the Trinity. Even in the terminology the Greek heritage is evident in Bede's cosmology. The Christianization of this concept ended up in a simplified form exemplified in the twelfth-century *Elucidarium* of Honorius of Autun, who distinguished three heavens: the corporeal heaven which we see; the spiritual heaven where dwell the spiritual substances, that is to say the angels; and the intellectual heaven where the blessed gaze on the Holy Trinity face to face. More scientific systems went back to the Aristotelian scheme which saw the universe as a complicated arrangement of 55 spheres, to which the scholastics added a supplementary exterior sphere, that of the first cause where God set the whole system in motion. Some men, such as William of Auvergne, bishop of Paris in the first half of the thirteenth century, pictured another sphere beyond that of the first cause, an immobile Empyrean, the resting place of the saints.

The essential thing was that, in spite of the care taken by the theologians and the Church to affirm the spiritual character of God, the language used allowed Christians to picture God to themselves in concrete form. There was a two-fold anxiety, to safeguard divine immateriality and not to shock naïve beliefs in the reality of God, described as substantial, which was equivocal enough to satisfy doctrinal orthodoxy and the thinking habits of the masses simultaneously. Honorius is a good witness to the somewhat delicate wish to conciliate.

'Where does God live?' asked the disciple.
'Everywhere in power, and in the intellectual heaven in substance', answered the master. But the disciple returned to the charge. 'How can one say that God is everywhere at the same time and always, and that he is also nowhere?'
'That is because God is incorporeal' answered the master, 'and consequently "not localized" – *illocalis*'.

The disciple contented himself with this because he knew from elsewhere that God existed in substance in the intellectual heaven.

However, as far as the masses were concerned, God existed in the corporeal form in which Christian iconography had represented him from early on. This material image of God had been inherited by medieval Christians from Judaism.

Of course, this God never showed himself to men. 'Thou canst not see my face,' he told Moses, 'for there shall no man see me and live' (Exodus 33.20). But the ancient Jews imagined God seated on a throne, looking down on men from the top of heaven; and where, in Genesis, it is said that God made man in his own image, the Jews, followed by most medieval Christians, took this resemblance to be chiefly a physical one, and portrayed God with human features.

Christianity, especially after the Council of Nicaea in 325, offered a three-person God, the Holy Trinity, to the adoration of the faithful. The Trinity excited theological difficulties: many theologians in the medieval west fell into anti-Trinitarian heresies, and the nature of the Trinity was one of the causes of hostility to Roman Catholicism felt by other forms of Christianity such as Byzantine orthodoxy. Furthermore it posed an enigma to the masses corresponding to the *mysterium theologicum*. The theme of the Trinity seems to have exercised an attraction chiefly over learned theological circles, finding only a limited echo among the masses. In the same way, devotion to the Holy Spirit seems to have been predominantly practised by the learned, at all events before the late middle ages, when confraternities and hospitals placed under the patronage of the Holy Spirit became common. It was Abelard who in 1122 founded a monastery dedicated to the Holy Spirit, the Paraclete or Consoler, which drew down sharp attacks on him. 'Many who heard the name were astonished, and several people violently attacked me, on the grounds that it was not permissible for my church to be assigned specifically to the Holy Spirit any more than to God the Father, but that it must be dedicated according to ancient wisdom either to the Son alone or to the whole Trinity' (Abelard, 1974, p. 91).

The universities celebrated masses of the Holy Spirit, the inspirer of the Liberal Arts, at the official start of their year, but here too this devotion was confined within a very orthodox, balanced Trinitarian piety, the prerogative of learned circles. The Oxford statutes of before 1350 prescribe, for example,

Since the good progress of all affairs depends on the opinion held by God at their beginnings and since no good construction exists where Christ is not the foundation, by common consent the masters ordain that every year on the first day of the resumption of lectures after Michaelmas, all the regent masters are to come together to celebrate a Mass of the Holy Spirit . . . and that on the last day of the last term they should solemnly celebrate a Mass in honour of the Trinity and should offer thanks.

In the writings of certain great mystics such as William of St Thierry, the Trinity was the centre of spiritual life. Asceticism was a route by which man succeeded in regaining the image of God which he had lost through sin. The three persons of the Trinity corresponded to three paths or three means of spiritual progress, whose method of operation was, however, the same. The Father presided over the path of memory, the Son over that of Reason, and the Spirit over that of love. Thus the mystery of the Trinity turned inwards to teach the faculties of the soul at the same time as it made spiritual dynamism supernatural. On the other hand, in certain popular circles, devotion to the Holy Spirit declined into a cult of the Spirit as a saint or the Holy Dove, both personifications of the third person of the Trinity.

Popular devotion was relatively unfamiliar with the Trinity or the Holy Spirit, which were perceived more easily by theologians and mystics. It swung between a purely monotheistic vision of God and an imaginative dualism going from Father to Son. Medieval art and sensibility had found it hard to triumph over the old Jewish taboo forbidding realistic representation, that is to say anthropomorphic representation, of God. To begin with, God was represented by symbols which continued to occur in iconography and probably in the subconscious for a long time after the human images of God had triumphed. These symbolic representations of God have very early on a tendency to designate either the Father or the Son rather than God in unity. Thus the hand descending from heaven coming out of a cloud was really that of the Father. It was originally a sign of command, since the single Hebrew word *iad* means hand and power. This hand could become eloquent in certain scenes or soften itself in a benign gesture, but it remained predominantly a materialization of the threat constantly suspended above man. Chirophany always surrounded itself in an atmosphere of sacred respect if not of fright. Medieval kings, who inherited from this their lawgiving hand, benefited from the intimidating power of this divine hand.

As for Christ, he was, in early Christianity, more particularly represented in the form of the lamb holding the cross or the banner of the resurrection. But this abstract portrayal was soon attacked because it hid Christ's humanity, an essential attribute. The thirteenth-century liturgist William Durand, bishop of Mende, bore witness to this highly significant attitude.

Because John the Baptist pointed out Christ with his finger and said, Behold the Lamb of God, some people paint Christ in the form of a lamb. Yet because Christ was a real man, Pope Adrian declared that we must paint him in human form. In fact it is not the Lamb which should be painted on the Cross, but after the man has been depicted, there is nothing to prevent one from showing the Lamb either at the foot or on the back of the Cross.

We shall return later to the subject of Christ's humanity, the foundation of a freedom-giving humanism. It was essential to the evolution of the west.

However, divine anthropomorphism for a long time worked in favour of God the Father. In the struggle against Arianism from the fifth to the seventh centuries, the desire to insist on Christ's divinity almost led people to confound the Son and the Father. The Carolingian period, which was more inclined to manifestations of power than to expressions of humility, left in the shadow everything which could appear as weakness in Christ: the attractive episodes in His life, His closeness to the poor and workmen, and the real, suffering aspects of His Passion were passed over in silence. God, Father or Son, or Father and Son at once, *junger Mensch und alter Gott*, young man and old God, to quote Walter von der Vogelweide, became a God of majesty. God enthroned as sovereign (Pantocrator) with the mandorla around his head carried to the highest point the inherited imperial ceremonial which Christianity had attributed to him when it triumphed in the Late Empire. This was a God whose power was manifested in the Creation (Genesis eclipsed all the other books of the Bible in theology, religious commentaries and art), in the Triumph (the Lamb and Christ became symbols of glory and not of humility), and Judgement (from the Christ of the Apocalypse with the sword between his teeth to the Judge of the Romanesque and Gothic tympana).

God had become a feudal lord or *Dominus*. The *Libri Carolini* repeated a phrase of St Augustine to give it its full meaning with reference to the existing social state of affairs: 'The Creator is called creator with respect to his creatures just as the master is called master with respect to his servants'. Ninth-century poets made God into the master of the celestial fortress, which bore a strange resemblance to the palace of Aachen. This God of majesty was the God of the *chansons de geste*, which were an expression of feudal society: *Damedieu, Dominus Deus*, the Lord God, and, even more explicitly: 'I conjure you, by the God of majesty . . . / I conjure you to salute me,' said Oberon to Huon of Bordeaux, and when he was satisfied, he went on: 'Never was greeting, in truth / Recompensed by the God of majesty / Better than yours will be, God knows!' The whole of the language of St Anselm's *Cur Deus Homo* of the late eleventh century was feudal. God appears there as a feudal lord who commands three types of vassal: the angels who hold fiefs in exchange for a fixed, perpetual service; the monks who serve in the hope of recovering the heritage lost by their wicked kinsmen; and the laymen plunged into a hopeless servitude. What all of them owe God is the *servitium debitum* or vassal service. What God is seeking in his behaviour towards his subjects is conformity to his seigneurial honour. Christ offers his life *ad honorem Dei*, the punishment of the sinner is willed by God *ad honorem suum*.

In fact God is a king rather than a feudal lord, *Rex*, even more than *dominus*. The royal sovereignty of God inspired pre-Romanesque and Romanesque church-building. The church was conceived as a royal palace. Arising from the Persian royal rotunda it converged on the dome or on the apse where the Pantocrator is enthroned. It moulded the iconography of God in majesty with his royal attributes, the throne, the sun and the moon, and the Alpha and Omega as insignia of universal power, the court of the elders of the Apocalypse or of the angels, and sometimes a crown.

This royal, triumphant vision of God did not spare Christ. There was Christ in judgement who bore the wound of the crucifixion uncovered on his side, but as a sign of victory over death, Christ on the Cross, yet wearing the crown. There was Christ on royal coins, such as the *écu* of Louis IX, as late as the thirteenth century, with the meaningful legend: *Christus vincit, Christus regnat, Christus imperat* – Christ conqueror, king, emperor. It was a monarchic concept of God, whose impact, by inspiring a type of devotion suited to subjects rather than to vassals, was of immense importance for the political character of western medieval society. With the help of the Church, the earthly kings and emperors, images of God here below, were to find in this a powerful assistance in triumphing over precisely that feudal concept which was trying to paralyse them. Finally, should we follow Norman Cohn and look behind this authoritarian God for a psychoanalytical image of the Father whose weight, whether that of his tyranny or of his goodness, might explain so many collective complexes of men in the middle ages, whether they were obedient sons or disobedient sons who followed Antichrist, the prototype of the rebellious son?

However, by the side of this Monarch-God, a Man-God of a humble, everyday humanity was slowly opening up a path into men's souls. This God near to man could not be the Father, who, even in his paternalistic form as the Good God, remained too distant – at the most condescending. Rather, it was the Son. The evolution of the image of Christ in medieval devotion is not simple. The early iconography of Christ was itself complex. By the side of Christ the Lamb, an anthropomorphic Christ appeared early on, Christ the Shepherd or Christ the Teacher, the head of a sect which had to be guided and taught in the midst of the persecutions. Medieval Christianity tended, as we have seen, to reduce the Lamb to an attribute of Christ as Man; it let the image of the Good Shepherd fall into disuse and kept the figure of Christ as teacher. It increased the number of Christological symbols and allegories: the mystical mills and wine-presses which signified Christ's fructifying sacrifice; a cosmological Christ, inheriting solar symbolism, appearing, as in a twelfth-century window at Chartres, at the centre of a wheel; symbols of the wine and of the bunch of grapes, animal symbols such as the lion and the eagle, which were signs of power, or the unicorn, which was a sign of purity, the pelican, a sign of sacrifice, and the phoenix, the sign of the resurrection and of immortality. Christ's emergence into medieval devotion and sensibility followed other basic paths. The first was of course the path of salvation. At the very moment when the humanity of Christ was suffering an eclipse, in the eighth and ninth centuries, a cult of the Saviour grew up which invaded religious liturgy and architecture. The so-called porch-church of the Carolingian period, which has rightly been seen as the point of departure for the development of the western façade or front (the *Westwerk*) of Romanesque and Gothic churches, is a response to the development of the cult of the Saviour. It formed the framework for the liturgy of the Resurrection and of another liturgy linked to it, that of the Apocalypse. It was the architectural respresentation of the heavenly Jerusalem joined to the earthly Jerusalem in one of those osmoses so typical of medieval attitudes and feelings in which celestial and earthly realities were merged. Yet the Christ the Saviour of the Carolingian period was still associated with a piety shut in on itself, and the dominant type of church then was a closed church, a rotunda, an octagon or a double-apsed basilica, which carried on beyond Carolingian art into Ottonian art and even into the great Rhenish imperial churches of the Romanesque period.

From the twelfth century Christ the Saviour opened his arms wider to mankind. Christ became the door by which people reached Revelation and Salvation. Suger, the builder of St Denis, said of Christ that he was the true door: '*Christus ianua vera*'. 'O thou who hast said: "I am the door, and he who enters by me shall be saved" ', said William of St Thierry to Christ, 'show us with what evidence of what dwelling thou art the door, at which moment and who they are to whom thou wilt open it. The house of which thou art the door is . . . the Heaven where thy Father dwells'. Thus the church opened wide, as both a symbol of the heavenly house and an approach to heaven. The door swallowed up the façade, as in Romanesque tympana, the porch of Glory at San Diego de Compostela, and the great Gothic doorways. This Christ who was nearer to man could come even closer to him by taking the form of a child. The theme of the Christ-child triumphantly asserted itself in the twelfth century, going hand-in-hand with the success of the Virgin Mary. We shall return to the state of events which supported this success and made it irresistible. As the Man who restored man, Christ became the new Adam by the side of the Virgin, the new Eve.

Yet above all Christ increasingly became the suffering Christ, the Christ of the Passion. The Crucifixion was increasingly portrayed, and increasingly realistic. Naturally it preserved some symbolic elements, but they often coincided with the new significance of the devotion to the Crucified, such as the link between Adam and the Crucifixion witnessed by iconography. Adam's skull was depicted at the foot of the Cross, and there was the legend of the Holy Cross being made of wood from the tree planted on Adam's grave. It would also be possible, by following the evolution of devotion to the Cross itself, to explore how it turned from being a symbol of triumph (it still had this meaning for the crusaders at the end of the eleventh century) into a symbol of humility and suffering. This symbolism, in fact, met with resistance, often in popular circles, especially in heretical groups. Under the direct influence of easterners such as Bogomils, for example, or by a chance encounter with heretical tradition, they refused to venerate a piece of wood which was a symbol of an ignominious torture reserved for slaves. It was an insupportable and inconceivable humiliation of God. By a curious turn of events, Marco Polo was to find this hostility in the Mongol Great Khan, who, influenced by Nestorian Asiatic Christianity, rejected this sacrilege in western Christianity before all else. 'He does not allow the Cross to be borne before him at any cost, because on it suffered and died so great a man as Christ'. It was literally a crime of *lèse-majesté*, which people often resented if they were attached to traditional forms of devotion, which were slower to adopt new outlooks and feelings.

Of course, devotion to the suffering Christ created new symbols and new objects of devotion. From the thirteenth century, in addition to the veneration for the relics of the Passion, appeared the cult of the instruments of the Passion. Not only did these instruments retain a concrete, realistic form, but in particular they manifested the substitution of new insignia for traditional monarchical insignia. From now on the kingship of Christ was chiefly that of the Christ crowned with thorns, announcing the theme of the *Ecce Homo* which swept spirituality and art in the fourteenth century. Finally the pre-eminent position of the suffering Christ became integrated into an evolution which brought the whole human life of Christ into the foreground. Realistic cycles, which traced the earthly existence of God made Man from the Annunciation to the Ascension, appeared in art from the thirteenth century; they owed much to the growing taste for 'histories' and to the evolution of religious drama. The fourteenth century, again, was to emphasize this tendency. The cycle of the Life of Christ painted by Giotto in the Arena Chapel in Padua in 1304–6 is iconographically of great importance.

We shall examine later the decisive evidence for a new sensibility, an expression of a new society which was provided by the appearance of the individual portrait in the thirteenth, and particularly in the fourteenth century. The first portrait in the middle ages was that of Christ. The archetype seems to have been the *Santo Volto* in Lucca. In the fifteenth century St Luke, who was celebrated for painting Christ's portrait even more than for painting that of the Virgin, became the patron saint of artists.

X

A powerful figure contested power with God in heaven and on earth; this was the devil. In the early middle ages Satan had not had an important role;

much less had he had a pronounced personality. He emerged with our middle ages and asserted himself in the ninth century. He was a creation of feudal society. With his myrmidons, the fallen angels, he was the very model of the felonious vassal or traitor. The devil and the Good God were the two figures which dominated medieval Christian life. The struggle between them served to explain all the detail of events to medieval men. According to orthodox Christian doctrine, of course, Satan was not God's equal but a creature, a fallen angel.

The great heresy of the middle ages was Manichaeanism, in a variety of forms and under a variety of names. The basic belief of Manichaeanism is the belief in two gods, a god of good, and a god of evil who is the creator and master of this earth. The great error of Manichaeanism, from the point of view of orthodox Christianity, was to put God and Satan, the good God and the devil, on the same level. The theologian St Anselm tried so carefully to avoid everything which could resemble Manichaeanism that he categorically rejected a traditional belief, that of the just power of the devil over man – of the 'rights of the devil'. However, the whole of the thinking and behaviour of medieval men was dominated by a fairly conscious, fairly concise Manichaeanism. As far as they were concerned, God was on one side and the devil was on the other. This great division ruled moral, social, and political life. Mankind was torn between these two powers, which did not know of compromise or agreements. If a deed was good, it was dependent on God, whereas a wicked deed came from the devil. At the Day of Judgement the good would go to heaven and the wicked would be thrown into hell. If people in the middle ages were aware of Purgatory they did not recognize it. They thus lacked an essential basis for gauging judgement, and they were forced by their latent Manichaeanism into intolerance. The implacable image of this intolerance is the separation of mankind into two groups on church tympana.

Thus reality for medieval men was black and white with nothing in between. Indeed, was not black the colour of the devil and white the colour of the angels who were the faithful servants of God? In the *Golden Legend*, St John the Almoner told the edifying story of a man called Peter: 'Peter fell sick and had a vision. He saw himself appearing at the Last Judgement, and coal black devils were depositing his sins on to one of the pans of the scales, while on the other side angels clothed in white stood sadly by . . . .'

Thus the men of the middle ages were constantly being shared out between God and Satan. The latter was no less real than the former and appeared even more often in incarnations and apparitions. Of course, iconography could show him in a symbolic form: he was the serpent who brought Original Sin, appearing between Adam and Eve; he was carnal or spiritual sin, together or separately, a symbol of intellectual or sexual appetite. But above all he appeared in various more or less anthropomorphic aspects. For medieval men there was a risk that he might show himself to them at any moment. He was the subject of that terrible anguish which gripped them almost every instant: to see him appear! Each man knew himself to be constantly watched by the 'ancient enemy of the human race'.

He appeared in two forms, probably as a result of his double origin. As a persecutor he showed himself in his terrifying form. As a seducer he clad himself in deceiving, alluring guises, showing himself most often to men whose force he could only overcome by ruse; here again this mirrored feudal life where in morals, just as in warfare, the valiant man could only be conquered by treachery. The most common disguise adopted by the devil was that of a young girl of great beauty, but the *Golden Legend* is full of tales of naïve or wearied pilgrims who succumbed to the devil appearing to them as a false St James. In general the devil as persecutor disdained to disguise himself, appearing to his victims in his repulsive aspect. The monk Ralph Glaber saw him 'one night before the office of Matins' in the monastery of St Léger of Champeaux, at the start of the eleventh century.

I saw a small man, horrible to look at, rise up at the foot of my bed. As far as I could judge, he was of medium height, with a skinny neck, a thin face, quite black eyes, a rugged, furrowed forehead, pinched nostrils, prominent mouth, thick lips, a receding, very narrow, chin, a goatee beard, hairy, tapering ears, bristly, shaggy hair, teeth like those of a dog, a pointed skull, a swollen chest, a humped back, shaking thighs and dirty clothes.

This last detail gives Ralph Glaber's vision a definite originality, for usually the devil as persecutor is completely naked. With women he tended to use force rather than ruse, though in any case he could easily resort to the former if the latter failed, as in the case of St Justina, according to the *Golden Legend*.

So he took the form of a handsome young man, came up to her in the bed where she was lying, and wanted to throw himself on her to embrace her. But Justina, guessing that he was the evil spirit, pushed him away with the sign of the cross. So the devil, with God's permission [notice in this formula the care to avoid all Manichaeanism] laid her low with fever . . . .

The unhappy male and female victims of Satan were often the prey of sexual assaults by demons, succubi and incubi. The cream of the victims underwent repeated assaults by Satan, who made use of all sorts of ruses, disguises, temptations, and tortures. The most famous of these heroic victims of the devil was St Anthony. His temptation remained throughout the middle ages and beyond a source of inspiration for the unbridled fantasy of artists and writers from Hieronymus Bosch to Flaubert.

Man was not only the object of dispute between God and the devil here below, but finally, on his death, he was the object of a final, decisive contest. Medieval artists were never tired of portraying the final scene of earthly existence where the soul of the deceased was torn between Satan and St Michael before being borne off by the conqueror to heaven or hell. Let us observe that here too, to avoid falling into Manichaeanism, the devil's adversary was not God himself but his lieutenant. But let us note especially that this image, with which medieval man's life closed, emphasized the passivity of his existence. It was the loftiest and most arresting expression of his alienation.

The supernatural powers enjoyed by God and Satan were not reserved to them exclusively. Some human beings were endowed with them to a certain extent. A higher level of medieval mankind was made up of individuals possessing supernatural gifts. The tragedy of the existence of the common mass of humanity lay in not being able to distinguish easily between the good and the evil, in being constantly deceived, and in taking part in the spectacle of illusions and misunderstandings which formed the medieval scene. Jacopo da Voragine quoted in the *Golden Legend* the words of Gregory the Great: 'Miracles do not make the saint but are only his sign,' and defined them further: 'One can work miracles without the Holy Spirit, because the wicked themselves have been able to boast of having worked miracles.'

What the men of the middle ages did not doubt was that not only could the devil work miracles, like God – with God's permission, of course, but this did not alter the effect produced on mankind at all – but also that this ability was linked with certain mortals, for good or evil. There was an extensive and ambiguous duality of black and white magic whose products were usually incapable of being told apart by the vulgar. It was summed up in the antithesis of Simon Magus and Solomon the Wise. On the one side, there was the maleficent race of wizards, and on the other the blessed troop of the saints. What was unfortunate was that the former generally presented themselves as saints in disguise, and belonged to the large deceitful family of pseudo-prophets. Of course, once they were unmasked, they could be put to flight by the sign of the cross, by an opportune invocation or a fitting prayer. But how were they to be unmasked? It was indeed one of the essential tasks of the true saints to recognize and drive out the doers of false or rather of evil miracles, the demons and their earthly minions, the sorcerors. St Martin was a past master in this respect. 'He shone by his skill in recognizing demons,' says the *Golden Legend*, 'he uncovered them in all their disguises.'

Mankind in the middle ages was full of the possessed, the unhappy victims of Satan lurking in their bodies, or of the spells of magicians. Only the saints could save them and force their persecutors to leave them. Exorcism was a saint's essential function. Mankind in the middle ages included a large number of people who were actually, or potentially, possessed, who were torn between a tiny number of evil sorcerors and an elite of good magicians. We may also note that although the good sorcerors were mostly drawn from the clergy, some eminent laymen could slip into the group. This is the phenomenon (to which we shall return) of the kings who worked miracles, the thaumaturgical kings. They bear witness to an archaic aspect of the struggle between priests and warriors. Some of the latter, more cunning, stronger or more lucky, had succeeded in taking to themselves part of the sorcerors' power. They personified the model of the king-priest whose relative rarity and lack of success in medieval society indicate that this society was of semi-primitive type.

XI

In fact in this society men had protectors who were more vigilant and constant than the saints or the healing kings, whom they did not have the chance of meeting at any moment. These indefatigable helpers were the angels. Between heaven and earth there was an incessant coming and going. The watchful choir of angels was drawn up against the cohort of demons who swooped on men whose sins called out to them. Jacob's ladder was erected between heaven and earth and on it the heavenly creatures climbed and descended ceaselessly in two columns, the rising column symbolizing the contemplative life and the descending column the active life. With the help of the angels men could hoist themselves on to the ladder, and their life was one long climb punctuated by falls and relapses. The *Hortus Deliciarum* of Herrad of Landsberg shows that even the best did not manage to climb over the final rung. This Christian version of the myth of Sisyphus was actually lived out in the delusive, if intoxicating, experience of the mystics. John of Fécamp acknowledged:

God cannot be seen directly. The contemplative life, which begins here below, will only attain perfection when God is to be seen face to face. The sweet, simple soul, when it is lifted up in speculation, and, breaking through the bonds of the flesh, contemplates heavenly things, cannot remain above itself for long, for the weight of the flesh draws it down again towards earth. Although it is struck by the immensity of the light above, it is quickly recalled to itself, but nonetheless it gathers great profit from the small amount of divine sweetness which it has been able to taste. Soon inflamed by a violent love, it hurries to take flight again. . . .

Each man had his angel, and the earth in the middle ages was inhabited by a double population, men and their celestial companions, or rather a triple population, for there was the world of demons on the lookout as well as the two groups of men and angels. We can read about this haunting company in Honorius of Autun's *Elucidarium*.

Do men have guardian angels?

Each soul, at the moment when it is sent into a body, is entrusted to an angel which is supposed always to urge it to good and to report all its actions to God and the angels in heaven.

Are the angels continuously on earth with those whom they guard?

If there is need, they come to help, especially if they are invited by prayers. They arrive immediately, for they can slip down from heaven to earth and return to heaven in an instant.

In what form do they appear to men?

In the form of man. Indeed man, who is corporeal, cannot see spirits. Therefore they assume an aerial form, which man can hear and see.

Are there demons watching on men?

Each vice is ordered by demons, and they have other innumerable demons under their orders, who ceaselessly urge on souls to vice and report the wicked deeds of men to their prince. . . .

Thus men in the middle ages lived under a constant double spy-system. They were never alone. No-one was independent. All were caught in a network of earthly and heavenly dependencies. Moreover the heavenly society of the angels was only the image of earthly society, or rather, as the men of the middle ages believed, the latter was only the image of the former, as asserted Gerard, bishop of Cambrai and Arras, in 1025: 'The king of kings organizes celestial and spiritual society into distinct orders just as much as the earthly and temporal society. He allots the functions of angels and men according to a marvellous order. It is God who has established sacred orders in heaven and on earth.' This angelic hierarchy, whose origins can be found in the writings of St Paul, was perfected by Pseudo-Denis the Areopagite whose treatise *On the Celestial Hierarchy* was translated into Latin in the ninth century by John Scotus Eriugena, although it only penetrated western theology and spirituality in the first half of the twelfth century under Hugh of St Victor. Its success was to be immense; it forced itself on thirteenth century university teachers, particularly Albert the Great and Thomas Aquinas. Dante was imbued with it. Its mystic theology quickly degenerated into popular imagery which assured it an enormous influence. This paralysing train of thought, which prevented men from laying hands on the edifice of earthly society without at the same time unsettling heavenly society, which imprisoned mortals in the meshes of the angelic network, put an extra weight on men's shoulders. Not only did they have the burden of their earthly masters, but they were also laden with the heavy angelic hierarchy of the Seraphim, the Cherubim, and the Thrones, Dominions, Virtues, Principalities, Powers, Archangels, and Angels. Men in the middle ages struggled between demons' talons and being entangled in those millions of wings which beat on earth as in heaven and made life into a nightmare of beating pinions. For the reality was not that the heavenly world was as real as the earthly world, it was that they only formed one world, in an inextricable mixture which caught men in the toils of a living supernatural.

XII

The middle ages not only confused heaven and earth – or, rather, treated them as a spatial continuity – but they treated time as merely a moment of eternity. There was thus temporal continuity analogous to that of space. Time belonged only to God and could only be lived out. To grasp it, measure it, or turn it to account or advantage was a sin. To misappropriate part of it was theft.

God's time was continuous and linear. It differed from time as seen by the philosophers and scholars of Graeco-Roman antiquity, who, if they did not all profess the same concept of time, were all somewhat tempted by the idea of a cyclical time which was always recommencing: the time of the eternal return. Of course, this idea of a time which was simultaneously perpetually new and exclusive of any repetition and thus of any knowledge (for one did not bathe twice in the same river) and always alike left its traces in medieval thought. Its most obvious and successful survival, out of all the circular myths, was that of the Wheel of Fortune. Someone is great today who tomorrow will be cast down; this man is at present humble whom Fortune's rotation will soon carry to the pinnacle. There were many variants. All said, in one form or another, like this legend from a fourteenth century Italian miniature: *Sum sine regno, regnabo, regno, regnavi* – ' I am without a kingdom, I shall reign, I reign, I have reigned.' The image probably came from Boethius, and enjoyed an astonishing popularity in medieval art. Written and pictorial encyclopaedias of the twelfth and thirteenth centuries assured its success: Honorius of Autun, the *Hortus Deliciarum*, Villard de Honnecourt's *Album*, and the *Somme le Roi*. The last-mentioned emphasized the success assured to the theme by the building programme of Gothic churches, 'these cathedral churches and royal abbeys where dwells Dame Fortune who turns everything upside-down faster than a windmill'. Fortune's wheel was the ideological frame of Gothic rose-windows, explicitly so at Amiens cathedral, St Etienne of Beauvais, Basel cathedral, and elsewhere, and in a stylized form, everywhere in the thirteenth century. We shall return to it as a symbol and expression of a world where insecurity reigned, and where the example of insecurity served as a lesson of resignation and opposition to progress.

The discouraging, reactionary myth of the wheel of fortune occupied a favoured place in the mental world of the medieval west. Even so it did not succeed in preventing medieval thought from refusing to go round in a circle and from giving time a direction, and not a roundabout one. The fundamental assertion was that history has a beginning and an end. This beginning and this end were simultaneously positive, normative, historical, and teleological. That is why every chronicle in the medieval west begins with the Creation, with Adam, and if out of humility it ends with the period when the author was writing it implies that the Last Judgement is the true conclusion. As has been said, every medieval chronicle is 'a dissertation on universal history'. According to the talent of the chroniclers, this framework could be turned into a profound causality or a formal mannerism of exposition. Even in the former case it could be, either consciously or unconsciously, an instrument of prejudice. Otto of Freising in the middle of the twelfth century used this aspect of time as continuity to prove what he saw as the providential character of the Holy Roman German empire. In all cases modern readers are usually struck by the contrast between the ambition to encompass everything and the paltriness of the actual horizon of medieval chroniclers and historians. We have already been struck by the example of Ralph Glaber at the start of the eleventh century, and dozens of other cases could be cited. At the start of his chronicle he rebukes Bede and Paul the Deacon for only having written 'the history of their own people and homeland', and asserts that his aim 'is to relate the events which have happened in the four parts of the world'. However, on the same page, he declares that he will establish 'the succession of time' from the dates of the reigns of the Saxon Henry II and the Capetian Robert the Pious. Soon the horizon of his Histories is revealed to be the limit of what he could see from Burgundy, where he spent most of his life, and particularly from Cluny, where he wrote most of the work. All the images which the western middle ages have passed down to us of themselves are constructed on this model; they veer from great plans to narrow frameworks (like the clearings in the forest which we mentioned earlier) which suddenly widen into lightning journeys to the infinite, within the dimensions of the universe and eternity. The all-encompassing terms of reference were the best aspect of medieval totalitarianism.

Therefore time, for the clerks of the middle ages and their audience, was history, and this history had a direction, but the direction of history sloped downwards in a decline. Various factors of periodization broke into the continuity of Christian history. One of the most effective was the scheme which modelled the division of time on that of the week. From St Augustine, Isidore of Seville, and Bede, this old Jewish theory passed into the middle ages which welcomed it at all levels of thought, as much in the doctrinal vulgarization of Honorius of Autun as in the high theology of Thomas Aquinas. The miniatures of the *Liber Floridus* of Lambert of St Omer of around 1120 manifest the success which this concept enjoyed. The macrocosm or universe fitted the pattern of the six weekdays by having six ages, like the microcosm, or man. The usual list divided time as follows: the creation of Adam, the law of Noah, the calling of Abraham, the kingdom of David, the Babylonian exile, the coming of Christ. Similarly there were six ages of man: childhood, youth, adolescence, maturity, old age, and decrepitude; according to Honorius these ended respectively at 7 years, 14, 21, 50, 70, 100 or death.

So the sixth age, at which the world had arrived, was therefore that of decrepitude. This was part of the fundamental pessimism which impregnated all medieval thinking and feeling. The world was restricted, the world was dying. *Mundus senescit*: the present age was the old age of the world. This belief, a legacy of the thinking of primitive Christianity in the midst of the tribulations of the Late Empire and the great invasions, was still alive and well into the twelfth century. Otto of Freising wrote in his chronicle: 'we behold the world . . . already failing and, so to speak, drawing the last breath of extremest old age' (Otto of Freising, 1928, p. 323). This *leitmotif* went beyond the banal repetition of a commonplace on the decadence of the present against the memory of a past which had been glorious, young, and virtuous. The middle ages were not *laudator temporis acti* because they abandoned themselves to a mental and literary tradition but by reference to an essential belief. Thus the beginning of the Life of St Alexis is just as forceful in its eleventh century version:

The age was good in the time of the ancients / Then one found faith, justice, and love / Belief too, of which very little remains; / Everything is changed, has lost its colour / Will never again be such as it was for our forebears / at the time of Noah and the time of Abraham / And of David whom God loved so dearly / The age was good; it will never have such worth again: / It is old and frail; everything is in decline, / has grown worse, no one does good any more –

as in its 'feudalized' version of the twelfth century:

The age was good in the time of the ancients, / Then one found faith, justice, and love, / Belief too, of which very little remains; / And it is so changed, has lost its worth / will never be again what it was for our forebears. / Goodness is now lacking, can no longer have strength. / The wife does not keep faith with her baron / nor the vassal to his liege lord; / In full knowledge, we lose our lord. / Life is frail, will not last many days. / In the time of Noah and in the time of Abraham, / And of David, whom God loved so dearly, / the age was good, it will never again have such worth, / it has grown worse, and goodness is dying; / The father does not keep faith with his child, / Nor the godson to his godfather at all, / And lords are deceiving their wives, / Decent people are keeping the law badly: / They transgress the holy commandments of God / and of the church, the daughter of Jerusalem, / They are growing absolutely feeble; / The faith of the age is getting very weak; / Life is frail, will not last long –

And the reworking in the thirteenth century, which gives the nouveaux riches their place, and draws them too towards a catastrophe which is even more certain and nearer:

Joy and gaiety are growing weaker: / Under heaven there is no man who has so much wealth / That he is not afraid of the morrow: / The end is nigh, to my own knowledge.

The same tone was struck in the milieu of the Goliards. The well-known poem of the Carmina Burana, *Florebat olim studium . . .* is a lamentation for the present. E. R. Curtius paraphrases it as follows:

Youth will no longer study! Learning is in decay! The whole world is topsy-turvy! The blind lead the blind* and hurl them into the abyss, birds fly before they are fledged, the ass plays the lute, oxen dance, ploughboys turn soldiers. The Fathers Gregory, Jerome, Augustine and the Father of monks, Benedict, are to be found in the alehouse, in court or in the meat market. Mary no longer delights in the contemplative life nor Martha in the active, Leah is barren, Rachel bleary-eyed. Cato haunts the stews, Lucretia has turned whore. What was once outlawed is now praised. Everything is out of joint.

Similarly in the framework of an urbanized history seen from a bourgeois milieu, Dante, the great reactionary of the middle ages, placed a lament about the decadence of towns and families in the mouth of his ancestor Cacciaguida. In growing old the world was growing tough and shrinking, like 'a cloak which quickly grows shorter' around which 'Time turns with his scissors' to use Dante's words. Men shrank too. When the pupil in the *Elucidarium* asked for details about the end of the world, the master said: 'The bodies of men will be smaller than ours, just as ours are smaller than those of the ancients.' 'Men of the bygone age were handsome and tall,' said Guiot de Provins at the start of the thirteenth century. 'Now they are children and dwarfs.' As in a play by Ionesco or Beckett, the actors in the medieval scene had the feeling of being stunted up to the imminent end of this *Endgame*.

*This is the subject of the famous painting by Breughel. Let us say here once and for all that the chief obsessions of medieval men can be found in two great artists who, chronologically, come a little later: Bosch (c.1450-1516) and Breughel (c.1525-69). Without failing to recognize everything that their painting owes to the lower levels of thought and feeling of their age, it should be especially emphasized that their work is an epitome of medieval mythology and folklore.

Even so, in this irreversible process of decline, in this single direction of history, there were, if not gaps, at any rate favoured moments. Linear time was cut in two by a central point, the Incarnation. Dionysius Exiguus in the sixth century laid the foundations of Christian chronology which went forwards and backwards from the birth of Christ, BC and AD. Chronology was pregnant with the whole history of salvation. Men's destinies were quite different according to whether they had lived on one side or the other of this central event. Before Christ there was no hope for the pagans; only the righteous who had waited in Abraham's bosom, whom Christ had gone to rescue by descending into Limbo, were to be saved. Moreover the theme of Christ's descent into Limbo only appears in the apocryphal Gospel of Nicodemus and only became widespread in the west late on, in the thirteenth century, particularly with the help of Vincent of Beauvais' *Mirror of History* and the *Golden Legend* of Jacopo da Voragine. If we set aside the crowd of the righteous from the Old Testament, the only people to be saved were certain isolated figures from antiquity, who were snatched from hell because of their popularity through some holy legend.

The most popular of these antique heroes was Alexander the Great, who inspired a whole romantic cycle, who explored the bottom of the seas in a bathyscaphe and the skies where he was borne by two gryphons. In addition to him there was Trajan who owed his salvation to an act of mercy recorded in the *Golden Legend*.

There was once in Rome a pagan emperor called Trajan, who, although a pagan, had shown great goodness. It is said that one day, when he was hastening to leave for a war, a widow came to find him, sobbing and saying to him: 'I beg you to avenge the blood of my son who has been killed unjustly!' Trajan had replied to her that if he came back from the war he would avenge the death of the young man. But the widow said, 'And if you die in the war, who will do me justice?'. Trajan replied: 'Whoever reigns after me!' The widow asked 'But you, what profit will you have, if it is another who does me justice?' Trajan said 'No profit.' The widow said 'Would it not be better for you if you do me justice yourself so as to assure to yourself the recompense for your good action?' And Trajan, moved with pity, had dismounted and had busied himself in doing justice in the case of the murder of the innocent.

It is also said that a son of Trajan, riding through the streets of the town, had killed the son of a poor woman, at which the emperor had given his own son as a slave to the victim's mother, and had given this woman a magnificent dowry. Then, one day when Gregory (Gregory the Great) was passing through Trajan's Forum he remembered the justice and goodness of that old emperor, so much so that when he arrived at the Basilica of St Peter, he wept bitterly over him and prayed for him. And lo, a voice from above answered: 'Gregory, I have accepted your request and freed Trajan from eternal punishment, but take great care for the future not to pray again for any damned soul!' According to Damascene, the voice is simply supposed to have said to Gregory: 'I grant your prayer and I pardon Trajan'. This point is absolutely beyond question, but people do not agree about the details surrounding the story. Some claim that Trajan was recalled to life, so that he could become a Christian and thus obtain his forgiveness. Others say that Trajan's soul was not completely freed from eternal torment, but that his punishment was simply suspended until the Day of Judgement. Others maintained that Trajan's punishment was simply softened at Gregory's request. Others assert that Gregory did not pray at all for Trajan, but merely wept for him. Some, finally, consider that Trajan was exempted from material punishment, which consists of being tortured in hell, but that he was not exempted from moral punishment, which consists of being deprived of the sight of God.

This is a long story which, through its variants and the unfolding of a long piece of casuistry on salvation, shows the difficulty with which, and then only in exceptional circumstances, a person could be put back into the right direction of history in the middle ages. Virgil, who, thanks to the Fourth Eclogue, benefited from a similar act of rescue, became a prophet and can be found in the Tree of Jesse in a twelfth-century German manuscript miniature. However, the characters of the ancient world were usually engulfed in the *damnatio memoriae*, in the mass-destruction of idols, and in the suppression of that historical aberration, pagan antiquity. Medieval Christianity carried this out as completely as possible, just as it destroyed pagan monuments. Here its only limitation was its ignorance and its lack of skills which obliged it to turn some of these temples, normally destined for demolition, to its own use. The vandalism shown by medieval Christianity was exercised at the expense of antique paganism just as much as it was at the expense of medieval heresies (whose books and monuments were pitilessly destroyed) and was only one aspect of the historical totalitarianism which made it wipe out all the weeds which were growing in the field of the past. Admittedly there was a Pleiades of ancient sages, whose names became symbolic – Donatus (sometimes replaced by Priscian), Cicero, Aristotle, Pythagoras, Ptolemy, Euclid, and, additionally, Boethius – who personified the seven liberal arts, sometimes on church doorways, such as at Chartres. However, when Aristotle or Virgil (if we discount the German miniature we mentioned earlier) escaped this ostracism and slipped into being portrayed in medieval churches, it was to be ridiculed in stories which circulated about them. Aristotle served as a mount to the young Indian Campaspa to whom he was paying court as a greybeard. Virgil was left hanging in a basket where a Roman lady who had given him a false rendezvous had left him exposed to jeers. One single symbolic figure, finally, remained out of this suppressed ancient history. This was the Sybil, who had foretold Christ, and who gave back to straying antiquity its historical direction.

Christian history was given its classic form by Peter Comestor (Peter the Eater) in the second half of the twelfth century in his *Historia Scolastica* which deliberately handled the Bible as a work of history.

Sacred history began with a primordial event, Creation. No book of the Bible had so much success or excited so many commentaries as Genesis, or rather the beginning of Genesis, dealt with as a history of seven days, the Hexaemeron. It was a natural history in which the sky and the earth, the animals and the plants appeared, and above all it was a human history with two protagonists who were to be the props and the symbols of mankind in the middle ages, Adam and Eve. Finally it was a history determined by the dramatic incident, the Temptation and Original Sin, from which all the rest was to flow. However, it was a history which thereafter divided itself into two great halves of a diptych, sacred history and profane history, each dominated by a central theme. In sacred history the dominant note is an echo. The Old Testament foretells the New, the parallels being pushed to the absurd. Each episode and figure prefigures corresponding ones. This history spills over into Gothic iconography, and spreads over the doors of cathedrals, over the doorway of the Ancestors of Christ, over the great figures, corresponding to each other, of the prophets and the apostles. It was the temporal incarnation of that essential structure of medieval thinking, a structure of analogy and echo. The only things and people who really existed were those which recalled something or someone who had already existed. In profane history the theme was that of the transfer of power. The world in every age had one heart; the rest of the universe lived according to its rhythm and impulse alone. The succession of the empires, based on Orosius' exegesis of the dream of Daniel, from the Babylonians to the Medes and Persians, then to the Macedonians and after them to the Greeks and the Romans, was the guiding thread of the medieval philosophy of history. It proceeded at a double level, that of power and that of civilization. The transfer of power, the *translatio imperii*, was above all a transfer of knowledge and culture, a *translatio studii*. Naturally this simplistic thesis was not content to twist history out of shape. It accentuated the isolation of Christian civilization by rejecting contemporary civilizations such as Byzantine, Muslim, and Asian civilizations. It could be bent to all passions and forms of propaganda.

Otto of Freising saw the Holy Roman German empire as its culmination. Supreme power had passed 'from the City (i.e. Rome) to the Greeks, from the Greeks to the Franks, from the Franks to the Lombards, from the Lombards to the Germans.' Chrétien of Troyes transported it to France in some well-known lines from the *Cligès*:

From such books which have been preserved we learn the deeds of men of old and of the times long since gone by. Our books have informed us that the pre-eminence in chivalry and learning once belonged to Greece. Then chivalry passed to Rome, together with that highest learning which now has come to France. God grant that it may be cherished here, and that it may be made so welcome here that the honour which has taken refuge with us may never depart from France. (Chrétien of Troyes, 1914, p. 91)

Richard of Bury in the fourteenth century shifted civilization to England:

The admirable Minerva made a tour of all the human races and carried herself from one extremity of the world to another to bestow herself on all peoples. We observe that she has already passed through the Indians, the Babylonians, the Egyptians, the Greeks, the Arabs and the Latins. She has already abandoned Athens, left Rome, forgotten Paris; she has just arrived happily in Britain, the most illustrious of the isles, the microcosm of the universe. . . .

As a bearer of national passion, the concept of the *translatio* above all inspired in medieval historians and theologians a belief in the rise of the west. This movement of history shifted the centre of gravity of the world ever westwards from the east, allowing the Norman chronicler Orderic Vitalis in the twelfth century to make his Norman compatriots the beneficiaries of this pre-eminence. Otto of Freising wrote: 'All human power or learning had its origin in the east, but is coming to an end in the west', and Hugh of St Victor wrote, 'Divine Providence has ordained that the universal government, which at the beginning of the world was in the east, has gradually, as the time approaches for its end, moved itself to the west to warn us that the end of the world is coming, for the course of events has already reached the edge of the universe'. This simplistic, simplifying concept did however have the merit of relating history and geography with each other. '*Loca simul et tempora, ubi et quando gestae sunt, considerare oportet*', 'it is necessary to consider together the places and the times where and when events have happened', to quote Hugh of St Victor again. It also emphasized the unity of civilization.

On the narrower scale of national history medieval clerks and their audience dwelt on the events which made their country progress in the general direction in which history was moving, and more particularly those which made it participate in the essential history of salvation. Thus, for France, three moments came to the fore: the baptism of Clovis, the reign of Charlemagne, and the first crusades, which were seen as a French exploit or *geste*, the *Gesta Dei per Francos*. In the thirteenth century, Saint Louis was to attempt a sequel to this providential view of French history. However, the intellectual climate had changed, and the holy king, although he was a new moment in a discontinuous history which overlooked unimportant episodes in order to put significant moments together, was also inserted into a new, continuous, historical web, that of the *Chroniques royales de Saint-Denis*.

Plate 1 Reliquary statue: St Foy of Conques

This famous statue, covered in gold plates and studded with precious stones, was probably made between 983, the date of a miracle which caused a stream of benefactions, and 1013, the year in which two clerks from Chartres, on a journey, complained about this idol's pagan appearance. The statue houses St Foy's cranium, lined with a layer of silver, in a hollow carved in the back.

(Conques, church of Sainte-Foy. Photograph reproduced by courtesy of Photographie Lauros-Giraudon.)

Plate 2 Restoration of the imperial idea in the tenth century: Otto II

This miniature, torn out of a manuscript of the Register of Gregory the Great executed *c.*984 for Egbert, archbishop of Trier, is one of the examples of the Ottonians' iconographic propaganda. The Byzantine influence (Otto II, who died in 983, was married to a Greek princess, Theophanu) is very obvious: note the regalia. However, the emperor was aiming at supremacy only in western Europe; the four women illustrated here representing the empire's satellite, if not subject, nations, are designated as Germania, Francia, Italia and Alemannia.

(Chantilly, Musée Condé. Photograph reproduced by courtesy of Photographie Lauros-Giraudon).

Plate 3 Anxiety for salvation: The Resurrection

This book of pericopes (Gospel passages to be read at Mass) was produced in the early years of the eleventh century in the abbey of Reichenau for the emperor Henry II who offered it to Bamberg cathedral, consecrated in 1012. We see here the dead rising from the tomb for the Last Judgement at the summons of the four angels blowing trumpets, escorted by the four winds. The Reichenau artist, an individualist, has dressed the dead who normally are shown naked in depictions of this scene.

(Munich, Bayerische Staatsbibliothek, Clm 4452, fo. 57. Photograph: Sächsische Landesbibliothek, Deutsche Fotothek.)

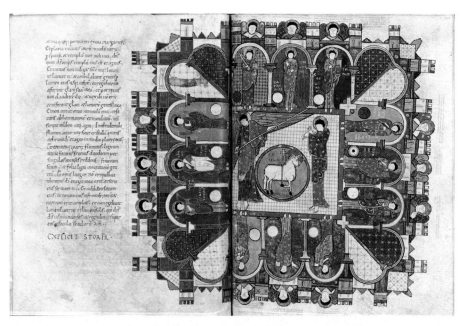

Plate 4 Heavenly Jerusalem

From the ninth century, with the fashion for the Revelation of St John (the Apocalypse) and eschatological beliefs and cults, the theme of the heavenly Jerusalem spread widely. Before it became the 'dream city' imagined by Romanesque and Gothic artists, it was viewed as a replica of the earthly Jerusalem and especially of the church of the Holy Sepulchre. The Apocalypse had become very popular in Spain as early as the seventh century; Beatus of Liébana's commentary on it written in 784 enjoyed a huge success. This copy was made in the mid-eleventh century in the monastery of St Sever in the Landes (Gascony). Four sets of three arches surround a square studded with stars. In the middle of the square is the Lamb bearing the Cross in a circle, with on one side St John the Baptist and on the other the angel holding the golden reed 'to measure the city, and the gates thereof, and the walls thereof'. The idea of Jerusalem was of central importance in forming men's conceptions of towns, and in creating the emotional complex which paved the way for the crusades and eschatological spirituality.

(Paris, Bibliothèque Nationale, Ms Lat. 8878, fos. 207v–8.)

anno incarnationis
dominice millesimo
xcv. indictione .iii.
viii. kl' nouembris.
dominus et uenerabil' VRBANVS
papa sedis. sacrauit altare pri
mum et mauis nom nri monas
terii in honorem dei. in memoria
beator apłor. Petri et Pauli. Sae
uit etiam ipse et altare sectm.
misse matutinalis. Lugdunen
sis aut archieps hugo. Pisanus
archieps dabtus. Eps signauit
bruno. eodem die ipso monas
terio iubente papa tria in trib'
pmus cancellis sacrarunt alta
ria. Tunc papa nr sacndo mis
sasq; agendo. p alia salutis hor
tamta. cora epis et cardinalibus
multorq; psonis. huiecemodi
... habuit ad plm.

Scm patres et maiores nri romani
pontifices. qui scē sedis aplice pre
federunt exquo locus cluniacus
institutus est. abinitio. et monas
terium istud fundatum tam
locum hunc quam rectores P
habitatores eius spensius. di
lexerunt. fouerunt. et cuaue
runt attentius. Et merito. Nam
pius ille Guillmus istius olim
monasterii institutor. nulli alii
aduocato. nulli patrono. nulli
regi uel principi curam ipsius
tutelamq; commendauit. nisi
deo et beato Petro eiusq; uica
riis. romanis scilicet pontificib'
quorum numero uel ordini diuina
me dignatio licet indignum af
sociauit. me olim monachum
prioremq; monasterii huius sub
domno ac uenerabili hugone

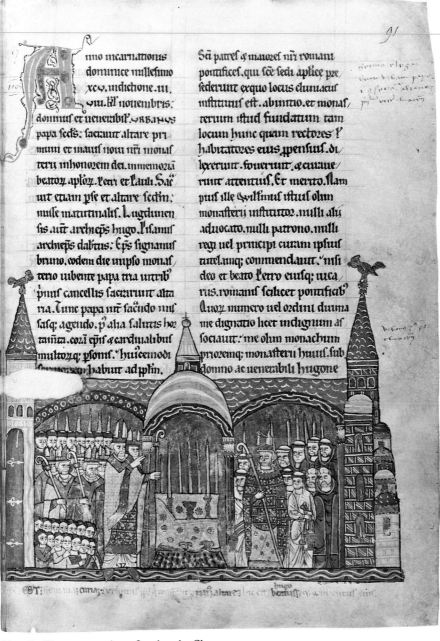

Plate 5 The consecration of a church: Cluny

This historical and liturgical compilation was composed around 1180–90 for the Cluniac prior of St Martin-des-Champs in Paris. In this illustration Pope Urban II, on his way to Clermont, where he preached the first Crusade on 27 November 1095, consecrates the new church (Cluny III) built by Abbot Hugh.

(Paris, Bibliothèque Nationale, Ms Lat. 17716, fo. 91.)

Plate 6 The devil devouring men

The devil is often portrayed in medieval iconography, in proportion to the constant fear which he inspired, but nowhere is he more dramatically present than in the twelfth-century Romanesque church of St Pierre de Chauvigny. The monstrous devil, squeezing his human prey in his claws and preparing to swallow it, is close to the devouring wolf-gods of peasant folklore.

(Chauvigny, Vienne, church of St Pierre. Reproduced by kind permission of Caisse Nationale des Monuments Historiques et des Sites; J. Feuillie/© C.N.M.H.S./S.P.A.D.E.M.)

Plate 7 Romanesque painting: the martyrdom of St Margaret

This detail from a twelfth-century altar frontal, in painted wood, from the Catalan church of Vilaseca, is characteristic of Romanesque sensibility and aesthetics. A taste for violence, particularly strong in Spain, is combined with an unusual sense of composition intended to emphasize the essential, which is the psychological and spiritual significance of the scene. Art tells a story and teaches a lesson. The contorted figure of the executioner, his eye inflamed with rage, is contrasted with the serenity of the saint, her eyes closed. God and Paradise are present in the dove representing the Holy Spirit, in the halo of sanctity and of reward, and the gesture of prayer and faith.

(Vich, Episcopal Museum. Photograph reproduced by kind permission of Yan Zodiaque.)

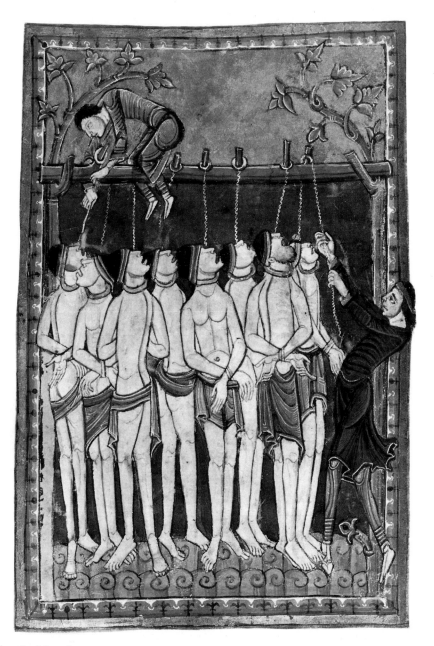

Plate 8 A hanging

This miniature illustrates a manuscript of the Life, Miracles and Passion of Saint Edmund made at the abbey of Bury St Edmunds in Suffolk between 1125 and 1150. Edmund, king of East Anglia from 855 to 870, was captured by the Danes, tied to a tree and riddled with arrows, then beheaded. When they became masters of England, the Danes venerated their victim; Cnut founded the abbey of Bury St Edmunds in 1020 on the site of the martyrdom.

(New York, Pierpont Morgan Library, Ms 736, fo. 19v.)

discrimina pmonochordū

BOE TIVS

Consul & geniꝰ servator phylosophiæ. Vt videat vocum
Iudicio aure sonum. pcurrens indice nervum.

Plate 9 A 'founder' of the middle ages: Boethius the musician

The philosopher Boethius (executed in 524), one of the principal 'mentors' of the middle ages, was often portrayed in medieval art. This miniature, from a mid twelfth-century Canterbury manuscript, represents Boethius as a musician. In the middle ages, music devoted to the service of God was still more than an art; it was a supreme instrument of culture and of spiritual formation, as it had been in ancient Greece or the world of Augustine. Boethius was a theoretician: 'less a musician than a mathematician and an acoustician' (Jacques Chailley). He is shown here testing the sounds on the Greeks' experimental instrument, the monochord (that is, an instrument with a single string). The ABCDEFG notation, preserved in the sol-fa of the modern English-speaking world, was probably later than Boethius. For centuries in the middle ages Boethius' musical theories were repeated, while living music was evolving in ignorance of them.

(Cambridge University Library, Ms Ll.3.12, fo. 61v.)

Plate 10 The pedestal of the St Bertin cross

The artists from the Meuse region were the most famous in the eleventh to thirteenth centuries for skills in metal-working. Suger, who had a passion for goldsmith's work, had made for St Denis a great golden cross in about 1140, by a group of goldsmiths from the Meuse region. The cross has disappeared but there remains a miniature copy of its base, a foot high, made some twenty years later in the style of one of the goldsmiths at St Denis, the famous Godefroy de Claire. It is a square pillar clad in enamelled plaques surmounted with a gilded bronze capital and standing on a base in the form of a flattened dome, decorated at its base with four seated figures, likewise in gilded bronze, representing the Evangelists. The enamel plaques on the column show scenes of the Old Testament prefiguring the Saviour's sacrifice: Moses before the brass serpent, Isaac bearing the wood for the sacrifice, Aaron marking the saving Tau symbol on the foreheads of the just, Caleb and Joshua carrying the bunch of grapes from Canaan slung from a rod. The capital is ornamented with figurines representing the earth and the sea, Moses holding the brass serpent and the centurion proclaiming the divinity of Christ. It is one of the earliest masterpieces of typological symbolism (see plate 22).

(Musée Hôtel Saudelin St Omer. Photograph reproduced by courtesy of Photographie Lauros-Giraudon.)

Plate 11 Human monsters: the peoples from the ends of the earth

Human monsters allowed medieval surrealism wide scope. This miniature illustrates the peoples of the ends of the earth (a subject conjured up by the inferior Roman vulgarizer Solinus in the third century and taken up again by Honorius Augustodunensis in the twelfth century). The manuscript was produced at Arnstein in the Rhineland in the second half of the twelfth century. (London, British Library, Harleian Ms. 2799, fo. 243.)

Plate 12 An emperor: Frederick Barbarossa

This miniature, drawn in 1188-9, from a manuscript of Robert of St Rémy's History of the First Crusade, shows Provost Henry of Schäftlarn offering the work to Frederick Barbarossa. It is an example of ecclesiastical iconographic propaganda; the emperor is indirectly being put in the service of the papacy through the expedient of the crusade. Frederick's orb (the imperial symbol), his chest, and his shield are all emblazoned with the cross. The inscription urges the emperor to make war on the Saracens.

(Vatican Library, cod. vat. lat. 2001, fo. I. Photograph reproduced by courtesy of Photographie Lauros-Giraudon.)

Plate 13 Rural economy: harvest

Here the harvest scenes, in spite of their apparently purely realistic character, have an allegorical meaning. The miniature, drawn in the late twelfth century in the middle Rhine territory, illustrates a manuscript of the Speculum virginum of Conrad of Hirsau (born in 1070). It shows the hierarchy of marriage, widowhood, and virginity. At the bottom the married woman, helped by their husbands, reap only 30 times what they have sown. In the middle the widows, whose merit is greater, reap 60 times what they have sown. Above, the virgins, whose state is highest, reap a hundredfold. The exaggeration of the yields displays one of the medieval peasant's obsessions. The tools are rudimentary. The stalks are cut half way up to leave stubble. ('Speculum virginum' by Konrad Hirsau, Rheinisches Landesmuseum, Bonn, no. 15328.)

Plate 14 A medieval castle: Château-Gaillard (Les Andelys, Eure)

This fortress is well known to us from written sources. Contemporaries were impressed by its site, its strength and the circumstances of its construction and destruction, which followed on each other swiftly. Built from 1196 onwards by Richard I of England as a threatening advance post against the king of France (one source referred to it as 'Boutavant'), the castle was captured and destroyed as early as 1202 by Philip Augustus who, according to the chronicler William le Breton, had called it 'Gaillard', a word meaning 'petulant'. This was the first step to the capture of Normandy. The sitings of castles give us valuable indications about medieval roads: castles controlled important points of passage, whether strategic or commercial – often both simultaneously.

(Reproduced by kind permission of Caisse Nationale des Monuments Historiques et des Sites: Lefevre-Pontalis/© Arch. Phot. Paris/S.P.A.D.E.M.)

Plate 15 Germanic legends in Christendom: the legend of Sigurd

The Scandinavian pagan legend of Sigurd Fáfnisbana depicted on the doorjambs of the wooden church at Hylestad in Norway (*c.*1200). The scene depicted at Hylestad is the one in which Sigurd, dressed as a knight, kills the smith (a figure who was both admired and accursed).

(Church of Hylestad, Setesdal, Norway. Reproduced by kind permission of © Universitetets Oldsaksamling, Oslo. Foto: Ove Holst.)

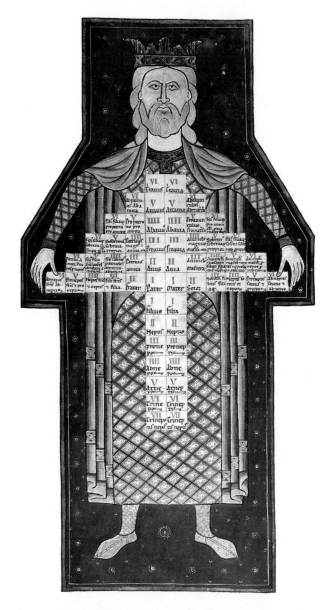

Plate 16 The family: Time holding the degrees of consanguinity

This miniature, from a thirteenth-century manuscript of Gratian's *Decretum* which belonged to the Grande Chartreuse, is typical of a whole series of illustrated juridical works. We can see scholastic anxiety for the order introduced by canon law into ecclesiastical justice, but the artist has fallen back on images from mythical iconography: Time is personified as a crowned king. The Church attached extreme importance to consanguinity out of faithfulness to the spirit of the Old Testament and its taboos. These allowed it to control society as a whole and the seigneurial classes in particular.

(Grenoble, Bibliothèque municipale, MS 34, fo. 185. Photograph reproduced by courtesy of Photographie Lauros-Giraudon.)

Yet even this Christianized, westernized history did not bring about optimistic joy in Christian medieval western Europe. The words of Hugh of St Victor which we quoted earlier say it neatly: this phase was a culmination, the sign of the imminent approach of the end of history. Indeed, the main thrust of the historical endeavours of medieval Christian thinkers consisted in trying to bring history to a stop or to complete it. Feudal society, with its two dominant classes, *chevalerie et clergie*, to quote Chrétien of Troyes, considered itself to be the culmination of history, just as Guizot in the nineteenth century was to see the crowning of historical evolution in the triumph of the bourgeoisie. The scholastics tried to affirm this stopping of history and they gave a rational basis for it by maintaining that historicity was fallacious and dangerous and that the only thing which counted was eternity outside time. The twelfth century was filled with the debate between the supporters of a progressively revealed truth (*Veritas, filia temporis*, Bernard of Chartres is supposed to have said) and the men who stuck to an immutable truth. Hugh of St Victor bitterly opposed Abelard for demanding explicit knowledge of the incarnation of Christ even from the righteous of the Old Testament. Hugh insisted on the *historia dispensationis temporalis divinae providentiae*. For him, the providential plan unfolded in time. However, Thomas Aquinas was to say a century later that the history of doctrines was useless; the only thing that was important was that part of the truth which they had been able to contain. This argument was doubtless partly polemic, and allowed the Angelic Doctor to borrow from Aristotle while avoiding any discussion of how he belonged in his pagan environment, but it also showed a deep-lying tendency to look for truth in immutability and to attempt to escape a historical, moving time.

In the face of these two tendencies, a historicism of decadence which led to historical pessimism, and a timeless optimism which was only interested in eternal verities, timid efforts were begun to stabilize the value of the present and the future.

The most important of these tendencies was the one which, while it accepted the system of the ages of the world and the diagnosis of old age applied to the present, emphasized the advantages of this old age. Thus Bernard of Chartres said, 'We are dwarfs mounted on giants' shoulders but we see further than they did.' Here the image of a historical shrinkage is cleverly turned to the profit of the present. Thus St Bonaventure also accepted the image of the ages and of the old age of the world to underline the growth of human knowledge which resulted from it. Pascal was later to make use of this too. Was this therefore the entire sentiment of progress of which the middle ages were capable? One feels, in examining the use of the terms *modernus, moderni, modernitas*, that something was getting ready to change in the twelfth century in the conception of time and in historical awareness. Of course these words had chiefly a neutral meaning. They designated contemporaries, over a period of time reckoned by Walter Map to be a hundred years, by contrast with the *antiqui* who had preceded them. Furthermore, the word and the concept were most often suspect, as Walter Map, again, notes: 'Every age has disliked its own modernity and each age has preferred those which have preceded it.' We shall encounter this aversion felt by the middle ages for modernity again.

And yet *modernitas* and the *moderni* of the twelfth century asserted themselves increasingly with a pride which one senses is heavy with defiance of the past and with promises for the future. The time was approaching when the term would become a platform, an affirmation, a banner. The Fourth Lateran Council of 1215 sanctioned an *aggiornamento* in Christian behaviour and feeling which was to open the doors to a self-conscious modernity if not to a self-conscious modernism. The mendicant orders were the champions of this reversal of values. As the *Annales de Normandie* said in 1215, 'These two orders, the Friars Minor and the Preaching Friars, were welcomed by the Church and the people with great joy because of the newness of their rule'. But this setting history in motion once more, this relaunch, had only been possible because new attitudes about time had taken root. These new attitudes arose out of the evolution of a time which was no longer the abstract one of clerics, but the actual one in whose network the men of medieval Christendom were entangled.

XIII

Marc Bloch coined a memorable phrase to sum up the attitude supposedly held by medieval men towards time: 'a vast indifference to time'. Chroniclers, who were sparing with dates (they were endowed with an insensitivity to precise numbers, to which we shall return), supposedly expressed this indifference in vague terms: 'at that time then', 'meanwhile', and 'a little after'. Above all, at the level of the collective mentality, past, present, and future were mixed together in a fundamental confusion. This confusion was particularly obvious in the persistence of collective responsibilities, which were a clear expression of primitivism. All living men bore equal responsibility with Adam and Eve for the Fall, all contemporary Jews bore equal responsibility for the Passion of Christ, and all the Muslims bore equal responsibility for Mahomet's heresy. As has been observed, the crusaders at the end of the eleventh century did not think that they were going to punish the descendants of Christ's executioners, but the executioners themselves. Thus the anachronistic costumes in art and on the stage (which continued for a long time, as we all know) are evidence not only that men confused different periods but above all that men in the middle ages felt or believed that everything which was fundamental for mankind was contemporary. Each year in the liturgy an extraordinary condensed form of sacred history was brought back to life. It was a magical mentality which turned the past into the present, because the web of history was eternity.

And yet the Incarnation made dating necessary. Since the life of Christ cut history into two and the Christian religion was founded on this event, this resulted in a basic inclination and feeling for chronology. Yet this chronology was not set up to follow a period of time which could be divided into equal, exactly measurable moments, what we would regard as an objective or scientific time. It was a chronology of significant moments. The middle ages were as keen to use dates as we are, but they did not do so according to the same norms or the same needs. The events which medieval men thought it important to date differed from what we think it important to date. Once we have allowed this, admittedly basic, difference, it seems to me that, far from being indifferent to time, men in the middle ages were singularly sensitive to it. It is merely that, when they were not precise, it was because they did not feel the need to be so, since the terms of reference of the event mentioned did not involve figures. However, it was rare for there to be no reference to time at all, even in the *chansons de geste*. In *Mainet* the young Charlemagne, the hero of the poem, attacks his enemy Braimant on the Feast of St John. 'Barons, it was on the Feast of St John / That Mainet descended near the tent of Braimant.' Might it be an allusion to the young man's sword whose pommel enclosed a relic, a tooth of St John? Or was it a more or less conscious evocation of the rites of St John's Eve and the part that young people played in them? In any case, the poet is anxious to give a date. Adenet le Roi tells at the start of *Berthe au grand pied* (Bertha the Big Foot) how he had read the adventures of his heroine in the *Livre aux histoires* at the abbey of St Denis: 'I was in the city of Paris on a Friday. / As it was Friday the thought struck me / That to pray to God I should go to St Denis. . . . / At St Denis I stayed from then until the Tuesday.' In fact these ways of recording dates, which here take the form of the days of the week, depend on the different systems of chronological reference which coexisted in the minds of men in the middle ages. The truth was that there was no unified time or chronology. The medieval mind accepted a multiplicity of methods of reckoning time as normal.

However, let us first of all deal with the need for chronology, which was never stronger than in sacred history. Everything which was connected with Christ was marked by a need to measure the time. Thus, in the *Elucidarium* the chronology of Jesus' life on earth is exposed in detail: the period of gestation: *Cur novem menses fuit clausus in utero?* 'Why did he remain nine months shut up in the womb?'; the moment of his birth: *Qua hora natus est?* 'At which hour was he born?'; the duration of his hidden existence: *Quare in triginta annis nec docuit nec signumfecit?* 'Why did he remain for 30 years without teaching or working miracles?'; the length of his physical death: *Quot horas fuit mortuus? – Quadraginta* 'How many hours did he remain dead? 40'. Similarly the period of creation demanded a subtle chronology, a hebdomadary one for the seven days of Creation and also precise computation of the time of the Fall. 'How long did (Adam and Eve) stay in Paradise?' 'Seven hours.' 'Why not longer?' 'Because as soon as Woman had been created she was immediately disobedient: at Terce, Man, who had just been created, named the animals; at Sext, Woman, barely formed, immediately tasted the forbidden fruit and reached out death to the Man who for love of her ate some of it; and soon after, at Nones, the Lord drove them out of Paradise.'

Likewise there was a mania for the date from which creation could be dated and from which the more or less symbolic epochs of the Bible could be calculated. At the same time as they pushed allegorical exegesis to its limits, medieval men went to extremes in taking the data in Scripture literally. In particular everything which figured in the 'historical books' was understood as a real, dated fact. Universal chronicles began with these dates, which betray a true obsession with chronology. However, people were not unanimous about it. Jacopo da Voragine ingenuously admitted this when he wrote: 'People are not in agreement over the date of birth of Our Lord Jesus Christ in the flesh. Some say that it took place 5228 years after the birth of Adam, others that it took place 5900 years after this birth.' And he added prudently, 'Methodius was the first to fix on the date of 6000 years, but he discovered it by mystical inspiration rather than by chronological calculation.'

To be sure, medieval chronology properly so called, the means of measuring the time and of knowing the date or the hour, in short the chronological equipment, was rudimentary. Continuity with the Graeco-Latin world was here complete. Instruments for measuring the time remained tied to the vagaries of nature. The sundial, for example, could by definition only indicate the time in sunny weather. Or else timekeeping instruments measured segments of time taken without reference to continuity, such as the hourglass, the waterclock, and all those substitutes for watches that were unsuited for measuring datable, calculable time, but were suited for defining fixed stretches of time. Into this category fell candles which could each burn for a third of the night, or, for short periods, prayers such as the Miserere or the Pater which gave their names to the length of time taken to say them. These instruments were incapable of precision and were at the mercy of unforeseeable technical accidents such as cloud, an overlarge grain of sand, or ice. Again, human malice might make candles longer or shorter or speed up or slow down the recitation of a prayer. In addition there were different systems for computing the time.

The year began at different dates according to which country one was in, depending on which religious tradition was used from which to date the redemption of mankind – and the renewal of time – whether Christ's Nativity, the Passion, the Resurrection, or even the Annunciation. Thus various chronological 'styles' coexisted in the medieval west. In France it was normal to begin the year at Easter. In the future, as we know, men were to adhere to a style which was very little used, that of the Circumcision or 1 January. Likewise the day began at variable times, at sunset, midnight, or midday. The hours were of unequal length; they were the old Roman hours, somewhat Christianized: Matins (near midnight), and then, in groups of three of our modern hours, approximately speaking, Lauds (3 a.m.), Prime (6 a.m.), Terce (9 a.m.), Sext (noon), Nones (3 p.m.), Vespers (6 p.m.), Compline (9 p.m.).

XIV

In daily life, medieval men used chronological points of reference borrowed from different sociotemporal frameworks, which were imposed on them by various economic and social systems. In fact, nothing better conveys the way in which medieval society worked than its systems of measuring and the conflicts which hardened around them. Measures of time and space were an exceptionally important instrument of social domination. Whoever was master of them enjoyed peculiar power over society. The multiplicity of time schemes in the middle ages mirrored the social struggles of the age. Men fought in the countryside and the towns over measures of capacity, which determined their rations and their standard of living; they fought for or against the measures owned by the lord or the town. Equally the measurement of time led to struggles which usually succeeded in removing control over it from the ruling classes, the clergy, and the aristocracy. Like writing, the measurement of time remained for much of the middle ages the monopoly of the powerful, an element of their power. The masses did not own their own time and were incapable of measuring it. They obeyed the time imposed on them by bells, trumpets, and horns.

Yet time in the middle ages was chiefly an agricultural time. In this world where land was the essential thing, from which almost the whole of society, whether rich or poor, made its living, the chief chronological point of reference was a rural one. Rural time was principally that of the *longue durée*. Farming or peasant time entailed waiting, putting up with things, unchanging circumstances, starting things over again, slowness, and, if not ultraconservatism, at any rate resistance to change. It lacked events and did not need dates, or rather its dates were ones that fluctuated gently according to the rhythm of nature. For rural time was natural time. The great divisions were day and the night and the seasons. Peasant time consisted of contrasts that encouraged the medieval tendency towards Manichaeanism: the opposition of dark and light, of cold and heat, of work and rest, of life and death.

Night was full of menaces and dangers in this world where artificial light was scarce (techniques of lighting, even in the daytime, were only to make progress with window glass in the thirteenth century). Moreover, artificial light was dangerous as it was a cause of fires in a world of wood. We only have to read, although there are many other stories on this subject, Joinville's description of the start of the fire which broke out at night in the cabin of the queen of France on board the ship taking her and Louis IX home from the Holy Land. Light was monopolized by the powerful: the clergy's big candles and the lords' torches eclipsed the little rushlights of the people. Doors were shut against human menaces; watches were alert in churches, castles, and towns. Medieval legislation punished misdemeanours and crimes committed at night with extraordinary force. Night was the great aggravating circumstance of justice in the middle ages.

Above all, the night was the time of supernatural dangers. It was a time for temptations, ghosts, and the devil. The German chronicler Thietmar at the beginning of the eleventh century told many stories of ghosts and asserted that they were authentic. 'Just as God has given the day to the living, he has given the night to the dead.' Nighttime was for sorcerers and demons. On the other hand for monks and mystics it was the finest hour of their spiritual combat. Vigils and night prayers were outstanding spiritual exercises. St Bernard quoted the words of the Psalmist 'At midnight I will rise to give thanks unto thee.' It was a time of struggle and victory, and every night recalled the symbolic night of Christmas. Let us open the *Elucidarium* at the chapter on Christ: 'At what hour was he born?' 'In the middle of the night.' 'Why during the night?' 'To lead those who wander in the night of error into the light of the truth.' In epic poetry nighttime is the time of distress and adventure, often connected with that other dark space, the forest. Nighttime in the forest was the scene of much medieval anguish, as in the case of the distraught Bertha (*Berthe au grand pied*). 'The lady was in the forest, and wept bitterly . . . / When night had come she began to sob / Ah! night, how long you are! I must fear you greatly.' This was echoed, at a time when the theme had become a somewhat sugared commonplace, by Chrétien of Troyes in *Yvain*: 'The night and the woods cause her great distress . . . .' On the other hand everything that was 'fair', or light – a key word in medieval literature and aesthetics – was beautiful and good, whether it was the sun shining on the armour and the swords of the warriors or the light blue eyes and the fair hair of the young knights. 'Fair as the day': the expression was never felt so strongly as in the middle ages. And the hope uttered by Laudine, impatient to see Yvain again, was commonly expressed: 'Let him turn night into day.'

Another contrast was that of the seasons. In fact, the medieval west knew only two seasons, winter and summer. When the word 'spring' appears, it occurs in learned Latin poetry, that of the Goliards. The poem *Omnia sol temperat* – the sun tempers all things – exalts the 'power of the spring', *veris auctoritas*. Another poem contrasts spring and winter: *Ver etatis labitur, / Hiemps nostra properat*. 'The springtime of life is flowing away / Our winter is approaching.' But here too the confrontation is only between two seasons, the customary summer and winter. In any case summer was, in vernacular literature, the time of renewal, the spring of Latin poetry. Marie de France in the *lai* of *Laostic* speaks of 'a summer evening when the woods and the meadows were growing green and the orchards were in flower'. The contrast between winter and summer was one of the great themes of *Minnesang*. *Sommerwonne* or the pleasure of summer was contrasted with *Wintersorge* or the anxiety of winter. Walter von der Vogelweide, in a famous poem, praised summer which 'hunts down and lays low winter with its triple care'. These cares were the disappearance of colours, the silence of the birds, and the end of pleasures in the fresh air. As day drove out night, so summer drove out anguish, *Anger*, the fruit of winter, as Conrad von Würzburg said: *Sumerzit / fröude git* – 'summer time gives joy'. Neidhart, who was nearer to the peasant outlook on life, called upon winter to flee, as was done in certain traditional peasant rituals: 'Go away, winter, you do harm.' Summer was personified in *Minnesang* in the month of May, the month of renewal, which confirms the absence of spring, or rather, its absorption by summer: 'Lord May, the prize to you / Let winter be ashamed' ran one of the earliest poems of *Minnesang*. The 'feeling of May' was so strong in medieval sensibilities that *Minnesang* forged the verb '*es maiet*', 'it is maying', to sum up the sense of deliverance and joy.

Nothing better expressed the medieval feeling that time was rural than the everywhere repeated theme of the months – in sculpture on church tympana, in frescos and miniatures, in literature, in a special genre of poetry. The twelve months were represented by rural occupations: from pruning trees to the fall of acorns for the pigs, to the slaughter of these pigs at the very start of winter and to the bacon stored in the chimney corner promising feasts to come. Variations might appear in the treatment of the theme which were associated with iconographical traditions and geographical differences in the rural economy. Harvest was often later in the northern cycles and occupations connected with viticulture did not always appear. It has often been remarked that April often holds the place in French poetry that May holds in German poetry, and thus the poem of Heinrich von Veldeke praising April has been attributed to French influence: '*In den Aberillen so die Blumen springen*', in place of the May habitual in *Minnesang*. Yet everywhere the cycle remained one of rustic tasks, although it should be noted that almost always there was a courtly, seigneurial incursion or hiatus in this rural sequence, this peasant cycle, in April or May. It was when the lord rode out, usually the young lord, young like the spring, or it was the lords' hunt. Thus an upper-class theme slipped in among the agrarian ones.

XV

This was because at the side of, or rather with, rural time, other social views of time were imposed, seigneurial and clerical time. Seigneurial time was chiefly to do with fighting. It exalted the time of year when fighting began again and vassal service was exacted. It was the time of the feudal army or '*ost*'. Seigneurial time was also the time when peasants were supposed to pay their dues. The points of reference throughout the year were, as we shall see, the great feast days. Some of these activated the sense of time among the peasant masses; these were the feudal term-days when dues were paid in kind or cash. These dates varied from region to region and from manor to manor, but one time of year stood out in this sequence of term-days: the end of summer when the bulk of the dues owing from the harvest was paid to the lords. The most important term-day was Michaelmas (29 September), though sometimes Martinmas (11 November) took its place.

XVI

Above all, medieval time was religious and clerical. It was religious time because the year was the liturgical year. The liturgical year was an essential feature of the medieval outlook on life and followed the drama of the Incarnation and the story of Christ from Advent to Pentecost, though it had been padded out little by little with important days borrowed from another cycle, that of the saints. The feasts of the greater saints had come to be intercalated into the Christological calendar, and the feast of All Saints (1 November) had become, in addition to Christmas, Easter, Ascension, and Pentecost, one of the great dates of the religious year. What made medieval people pay keener attention to these feasts and what definitively fixed them as dates was that, beyond the special, often spectacular, religious ceremonies which marked them out, they were the points of reference for economic life. They were the dates for paying agricultural dues, and holidays for craftsmen and workmen.

Medieval time was clerical because the clergy was, through its education, the master of the measurement of time. Only the clergy needed to measure time, for the liturgy, and it alone was capable, at any rate approximately, of doing so. Ecclesiastical computation, principally the calculation of the date of Easter (over which in the early middle ages there had been a long disagreement between an Irish style and a Roman one), lay at the origin of the earliest progress in measuring time. Above all the clergy were in charge of the signals indicating time. Medieval time was punctuated by bells. The peals rung for clerks and monks for the offices were the only points of reference throughout the day. The ringing of bells let people know the only time of day which was even approximately measured, that of the canonical hours by which men ordered their lives. The peasant masses were so enslaved to this clerical time that John de Garlande, a university lecturer at the beginning of the thirteenth century, gave a fantastic but revealing etymology for the word *campana* or bell which ran as follows: '*Campane dicuntur a rusticis qui habitant in campo, qui nesciant judicare horas nisi per campanas*'. 'Bells (*campanae*) are called after the peasants who live in the country (*in campo*), who do not know how to tell the time except by bells'.

The definitive feature of agricultural, seigneurial, and clerical time was their narrow dependence on natural time. While this is self-evident for agricultural time it is also, if one thinks about it, obvious for the other two. The military year was closely linked with the natural year. Warfare only began with the summer and ended with it. It is well-known that feudal armies were disbanded as soon as the three months of army service were over. This dependence on natural time was accentuated by the fact that the medieval army was made up of cavalry. A capitulary of Pippin the Short in 751 sanctions this evolution. From now on the *ost* was to be summoned in May and not April to allow the horses to feed in the fields once the fresh grass had grown. Courtly poetry, which borrowed its vocabulary from chivalry, called the time when the lover paid court to his lady 'summer service'.

Clerical time was no less submissive to this rhythm. Not only did most of the great religious feasts succeed to pagan feasts which themselves were in direct relation to the natural cycle of the year (to take the best-known example, Christmas was established in the place of a sun festival at the moment of the solstice), but more especially the liturgical year was in agreement with the natural rhythm of agricultural tasks. The liturgical year, from Advent to Whitsun, occupied the countrymen's period of rest. The summer and part of the autumn, times of agricultural activity, remained free of great feasts with the exception of a break at the Feast of the Assumption of the Virgin Mary

(15 August). This feast, however, only came slowly to prominence, did not enter into iconography until the twelfth century and does not seem to have gained recognition until the thirteenth century. Jacopo da Voragine testifies to a significant fact: the original date of All Saints was moved so as not to inconvenience the farming calendar. This feast, which was proclaimed in the west by Pope Boniface IV at the start of the seventh century, had then been fixed on 13 May, following the example of Syria, where the feast had emerged in the fourth century in the framework of a Christianity which was basically urban. It was moved at the end of the eighth century to 1 November, for, said, the *Golden Legend*, 'the pope judged it better that the feast be celebrated at that point of the year when, the grapes and the corn having been harvested, the pilgrims could more easily find something with which to feed themselves'. The turn of the eighth and ninth centuries, which was also the time when Charlemagne gave the months new names which mostly evoked rural tasks, seems indeed to have been the decisive moment when, as we have seen, the medieval west became ruralized.

The basic character of this dependence of the medieval attitude to time (the outlook of a primitive rural society) on natural time, did not show itself anywhere more clearly than in the works of the chroniclers. Among the principal events they noted exceptions to the natural order: bad weather, epidemics, and famines. These remarks, which are so valuable to the economic and social historian, flowed directly from the medieval concept of time as a natural duration.

This dependence of medieval time on natural time can be found even in the world of industry and commerce, which in appearance were more detached from this servitude. In the world of crafts, the contrasts between day and night, winter and summer can be found in the rules of the corporations. It was to a large extent from this that the habitual ban on working at night derived. Many professions had a rhythm of activity which varied from winter to summer; for example, the masons at the end of the thirteenth century received different rates of pay according to whether it was winter or summer. In the world of commercial activity, merchant shipping, which has been viewed as one of the driving forces of the medieval economy, came to a stop in the winter, or at any rate it did so until the end of the thirteenth century; the time when the use of the compass and the rudder with steering post became widespread. Ships were tied up and remained at anchor, even in the Mediterranean, from the start of December to the middle of March, and often longer in the northern seas.

Doubtless the medieval concept of time changed – slowly as yet – in the course of the fourteenth century. The success of the urban movement and the progress made by the bourgeoisie, which consisted of merchants and employers, who felt the need of measuring more exactly the time of work and of commercial operations (especially banking ones before the development of letters of change) cut across traditional views of time, unifying them. Already in the thirteenth century the watchman's cry or horn marked the start of the day, and soon bells to summon people to work appeared in mercantile towns, especially those which produced textiles, in Flanders, Italy, and Germany. Above all, technical progress broke up time and made it discontinuous. It was supported by the evolution of a science which was critical of Aristotelian and Thomist physics. Science also allowed the appearance of clocks which measured the hour in the modern sense as the 24th part of the day. Gerbert's clock of around the year 1000 was certainly only a waterclock, just like the one which Alfonso the Wise, king of Castile, described in the thirteenth century, though Alfonso's was of course an improved model. However, it was at the end of the century that the decisive advance was made with the invention of the escapement mechanism, from which were born the earliest mechanical clocks which spread through Italy, Germany, France, and England, and then through all Christian Europe, in the fourteenth and fifteenth centuries. Time was becoming laicized, and a secular time from clocks in corporation belfries asserted itself in the face of the clerical time of church bells. These mechanisms were as yet fragile and often broke down, and they remained dependent on natural time because the starting-point of the day varied from one town to another and quite often was based on that ever-variable moment, sunrise, or sunset. It is still true that the shift from one system to the other was sufficiently great for Dante, that *laudator temporis acti*, to feel that a whole way of measuring the time was in the course of disappearing, and with it a whole society, that of our middle ages. Again, it was Cacciaguida who uttered the lament over this departed time: *Fiorenza, dentro della cerchia antica / ond' ella toglie ancora e terza e nona, / si stave in pace, sobria e pudica*, 'Florence, within the circle of her ancient walls / where terce and nones were still rung / was peaceful, sober and virtuous.'

XVII

However, before this great shift took place what was important to people in the middle ages was not what changed but what endured. As has been said, 'for the medieval Christian, to feel himself to exist was to feel himself to be, and to feel himself to be was to feel himself not to change . . . but to feel himself to continue to exist'. Above all it was to feel that one was being directed toward eternity. For the medieval Christian the essential time was the time of salvation. Between heaven and earth, although they were so closely linked to each other, indeed, so inextricably mixed, an extraordinary tension existed in the medieval west. To gain heaven from here below was an ideal which conflicted in minds, hearts, and behaviour, with an equally violent, but contradictory desire: to make heaven descend to earth.

The first movement was that of flight from the world or *fuga mundi*. We know the point from which it dates in Christian society. In doctrine it was present from the beginning; in its social incarnation, from the moment when, once Christianity had won its case in the world, zealous beings declared in favour of the eremitic life for themselves and their brothers. This began in the fourth century and was constantly repeated. The east, especially Egypt, provided the great example. The *Vitae Patrum*, the lives of the desert fathers, enjoyed an extraordinary success. Contempt for the world, *contemptus mundi*, was one of the great themes of medieval thought. It was not a monopoly of mystics, or theologians (Innocent III, before he became pope, wrote a treatise at the end of the twelfth century called *De contemptu mundi* which was the ideological quintessence of this feeling), or even of poets: we know, among many others, of poems by Walter von der Vogelweide and of Conrad von Würzburg and other *Minnesänger* about Frau Welt, or the world personified by a woman with deceptive charms, seductive seen from the rear but repulsive from the front. Contempt for the world was deeply rooted in the feelings of common people.

This deeprooted tendency, which not everyone managed to put into effect in their lifetimes, was incarnated by a few people who offered themselves as examples and guides. These were hermits. From its very beginnings in Egypt, eremiticism gave birth to two currents, that of individual solitude expressed by Saint Anthony, and that of communal solitude in monasteries, a cenobitic current represented by Saint Pachomius. The medieval west knew both these currents, but only the former was truly popular. Of course orders of eremitical origin such as the Carthusians or the Cistercians temporarily enjoyed a spiritual prestige superior to that of the traditional monks, who were more involved with the world, that is the Benedictines, even the reformed ones of Cluny. The white monks (their white habit was truly a banner, a symbol of humility and purity because it was made of unbleached, undyed cloth) contrasted themselves with the black monks and to begin with exercised a greater charm over the people. But soon popular suspicion joined them to the mass of monks and even secular clergy. The model holy man was the isolated hermit, the man who in the eyes of the lay masses truly realized the solitary ideal, and who was the highest manifestation of the Christian ideal.

It is true that circumstances had to be right for eremiticism; certain periods were rich in hermits. At the moment when the western world was tearing itself free from the stagnation of the early middle ages, and was beginning a period of growth rich in demographic, economic, and social successes from

the late tenth to the late twelfth century, a great eremitical current sprang
up as a counterpoint, to balance, if not to protest at this worldly success. It
probably originated in Italy; it had connections, through Byzantium, with the
great oriental tradition of eremiticism and cenobitism. There was St Nilus of
Grottaferrata, St Romuald, the founder, at the start of the eleventh century, of
the Camaldolensians near Florence, and St John Gualberti and his community
of Vallombrosa. This movement culminated in the orders of Prémontré,
Grandmont, Chartreuse, and Cîteaux, though, in addition to these great
successes, it encompassed more modest achievements such as Robert of
Arbrissel's foundation of Fontevrault, and above all innumerable solitaries,
hermits, anchorites, and anchoresses. These, who were less bound to a rule
or an ecclesiastical system, were nearer to a certain anarchical idea of religious
life, were more easily confused by the people with magicians, and were in
any case easily transformed by the former into saints. They peopled the
deserts, that is to say the forests, of Christian Europe. The hermit was the
model, the confidante, and the teacher par excellence. To him turned souls
in torment, knights or lovers tortured by some misdeed. In the *chansons de
geste* and the romances hermits crop up in every corner of the forest, such
as the old Ogrin whom Tristan and Iseult consulted. 'The hermit Ogrin
reprimanded them much, / Gave them counsel of repentance. / The hermit
often told them / The prophecies of Scripture / and often recalled to them
/ the judgement of God.' For men of the middle ages the hermit was the refuge
of the Christian ideal when the Church seemed to be betraying it. We may
recall Walter von der Vogelweide who abused the *Pfaffen* (priests) and
contrasted them with the hermit weeping over the church and its pope, the
too-young Innocent III, and asking the Lord to help Christendom. '*Da weinte
ein klosenaere. . . .* There wept a hermit. . . . ' Hermits sometimes ended by
becoming spiritual agitators and often popular leaders. Transformed into
itinerant preachers, placed at crossing-places on roads, forest crossroads, or
bridges, they might in the end abandon the desert for public squares in towns,
where they caused great scandal, for example to the Chartres cleric Payen
Bolotin in the early twelfth century. He wrote a vengeful poem against these
'false hermits', while the famous canonist Ivo of Chartres extolled the cenobitic
life in opposition to the hermit Rainaud, the supporter of the solitary life.

However, right through the middle ages, outside the moments when
eremiticism was in fashion and booming, solitaries were ever-present and ever-
fascinating. Iconography shows them such as they were in real life, a living
declaration of a show of savagery in the face of a world which was succeeding,
establishing and civilizing itself. They had bare feet and were clad in the skins
of animals (usually goats). They held a T-shaped staff in their hand, the stick
used by the pilgrim and the wanderer and also the instrument of magic and

salvation. The tau sign made by this staff was a protection, in imitation of the saving sign announced by Ezekiel (Ezekiel 9.6) – 'come not near any man upon whom is the mark' – and by Revelations (7.3). They exercised their fascination on the model of their patron saint, Anthony, the great conqueror of all temptations, and through him, the initiator of desert spirituality, St John the Baptist.

Not all could make themselves hermits. Yet many tried to achieve this ideal, at least symbolically, for it seemed to be a guarantee of salvation. The practice of clothing onself in the monastic habit when in *articulo mortis*, which was common among the great, shows the desire to identify oneself with the example of monastic, and more particularly eremitical, perfection. The theme of the knight retiring to become a hermit was another great theme of the *chansons de geste*, which often included an episode of '*moniage*', that is to say the knight taking the monastic habit before his death, the best known example being the *Moniage Guillaume*, when William of Orange took the habit. The example was followed by the class of the great merchants. Sebastiano Ziani, doge of Venice, who had become proverbially rich by trade ('as rich as Ziani' was a phrase of the time) retired in 1178 to the monastery of San Giorgio Maggiore, as his son, Piero Ziani, who also became doge, was to do in 1229. The great Sienese banker, Giovanni Tolomei, founded the monastery of Monte Oliveto Maggiore in 1313, where he shut himself up to die. At the start of the twelfth century St Anselm wrote to Countess Matilda of Tuscany: 'If you feel death to be imminent, give yourself entirely to God before leaving this life, and for that always have a veil secretly prepared near you'.

Sometimes indeed a man of the people might be affected by the appeal of the desert, to which might be joined a certain taste for adventure, or even exoticism. For example there was the sailor employed by Louis IX whose sudden vocation on the way home from the Holy Land is recorded by Joinville.

After taking in a supply of drinking water and other such things as we required, we left the island of Cyprus, and sailed to another island called Lampedusa, where we caught a great number of rabbits. We found there an old hermitage among the rocks, with a garden which the hermits who had lived there long ago had laid out. It was planted with olive trees, fig trees, and vines, and other trees and bushes of various kinds. A stream that rose from a spring ran through the garden. The king and all the rest of us went to the bottom of the garden, where we found, in the first cave we came to, an oratory with whitewashed walls that contained a terracotta cross. On entering the second cave we found two bodies of dead men from which the flesh had rotted. Their ribs still held together, and the bones of their hands were on their breasts. Their bodies had been laid towards the east, in the same way as those that are consigned to earth. When we got back to our ship we found that one of our sailors was missing; our captain thought he must have remained on the island to be a hermit.

So Nicholas de Soisi, who was the king's chief sergeant, left three bags of biscuits so that the man might find them and have something to sustain him (Joinville, 1971, pp. 323-4).

Finally, for those who were not capable of this final act of penance, the Church allowed for other means of ensuring salvation. There was the practice of charity, of works of mercy, gifts, and for usurers and those whose wealth had been wrongly acquired, restitution *post mortem*. Thus the will became a passport to heaven.

If we do not keep the obsession with salvation and the fear of hell which inspired medieval men in the forefront of our minds we shall never understand their outlook on life. Without this understanding we would be stupefied at how people stripped away all the endeavour of a lifetime spent acquiring, at how they stripped away power and riches; this provoked an extraordinary mobility of fortunes. It is evidence of how the men who were most greedy for worldly goods in the middle ages, always ended up by despising the world, even if it was only literally *in extremis*. This mental trait which operated against the accumulation of fortunes helped to distance medieval men from the material and psychological conditions in which capitalism might flourish.

XVIII

A head-over-heels flight from the world was not, however, the only way in which men in the middle ages aspired to the grace of salvation or eternal life. Many were impelled by another, equally powerful, current towards another hope, another desire. They wanted to achieve eternal happiness on earth; they wanted to return to a golden age, to the lost paradise. This current was millenarianism, a dream that the millennium, a period of 1000 years, but in fact eternity, would be established, or rather, re-established, on earth. The historical detail of this belief is complex. Millenarianism is an aspect of Christian eschatology; it grafted itself on to the apocalyptic tradition and is closely linked with the myth of Antichrist. It was formed and was slowly enriched on a basis of the Apocalypse. Of course, Revelations evokes terrible tribulations, but this dramatic climate found an outlet in a message of hope. The Apocalypse fed an optimistic belief. It affirmed a decisive renovation: *Ecce nova facio omnia.* 'Lo,' says God on Judgement Day, 'I make all things new.' Above all, the vision of the author of Revelations would be realized and the heavenly Jerusalem would descend on earth. *Et ostendit mihi civitatem sanctam Jerusalem, descendentem de caelo a Deo*; 'And he showed me the holy city, Jerusalem, coming down from God in heaven' and this vision was accompanied by all the splendour of all those lights, which, as we have already seen, had great fascination for medieval men. The heavenly Jerusalem appeared *habentem claritatem Dei, et lumen ejus simile lapidi pretioso tamquam lapidi jaspidis, sicut crystallum,* 'having the brightness of God, and his light similar to a precious stone, as if a jasper, like to crystal'. *Et civitas non eget sole, neque luna, ut luceant in ea: nam claritas Dei illuminavit eam et lucerna ejus est Agnus.* 'And the city does not need the sun or the moon that they shine in her: for the brightness of God has illumined it and his lamp is the Lamb'.

However, in this process culminating in the victory of God and in the salvation of mankind, it was the tribulations which were to be unleashed on earth during the preliminary phase which soon monopolized the attention of men in the middle ages. Other texts interposed themselves, borrowed from the Gospel: Matthew 24, Mark 13, and Luke 21. This was the description of the events which were to precede the arrival of the Son of Man. Let us quote from Matthew the terrible prophecy: *Consurget enim gens in gentem, et regnum in regnum, et erunt pestilentiae, et fames, et terraemotus per loca: haec autem omnia initia sunt dolorum,* 'For nation shall rise against nation, and kingdom against kingdom: and there shall be famines, and pestilences, and earthquakes, in diverse places. All these are the beginning of sorrows', of 'the abomination of desolation'. The presaging of the end of time through wars, epidemics, and famines seemed close to the men of the middle ages. The massacres of the barbarian invasions, the Great Plague of the sixth century, and the terrible famines repeating themselves every now and then helped to keep up the anguished anticipation. Fear and hope were mixed, but chiefly, and increasingly, fear, a panic, a collective fear. The medieval west was, in the wait for its hoped-for salvation, a world of certain dread. We may observe several different stages in this long history of a fear which was gradually elaborated doctrinally, and which was experienced in the guts of generation after generation.

At the end of the Great Plague of the sixth century, when the recurrence of the scourge made people believe in the imminence of the Last Judgement, Gregory the Great, who had become the successor of a series of impotent popes in 590, in the middle of an epidemic (had not the Roman populace pursued one of his predecessors, according to the *Liber Pontificalis,* with the cry *Pestilentia tua tecum! Fames tua tecum!* May your plague and your famine be on you!), bequeathed to the middle ages a spirituality of the end of the world, born out of an appeal to a grand collective penance.

Yet within this web of terrible events, one theme gradually came to the forefront, that of the Antichrist. Antichrist occurs in embryonic form in the prophecy of Daniel and in Revelations and the two epistles of St Paul to the Thessalonians. St Irenaeus at the end of the second century, Hippolytus of

Rome at the beginning of the third century, and finally Lactantius at the start of the fourth century, gave him a personality and a history. We may note that all these catastrophic predictions were forged in the midst of historical ordeals such as the Jewish war, the economic crisis at the end of the first century at the time of the Apocalypse of St John the Divine, the great crisis of the Roman world in the third century, and the bubonic plague in the sixth century. Let us summarize the story. On the eve of the end of time a diabolical figure will come to play the role of conductor in these catastrophes and will try to drag down mankind into eternal damnation. This, the antithesis of Christ, is Antichrist, and against him will stand up another figure who will try to reunite the human race under his leadership to lead it to salvation. This is to be the Emperor of the end of the world, who will in the end be laid low by Christ when he redescends to earth.

The figure of Antichrist was perfected in the eighth century by a monk called Peter, who took the character out of a short seventh-century Greek work which he attributed to a certain Methodius. Then the theme was picked up again in the tenth century by Adso for Queen Gerberga, the wife of Louis IV of Outremer, and after the year 1000 by Albuin who adapted to the west the predictions of the Sibyl of Tibur created during the fourth to fifth centuries in a Byzantine milieu. From then on Antichrist became a favourite hero for theologians and mystics. He haunted Cluny under the holy abbot Odo at the start of the tenth century and again when the monk-poet Bernard of Morval was there in the middle of the twelfth century. He found a particularly welcoming field in twelfth-century Germany, with Anselm of Havelberg, Gerhoch of Reichersberg, Otto of Freising, and Hildegard of Bingen. The holy nun saw him in a dream as a copy of Satan: 'A beast with a monstrous head, black as coal, with flaming eyes, wearing asses' ears and with gaping jaws decorated with iron hooks'.

What was most important was that Antichrist and his adversary, the Emperor of the End of Time, lent themselves to all sorts of religious and political uses and seduced the popular masses as much as the clergy. The idea (in this world where the duel, as we have seen, was a dominant image in the spiritual life) of a single adversary of Christ and the easy application to real situations of episodes of the story of Antichrist favoured the adoption of the belief by the people. Finally, very early, at least from the twelfth century, the great publicizing artistic medium of the middle ages, the mystery plays, took over the figure and made him familiar to all. The *Ludus de Antichristo* or *Play of Antichrist* was played all over Christian Europe. We possess particularly interesting versions of it from England and Germany, one in a manuscript of the abbey of Tegernsee in Bavaria from as early as the second half of the twelfth century. However, the two essential roles were Antichrist and his enemy, the *rex justus* or just king. Interests, passions, and propaganda took possession of famous figures of the medieval scene and to suit the needs of a particular cause they were identified by their supporters with either the just king or Antichrist. National propaganda in Germany made Frederick Barbarossa and Frederick II the good emperor of the end of the world; on the other hand, the propagandists of the kings of France, relying on a passage in Adso, prophesied the reunion of Christianity under a French king, propaganda from which Louis VII in particular benefited at the time of the Second Crusade. Then again, the Guelf faction, which supported the popes, made Frederick II into Antichrist, while Boniface VIII was to be an Antichrist seated on the throne of St Peter for his lay enemies. We know what was to become of this publicity instrument, the epithet 'Antichrist', in the fifteenth and sixteenth centuries. Savonarola was Antichrist to his enemies and so were the popes of Rome to the Protestant reformers.

In addition there was social propaganda which saw the saviour of the world in various political leaders. Thus, at the start of the thirteenth century in the west, Baldwin of Flanders, the Latin emperor of Constantinople, became 'a superhuman figure, a fabulous creature, half-angel, half-demon'.

Most of the legends created around historical figures arose out of the myth of the 'sleeping emperor', an echo of the eastern myth of the 'hidden emir'. Barbarossa, Baldwin, and Frederick II were not dead to the masses, who were avid for millenarian myths. They were sleeping in a cavern or living disguised as beggars, waiting for the moment to wake up or reveal themselves and lead mankind to happiness. Some revolutionary leaders shone with this aura, for example Tanchelm in Zealand and Brabant, around 1110. He began by preaching in the open fields dressed as a monk. It is said that crowds came to hear him, this man of an extraordinary eloquence, like an angel of the Lord. He was just like a saint and it was not a coincidence if his mortal enemies in the cathedral chapter of Utrecht complained that 'the Devil had clad himself in the appearance of an angel of light'. One should read the story of Tanchelm in the letter written by the chapter of Utrecht in 1112 or in Norman Cohn's book *The Pursuit of the Millennium*. Again, we find the same theme at the time of the movement of the Pastoureaux in France, in 1251, attached to the leader of the movement, an apostate monk called the Master of Hungary. Sometimes pure usurpers made themselves pass for these earthly Messiahs at the anticipated awakening. False emperors arose like the false Dimitris in Russia at the time of the troubles or false Louis XVIIs in France in the beginning of the nineteenth century. The most famous was the false Baldwin at the start of the thirteenth century in Flanders and Hainault, who was none other than an example of a familiar type of personality: a mendicant hermit who became 'a prince and a saint so revered that the people kissed his scars which witnessed to his long martyrdom, fought each other for one of his hairs or for a scrap of his clothing, and drank his bathwater, as people had drunk Tanchelm's several generations before'. In 1225 when a terrible famine was raging he received from his faithful the title of emperor.

The Church, often with little success, would denounce these agitators as being either Antichrist himself or one of those pseudo-prophets who, as even the Gospel and the millenarian texts said, were to accompany him and seduce the people with false miracles.

The millenarian current was a complicated one. Firstly it polarized the feelings of the time around certain phenomena which thereby became essential for the medieval mentality. At the start of the *Golden Legend*, Jacopo da Voragine listed the signs which would announce the arrival of Antichrist and the approach of the end of the world:

The circumstances which will precede the Last Judgement are of three sorts: terrible signs, the imposture of Antichrist, and an huge fire. The signs which must precede the Last Judgement are five in number, for St Luke said, 'There will be signs in the sun, in the moon and the stars, on earth the nations will be consternated and the sea will make a frightening noise by the crashing of its waves.' All these are things commented on in Revelations. St Jerome, for his part, found fifteen signs preceding the Last Judgement in the annals of the Hebrews: (1) on the first day, the sea will rise to forty cubits above the mountains, and will stand upright immobile like a wall; (2) on the second day, it will sink so low that one will barely be able to see it; (3) on the third day, sea monsters appearing on the waves will utter roars which will rise up to heaven; (4) on the fourth day the water in the sea will burn; (5) on the fifth day, the trees and all the plants will exude a dew of blood; (6) on the sixth day, buildings will fall down; (7) on the seventh day, the stones will break into four pieces which will all clash against each other; (8) on the eighth day a universal earthquake will take place, which will lay men and animals low on the ground; (9) on the ninth day, the earth will make itself level, turning mountains and hills to dust; (10) on the tenth day, men will come out of caverns and wander like madmen, without being able to speak to each other; (11) on the eleventh day the remains of the dead will come out of the tombs; (12) on the twelfth day the stars will fall; (13) on the thirteenth day all living beings will die to be resurrected again with the dead; (14) on the fourteenth day the heavens and earth will burn; (15) on the fifteenth day there will be a new heaven and a new earth, and all will be resurrected.

In the second place, the Last Judgement will be preceded by the imposture of Antichrist, who will try to deceive men in four ways; (1) by false exposition of the Scriptures, from which he will try to prove that he is the Messiah promised by the Law; (2) by the accomplishment of miracles; (3) by the distribution of gifts; (4) by the infliction of tortures.

In the third place, the Last Judgement will be preceded by a violent fire lit by God to renew the world, to make the damned suffer and to set the elect in the light.

Let us leave for a moment the social and political events associated with Antichrist. Let us concentrate on the extraordinary list of geographical and meteorological portents which accompany the coming of the Last Day in this sample description. In this way all the portents of Graeco-Roman tradition can be found linked as much to the world of Ouranos as to the world of Chthonos. In this way could be nourished an exceptional feeling for natural 'signs' among medieval men. These signs were so full of terrors and promises for them. Comets, raining mud, shooting stars, earthquakes, and tidal waves unleashed a collective fear which was much less frightened by the natural cataclysm than by the end of the world which it might announce. Yet these signs also were, beyond the time of ordeal and fear, a message of hope in the anticipation of the final resurrection. Thus medieval time became a time of fear and hope.

It was a time of hope, for the myth of the millennium became more precise and took on revolutionary dreams. As we have seen it inspired ephemeral popular movements. At the start of the thirteenth century a Calabrian monk, Joachim of Flore, gave it an explosive content which was to move a section of the regular clergy and the lay masses for the whole century. The teaching of Joachim was bound up with a religious division of history which was in competition with the more orthodox division into six ages. It meant a division into three ages: *ante legem, sub lege, post legem,* the ages of the Father, the Son, and the Holy Spirit, of the Old Testament which is accomplished, of the New Testament which is in the process of being fulfilled, and of the 'Eternal Gospel', announced by Revelations, which was on the eve of being fulfilled. Joachim of Flore even gave the date when it would arrive – the middle ages were keen on dates – 1260. The main point was that the content of Joachim's teaching was profoundly subversive. Indeed, in the eyes of Joachim and his disciples the Church was rotten and damned with the existing world. She would have to make way for a new Church, the Church of the saints, which would repudiate wealth and would make equality and purity reign. What is significant here is that a mob of disciples, clergy, and laity, neglected a host of theological subtleties and a basically very conservative mysticism, and retained from Joachimite teaching only this anticlerical, antifeudal, and egalitarian prophecy. The influence was so great that before he embarked for the Holy Land St Louis, always on the lookout for religious movements, went to talk to a Joachimite Franciscan, Hugh of Digne, who drew great crowds to Hyères, where he had retired. Joachimism, which disturbed the university of Paris in the middle of the thirteenth century, survived to the year 1260, as we know, and inspired a group of Franciscans who were soon declared heretical: the Spirituals, later the Fraticelli. One of them, Peter John Olivi, wrote a commentary on Revelations at the end of the thirteenth century. Another,

Jacopone da Todi, wrote the *Laudi*, the highest point of medieval religious poetry.

Joachimite millenarianism rediscovered a current of thought from the ancient world which sprang up again in the thirteenth century: a belief in the egalitarian Golden Age, which was unaware of all government, and all class division. Jean de Meung describes it in the second part of the *Roman de la Rose*. This long and fine work should be read in full, but we may recall the chief points.

Once, in the time of our earliest fathers and our earliest mothers, as the writings of the ancients testify, people loved with a fine and faithful love, and not out of covetousness and the desire of rapine, and goodness reigned in the world. . . .

The earth then was not cultivated, but it was as God had formed it, and itself bore that from which each might draw his subsistence.

This is an almost Rousseau-like theme of original happiness based on equality.

No king or prince had yet criminally seized other men's goods. All were equal and had nothing of their own; they knew well that maxim that love and authority never go together and live together, that they are disunited by him who rules.

From this a critique of the social and political order is developed.

The Ancients kept company together, free of all bonds and constraints, peacefully and honestly, and they would not have given their liberty for the gold of Arabia or Phrygia. At that time there was no pilgrimage; no-one left his country to go and explore foreign countries; Jason had not yet built his ships and crossed the sea to win the Golden Fleece.

However Barat [deception] came, with his lance in rest, with Sin and Unhappiness, who did not care about sufficiency; Pride, which disdained it equally, appeared with his train: Covetousness, Avarice, Envy and all the other vices. They made Poverty leave hell, where she had stayed so long that no-one knew anything about her. Cursed be that wretched day when Poverty came to earth! . . .

Soon these wretches, frenzied with rage and envy at seeing men happy, invaded all the earth, sowing discord, chicanery, differences and litigation, quarrels, disputes, wars, slander, hatred and rancour; and since they doted on gold, they had the earth scoured to drag its hidden treasures out of its entrails – precious metals and stones.

As soon as the human race became the victim of this band, it changed its earlier form of life. The men did not cease to do wrong. They became false and cheating, they became attached to possessions, they even shared out the ground, and in this sharing they set up boundaries, they fought with each other, taking away what they could, and the strongest had the largest shares. . . .

And here is the emergence of political authority.

Then it was necessary to find someone who would guard the huts, arrest the wrongdoers and do justice to plaintiffs, so that no one would contest his authority; then they assembled to elect him. They chose among themselves a great thug, the biggest-built, the broadest-backed and strongest whom they could find, and they made him ruler and lord. He swore to preserve justice and to defend their shacks, provided that each would personally, from his own means, give him something to live on, and they agreed . . . . The people had to be assembled again so that taxation could be imposed on each, so that the ruler could have sergeants. Then they were taxed generally, and paid him dues and tributes and granted him vast territories. This was the origin of kings, of earthly rulers . . .

At this moment men amassed treasures. With gold and silver, precious and malleable metals, they made vessels, coins, clasps, rings, and belts; with resistant iron they forged weapons, knives, swords, guisarmes, lances and coats of mail to fight their neighbours with. At the same time, they built towers and lists and walls with cut stones; they fortified citadels and castles and made great sculpted palaces, for those who held these riches feared greatly that they would have them taken away secretly or by force. From then on they were much more to be pitied, these men of misfortune, since they no longer had any security from the day when they appropriated out of greed what had previously been common to all like the air and the sun.

Thus millenarianism, which expected the return of the Golden Age, was the medieval form of the belief in the coming of a society without classes where the State would have withered away completely and there would no longer be any kings, or princes, or lords. To make heaven descend on earth, to bring heavenly Jerusalem here below, was the dream of many in the medieval west. If I have spent some time in evoking this myth (although in an oversimplified way), it is because, although it was masked and combated by the official Church, it bowled over minds and hearts. It reveals to us in their depths the popular masses of the middle ages, and their economic and physiological anxieties in the face of the permanent conditions of their existence: their subjection to the changeability of nature, to famines and epidemics; their revolts against a social order which crushed the weak and against a Church which benefited and guaranteed that order; their dreams – a religious dream which drew heaven down to earth and only caught sight of hope at the end of unutterable terrors. The piercing desire which it reveals of going 'to the end of the unknown to find the new' (*ecce fecit omnia nova*) did not succeed in picturing a truly new world. The Golden Age of the men of the middle ages was only a return to their origins. Their future was behind them. They walked on with their heads turned backwards.

7

Material Culture
(Tenth to Thirteenth Centuries)

I

THE MEDIEVAL west was a world poorly equipped. It is tempting to say underequipped, but it must be stressed that the middle ages cannot be spoken of as being *under*equipped, and still less of being underdeveloped; for although Byzantium, the Muslim world, and China surpassed the west in the lustre of monetary economies, urban civilization, and the production of luxury goods, the standard of technology there was low too. In this respect the early middle ages had probably undergone a certain regression in relation to the Roman empire. On the other hand, important technological improvements emerged, developing from the eleventh century, and although invention between the fifth and the fourteenth century was limited, it is still true that progress, basically of a quantitative rather than qualitative character, was not negligible. The positive aspect of technical evolution in the medieval west was the diffusion of tools, machines, and skills that had been known from classical times but that had remained in effect rarities or curiosities, rather than innovations.

The two most spectacular and revolutionary of the 'medieval inventions' dated from antiquity, but for the historian their date of birth, which is that of their diffusion not of their discovery, certainly lies in the middle ages. The watermill, for example, was known in Illyria as early as the second century BC, in Asia Minor from the first century BC, and it existed in the Roman world. Vitruvius described it, and his description shows that the Romans had made a notable improvement to the early watermill by replacing the original horizontal wheels with vertical wheels and gearing which linked the horizontal axis of the wheels to the vertical axis of the millstones. However, the hand mill turned by slaves or animals remained the norm. In the ninth century the watermill was already widely known in the west; 59 are mentioned in the polyptych of the wealthy abbey of St-Germain-des-Prés. Yet as late as the tenth century the *Annals* of St Bertin describe the construction by the abbot of a watermill near St Omer as 'a wonderful spectacle in our age'. The boom in watermills took place between the ninth and the fourteenth centuries. In one part of Rouen there were two mills in the tenth century, five new ones appeared in the twelfth century, ten others in the thirteenth, and another fourteen in the fourteenth.

Similarly the medieval plough almost certainly derives from the wheeled plough described by Pliny the Elder in the first century AD. It became widespread and gradually underwent improvements during the middle ages. Linguistic studies suggest that it is very probable that the wheeled plough became fairly common in the Slav lands early on – in Moravia before the Hungarian invasion at the beginning of the tenth century, and even perhaps over all the Slav lands before the Avar invasion of 586, since vocabulary relating to it is common to different Slavonic tongues and is therefore earlier than the Avar advance which led to the splitting up of the Slav groups. Yet as late as the ninth century it is difficult to say what type of instrument the *carrucae* mentioned in Carolingian capitularies and polyptychs refer to. Equally, for example, in the area of small tools, the plane whose invention has often been attributed to the middle ages had been known from the first century.

On the other hand it is likely that a fair number of 'medieval inventions' not inherited from the Graeco-Roman world were borrowed from the east. Although it cannot be proved, it is probably true of the windmill, which was known in China and then Persia in the seventh century, is recorded in Spain in the tenth century and did not appear in Christian Europe until the end of the twelfth century. However, the earliest western windmills known to us were sited in a restricted area around the English Channel (Normandy, Ponthieu, and England); and generic differences between the oriental mill, which lacked sails but which had tall loopholes to concentrate the wind movement on to big vertical wheels, the western mill with four long sails, and the Mediterranean mill with many triangular pieces of canvas stretched out with ropes, as one can still see on Mykonos or in Portugal, make it quite possible that the windmill appeared independently in these three geographical zones.

Whatever the importance of the diffusion of these technical advances, the feature that above all characterized the technical world of the medieval west, even more its lack of inventive flair, was the fact that it was rudimentary. The medieval west was held back in a primitive state chiefly by a combination of technical inadequacies, handicaps and bottlenecks. Clearly the framework of society and thought was broadly responsible for this technical poverty and stagnation. A dominant minority of lay and ecclesiastical lords was the only

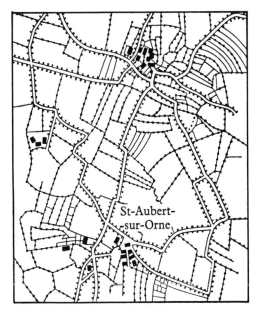 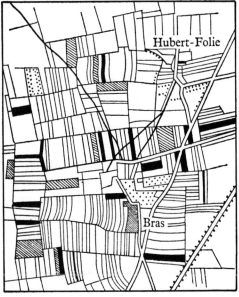

17 St-Aubert-sur-Orne
(after M. Bloch, *Les caractères originaux de l'histoire rurale française*)

18 Bras and Hubert-Folie
(after M. Bloch, ibid)

Figures 17, 18 'Bocage' and open country

In his poem on the Norman peasant revolt of 997 (see p.299), the poet Wace (circa 1170) names the two chief types of rural landscape in medieval Normandy: the 'plain' with open, long fields and the 'bocage' with enclosed, irregular-shaped fields; (17) is the plan of a 'bocage' landscape at St-Aubert-sur-Orne (Orne) and (18) shows a landscape characteristic of the plain around Caen with the villages Bras and Hubert-Folie (Calvados). These drawings from plans of the early eighteenth century show how the extreme medieval fragmentation had been preserved.

group which felt the need for luxury goods and was the only one able to satisfy this need. They could acquire foreign products such as fine cloth or spices by importing them from Byzantium or the Muslim world; game and furs, products of the chase for the table or for clothing, they could procure without any artisanal or industrial preparation; ironwork and goldsmithery they could demand in small quantities from a few specialists. Although the mass of the population did not provide the lords with a workforce as cheap and exploitable as had been the slaves in the ancient world, it was still large and amenable enough to economic necessities to support the upper classes and to keep itself in a fairly wretched state by using very backward equipment. It was not the case that the dominance of the lay and clerical aristocracy had a merely negative, inhibiting effect on the field of technology. In some areas its needs or its tastes favoured a certain progress. The clergy and above all the monks were obliged to have as few contacts as possible with the outside world, including economic relations, and above all they desired to be freed from material tasks to have time for the *Opus Dei* and for properly spiritual occupations (offices, prayers), and for their works of charity, which obliged them to provide for the economic needs not only of their numerous *familia* but also of the poor and of wandering beggars by distributing foodstuffs. This encouraged them to develop equipment of a certain technical standard. If one is looking for the earliest mills, watermills or windmills, or for progress in farming techniques, one often sees the religious orders in the vanguard. It was not a coincidence if here and there during the early middle ages men attributed the invention of the watermill to a saint who had introduced it into a region, for example St Orens of Auch who had a mill built on the lake of Isaby in the fourth century, or Caesarius of Arles who set one up at St Gabriel on the Durançole in the sixth century.

The evolution of weaponry and of military skill, essential to a warfaring aristocracy, brought in its wake progress in both metalworking and ballistics. As we have seen, the Church encouraged improvements in the measurement of time for the needs of ecclesiastical computation. The building of churches – the first great buildings of the middle ages – gave a stimulus to technical progress, not only in building techniques, but also in the tools used, in methods of transportation, and in the auxiliary skills such as glasswork.

Even so, the attitude of the ruling classes was hostile to technology. For the greater part of the middle ages, until the thirteenth century and even (to a smaller degree) beyond, tools, instruments, and work in its technical aspects appear in literature and art merely as symbols. It is to Christological allegories of the mystic mill or press and to Elijah's chariot that we owe the representations of the mill, the press, and the cart, such as those seen in the *Hortus Deliciarum* of the twelfth century. A tool will appear only as the symbolic attribute of a saint. The shoemaker's awl owed its fairly frequent

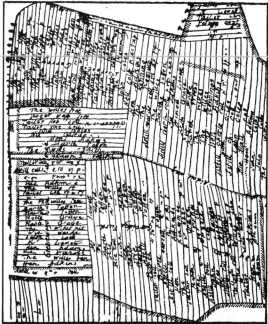

19 Weston Pinkney
(from Beresford, *Lost Villages of England*)

20 Weston Pinkney
(aerial photograph, from Beresford, ibid).

Figures 19, 20 Medieval plough-rigs in the 'open field' system

Weston Pinkney, Northants, is a classic example of a medieval open field with a pattern of ridges and furrows; (19) is a sketch after the plan made in 1593 for All Souls College, Oxford, in which one can observe the tenants' names written on each strip of land; (20) is the same landscape from an aerial photograph which shows up the lines of the medieval fields.

portrayal in medieval iconography to the fact that it formed part of the tortures which according to tradition had been inflicted on certain martyrs, such as St Benignus of Dijon or the shoemakers' patron saints themselves, Crispin and Crispinian. Saint James the Less is shown until the fourteenth century with the fuller's club with which one of his executioners is supposed to have shattered his skull in Jerusalem. At the end of the middle ages, artists substituted for the fuller's club, as the instrument of martyrdom, a craftsman's tool, a triangular bow which was a sort of carding tool. Society and attitudes had changed.

Probably there was no sector of medieval life where the horror of 'novelties', another mental characteristic of the period, acted with more force against progress than in the technical domain. Innovation in technology was, more even than elsewhere, a monstrous act, a sin. And since, as we shall see, new advances turned to the lord's benefit, they ran into violent or passive opposition from the masses. For a long time no-one in the western middle ages composed a technical treatise, these being unworthy of the written word or dependent on a secret which must not be repeated. When at the start of the twelfth century the German monk Theophilus wrote *De diversis artibus*, claimed to be the earliest technological treatise of the middle ages, he was less preoccupied with teaching craftsmen and artists than with showing that the technician's cunning is a gift of God. The English treatises of the thirteenth century on agriculture, the manuals of *Housebondrie*, the most famous of which is that by Walter of Henley, or the *Seneschaucy*, were as yet no more than works of practical advice. We must wait for the *Ruralium commodorum opus* of the Bolognese Pietro de Crescenzi at the beginning of the fourteenth century for the tradition of the Roman agronomists to be renewed. Otherwise, works claiming to be technical are only erudite compilations, often pseudoscientific ones, with little use as sources for the history of skills. Examples of these are the dictionary of John de Garlande, Alexander Nequam's *De nominibus utensilium*, Albert the Great's *De vegetalibus*, and also the *Regule ad custodiendum terras*, composed by Robert Grosseteste around 1240 for the countess of Lincoln.

II

The feebleness of medieval technological equipment was most apparent in such basic aspects as the predominance of tools over machines, the limited effectiveness and inadequacy of the tools and of farming techniques which produced only very limited returns, and the inferiority of transportation, of financing and commercial skills, and of the means for harnessing energy.

There was practically no qualitative development in the use of machinery during the middle ages. Almost all the machines then in use had been described by scholars in the Hellenistic period, especially the Alexandrians, who had also often sketched out the scientific principle on which they operated. In particular, the medieval west barely made any innovations in the systems of the transmission and of the transformation of movement. Five 'cinematic sequences' – the screw, the wheel, the cam, the ratchet, and the pulley – had been known in antiquity. Only the sixth of these sequences, the crank, seems to have been a medieval invention. It appears during the early middle ages in simple mechanisms like the turning millstone described in the Utrecht Psalter in the middle of the ninth century, but does not seem to have become widespread before the end of the middle ages. In any case its most effective form, the system of connecting rod and crank, only appears at the end of the fourteenth century. It is true that many of these mechanisms or machines had often only been known to antiquity as curiosities or games (such as the Alexandrian automata) and they became widespread and really effective only in the course of the middle ages. Medieval workmen were also able to compensate their ignorance to some extent with a certain empirical cunning. Thus the combination of a camshaft and a spring allowed people to operate percussion tools such as hammers and mallets and to some extent compensated for the as yet unknown crank and connecting rod system.

If this stagnation in techniques for transforming movement cannot be explained by men's attitudes, can it at least be related to some scientific and theological concepts? Aristotle's mechanics were not his most fruitful aid to science, in spite of the works of Jordanus Nemorarius and his school in the thirteenth century; the treatise *De mechanica*, whose author remains unknown, should not be attributed to Aristotle as it was in the middle ages. In the fourteenth century scholars such as Bradwardine, Buridan, and Oresme, the theoreticians of the *impetus*, subjected Aristotle's physics and more especially his mechanics to fairly vigorous criticism. Yet they remained, like Aristotle, prisoners of a metaphysical concept which vitiated their idea of dynamics from the root. The *impetus*, like the *virtus impressa*, remained a 'virtue', a 'motive force', a metaphysical notion from which the process of movement was made to arise. Moreover the basis of these theories of movement was still formed by theological questions.

A significant example of this way of thinking was provided in 1320 by François de la Marche. He asked 'if there is in the sacraments some super-natural virtue which might be formally inherent in them'. This suggested to him the problem of knowing 'if there could be in an artificial instrument, or be received from an exterior agent, a virtue inherent to this instrument'. Thus he studied the example of a stone thrown violently into the air and then, as has been rightly said, laid 'the foundations of a physics of *impetus*'. This handicap of seeing things both theologically and metaphysically was accompanied by a certain indifference to movement, which was characteristic of the medieval outlook. I suspect that it was greater than the medieval indifference to time, although the two were connected, because for Thomas Aquinas as for Aristotle 'time is the number of movement'. What interested men in the middle ages was not what moved but what was still. What they were seeking was rest, *quies*. Everything which by contrast entailed agitation and pursuit seemed to them to be vain (the adjective commonly attached to these nouns) and a little bit diabolical.

It would be wrong to exaggerate the influence of these existential doctrines and tendencies on the stagnation of skills. The inferiority of medieval machines was chiefly dependent on the general state of technology linked to the economic and social situation. When certain improvements appear, as in lathes, either their use was limited to work on substances which were not longlasting, which explains why we possess very few objects turned on the lathe from the middle ages, or they came late. For example, the system of a spindle with a crank only came into use in spinning wheels in about 1280 against the background of the crisis in the luxury textile industry, and the spinning-wheel was still operated manually by a spinner who usually had to stand to work. This was because of the absence of the pedal which was only to appear with the crank and connecting rod system. The potter's wheel went back to prehistory, and the pole lathe existed in classical antiquity. The lathe with a pulley and double pedal which can be seen in a thirteenth-century window at Chartres was perhaps an improvement of the medieval period, but even then only of limited significance.

The use of lifting appliances and powered mechanisms was stimulated by the growth in building, especially the construction of churches and castles. Even so the inclined plane was without any doubt the most frequent method for lifting materials. Lifting machines, which barely differed, at least not in their principles, from the machines of antiquity – the simple block and tackle and cranes with a treadmill – remained curiosities or rarities which only princes, cities, or church fabric funds could use. An example of this was the engine, not well known to us, called the 'vasa' which was used at Marseilles to launch ships. At the end of the twelfth century the monk Gervase marvelled at the talent of the architect William of Sens who had first-rate Caen stone brought to rebuild Canterbury cathedral which had been destroyed by fire in 1174. 'He built ingenious machines to load and unload the ships and to raise the stones and the mortar.' But what were these machines? A crane with a treadmill was still a novelty; a given place would have only one. In the fourteenth century it was part of the equipment of certain ports and seemed marvellous enough to be shown in several pictures. Bruges had one of the earliest and one can still see restored examples today in Lüneburg and Gdansk. The earliest jack, known to us from a drawing of Villard de Honnecourt from the first half of the thirteenth century, was still a curiosity.

Before firearms, artillery itself was only a continuation of the Hellenistic artillery which had already been improved by the Romans. It was not the ballista or the catapult so much as the scorpion or onager, described by Ammianus Marcellinus in the fourth century, which was the ancestor of the trebuchets and mangonels of the middle ages. The trebuchet launched projectiles over high walls whereas the mangonel, which moreover could be better regulated, sent its ammunition less high but further. However, the principle remained that of the sling.

In fact, the word machine (as in the Late Empire where the *mechanici* were the military engineers) was in the medieval west almost exclusively applied to siege engines which were generally lacking in any technical ingenuity. One such was described by Suger in his *Life of Louis VI* when recounting the attack by the king on the castle of Gournay in 1107:

Without intermission, they used war-engines to demolish the castle: a tall machine, towering over the combatants with its three storeys, rose up, intended, by looking down on the castle, to prevent the archers and cross-bowmen of the first line of defence from moving around or from showing themselves within the wall. Then the besieged, ceaselessly pressed day and night by these engines, could no longer stand on their ramparts. They tried to place themselves prudently in the shelter afforded by holes dug below the surface, and by making their archers shoot unseen, they counted on the mortal danger run by those who were looking down on them from the highest battlements of the engine. To this machine, which rose up into the air, was attached a wooden bridge, which, by rising up high enough, was supposed, on being lowered slightly on to the wall, to effect an easy entry to the combatants who would walk down it. . . .

There remained the use of the watermill for small-scale or even large-scale industrial purposes. Here, and in the modern system of harnessing, are to be found the greatest technical advances of the middle ages.

III

The middle ages was a world of wood, in those days the universal material. Furthermore it was often poor quality wood: at any rate the pieces used were restricted in size and poorly worked. The large pieces from a single bole, or beams, which were used for the construction of buildings, ships' masts and wood roofs, were hard to cut and shape, and were expensive, if not luxury, materials. Suger, when he was looking for trees of a large enough diameter and tall enough for the roof of St Denis in the middle of the twelfth century thought it a miracle to find the wood he desired in the valley of Chevreuse. A similar miracle was attributed in the early fourteenth century to St Ivo. Wood itself was precious. A trunk of great height was something rare enough for a miracle to be necessary to avoid wasting one as a result of a mistake in cutting.

St Ivo, having remarked that the cathedral of Tréguier was threatening to fall down, went to find the powerful and magnificent lord of Rostrenen and made known the needs of the church to him. The lord . . . granted, among other things, all the wood necessary which could be found in the woods and forests. The saint sent woodcutters to cut and transport the finest and most desirable trees. The beams consecrated for this pious and sacred work were cut down and taken away . . . . When the skilful chief mason designated by the saint had taken the measurements of the church, he had the beams cut according to geometric rules in the proportions which seemed suitable to him. But he found that the boles had been cut too short. He lamented, tore his hair . . . went red with confusion, took a rope in his hands and went to find the saint, threw himself at his knees and in the midst of his cries, tears, and groans told him: 'What can I do? How shall I dare to appear before you again? How could I suffer such a dishonour and repair the immense damage which I have caused to the church of Tréguier? Here are my body, my neck and this rope. Punish me for having through my negligence lost and made useless the tree-trunks procured by your care by having them cut two feet too short.'

Of course the saint reassured him and miraculously lengthened the beams to the necessary size.

Wood (together with the produce of the earth) was a material so precious in the middle ages that it became the symbol of earthly goods. Among the souls who went to Purgatory the *Golden Legend* mentions those who when dying took with them 'wood, hay, and stalks', that is to say, those who, while still adoring God, remained attached to earthly goods. Although it was difficult to find it in the form of large tree-trunks, wood remained the most common product of the medieval west. The *Roman de Renart* tells us that the fox and his companions, always in search of material goods which they lacked, had more than enough of one single substance, wood. 'They lit a large fire, for logs were not lacking.' Indeed, wood provided the medieval west very early on with one of its principal exports, for it was in demand in the Muslim world, where, as we know, trees, except in the forests of Lebanon and the Maghreb, were rare, in contrast to the west. Wood was the greatest traveller in the medieval west, and like other travellers it travelled by water as much as possible whether on board ship or in rafts.

Another product exported to the east, from the Carolingian period, was iron in the form of swords. Frankish swords abound in the Muslim sources for the early middle ages. But this was a matter of a luxury product, a highly worked product, the result of the skill of barbarian smiths, who were, as we have seen, experts in metalworking techniques which had come by way of the steppes from Central Asia, the home of metals. Iron, unlike wood, was rare in the medieval west. We should not be astonished that in the early middle ages iron was rare enough for a monk of St Gall to record that the Lombard king Desiderius observing Charlemagne's army all clad in iron, from the top of the ramparts of Pavia in 773, cried out in terror and stupefaction '*O ferrum! heu ferrum!* – Oh iron, alas, iron!' Yet as late as the thirteenth century, the Franciscan Bartholomaeus Anglicus treated iron as a precious substance in his encyclopaedia *De proprietatibus rerum*:

From numerous points of view, iron is more useful to man than gold, although greedy creatures covet gold more than iron. Without iron, the people could not defend itself against its enemies, nor let the common law prevail: innocents ensure their defence thanks to iron [that is, the ordeal of hot iron] and the impudence of the wicked is punished thanks to iron. Equally all manual work demands the use of iron without which no-one could cultivate the ground or build a house.

Nothing better proves the value of iron in the middle ages than the attention paid to it by St Benedict, the master of the medieval material life as of the spiritual life. In his Rule he consecrated a whole chapter, the 27th, to the care which the monks must take of the *ferramenta*, the iron tools owned by the monastery. The abbot must only entrust them to monks 'in whose lives and whose hands he has complete trust'. To spoil or lose these instruments was a serious breach of the Rule and called down a severe punishment. The miracles of St Benedict haunted the minds of men in the middle ages after Gregory the Great had bequeathed them as a basic source of instruction, in a tradition which continued up to Jacopo da Voragine, and among them there was one which brings out the value of iron in the medieval world. The miracle is sometimes attributed to Solomon, which is not at all astonishing because he was considered in the middle ages to be the great master of technical and scientific secrets, and it had been worked in the Old Testament by Elisha (2 Samuel, 6.5-7). Let us read the story in the *Golden Legend*: 'One day a man was scything thorns near the monastery, when the blade of his scythe came off the handle and fell into a bottomless hole, which made the man very distressed. But St Benedict put the handle of the scythe into the hollow of a spring, and soon the blade, emerging from the rock, came up to the handle.'

In his chronicle of the first dukes of Normandy, written at the start of the eleventh century, Dudo of St Quentin records the value which these rulers attached to ploughs, and the exemplary punishments which they laid down for the theft of these instruments. In his *fabliau*, *Le vilain de Farbu*, the Arras poet Jehan Bodel recounts at the end of the twelfth century how a blacksmith had put a hot iron in front of his door as a trap for the unwary. A passing villein asked his son to seize it, for a piece of iron was a nice windfall. Moreover, the greatest part of the limited iron production in the middle ages was destined for armaments and military use. What remained for ploughshares, the blades of sickles and scythes, and the cutting edges of spades and other tools, was only a tiny proportion of a deficient output, even though it increased from the ninth century. However, in general, the findings of Carolingian inventories, which, after listing several iron tools, mentioned the bulk of the agricultural equipment en bloc under the rubric *Utensilia lignea ad ministrandum sufficienter* – 'Wooden tools in sufficient number for the work', held good for the middle ages. Again it must be noted that a large number of iron tools, or of partly iron tools, such as axes, hatchets, augers, and pruning-knives, were used for working on wood. Nor should it be forgotten finally that among these iron tools the largest part were instruments of restricted size and efficacity. The basic tool, not only of the medieval joiner or the carpenter, but even of the woodcutter, was that very ancient and simple tool, the axe – used in the great medieval land-clearances, which attacked brushwood and bushes rather than full-grown timber, against which tools were usually powerless.

So it was not at all astonishing that iron was, as we have seen, the object of attention which went so far as to make it an occasion for miracles. There was nothing astonishing if the blacksmith was from the early middle ages an extraordinary figure, almost a sorcerer. Doubtless he owed this aura above all to his work as a maker of weapons, as a swordsmith, and to a tradition which made of him, with the goldsmith, a sacred being bequeathed by barbarian Scandinavian and Germanic tradition to the medieval west. The sagas glorified the blacksmiths with their superior powers – Alberic, Mime, Siegfried himself, who forged Nothung, the sword without equal, and Völund who is shown at work in the saga of Thidrek:

The king said, 'The sword is good', and he wanted it for himself. Völund replied, 'It's not particularly good; it must be made better; I shall not stop before I have done so'. . . . Völund went back to his forge, took a file, cut the sword into very small shavings and mixed them with flour. Then he made some caged birds fast for three days and gave them this mixture to eat. He put the birds' excrement in the hearth of his forge, melted them down and made all the dross that the iron still contained come out, and he then forged a new sword; this was smaller than the first . . . . It could be held just as well in the hand. The first swords which Völund had made had been bigger than was normal. The king sought out Völund once more, gazed at the sword, and declared that it was the sharpest and the best that he had ever seen. They went down to the river; Völund took in his hand a tuft of wool three feet thick and the same length and threw it in the river; he kept the sword in the water without moving it; the ball of wool was carried against the cutting edge, and the sword sliced through the ball as smoothly as the current of the water itself. . . .

Might the evolution of the figure of Joseph, whom the early middle ages tended to see as a *faber ferrarius*, a blacksmith, and who then became the incarnation of the human condition in the wooden middle ages, a carpenter, manifest this medieval feeling about raw materials? Also, finally, perhaps one should again think here of a possible influence of an outlook linked to a form of religious symbolism on the evolution of skills. In the Jewish tradition wood was good and iron was wicked, wood was the word which brought life, and iron the flesh weighing one down. Iron must not be used alone; it must be joined to wood which took away its power to harm and made it serve a good purpose. Thus the plough was a symbol of Christ as the ploughman. Medieval tools were essentially made of wood and consequently were of limited strength and poor resistance.

Moreover the raw material which rivalled wood in the middle ages was not iron, which usually only provided a very small contribution (the cutting edges of tools, nails, horseshoes, braces and clamping to strengthen walls); it was stone. Wood and stone were the two basic raw materials in medieval technology. Indeed architects were simultaneously *carpentarii et lapidarii*, carpenters and masons, and building workers were often entitled *operarii lignorum et lapidum*, workers in wood and stone. For a long time stone was a luxury in relation to wood. From the eleventh century the great boom in building, a phenomenon which was essential in the development of the medieval economy, very often consisted of replacing a wooden construction with one in stone – whether churches, bridges, or houses. Stone, in relation to wood, was a noble material. To have a stone house was a sign of wealth and power. God and the Church and the lords in their castles were the first to have stone dwellings. Then, having a stone house soon became a sign of the rise of the richest burgesses. Urban chronicles are careful to mention this manifestation of city progress and of the ruling class in the towns. Suetonius' words about Augustus boasting of having found Rome made of brick and having left it made of marble were quoted by many chroniclers in the middle ages, who applied it to the great building abbots of the eleventh and twelfth centuries, though brick and marble here were replaced by wood and stone. In the middle ages, to find a church in wood and leave it in stone was progress, honour, and an achievement. And we know that one of the great forms of technical progress in the middle ages was to rediscover how to vault in stone and to invent new systems of vaulting. For some eleventh-century buildings now in ruin the problem always arises of knowing whether the builders had advanced beyond roofing in wood to vaulting in stone; thus the abbey of Jumièges, for example, still remains a riddle in this respect for historians of craft and art. Even in buildings built and vaulted in stone the proportion of the building made of wood, above all the roofbeams, remained considerable, hence their vulnerability to fire. A fire that began in the roof destroyed Canterbury cathedral in 1174; the monk Gervase records how the fire after having smouldered under the roof-tree, suddenly burst out: *Vae, vae, ecclesia ardet* – 'Woe, woe, the church is burning', the lead sheets on the roof melted, the beams turned to cinders, fell into the choir and set fire to the stalls. 'The flames, fed by all this mass of wood, rose up to fifteen ells and demolished the walls and above all the pillars of the church'. Scholars have drawn up a long list of medieval churches that burned down because of their wooden roofs. Jules Quicherat noted in northern France alone the cathedrals of Bayeux, Le Mans, Chartres, and Cambrai, and the abbey churches of Mont St Michel, St Martin of Tours, St Vaast of Arras, and St Riquier of Corbie.

Time, which idealizes everything, idealizes the material past only by letting the durable parts survive and by wiping out the perishable parts that were almost everything. To us the middle ages is a glorious collection of stones: cathedrals and castles. Yet these stones represent only the tiniest part of what once existed. They are a few bones remaining of a body of wood and materials even humbler and more perishable, such as straw, mud, and cob. Nothing better shows the fundamental belief of the middle ages in the separation of the soul from the body and the survival of the soul alone. What the age has left to us, once its body had crumbled into dust, is its soul incarnated in durable stone. Yet we should not be deceived by this illusion produced by time.

IV

The most serious aspect of this inferior technical equipment is to be found in the agricultural sector. Land and the agrarian economy were effectively the basis and the essence of material culture in the middle ages and of everything conditioned by it; wealth, social and political power. However, land in the middle ages was barren because men were incapable of getting much out of it.

First, this was because the implements were rudimentary. Second, the earth was not well worked. Third, ploughing did not go deep; the ancient swingplough, which in any case was and remained suited to the shallow soils and hilly landscapes of the Mediterranean area, persisted for a long time in many places. Its symmetrical share, sometimes tipped with iron but often made of wood which had merely been hardened in the fire, scratched the soil rather than cut through it. The wheeled plough with an asymmetrical share and a mouldboard with a movable wheeled front pulled by a stronger team, which became widespread in the course of the middle ages, represented a definite, considerable advance. It is still true that the heavy clay soils, the most fertile when properly worked, put up a stiff resistance to medieval farm implements. Deeper ploughing in the middle ages was more a result of repeating the work than of improving the equipment. The practice of ploughing three times became widespread; at the turn of the thirteenth and fourteenth centuries four ploughings were common. Yet additional work remained necessary, even though of limited use. After the first ploughing the clods were often broken up by hand, as we see in a miniature in the Luttrell Psalter of the start of the fourteenth century, where we can see that weeding, which was not done everywhere, used rudimentary tools, such as forks and sickles mounted on rods, to cut thistles and other weeds. The harrow, one of the first pictures of which appears in the late eleventh-century Bayeux Tapestry, became common in the twelfth and thirteenth centuries. Every now and then it was still necessary to dig the field up deeply with a spade. The earth, badly dug into, badly turned over, badly aerated, did not reconstitute itself quickly in fertilizing substances. This lack of equipment might have been remedied to some extent by improving the soil with manure. However, the weakness of medieval agriculture in this area was even more flagrant.

Artificial chemical fertilizers, of course, did not exist. And natural fertilizers, although available, were very limited. The main reason for this was the limited number of animals. There were secondary causes for this such as the ravages caused by disease, but the main cause was that pasture took second place after the ploughed fields, cereal growing, and what was required to grow plants for food. Meat was partly furnished by game. In any case people were happier to rear animals that lived in the forest, such as pigs and goats whose dung was mostly lost. Dung from other animals was carefully gathered, as far as was possible, given that the flocks, which were allowed to wander, fed mostly in the open air and were rarely shut up in the byre. Droppings from dovecots were used carefully. A 'pot of dung' was a heavy due sometimes owed by the tenant to the lord. On the other hand, some privileged seigneurial agents, such as the prebendaries who managed certain estates, for example Münchweiler in Germany in the twelfth century, received as a salary 'the dung of one cow and the sweepings of the house' for using on the land which they held.

Apart from clay soil used in marling, vegetable compost provided a large proportion of the fertilizer available. There were rotting grass and leaves, and stubble which the animals had not eaten after the harvest. For, as one can see in many miniatures and carvings, when people cut corn with the sickle they did it near the ear and in any case halfway up the stalk, so as to leave the greatest possible quantity of straw first to feed the animals and second for fertilizer. Fertilizer was often reserved for delicate or speculative cultivation, for orchards, vineyards, and gardens. There was a striking contrast in the medieval west between the small pockets of land devoted to gardening which monopolized most of what agricultural refinement there was, and the large areas abandoned to rudimentary techniques.

The result of inferior equipment and the lack of fertilizer was chiefly that farming, instead of being intensive, was to a large extent extensive. Even outside the period of the eleventh to the thirteenth century, when population growth had brought with it an increase in the surface area under cultivation by means of land clearances, medieval farming was notably shifting. For example, in 1116 the inhabitants of a village in the Ile de France received permission to clear certain parts of a royal forest but on condition 'that they cultivate them and receive the fruits for two harvests only, since they would then go into other parts of the forest'. Slash and burn or the cultivation of burnt patches, which implies a certain agricultural nomadism, was very common on poor soils. Clearances themselves were often pieces of land temporarily taken into cultivation, on *assarts* which are so common in medieval place names and which occur so often in literature when the countryside is the background: 'Renart came along into an assart. . . . '

The consequence of this was that the land was both badly worked and poorly enriched. Thus it was often necessary to let it rest and reconstitute itself. Letting land lie fallow was extensively practised. One advance, probably made between the ninth and the fourteenth century, consisted in replacing, here and there, biennial crop-rotation with triennial rotation which succeeded in only leaving land infertile one year out of three rather than one year out of two, or rather in using two-thirds of the cultivable surface area instead of only half. However, triennial rotation seems to have spread more slowly and less commonly than has been claimed. In the Mediterranean area and on poor soils biennial rotation persisted. The author of one thirteenth-century English agricultural treatise prudently urges his readers to prefer one single good harvest every two years to two poor ones every three. In Lincolnshire there is no definite example of triennial crop rotation before the fourteenth century. In Forez, at the end of the thirteenth century, the lands produced harvests only three times in 30 years.

We may add that other factors which one can come across contributed to the restricted productivity of the land in the middle ages. For example there was the tendency of medieval manors to autarky, which was a consequence of economic realities and of habits of thinking simultaneously. To have recourse to the outside world and not to produce all that one needed was not only a weakness, it was a dishonour. In the case of monastic properties, to avoid all contact with the outside world flowed directly from the spiritual ideal of solitude, and economic isolation was a condition for spiritual purity. Even the moderate Rule of St Benedict recommends it: 'The monastery should, if possible, be so arranged that all necessary things, such as water, mill, garden, and various crafts may be within the enclosure, so that the monks may not be compelled to wander outside it, for that is not at all expedient for their souls' (McCann, 1976, p. 74).

When the Cistercians built mills for themselves, St Bernard threatened to order their destruction because they formed centres for human relations, contacts, meetings and, worse still, prostitution. Yet these moral prejudices had a material basis. In a world where transport was expensive and hazardous, and the monetary economy, which was necessary for exchanges, little developed, producing everything which one needed was a sound economic calculation. As a consequence, the medieval rural economy was dominated by the practice of growing many different crops, which meant that conditions of production, whether to do with geography, soil, or climate, were abused as much as possible. For example, the vine was grown in the most unfavourable climates, far to the north of its modern limit of cultivation. Vines were sometimes grown in England, the Parisian region possessed a large vineyard, and Laon could have qualified as a 'wine capital' in the middle ages. Bad land was put under cultivation, and crops were grown on unsuitable soils.

The result of all this was the weakness of agricultural yields. In the Carolingian period it seems likely that renders had been close to 2-2.7-fold on the royal estate at Annapes (France, *département* Nord) at the start of the ninth century, sometimes barely rising above 1, that is to say producing purely and simply what had been sown. A notable advance was achieved between the ninth and the fourteenth century, but production was still low. According to the English agronomists of the thirteenth century the normal levels were eightfold for barley, seven for rye, six for leguminous plants, five for wheat, and four for oats. The reality seems to have been less rosy. On the good lands of the episcopal estates of Winchester the levels were 3.8 for wheat and barley, and 2.4 for oats. The proportion of 3 or 4 to 1 seems to have been the norm for wheat.

Again, the variability of the production was considerable, particularly between different kinds of soil. In the mountains the level remained not much changed from the Carolingian period, 2:1; In Provence it rose to 3 or 4:1; on certain alluvial plains, in Artois for example, it could rise to above 10 and go as high as 18, that is to say that it could approach modern production from poor land. Yields also varied from year to year, which was all the more serious in that the variations could be considerable. At Roquetoire in Artois wheat yield was 7.5 in 1319 and 11.6 in 1321. Finally, on a single estate, the yield could differ greatly from one commodity to another. On one manor of the abbey of Ramsey the barley yield oscillated between 6 and 11 while that for oats barely exceeded what was sown.

V

Although there was a notable advance in the development of sources of energy with the diffusion of mills (especially watermills and various applications of water-power such as fulling-mills, hemp-mills, tanning-mills, beer-mills, and grinding-mills) it must be noted that the chronology of the appearance and diffusion of these machines must urge us to be cautious. As far as fulling-mills are concerned, for example, the thirteenth century saw a decline in their use in France, and in England, where they have been seen as the instrument of a veritable 'industrial revolution' they only underwent a real growth at the end of the thirteenth century. In Italy they did not spread rapidly throughout. Florence sent its cloth to Prato to be fulled in the thirteenth and fourteenth centuries. In Germany the first mention of a fulling-mill only dates from 1223, at Speyer, and they seem to have been rare in the thirteenth century. The mills which were most important for industrial development only appear at the end of our period; the forge-mill was a rarity before the thirteenth century. The one recorded at Cardadeu in Catalonia is not definite, although the growth of the so-called Catalan forges in the second half of the twelfth century is perhaps linked with the diffusion of the forge-mill. The first definite mention of the latter dates from 1197 for the monastery of Soroë in Sweden. Papermills, attested from 1238 at Jativa in Spain, did not spread in Italy before the late thirteenth century (Fabriano in 1268). The first French papermill, at Troyes, dates from 1338; the first German one, at Nuremberg, was in 1390. The hydraulic saw was still a curiosity when Villard de Honnecourt drew one in his album in about 1240. The watermill was still chiefly used to grind grain. From Domesday Book, written in 1086, we can see that as early as the end of the eleventh century there were more than 6000 in England.

In spite of the advances made in the application of water and air power, energy in the medieval west still came mainly from men and animals. Here too important advances were made. The most spectacular and the one with the most consequences was probably what Commander Lefebvre des Noëttes and M. Haudricourt called 'the modern harness'. This is a group of technical advances which allowed men around the year 1000 to make better use of animal traction and to increase the work-output of the beasts. Most importantly, these innovations allowed people to use the horse as a draught and plough animal, as it was quicker than the ox and this meant that tasks such as ploughing and harrowing could be done faster and more frequently. Ancient harnessing (throat and girth) which made the chest carry the traction compressed the chest, making breathing hard for the animal and tiring it rapidly. Modern harness essentially meant that weight of the traction was carried on the shoulders. In addition to shoulder-collars horseshoes with nails were introduced which helped the animal to move faster and protected its feet. Finally, animals were now harnessed in line, which made it possible to haul heavy loads, and was very important for the building of large religious and secular buildings. The first certain picture which we have of the shoulder-collar (the decisive element in modern harnessing) is to be found in a manuscript in the Stadtbibliothek in Trier dating from about 800, but the new system only became widespread in the eleventh and twelfth centuries.

Again, we must chiefly bear in mind that the size and strength of medieval work-animals were quite inferior to those of modern animals. The plough-horse was generally of a smaller breed than the war-horse, the heavy charger which had to carry, if not a caparison, at any rate a heavily armed rider whose weight could play an important role in the charge. Here we can once more observe the primacy of the military and the warrior over the economic and the producer. The retreat of the ox before the horse was not general. The advantages of the horse were such that already in 1095 Urban II in proclaiming the Peace of God in advance of the First Crusade placed horses used for ploughing and harrowing under divine protection: *equi arantes, equi de quibus hercant*; the superiority of the horse was recognized from the twelfth century by the Slavs to such an extent that according to the Chronicle of Helmold the plough unit was what one pair of oxen or one horse could achieve in a day, and that in Poland in the same period a plough-horse was worth two oxen. Furthermore modern farming experts have calculated that the medieval ox, taking the fact that its output was lower, cost 30 per cent more per working day than the horse. Yet it was still the case that many peasants or lords were put off by two disadvantages of the horse: its high nominal price, and the difficulties of having to feed it on oats. Walter of Henley in his *Treatise of Housebondrie* in the thirteenth century recommends people to use not the horse but the ox whose fodder was less expensive and which in addition to its labour provided meat. In England, after a period at the end of the twelfth century when the horse made definite progress, especially in East Anglia and the East Midlands, its advance seems to have been halted in the thirteenth century probably due to the return to direct land management and peasant labour-services. In Normandy, ploughing with horses seems to have been habitual in the thirteenth century, as evidenced by an item in the visitation register of Eudes Rigaud of 1260 when he had some horses seized which he saw working on St Mathias' Day, and this must have also been the case on the lands of the lords of Audenarde because only horses appear in the illustrations to the *Vieil Rentier* of around 1275. Yet not only did the ox remain master of the field in the South of France and in Mediterranean regions where oats were difficult to cultivate, but one still finds plough-oxen in Burgundy in the middle of the thirteenth century and in Brie in 1274. If we want to know how much a horse cost a peasant (even in a favoured region, Artois around 1200) we should read Jehan Bodel's *fabliau, Les deux chevaux*, in which the horse which is good *'en charrue et en erce'* – harnessed to the plough and the harrow – is contrasted with the *'maigre roncin'* or skinny nag.

In addition to the horse and the ox, it should not be forgotten that in the medieval west, even outside the Mediterranean zone, the donkey played a considerable part in agricultural work. A document from Orléans lists work-animals 'whether ox, horse, or ass'. The text from the Brie area of 1274, mentioned above, demands that peasants forced to plough as a labour-service should use oxen, horses, and asses. In fact, the humble and normal reality of medieval work-animals meant, as at the Nativity, the presence of ox and ass.

Even more, human energy remained fundamental. In the countryside or in the workshops, and even on board ship, where sails were only a poor addition to the power of the oar, that is to say human power, human manual work remained the principal source of energy. Again, the productivity of these human sources of energy, or 'biological converters' to quote Carlo Cipolla, was limited, for, as we shall see, the producing class coincided almost exactly with that portion of society which was badly fed, if not undernourished. 'Biological converters' (plants and animals together) provided, according to K. M. Mather and Carlo Cipolla, at least 80 per cent of the energy in the medieval preindustrial society, but the disposable energy which could come from them was limited: about 10,000 calories per day per person (100,000 in a modern industrial society). We should not be surprised if human capital was precious to medieval lords, to the point where some of them, for example in England, imposed a special tax on young unmarried peasants. The Church, in spite of its tradition of exalting virginity, increasingly put the accent on the text 'Grow and multiply', a slogan which was chiefly a response to the technological limitations of the medieval world. There was a similar handicap in the area of transportation. Certainly portage services, a remnant of antique slavery, became less and less numerous and seem to have disappeared after the twelfth century. Yet as late as the eleventh century the monks of St Vanne exacted from their serfs living at Laumesfeld in Lorraine 'the obligation of carrying corn for six miles on their shoulders', or rather on the napes of their necks, as the Latin text says: '*cum collo*'.

The portage labours demanded as a penance or pious work for the building of cathedrals from the different classes of society had not only a psychological and spiritual character but also a technical and economic significance. In Normandy the year 1145 saw an explosion of this particular form of devotion. Among numerous references, that of Robert of Torigny, talking about the building of Chartres Cathedral, is famous:

That year men began – firstly at Chartres – to draw on their shoulders waggons loaded with stones, wood, food and other products for the fabric of the church, the towers of which were then being built . . . . But this phenomenon did not only happen there, but also in practically all of the Ile de France and Normandy and in many other places. . . .'

In the same year the abbot Haimo described a similar spectacle at St-Pierre-sur-Dives in Normandy:

Kings, princes, men powerful in the world, loaded with honours and riches, men and women of noble birth bent their proud and swollen necks to harness themselves to the waggons and draw them with their loads of wine, wheat, oil, lime, stones, wood and other products necessary to sustain life or for building churches right up to the refuge of Christ, in the manner of animals.

We find the same things said in the chronicle of Mont St Michel and the chronicle of Rouen and elsewhere. Perhaps the campaign of human portage of this year 1145 had been exceptional in its scale and through the fact that all classes of society participated. 'Who has not seen these scenes, will never see any like them,' wrote Robert de Torigny. Yet scenes on a more limited scale but with equally spectacular participants were repeated under Louis IX in the thirteenth century, whether in the Holy Land or at the abbey of Royaumont, where the king and his brothers (whether the latter liked it or not) carried the raw materials.

It is still true that human portage remained an essential form of transport. Roads were in a poor state, there was a limited number of carts and waggons, which were expensive, and useful vehicles were absent. The wheelbarrow, for example, probably first appeared on building sites in the thirteenth century, but it only became widespread at the end of the fourteenth century and seems to have been of limited manoeuvrability. Human labour, therefore, remained in first place. Miniatures show us men bent double under nets, baskets, and hods. Animals were important too: in addition to the draught animals which one sometimes sees honoured after their toils like the stone oxen on the towers of Laon Cathedral, pack animals played an important role in medieval transport. Not only were the mule and the ass irreplaceable for crossing mountains in Mediterranean lands, but using pack-animals was common far beyond those regions whose hilly terrain made it essential. In contracts drawn up in 1296 at the Fairs of Champagne between Italian merchants buying broadcloth and linen and their carriers, we see the latter engage to 'take the merchandise with their beasts to Nîmes in a 22-day period without a cart', and again there is a reference to 'ten bales of French broadcloth which he (the carrier) has promised to bring and to carry to Savona by the direct roads of my lord the king of France and my lord King Charles and by the Riviera of Genoa and to perform the stage each day without a cart, over a period of 35 days. . . . ' The vocabulary of weights and measures teaches us the importance of pack animals and human porters: for salt, for example, the basic measurement was the load that could be carried by a pack-animal.

VI

Sea transports, again in spite of considerable technical improvements, remained insufficient, whether because these improvements had not yet had their full effect before the fourteenth century or later, or because their scope remained limited. To start with, the tonnage of the fleets of medieval western Europe was small. Individual ships were also small, even though there was an increase in tonnage in the twelfth and thirteenth centuries, especially in the north where the ships had to transport bulky products such as grain and timber. Here the Hanseatic *kogge* or cog appeared, whereas in the Mediterranean galley-ships (*galee da mercato*) of larger dimensions were built at Venice. Is it possible to give figures? Capacities of more than 200 tons seem to have been exceptional. There were few ships in total. The number of 'great ships' was very limited. At the start of the fourteenth century, the convoys which Venice (the first maritime power of the age) commissioned to sail to England and Flanders, about one or two a year, consisted of two or three galleys. The total number of *galee da mercato* in service on the three principal commercial routes in the 1420s was about 25: in 1328, for example, eight sailed for Outremer, that is to say Cyprus and Armenia, four for Flanders, and ten for Romania, that is to say the Byzantine Empire and the Black Sea. In August 1315, when the Great Council, having received alarming news, ordered its ships in the Mediterranean to form themselves into a convoy, it made an exception for the large ships which were too slow to be suited to sail in convoy: there were nine of them. Moreover, the size of these ships was limited by law, for they had to be able to be converted for military purposes and not be handicapped by being too big and too slow. Frederic C. Lane calculated that in 1335 the 26 ships of an average tonnage of 150 tons which made up the Venetian convoys represented 3900 tons in all, and if one applies a multiplier of 10 to this figure, which would more or less be valid for the sixteenth century, the total tonnage of the Venetian fleet would go up to about 40,000.

The progressive introduction of the stern-post rudder in the course of the thirteenth century, which made ships easier to steer, was probably of less importance than has been thought. As for the use of the compass, which resulted in more exact mapmaking and allowed navigation during the winter, it only became common after 1280. Finally, the middle ages had no knowledge of the quadrant and the nautical astrolabe, instruments which were introduced in the Renaissance.

VII

Then, too, there were deficiencies in mining. Engines for digging and lifting were poor and this, together with the fact that it was technically impossible to evacuate water, limited extraction to surface or fairly shallow veins. Iron mining did, it is true, make some progress from the twelfth century. Copper was mined, and so was lead, which is well-documented in a mining code of the early thirteenth century for the region of Massa Marittima in Italy. Coal was possibly known in England as early as the ninth century, and was definitely mentioned in Forez in 1095, though it only began to be really exploited in the thirteenth century. For salt there were wells and mines such as those of Halle in Germany and Wielicka or Bochnia in Poland, which do not seem to have been exploited before the thirteenth century. We know nothing about the extraction of tin, which was chiefly produced in Cornwall. Mines for gold and silver soon showed themselves to be incapable of supplying the demand of an increasingly monetary economy, and their failure to meet this demand, in spite of intensified exploitation (notably in central Europe, for example at Kutna Hora in Bohemia), brought about the monetary famine of the end of the middle ages which only ended with the influx of American metals in the sixteenth century. All these minerals were produced in insufficient quantity, and, in most cases, treated with rudimentary equipment and techniques. Blast furnaces (the bellows were operated by hydraulic power) appear at the end of the thirteenth century in Styria, and in the Liège area around 1340. The blast furnaces of the end of the middle ages did not, however, immediately revolutionize metal-working. As we know, it was not until the seventeenth century that decisive progress was made, through the use of coke in iron-working and steam-power for underground pumping, and these practices did not become widespread until the eighteenth century.

Finally, the most important technical advances in the 'industrial' field concern particular or peripheral sectors only, and again their diffusion only took place at the end of the middle ages. Of course the most spectacular was the arrival of gunpowder and firearms. But their military effectiveness was slow to assert itself. During the fourteenth century and even afterwards, the earliest cannons spread terror among the enemy more through their noise than their ability to kill. Their importance above all stemmed from the fact that from the fifteenth century the development of artillery encouraged a boom in the metal industry.

Oil-painting, known from the twelfth century, only made decisive progress at the end of the fourteenth century and the beginning of the fifteenth. According to tradition its use was strengthened by the Van Eyck brothers and Antonello da Messina, but it did not revolutionize painting so strikingly as did the discovery of perspective. Glass, known since antiquity, reappeared as an industry in the thirteenth century, especially in Venice, and took on the form of a manufacturing industry in Italy in the sixteenth century; at the same time, paper use triumphed with printing. Glass, in the middle ages, was essentially leaded window glass, and Theophilus' treatise at the start of the twelfth century, *De diversis artibus*, 'the first technical treatise of the middle ages', shows how it was in the process of rising in Christian Europe; but the treatise clearly reveals the limits of medieval technology. For a start it was essentially a technology in the service of God. The processes described by Theophilus are those used in monastic workshops and they were above all destined for building and adorning churches. The first book is devoted to the preparation of colours, both for illuminating manuscripts and, secondarily, for frescos; the second book is about stained glass; and the third is about metal-working, especially goldsmithery. Furthermore, it was a technology for luxury products, just as in the textile industry, where the basic garments were made in the home, and luxury fabrics were made in workshops. Finally, it was a technology of artist-craftsmen, who applied traditional formulas to the production of individual pieces with rudimentary tools. Technicians and inventors in the middle ages were in fact craftsmen. This is equally true of the men whom some people have preferred to see as an intellectual elite with a mastery of subtle skills: the Italian and Hanseatic merchants sometimes described as possessing an 'intellectual supremacy'. But for a long time the principal task of the merchant was to move around, which required no special qualifications, and be merely yet another of those wanderers on the medieval roads. In England he was called the 'piepowder' or *pied poudreux* (dusty-foot), covered with the dust of the roads. He appears in literature, for example, in the *fabliau* of Jehan Bodel, *Le souhait fou*, from the late twelfth century, as a man who stays away from his home for months 'to seek his merchandise' and who returns 'gay and joyous' after having remained for a long time 'outside the country' – far from his home. Sometimes this itinerant, if he were rich enough, would manage to carry out a large part of his business at the Fairs of Champagne, but if an 'intellectual' intervened in this business – and then only in southern Europe – it was the notary who drew up contracts for him. Usually these were very simple contracts, whose principal merit was to serve as a testimony, on the model of feudal charters. Even the Church, which forced the merchant to employ a certain complexity and subtlety in his dealings by condemning all credit-operations under the name of usury, did not manage to make the merchant's techniques progress in a decisive fashion. In any case the two instruments which marked a definite progress in commercial practices, although only of a limited technical level, the letter of change and double entry book-keeping, only became widespread from the fourteenth century. Commercial and financial techniques were more rudimentary than many other medieval skills. Exchange, the most important, was limited to the exchange of coins.

Perhaps only one technician, the architect, attained a higher level. Certainly, his field was the only one in the middle ages with an undeniably industrial aspect. In fact it was only in the Gothic period, and even then not throughout the whole of Christian Europe, that the art of building became a science and the architect a scientist. This learned architect, who indeed called himself 'master', even 'master in stones' (*magister lapidum*), just as other men were masters of arts or masters of canon law, and who calculated according to rules, set himself up against the architect-craftsman or mason who applied traditional formulas. The two types of constructors continued to coexist and to confront each other, as we know, up to the end of the middle ages. It was on the building site of Milan Cathedral, at the turn of the fourteenth and fifteenth centuries, that the revealing debate occurred between, on the one hand, the French architect, in whose eyes there was no 'skill without science' (*Ars sine scientia nihil est*), and, on the other, the Lombard masons for whom science was only skill (*Scientia sine arte nihil est*).

Medieval craftsmen displayed artistic genius, skill, and daring (the cathedrals are there to prove it, and not only them – Joinville marvelled at the covered markets of Saumur, 'constructed on the model of a cloister in a Cistercian monastery'), but do we need to be reminded that the buildings put up in the middle ages were generally technically of poor quality, contrary to what is too often believed? The middle ages had constantly to repair, replace, and reconstruct. Church bells were always having to be refounded. Buildings, especially churches, often fell down. The collapse of the choir of Beauvais

Cathedral in 1284 (it was the tallest in medieval Europe) was doubly symbolic. It signalled a halt to the rise of Gothic architecture, but even more it showed the fate that was common to many a medieval building. Indeed, estimates of the repairs to be carried out on churches, notably cathedrals, became one of the principal resources of architects at the end of the thirteenth century, and most of the masterpieces of medieval architecture owe the fact that they are still standing to the repairs and restoration work carried on them through subsequent ages.

The middle ages invented little and did not even greatly enlarge the number of plants grown for food – rye, the most important food source introduced in the middle ages, which has almost disappeared from western Europe, was only a transitory addition to the agricultural repertoire. Yet even so the period marked a stage in the conquest of nature by human skills. Of course its most important development, the mill (or rather, but this is the essential point, its diffusion) could not escape whims of nature such as a lull in the wind, the drying up of watercourses in the south or the freezing up of water in the north. But, as Marc Bloch put it:

Mills driven by water or by wind; mills for corn-grinding, for tanning, for fulling; hydraulic sawmills, blacksmith's drop-hammers; shoulder-collars; the shoeing of draught-animals, harnessing in line; even the invention of the spinning-wheel: all these represent progressive steps towards a more effective use of natural forces, animate or inanimate, and hence led to economies in human labour, or – what comes to much the same thing – a more productive return. Why was this? Perhaps because there were fewer men available, but most of all because the master had fewer slaves. (Bloch, 1967, pp. 181-2)

Even though the middle ages did not count technical progress as a virtue, some people then became aware of this link between human progress and technical progress. Some deplored it, for example Guiot de Provins in the early thirteenth century, who regretted that in his time, even in the field of warfare, the 'artists' had to yield place to the 'technicians', the 'knights' to the 'cross-bowmen, sappers, operators of stone-throwing machines and engineers'. Others, on the contrary, rejoiced, particularly a monk of Clairvaux who intoned a veritable hymn to the liberating powers of mechanism. We might remember that this progress had already been celebrated in the classical period, in an epigram from the Palatine Anthology, on the appearance of the earliest mills. 'Cease from grinding, ye women who toil at the mill; sleep late, even if the crowing cocks announce the dawn. For Demeter has ordered the Nymphs to perform the work of your hands' (Paton, 1906-8, iii, p. 233). Already in the fifth century the abbot of Loches was rejoicing in the fact that a mill belonging to the abbey allowed 'one single brother to accomplish the work of several' and brought relief to the monastic community. Yet our monk of Clairvaux enthused within a context of industrial applications and of the noise of machines which truly make his text into one of the earliest hymns to the glory of mechanism:

A branch of the Aube, running across the numerous workshops of the abbey, everywhere makes itself blessed by the services which it renders. The Aube is raised up here through a great labour, and if it does not arrive absolutely complete, at least it does not remain idle. A riverbed whose curves divide the valley floor in two has been dug not by nature but by the industry of the monks. By this route the Aube transmits half of itself to the abbey, as if to greet the monks and to excuse itself for not coming in its entirety, since it has not been able to find a channel large enough to contain it. When sometimes the river is in spate and pushes too much water beyond its normal limits, it is repulsed by a wall which is built against it, and under which it is forced to flow. Then it turns back in its tracks, and the water which was following its old course welcomes the water which flows back in its embrace. However, the river which is admitted into the abbey to the extent that the wall, acting as a porter, permits, throws itself first impetuously into the mill, where it is very busy and takes plenty of exercise, as much to grind the wheat under the weight of the mills as to shake the fine sieve which separates the flour from the bran. Behold it already in the next-door building. It fills the cauldron and gives itself up to the fire which cooks it to prepare drink for the monks, if, by chance, the vine has given the vine-grower's industry the evil answer of sterility, and if, the blood of the grapes being absent, it has been necessary to compensate for it with the daughter of the corn-ear. Yet the river does not consider itself to be discharged. The fullers, set up near the mill, call the river to them. In the mill it is busy preparing the brothers' food; it is therefore justifiable to demand that now it should think of their clothes. It does not contradict, and refuses to do nothing that is ordered of it. It raises and drops alternately those heavy pestles or mallets, or, to put it better those wooden feet (for this noun more exactly expresses the hopping work of the fullers), and spares the fullers a great labour. Merciful God! What consolations you grant to your poor servants to prevent too great a sadness from overcoming them! How much you relieve the difficulties of your children who do penance, and how you take the extra burden of work away from them! How many horses would be exhausted, how many men would tire their arms in the labours which, without any work on our part, are done for us by this gracious river to which we owe our clothes and our food! It combines its efforts with our own, and after it has borne the heat and burden of the day, it expects only one reward for its work: this is permission to go away free after having carefully performed all that it has been ordered to do. When it makes so many swift wheels turn so quickly and giddily, it comes out foaming; it looks as though it has ground itself and has become softer. . . . Coming forth from there it goes into the tannery where, to prepare the materials necessary for the monks' shoes, it shows as much activity as care. Then it splits itself up into a crowd of little branches, and goes on its ever-obliging course to visit the different departments, seeking diligently everywhere those which need its ministry for whatever purpose it might be, whether it is a question of cooking, filtering, rotating, crushing, spraying, washing or milling, offering its assistance and never refusing it once . . . !

VIII

The aim of the medieval economy was human subsistence. It did not go further than this. If it seems to have gone beyond satisfying this pure and simple need, this is because subsistence is of course a socioeconomic notion, not a purely material one. Subsistence varies according to social classes. For the masses subsistence in the strict sense of the word, that is to say what they needed for their physical support, sufficed: food first and foremost, and then clothing and shelter. Thus the medieval economy was essentially agricultural and based on the land which provided necessities; so much so that the demand for subsistence lay at the basis of the medieval economy and, in the early middle ages, when it was coming into being, there was an attempt to establish each peasant family (the socioeconomic unit) on a uniform portion of land, that which could support a normal family: the *mansus*, or, as Bede put it, the *terra unius familiae*. For the upper classes, subsistence included the satisfaction of larger needs; it had to allow them to maintain their rank and not lose standing. Their subsistence was provided to a small extent by imports from abroad and the rest by the work of the masses.

The aim of work was not economic progress, whether individual or collective. It had religious and moral ends such as avoiding idleness, which left the door open for the devil, doing penance through toil, or humiliating the body, and its economic aims were ensuring one's own subsistence and that of the poor who were unable to procure their own property. Thomas Aquinas restated this in his *Summa theologica*: 'Work has four aims. First and foremost it must provide necessities of life, secondly it must chase away idleness which is the source of many evils, thirdly it must restrain concupiscence by mortifying the body, fourthly it allows one to give alms. . . . '

The economic aim of the middle ages was providing what was necessary, *necessitas*. Necessity legitimized work and even brought with it exemptions from certain religious rules. Work on Sundays, normally forbidden, was allowed in case of *necessitas*; the priest, to whom numerous occupations were prohibited, was sometimes authorized to work for his living, and men who stole out of necessity were even 'excused' by certain canonists. Raymond de Peñaforte wrote in his *Summa* in the 1230s: 'If someone steals food, drink, or clothing because of the necessity of hunger, thirst, or cold, does he really commit a theft? He does not commit a theft or a sin if he acts out of necessity.' But trying to procure for oneself more than what was necessary *was* a sin; it was the economic form (one of the most serious forms) of *superbia* or pride. The economic ideal laid down in the Carolingian period by Theodulf, who was careful to remind all workers of the spiritual goals of economic activity such as tithes and alms, remained valid for the central middle ages. It was necessary to remind those who give themselves up to business and merchandise that they ought not to desire earthly profits more than eternal life. . . . Just as those who undertake work in the fields and other tasks to acquire food, clothing and other necessities must give tithes and alms, so those who engage in commerce to supply their needs must do the same. God has in fact given each man an occupation so that he may live by it, and each must also draw from his occupation, which provides him with what is necessary for his body, a support for his soul, which is even more necessary.

All economic calculation which went beyond providing necessities was severely condemned. Of course landlords tried to get to know, to foresee, and to improve the production-levels of their lands. This was particularly true of ecclesiastical landlords, notably abbeys which had a better educated personnel at their disposal. As early as the Carolingian period, this interest in the economy is shown in capitularies, polyptychs, and imperial or ecclesiastical inventories, the most famous of which is the polyptych which Irminon, abbot of St-Germain-des-Prés, had drawn up in the early eleventh century. Whereas Suger's treatises on the management of his abbey of St Denis in the middle of the twelfth century betray the constantly empirical character of his administration, from the end of the twelfth century the administration of the great estates, especially ecclesiastical ones, was taken in hand by specialists. On the manors of the most important English abbeys the villein in charge of the management, the reeve, had to provide accounts for the clerks who came to record them at Michaelmas before submitting them to be verified by auditors. Yet this still meant continuing to produce what was necessary, by better administration and calculation in the face of an advancing crisis. In addition, people were coming to terms with the progress made by the monetary economy. Distrust of calculation continued to reign for a long time, and we know that it was not until the fourteenth century that a true care for quantification emerged, for example in the statistics, as yet rather inexact, made by Giovanni Villani for the Florentine economy. Again, this attention to numbers was, when all is said and done, born out of the crisis that was affecting the towns and obliging them to keep reckonings, rather than out of a desire for calculated economic growth. Well into the thirteenth century, the famous Italian collection of narratives, the *Novellino*, bore witness to this hostile state of mind to recording figures, to numbers.

King David, being king by the grace of God, who had turned him from a guardian of the flocks to a lord, was one day anxious to know, all things considered, what was the number of his subjects. And this was an act of presumption, and thus he much displeased God who sent his angel to him and caused him to speak thus: 'David, you have sinned. This is what your Lord has sent to say to you: Do you wish to stay three years in hell, or three months in the hands of your enemies, or do you rather wish to place yourself in the hands of your Lord for judgement?' David replied, 'I wish to place myself in the hands of my Lord: let him deal with me as he pleases.' So, what did God do? He punished him for his sin. Since he had been puffed up with pride at so great a number . . . it happened one day that, while he was riding along, David saw the angel of God with a naked sword, who was going along and killing. . . . David immediately dismounted and said, 'Sir, mercy for God's sake! Do not kill the innocents, but rather kill me who am the culprit.' Then, for the good nature of these words, God had mercy on the people and halted the massacre.

When there was economic growth in the medieval west – as happened, as we have seen, in the eleventh and twelfth centuries – this growth was only the result of a growth in population. It was a question of coping with a larger number of people to feed, clothe, and house. Land clearances and the increase in the area cultivated were the principal remedies sought for the extra population. Increasing the yields by intensive forms of farming such as triennial crop rotation, manure, or improving tools, was only a secondary aim. Even the size of the large Romanesque and Gothic churches was chiefly simply a response to the need to accommodate an enlarged Christian population. In any case monastic land management, which led the way economically and which acted as a barometer for the economy, often intensified or slackened production depending on variations in the number of monks. At Canterbury in the second half of the twelfth century, dues paid by peasants in kind decreased at the same time as the number of monks.

It was normal that this indifference and even this hostility to economic growth should be reflected in the monetary economy sector and should put up strong resistance to the development within this sector of a spirit of profit of precapitalistic type.

The middle ages, like antiquity, for a long time knew loans for consumption as the principal, if not the only, form of loan, loans for production remaining almost non-existent. Interest made on loans for consumption was forbidden between Christians and constituted usury pure and simple, which was condemned by the Church. Three biblical texts (Exodus 22.25, Leviticus 25.35-7, and Deuteronomy 23.19-20) condemned lending with interest between Jews, as a reaction to the influences of Assyria and Babylon, where the practice of advancing loans against crops was highly developed. These prescriptions, although they were not observed carefully by the ancient Jews, were taken up by the Church, which based its position on a saying of Christ: 'Lend, hoping for nothing again; and your reward shall be great' (Luke 6.34-5). In this phrase Christ had only indicated an ideal for the most perfect of his disciples, but in concentrating on it the Church put to one side all the passages where Christ had alluded without condemnation to financial practices condemned by the medieval Church as usurious. The whole of Christ's attitude to Matthew, the tax-gatherer or banker, a money-man in any case, confirmed that Christianity could be indulgent to finance. It was almost totally ignored or passed over in silence by the middle ages. On the contrary, medieval Christianity condemned loans for consumption between Christians (another proof of how it was defining itself as a closed group) and abandoned the role of usurer to the Jews, although this did not prevent the great abbeys of the early middle ages from acting to a certain extent as 'hire-purchase companies'. It was also for a long time opposed to the loans for production. More generally, all forms of credit were condemned as usury – and credit was a stimulus to, if not a precondition of, economic growth. The scholastics, such as Thomas Aquinas (who, contrary to what has sometimes been argued, was not very understanding towards merchant circles and who was imbued with the economic ideas of the lesser landowning aristocracy from which he sprang) summoned Aristotle to the rescue. They took up his distinction between economy, of a family-based, autarkic type, and wealth of a commercial type, or rather, between a natural wealth aiming at the simple use of goods – that is, subsistence – which was therefore praised, and monetary wealth, which was a practice against nature and therefore condemned. The scholastics borrowed from Aristotle the assertion that money did not come into being naturally, and therefore ought not to reproduce: *Nummus non parit nummos*. Any credit operation producing interest stumbled against this teaching for a long time.

In fact, all medieval social categories were subjected to strong economic and psychological pressures, the effect if not the aim of which was to oppose all accumulation appropriate to bring about economic progress. The peasant masses were reduced to the living minimum by exactions on the fruits of their labours. These were imposed by their landlords in the form of feudal rent and by the Church as tithes and alms. The Church itself spent a portion of its ostentatious wealth to the profit of some of its members – the higher clergy, that is the bishops, abbots, and canons, sterilized another portion to the glory of God in the construction and adornment of churches and in liturgical pomp, and used the rest for the subsistence of the poor. As for the lay aristocracy, it was called on to squander its surpluses in gifts and alms and in shows of munificence in the name of the Christian ideal of charity and of the chivalric ideal of largesse whose economic importance was considerable. The dignity of honour of lords consisted in spending without counting the cost; the consumption and waste appropriate to primitive societies used up almost all of their income. Jean de Meung was quite right to couple and condemn together '*largesse*' and '*pauvreté*' in the *Roman de la Rose*; the two were jointly responsible for paralysing the medieval economy. When, finally, there was any accumulation, it took the form of hoarding. Hoarding sterilized precious objects, and apart from its function of boosting a man's status it had only a non-creative economic function. Precious vessels and hoards of money, which were melted down or put into circulation when catastrophe or crisis struck, came to satisfy bare survival at critical moments, and did not feed a regular, continuous productive activity.

IX

The inferiority of production techniques, backed up by habits of thought, condemned the medieval economy to stagnation, to the sole satisfaction of subsistence and of prestige spending by a minority. Obstacles to economic growth came above all from the feudal system itself, which, moreover, was the cause of the low technological level too. Of course the feudal system was not identical with the manorial system, but it rested on a method of economic management whose pattern was basically the same across different regions and periods of time. The feudal system was essentially the appropriation by the seigneurial class, ecclesiastical and lay, of all the surplus agricultural production achieved by the peasant masses. This exploitation was carried out in conditions which deprived the peasants of the means of assisting economic progress without the beneficiaries of the system themselves having much greater possibilities of productive investment.

Of course, as we have seen, the feudal income, that is to say the combined revenues which the seigneurial class drew in from the exploitation of the peasants, did not always have the same composition or the same value. According to the period the relation between the two parts of the lord's estate varied. On the one hand there was the demesne, which was directly managed by the lord, thanks chiefly to labour services performed by some of the peasantry; on the other hand there were the holdings granted to villeins in return for services to be performed and dues to be paid. Even the proportion between labour services and dues and between dues in kind and in cash varied. Possibilities of disposing of the natural or monetary surpluses also varied considerably according to social class. If most lords were 'rich', that is to say that they had something with which to procure their subsistence and an excess necessary to maintain their rank, there were also 'poor knights', such as the one mentioned by Joinville, who seemed to be unable even to provide for the needs of himself and his family: 'A poor knight and his wife, with their four children, arrived in a ship. I gave them a meal in my quarters. After we had finished eating I called together all my important guests and said to them: "Let's perform a deed of charity and relieve this poor man of his children, each of you taking charge of one, while I take one myself" ' (Joinville, 1971, p. 313). Or there was Du Clusel, a knight in Forez in the fourteenth century, discovered by the historian Edouard Perroy, who was so poor that to live he became rector of the parish and village notary. On the other hand, while the majority of the peasantry maintained themselves with difficulty around the survival level, some achieved greater ease. We shall return to this theme.

Variations in the forms taken by seigneurial exploitation did not all tend in the same direction. Of course labour services tended to decline and even to disappear in the twelfth and thirteenth centuries, but this was not true everywhere, and we know that to the east of the Elbe, in Prussia, Poland, and beyond, in Russia, a 'second serfdom' came into being at the end of the middle ages which was to last until the nineteenth century. Again, dues paid in cash also became increasingly important in the course of the same period, the twelfth and thirteenth centuries, in contrast to dues in kind, to the point where dues in cash reached, to take an example, 76 per cent of the feudal income in Buckinghamshire in 1279. However, Georges Duby has clearly shown that at Cluny, especially after 1150, the proportion of dues paid in kind rose among the dues from the estates dependent on the abbey.

Yet in all regions and in all periods, at least until the fourteenth century, the seigneurial class used up its revenues on unproductive expenditure. These were the revenues assured to it by the peasant masses which were thus reduced almost entirely to the satisfaction of essential needs. It is admittedly very difficult to establish a typical budget for a lord or for a peasant. Documents are scarce and lack details, the levels of wealth varied considerably, and methods of making a numerical calculation of the different elements of the budget are hard to fix. However, it has been possible to establish with a good degree of probability the budgets of some big English lordships at the end of the thirteenth and beginning of the fourteenth centuries. The balance between revenues and expenditure (on subsistence, military equipment, building, and spending on luxuries) allowed the richest among them the possibility of investing between 3 and 6 per cent of the revenues, but only just. As for the revenues, they are almost exclusively made up of feudal income, that is to say exactions imposed on the work and produce of the work of peasants. It was only at the end of the thirteenth century and in the fourteenth that the crisis in the feudal income led, as we have seen, the lords who were capable of so doing to seek resources outside the reorganization of seigneurial management, in fiefs paid in money, (*fiefs de bourse* or *fiefs-rentes*), or in profits of warfare (ransoms), or more rarely in a more advanced marketing of agricultural surpluses or in buying rents. When, finally, they appear to have favoured economic progress, it was in a way in spite of themselves, for, adhering to the logic of the feudal system, they did not favour progress with a view to economic profit, but to a fiscal exaction or a feudal right. When they built a manorial mill, press, or oven, it was to force the peasants on their lands to use them, at a cost, or to obtain exemptions from such obligations by paying a tax. When the lords patronized the building of a road or a bridge, or the establishment of a market or a fair, it was, again, so that they could derive from this the levying of rights such as tolls.

On the other hand, the peasant masses were dispossessed of their surpluses and sometimes of what they needed by the exaction of feudal dues. Not only did they owe the lord a sizable portion of the fruits of their toil in the form of payments in kind or cash, but their productive capacity was reduced by labour services demanded by the lord or by payments for the right to be exempt from these; in addition the lord generally reserved the best lands and most of the manure for himself and even secured the tiny part of the peasant budget which was consecrated to relaxation, that is to say, to frequenting the village inn, which, like the press, the mill, or the oven, belonged to the manor. Sir Michael Postan estimated that in England in the second half of the thirteenth century, the feudal income took away 50 per cent or slightly more of the peasant income, and for the unfree classes left each villein with barely enough to support himself and his family.

In any case, when a peasant managed to increase his land-holding, it was not generally to increase his resources directly but to be able to produce enough to feed himself and pay the feudal dues, to reduce the necessity with which he found himself faced of selling part of his harvest at any price to pay off his dues to his lord, and thus to limit his dependence with regard to the market.

Even if there were (as we shall see) better-off sections of the peasantry, one should not believe that the possessors of a free piece of land or an allod, who were not burdened with services or rights, formed a section of the peasantry which escaped the feudal economic system. It is true that these allod-holders, owners of a small piece of land, for allods were usually small, were more numerous in the middle ages than has often been said. Firstly, more allods than were previously believed seem to have escaped the process of feudalization. Furthermore, the peasant allod – except in England, where, however, the freeholders were not very different from allod-holders – partially re-established itself in the eleventh and twelfth centuries in several ways: by contracts of 'complant' or joint plantation which joined a peasant to a lord to create a freely held vineyard; by the hidden appropriation, as a result of the negligence of lords and their officers, of a piece of land which was held as an allod after several years of free possession, or again through the cunning of certain peasants in creating for themselves a few patches of free fallow land on the edge of seigneurial clearances.

Finally, if the adage coined by lawyers '*nulle terre sans seigneur* – no land without a lord', which is closer to theory than to reality, is false even in France, it is even more false in regions such as Italy where urban continuity maintained, in the immediate environs of towns, 'cases of independence' to use the phrase of Gino Luzzatto. Likewise in Spain the special conditions of the Reconquista kept a number of the occupants of reconquered lands outside seigneurial dependence, and in certain parts of Poland and Hungary the disruption caused by the Tartar invasion of 1240-43 allowed certain peasants to free themselves. After the turmoil one can see Cistercian abbeys reconstituting their lordships with some difficulty. The vill of Sconewalde (Schönwalde), belonging to the abbey of Henrykow in Silesia, had been occupied in this way by a Polish noble, Peter of Piotrowice, who had installed a bailiff or *villicus* called Sibodo. For five years, the abbot of Henrykow solicited Duke Boleslaw for the restitution of this village in vain. When Peter of Piotrowice finally had to give in, Sibodo resisted in his turn, and the abbot had to buy him out, though in fact for only four marks, since Sibodo had not yet cleared the forest.

However the independence of the allod-holders should not give us illusions. Economically they were subjected to seigneurial domination, for exactions burdened them personally, whether directly or indirectly through an intermediary in the form of the judicial and public legal rights enjoyed by the lord of the region and they had to pay these levies by sacrificing some of the produce ·of their land. They were even more surely dependent on the lord because he controlled the local market and, what was more, the economy of the region as a whole. Thus the allod-holders themselves did not escape the economic exploitation of the seigneurial class. They were barely distinguishable from the mass of the peasantry, the majority of whom were exposed through the exaction of feudal dues to poverty and sometimes to want, that is to say to the lack even of subsistence, to hunger.

X

The combination of poor technological equipment and a social structure which paralysed economic growth meant that the medieval west was a world on the edge of the brink. It was constantly threatened by the risk that its subsistence might become uncertain. It was only just in a state of equilibrium. First of all the medieval west was a world ravaged by the fear of hunger, and, too often, by hunger itself. In peasant folklore, myths of feasting exercised a particular fascination. The dream of the Land of Cockayne was a literary theme in the thirteenth century, both in the French *fabliau Cocaigne* and in the English poem *The Land of Cockaygne*; later it was to inspire Breughel. The feeding miracles in the Bible, from the manna in the desert to the multiplication of the loaves, occupied men's imaginations. People could find them in the lives of almost every saint, as we can read on almost every page of the *Golden Legend*. To take an obvious example, here is a miracle of St Benedict:

The whole of Campania was being laid waste by a great famine, and in the monastery of St Benedict the brothers noticed one day that they possessed no more than five loaves. But St Benedict, seeing them afflicted, addressed to them a kindly word of admonishment to correct them for their faintheartedness; after which, to console them, he said to them, 'How can you be so anxious about such an unimportant matter? Bread is short today, but that is no evidence that you will not have bread in abundance tomorrow!' Then, the next day, two hundred *modii* of flour were found in front of the doors of St Benedict's cell, without it being possible to know, even today, to which messenger God entrusted the care of bringing them. At the sight of this miracle, the brothers, giving thanks to God, learned not to despair any longer in times of scarcity.

There was the miracle of St James who had to feed the poor pilgrim:

A pilgrim from Vézelay one day found himself short of money, and since he was ashamed to beg, he found under a tree, beneath which he had gone to sleep, a loaf cooked in the ashes. Moreover he had dreamed in his sleep that St James had taken it upon himself to feed him. And he lived off this loaf for a fortnight, until his return to his country. Although he ate his fill twice a day, but the next day he found the loaf entire once more in his sack.

Then there is a miracle of St Dominic:

When the brothers – there were forty of them – were assembled, they saw that they had nothing to eat but a rather small loaf. St Dominic ordered them to cut the loaf into 40 pieces. And, as each brother joyfully took his mouthful, two young people, exactly alike, entered the refectory bearing bread in the folds of their cloaks. They put down the bread at the head of the table without saying anything, and then disappeared, in such a way that no-one knew whence they had come, or how they had left. Then St Dominic, stretching his hands out to his brothers, said, 'Well, my dear brothers, here you have something to eat.'

All these miracles have bread as their object, not just in memory of Christ's miracle, but because bread was the basic food of the masses. Although the miracle of the wedding feast at Cana also bore the authority of Jesus, it did not enjoy so much popularity in a society where, for a long time, the upper classes were the only ones to drink much wine. Yet feeding miracles could concern other sorts of food which were economically important, such as a poor peasant's only cow.

While he (St Germanus) was preaching in Britain, the king of this country refused him hospitality, and refused it to his companions too. But a swineherd who was going home, having seen St Germanus and his companions exhausted with hunger and cold, welcomed them into his house, and killed for them the only calf which he possessed.

Then, after the meal, St Germanus had all the calf's bones put together again under its skin, and, at his prayer, God gave life to the animal.

When, in *Minnesang*, courtly inspiration gave way in the second half of the thirteenth century to a realistic, peasant vein, culinary themes became prominent and a genre of 'feasting poems' known as *Fresslieder*, appeared. This obsession with hunger occurred by contrast among the rich, to whom, as we shall see, luxurious eating-habits and ostentatious food expressed class behaviour at a basic level. In any case preachers were not mistaken when they said that gluttony or as it was better put in the middle ages, *gula* (original meaning, 'gullet'), was one of the typical sins of the seigneurial class. In this respect the *Roman de Renart* is an extraordinary document. A drama, an epic of hunger, it shows us Renart, his family, and his companions ceaselessly impelled by the call of their empty bellies. The driving force of almost all the branches of the cycle is omnipresent and omnipotent hunger – the motive for Renart's cunning. Thus impelled he steals hams, herrings, eels, and cheese from the crow, and chases hens and other birds.

It was when summer is at an end and the season of winter is returning. Renart was then in his house. When he had taken down his meat-safe, he was cruelly disappointed to find that there was nothing in it for him to take out . . . . Renart, who had set out early on his way, urged on by hunger . . . . Both made off along a path, both ready to faint, they were suffering from such great and harsh hunger. Then, by a marvellous piece of luck, they found a beautiful sausage of chitterlings on the edge of the lane. . . . Renart was in his house of Malpertuis without provender or victuals, to such a point that he was gaping with hunger and was suffering much in his body. . . . Renart was in his manor of Malpertuis, but how sad and full of care was his heart, for he did not have the least bit of food. He was thin and feeble, so much was hunger tormenting his bowels. He saw in front of him his son Rovel who was crying with hunger, and Hermeline his wife equally starving. . . .

Thus when, in this parody of a *geste*, Renart and his companions turned themselves into barons, the first thing they hastened to do was to have a feast and the banquet of animals changed into lords has been immortalized in a miniature: 'Dame Hersent joyfully made them a feast and prepared things for them to eat as well as she could: lamb, roasts, capons in a pot; she brought plenty to everyone and the barons ate their fill.' Already the *chansons de geste* had made way for giants with huge appetites – close to peasant legends, ancestors of Pantagruel, brothers of the ogres. The most famous appeared in *Aliscans*: Renouart *au tinel*, a giant of fabulous gluttony who ate a peacock in two mouthfuls.

Obsession with food occurred not only in hagiography but also in the mythical royal genealogies. Several medieval dynasties had as their ancestor a peasant-king, the purveyor of food. They remind us of the myth of the foodgiving kings and heroes of antiquity, such as Triptolemus or Cincinnatus. Thus among the Slavs there was Przemysl, the ancestor of the Przemyslids of Bohemia, who according to his chronicler Cosmas was torn from his plough to be made king, as we see in a fresco of the early twelfth century in the church of St Catherine of Znojmo. Piast, the ancestor of the first Polish dynasty, was described by Gallus Anonymus as a ploughman, *arator*, as a farmer, *agricola*, and also as a swineherd: *qui etiam porcellum nutriebat*. This is reminiscent of the story about the Britons in the *Golden Legend*: 'Saint Germanus, on God's orders, made the swineherd and his wife come forward, and, to the great astonishment of all, he proclaimed this man, who had given him hospitality, as king (Gallus Anonymus also calls Piast an *arator hospitalis*). From then on the nation of the Britons has been ruled by kings descending from a family of swineherds.' A ninth-century poem remarked of Charlemagne: 'Behold the great emperor / Good sower of a good harvest / And prudent farmer (*prudens agricola*).'

Perhaps the most terrible thing about this reign of hunger was that it was at once arbitrary and inescapable. It was arbitrary because it was tied to the unpredictability of nature. The immediate cause of famine was a poor harvest, that is to say an upset in the natural order: drought or flooding. However, not only was it the case that at long intervals an exceptionally harsh climatic phase would bring about a catastrophe in the food supply – a famine – but also that everywhere, fairly regularly, every three, four, or five years, a shortage of corn would produce a period of dearth. This would have more limited effects, which were less dramatic and less spectacular but none the less lethal. In fact, during every disaster, a vicious spiral developed. Thus at the start one might have a spell of unexpectedly bad weather with, as a result, a bad harvest. The rise in price of commodities which resulted made the poor poorer. Those who did not die of hunger were exposed to other perils. Eating food of poor quality, such as plants or flour unfit for consumption, damaged food, and sometimes even earth, without counting human flesh (and references to this should not be attributed to the propensity of some chroniclers to tell tall stories!), caused diseases which were often fatal, or a state of malnutrition which encouraged wasting illnesses that often killed people. The spiral happened thus: bad weather, shortage, rise in prices, epidemic, or 'mortality', that is to say an increase in the number of deaths.

Unexpected climatic changes produced a catastrophic effect chiefly because of the weakness of medieval technology and economy and above all the powerlessness of the public authorities. Of course, famines had existed in the ancient world, for example, in the Roman world. Here, too, limited harvests explained the absence or the limited quantity of surpluses which could have been stored to be distributed or sold in times of shortage. But the state and municipal organization established a rough and ready system of storing and distributing foodstuffs. We need only remember the importance of barns and granaries (*horrea*) in both Roman towns and villas. A well-maintained system of roads and communications and a unified administration also allowed people to some extent to transport food aid from an area of plenty or sufficiency to an area of shortage.

Practically nothing of this was left in the medieval west. Transportation and roads were insufficient, and there were thousands of 'customs barriers': taxes and tolls were charged by every minor lord at every bridge or obligatory point of passage, without counting brigands or pirates. How many obstacles there were to what was to be called in France up to 1789 'the free circulation of corn'! Of course the great lay lords and above all the great ecclesiastical lords - the rich monasteries - the rulers, and from the twelfth century, the towns built up stocks and in times of shortage or starvation made emergency distributions from these reserves or even tried to import foodstuffs. Galbert of Bruges records how in 1125 the Count of Flanders, Charles the Good, tried to fight against famine in his territories:

The count tried in every way possible to take care of the poor, distributing alms in the towns and throughout his domain, both in person and by his officials. At the same time he was feeding 100 paupers in Bruges every day; and he gave a sizable loaf of bread to each of them from before Lent until the new harvests of the same year. And likewise in his other towns he had made the same provision. In the same year, the lord count had decreed that whoever sowed two measures of land in the sowing time should sow another of peas and beans, because these legumes yield more quickly and seasonably and therefore could nourish the poor more quickly if the misery of famine and want should not end in that year. He had also ordered this to be done throughout the whole county, in this way making provision for the poor in the future as well as he could. He reprimanded those men of Ghent who had allowed poor people whom they could have fed to die of hunger on their doorsteps. He also prohibited the brewing of beer because the poor could be fed more easily and better if the townspeople and country people refrained from making beer in this time of famine. For he ordered bread to be made out of oats so that the poor could at least maintain life on bread and water. He ordered a fourth of a measure of wine to be sold for six pennies and not more dearly so that the merchants would stop hoarding and buying up wine and would exchange their wares, in view of the urgency of the famine, for other foodstuffs which they could acquire more quickly and which could be used more easily to nourish the poor. From his own table he took daily enough food to sustain 113 paupers . . . .

This text, apart from showing us one of those rare medieval attempts to go beyond simple charity by a food relief policy, reminds us of two important facts in addition to many others. Firstly men were afraid that bad harvests might be repeated. Providing food could barely extend beyond a year. The low yields, the slow introduction of triennial crop rotation which allowed winter corn to be sown, and the poor methods of conserving food let people hope at most that the gap between the harvest of the previous year and the new harvest might be bridged.

We have dozens of accounts of the bad conservation of produce and of its vulnerability to natural or animal destruction. The middle ages did not know how to keep wine, and were forced to drink it before it was a year old, or to fall back on processes which altered its flavour, but this was perhaps of little importance. Above all it was a question of taste, and wine, although it was consumed on a large scale, was not a product essential to subsistence. Peter Damian's complaints when he crossed France in 1063 to preside as papal legate at a council at Limoges were those of a great lord of the church, even though he was inclined to asceticism: 'Everywhere in France it is the practice to smear the inside of the barrels with pitch before putting in the wine; the French say that this gives the wine colour, but many foreigners are made sick by it. This wine very quickly made our mouths itch.' And we may note that although the problem of finding drinking water had not reached a crisis point as in semidesert lands or in big modern conurbations, it did sometimes occur in the medieval west. Peter Damian again, disgusted with French wine, added, 'Indeed, it is only with great difficulty that one sometimes finds water fit to drink in this country.'

Then there was the damage caused by rats which occurs in chronicles and legend. The *Annals* of Basel noted in the year 1271: 'The rats devastated the corn; great shortage'. The story of the *Rattenfänger* of Hameln, the Pied Piper, who in 1284 on the pretext of ridding the town of the rats which infested it is supposed to have removed the children of the town, mixed themes from folklore with the struggle against the evil rodents. Above all the chroniclers inform us of the damage made by insects in the fields. There were rare invasions by locusts, though after the great clouds which stretched from Germany to Spain in 873, there were practically none except in Hungary and Austria in the autumn of 1195, as the annalist of Klosterneuburg records. In 1309 and 1310 a swarm of cockchafers ravaged Austrian vines and orchards for two years, according to the Annals of Melk. However, noxious insects could destroy harvests much more effectively once they had been stored in the barn.

What therefore was really catastrophic was the repetition, two years and sometimes three years in a row, of a bad harvest. But what we also learn from texts such as those of Galbert of Bruges is that the habitual victims of these famines and of the epidemics which often accompanied them were of course the poor. These, indeed, since their surpluses were used up by the exactions of the lords, could not build up stocks for themselves. Lacking money, even when the monetary economy started to expand, they were incapable of buying foodstuffs at the prohibitive prices which commodities would reach at such times. Measures taken by certain authorities to fight against hoarders and speculators were rare and often ineffective, in particular because importing grain from abroad was, as we have seen, difficult. Of course, in 1025, for example, Bishop Meinwerk of Paderborn 'in a period of great famine sent men to buy wheat in Cologne and had it loaded on board two ships which brought it down into the low lands where he had it distributed'. According to a late and unreliable source, Charles the Good of Flanders had to deal severely with clerics forgetful of their duty to give alms in food at the time of the great grain shortage in 1125.

It happened that some merchants from the south brought a large quantity of grain in a boat. Learning this, Lambert de Straet, a knight, the brother of the provost of St Donatian, with his son, Boscard, bought all this grain from the south at a low price, and, in addition, all the tithes of the collegiate churches and the monasteries of St Winnoc, St Bertin, St Peter of Ghent and St Bavo. Their barns were full of corn and all sorts of grains; and yet they sold them so dear that the poor could not buy any. The complaints of the mob, and in particular those of the poor, reached the ears of the pious ruler Charles who summoned the provost and his brother Lambert and asked them how much grain they had in their barns, and reproached them for their inhumanity and their hardheartedness, and above all for their cruelty towards the poor. The provost then swore to the count that he had barely enough to feed his chapter on for seven weeks, and Lambert de Straet said that he did not have enough to feed his family and himself with for a month. The pious Charles declared that he wanted to have all their bread and that he would take it on himself to feed both the collegiate church of St Donatian, with the provost and his *familia*, and Lambert and his family for half a year. Then the pious count ordered Tammard, his almoner, to open all the barns belonging to the provost and to Lambert, and to sell grain to the people at an honest price, but to distribute it for the love of God to the poor and the sick, and finally to reserve a quantity sufficient to feed the collegiate church of the said provost and his brother Lambert and his family for a year. . . . When the grain was distributed the shortage ceased; the grain sufficed the towns of Bruges, Aardenburg and Oudenburg for a year.

Of course hunger was man's lot. It was the ransom for Original Sin, as the *Elucidarium* said.

Hunger is one of the punishments of Original Sin. Man was created to live without working, if he had desired it. But after the Fall he could only ransom himself by work. . . . God therefore imposed hunger on him so that he would work under the constraint of this necessity and so that he could by this means return to things eternal.

But just as servitude, another consequence of Original Sin, was concentrated in the serf class, so famine was limited, with a few exceptions, to the class of the poor. This social discrimination of calamities which struck the poor and spared the rich was so normal in the middle ages that everyone was astonished when a scourge arrived that killed all classes without distinction, the Black Death. It was exceptional for a famine to be so serious that it claimed victims from all classes. A rare example is mentioned by Ralph Glaber in 1032:

This vengeful sterility had its birth in the lands of the east; it laid Greece waste, arrived in Italy, and, from there it was communicated to Gaul and passed through this country on the way to all the peoples of England. Since the lack of foodstuffs struck the entire nation, the great and those of the middling sort shared the pallors of hunger with the poor; the brigandage of the powerful had to cease before the universal destitution.

In his book on medieval famines, *Hungersnöte im Mittelalter*, Fritz Curschmann brought together hundreds of quotations from chronicles which, right up to the great famine of 1315–17, pitilessly unfold the sad list of periods of bad weather, famines, and epidemics with their terrible episodes, cannibalism included, and their inevitable dénouement death, and their favourite victims, the poor.

Here is the famous passage of Ralph Glaber, monk of Cluny, from the early eleventh century, for the years 1032–4:

The famine started to spread its ravages and one could have feared the disappearance of almost the entire human race. The atmospheric conditions became so unfavourable that no suitable time could be found to sow seed, and that, especially because of the floods, there was no means of reaping the harvest . . . . Continual rains had soaked into all the soil to the point where during three years no one could dig furrows capable of taking the seed. At harvest-time, weeds and ill-omened tares had covered the whole surface of the fields. A *modius* of grain sown, where it gave the best yields, gave a sexter at harvest, and the sexter itself produced barely a fistful. If by chance one found some food for sale, the seller could charge an outrageous price just as he pleased. However, when they had eaten the wild beasts and birds, the people started, under the sway of a devouring hunger, to collect all sorts of carrion and other things which are horrible to mention to eat. Some in order to escape death had recourse to forest roots and water-weed. Finally, horror takes hold of us listening to the perversions which then reigned among the human race. Alas! O woe! Something rarely heard of throughout the ages: rabid hunger made men devour human flesh. Travellers were kidnapped by people stronger than they were, their limbs were cut off, cooked on the fire and eaten.

Many people who moved from one place to another to flee the famine, and who had found hospitality on the way, were murdered in the night, and served as food for those who had welcomed them. Many showed a fruit or an egg to children, enticed them into out-of-the-way spots, killed them, and devoured them. Bodies of the dead were in many places torn out of the ground and equally served to appease hunger. . . . Then people tried an experiment in the region of Mâcon which had never before, to our knowledge, been tried anywhere. Many people took out of the ground a white soil which looked like clay, mixed it with what flour or bran they had, and made out of this mixture loaves with which, they reckoned, they would not die of of hunger; this practice however brought only an illusory hope of rescue and an illusory relief. One only saw pale and emaciated faces; many people had a skin distended with swellings; the human voice itself became thin, like the little cries of dying birds. The corpses of the dead, who were so numerous that they had to lie scattered without burial, served as food for the wolves, who thereafter continued for a long time to seek their pittance among men. And since it was not possible, as we said, to bury each person individually because of the great number of the dead, in certain places men who feared God dug what were commonly called charnel pits, into which the bodies of the dead were thrown by the 500 or more, as many as there was space for, pellmell, half naked or without any covering; crossroads and the edges of fields served as cemeteries. Although some heard say that they would find it better to take themselves off to other regions, many were those who perished along the way of starvation.

Even in the thirteenth century when the great famines seem to have been rarer, the sinister litany continued: 1221–3: 'There were heavy rains and floods for three years in Poland, and a two-year famine resulted and many died'; 1233: 'There were great frosts and the harvests were frosted; whence a great famine resulted in France,' and in the same year: 'A very violent famine in Livonia, to the point where the men ate each other, and the thieves were taken down from the gibbets to be eaten'; 1263: 'There was a very severe famine in Moravia and in Austria; many died of hunger; people ate roots and the bark of trees'; 1277: 'In Austria, Illyria and Carinthia there was so great a famine that men ate cats, dogs, horses and corpses'; 1280: 'There was a great shortage of all things, grains, meat, fish, cheese, and eggs, to the extent that it was hard to buy two hen's eggs for a penny, when hitherto one could buy 50 eggs for a penny in Prague. And the winter sowing could not be carried out that year, except in regions distant from Prague, and where it was possible to sow, it was only a very little; so a severe famine struck the poor and many of the needy died of hunger'.

Famine and the poor started to afflict the towns to such an extent that urban legend dreamed up schemes for clearing out starving people which are reminiscent of the legend of the Pied Piper, but which were closer to the truth. Hence this story from Genoa in the thirteenth century:

There was at Genoa a great scarcity caused by a shortage of foodstuffs, and there were more vagabonds there than in any other country. So several galleys were hired as well as rowers who were paid, and then notice was given that all the poor should go to the shore and that they would receive bread from the commune. So many came that it was a wonder . . . all embarked. The masters of the ships were busy. They drove the oars through the water and unshipped the whole crowd in Sardinia. There there was food to eat. They abandoned them; thus the great scarcity in Genoa came to an end.

XI

Nor should we forget that livestock was particularly affected during these calamities. Animals suffered from their own shortages and illnesses (endlessly recurring epidemics). In addition, in time of famine, they were killed by men, firstly because they wanted to keep for themselves food which was normally reserved for the beasts (oats in particular), and then because the meat provided food for the starving. Indeed one can see the Church on such occasions authorizing people to eat meat in Lent: 'At that time,' (*circa* 1000) wrote Adhemar of Chabannes, 'ergotism flared up among the people of the Limousin. . . . Bishop Audouin, seeing the inhabitants of Evaux a prey to a shortage, decided, to stop them from dying from hunger, that they could eat meat.' In 1286 the bishop of Paris allowed the poor to eat meat in Lent, because of the severe shortage. This was a world on the edge of starvation, an underfed and badly fed world.

Hence, following in the train of famine, came epidemics caused by the eating of food unsuitable for consumption. The most spectacular of them was ergotism caused by ergot growing on rye, and probably on other types of cereal as well, which appeared in Europe at the end of the tenth century. In 1090, records Sigebert of Gembloux, 'there was a year of epidemic, especially in western Lotharingia. Many rotted from the effect of the sacred fire [erysipelas] which consumed the inside of their bodies, with their burned limbs turning black like charcoal, and either they died miserably, or else, once their hands and feet, which had gone rotten, had been cut off, they were spared to live yet more wretchedly. . . . ' In 1109 several chroniclers noted that the burning epidemic, *pestilentia ignearia*, 'once more ravaged human flesh'. In 1235, according to Vincent of Beauvais, 'a great famine reigned in France, especially in Aquitaine, so much that men ate grass in the fields, like animals. A sexter of corn rose to a hundred sous in Poitou, and there was a great epidemic: the poor were devoured by the sacred fire in such great numbers that the church of St Maxentius was full of those who were brought there.'

Ergotism was the basis of a peculiar devotion which led to the foundation of an order. As we have seen, the eremitical movement of the eleventh century venerated St Anthony. Some hermits in the Dauphiné claimed in 1070 to have received relics of the saint from Constantinople. At that time ergotism was raging in the region. The relics of St Anthony acquired a reputation for curing it and ergotism was christened 'St Anthony's Fire'. The abbey which preserved the healing relics became St-Antoine-en-Viennois and spread daughter-houses as far as Hungary and the Holy Land. The brothers of St Anthony received the sick, especially people lacking limbs, into their abbey-hospices; their great hospital at St-Antoine-en-Viennois was called the hospital of the 'dismembered'. Their convent in Paris gave its name to the Faubourg St-Antoine. It is interesting to see that although it was not founded, it was at least reformed in 1198 by Fulk of Neuilly, the famous preacher who began by inveighing against the usurers, the monopolizers of foodstuffs in time of famine. Fulk ended up preaching the crusade, and the earliest fanatical supporters of the crusading movement at the end of the previous century had been peasants decimated by the epidemic of sacred fire in 1094 and the other scourges of the time. The poor peasants of the first crusade in 1096 came above all from the areas most affected by this calamity – Germany, the Rhineland, and eastern France.

The arrival of rye ergot in the west, famines, and ergotism which generated convulsions and hallucinations, the action of the brothers of St Anthony, and popular fervour for the Crusade together formed a complex in which the medieval world can be perceived in its physical, economic, and social ills and in its most disorderly and most spiritual reactions. When we look at eating habits and the role of the miraculous in medieval medicine and spirituality we find these nexuses of miseries, disorder, and outbursts which were the lot of medieval Christian Europe in the depths of its lower classes. For, even outside the exceptional periods of catastrophe, the medieval world was doomed to a whole series of illnesses which united physical ills to economic difficulties and to emotional and behavioural breakdowns.

Poor food and limited medical knowledge, which could not find a place for itself between old women's simples and pedantic theories, brought about frightful physical wretchedness and high mortality, typical of underdeveloped countries. Life expectancy was limited, even if we try to reckon it without taking count of the appalling infant mortality and of the numerous miscarriages suffered by badly nourished women forced into difficult labours. Life expectancy, which has been established at about 70–75 years in contemporary industrial societies, is supposed barely to have exceeded 30 years in the medieval west. William of St-Pathus, naming the witnesses in the canonization hearing for St Louis (Louis IX of France) called a man of 40 a man 'of discreet years' and a man of 50 'a man of great age'.

Physical failings, especially in the early middle ages, could be found even among the higher classes; the skeletons of Merovingian warriors have revealed serious dental caries, a result of bad nutrition, and even royal families suffered high death rates among babies and children. St Louis lost several children young or at an early age. But bad health and untimely death were chiefly the lot of the poor classes who were forced by feudal exploitation to live on the edge of starvation. A bad harvest could plunge them into famine, which was less easy for them to bear in any case because their constitutions were more vulnerable. We have seen the role played by saints who fed and healed people. Here let us just draw up the sad list of the great medieval illnesses whose connection with insufficient and poor quality food is evident. The most widespread and lethal of endemic illnesses in the middle ages was probably tuberculosis, which is likely to have been the *languor* mentioned in so many sources. Skin diseases came next, firstly the terrible leprosy to which we shall refer again. However, abscesses, gangrene, scabies, ulcers, tumours, cankers, eczema (St Laurence's fire), and erysipelas (St Sylvanus' fire) are shown in many miniatures in devotional texts. Two pitiable figures often occur in medieval iconography, Job (turned into a saint at Venice where there was a church of San Giobbe, and at Utrecht where a hospital was founded in his honour), who was covered with ulcers, and scraped his boils with a sherd, and poor Lazarus seated at the door of the wicked rich man with the dog who licked his sores. In this image sickness and poverty were appropriately united. Scrofula (or ulcers, often tubercular) was so representative of medieval illnesses that according to tradition it was cured by kings of France endowed with healing powers. Deficiency diseases and malformations were no less frequent. The medieval west was full of blind people with sunken eyes and empty pupils who would come to stare out at us in the frightening picture by Breughel; the middle ages were full of the maimed, hunchbacks, people with goitres, the lame, and the paralysed.

Mental illnesses formed another striking category: epilepsy (or St John's disease), the dance of St Guy for which one could also invoke St Willibrord, who was the patron saint of a *Springprozession* at Echternach in the thirteenth century, a processional dance on the fringes of medieval witchcraft, folklore, and religiosity. With ergotism one penetrates further into the world of breakdowns and madness. There were the gentle and furious madnesses of lunatics, frenetics, and the insane. In the face of these the middle ages hesitated between repulsion which people tried to appease with a superstitious form of therapy (exorcising the possessed) and sympathetic tolerance. This spilled over into the courtly world (clowns were employed by lords and kings), or into games (*fous des échecs* – chess bishops), and on to the stage (the young mad peasant, the *dervé* of the *Jeu de la Feuillée* in the thirteenth century announced the satirical farces of the end of the middle ages). The Feast of Fools prepared the way for the great unbridling of the Renaissance when madmen frolicked from the Ship of Fools to the comedies of Shakespeare, before they were cast into shadow in the repression of the classical age, in 'the great seclusion' of the prison-type hospitals denounced by Michel Foucault in his *Histoire de la Folie*.

And, in the very earliest years, there were innumerable childhood illnesses which so many patron saints tried to relieve, a whole world of childhood suffering and distress. St Agapitus soothed toothache; St Cornelius, St Giles, and many others took care of convulsions; St Aubin, St Fiacre, St Firmin, and St Macou cured rickets; St Agapitus, again, in company with St Cyr or St Germanus of Auxerre, healed colic.

We must be mindful of men's physical frailty. It was a physiological terrain made to entertain diseases of mind and body and extravagances of religious behaviour in the shortlived flowering of collective crises. The middle ages was the realm par excellence of the great collective fears and of the great, collective public and physical penances. As early as 1150 the processions of people carrying stones to cathedral building sites stopped from time to time for sessions of public confession and mutual flagellation. In 1260 a new crisis made flagellants break out in Italy, and then in the rest of Christian Europe, before the Black Death in 1348 unleashed hallucinated processions (recreated by the imagination of the contemporary film-maker Ingmar Bergman in *The Seventh Seal*). At the level of daily life itself, underfed and badly fed bodies were predisposed to all the wanderings of the mind – dreams, hallucinations, and visions. The Devil, the angels, the saints, the Virgin, and God himself could appear. The bodies were ready to perceive them and they caused the minds to accept them.

XII

The middle ages lived under the perpetual threat of this limit. The inferior technology and equipment created strangleholds as soon as conditions became abnormal. In the area round Worms in 1259 an exceptionally abundant wine harvest suffered because there were not enough vats to contain it, 'so much that the vats were being sold for more than the wine'. In 1304 in Alsace an especially generous harvest of cereals and wine provoked a fall in local prices, exacerbated because no bread could be made because the rivers dried up and the mills were useless, and because transporting the wine was impossible. The level of the Rhine was so low that it could be forded at several points between Strasbourg and Basel, and the shortage and expense of overland transportation meant that it could not make up for the lack of the river.

We have seen that, in spite of progress brought about by the plough, triennial crop rotation, more frequent ploughing and hoeing, the limit of the soil's fertility was quickly reached, yields remained low, and men in the middle ages had to look for an increase in resources more by enlarging the cultivated surface area than by raising the yields. Medieval agriculture was condemned to be extensive. But rapaciously exploiting space in this way also destroyed wealth. For man was incapable of reconstituting the riches which he was then destroying, or of waiting for them to grow back again naturally. Clearances, especially by burning, which devoured waste land, exhausted the soils and above all destroyed timber, that apparently unlimited wealth of the medieval world. One source among very many others shows how quickly the medieval economy became powerless against nature, for nature responded to the technological progress which in exceptional circumstances did violence to it by becoming impoverished. Thus progress was reversed. At the end of the thirteenth century, in the territory of Colmars in the lower French Alps, the town consuls ordered that hydraulic saws, which were leading to the disafforestation of the area, should be destroyed. The result of this measure was that the woods were invaded by a crowd of 'poor and needy people', *homines pauperes et nichil habentes*, armed with hand saws, who committed 'a hundred times more damage'. Documents and measures increased to protect the forests whose shrinkage or disappearance not only meant a diminution of essential resources such as timber, game, and wild honey but also, in certain regions and on certain soils, especially in the Mediterranean region, encouraged streams to carry off the topsoil, often with disastrous results. On the southern edge of the Alps, from Provence to Slovenia, one can see some protection of the forests being organized from about 1300. On 30 March 1315 the general assembly of the men of Folgara, in the Trentino, summoned in the public square, issued the following edict:

If anyone is caught cutting wood on the hill 'At the Galilena' as far as the path of the men of Costa which leads to the hill, and from the summit down to the plain, he will pay five shillings per stump. Let no-one dare cut larch stems to make fire-wood on this hill, on pain of five shillings per trunk.

Man was not the only culprit in this process. Livestock wandering in the fields or the meadows was destructive. The number of places closed off against the wandering and pasture of animals, especially goats, the great enemies of the medieval peasants, increased. At Folgara, for example, we find:

If someone is found among the vines with a flock of goats and sheep, he will pay twenty shillings for the whole flock, and five shillings if it is in another place. If someone is found away from the public road and crossing someone else's meadow with oxen or cows harnessed to a cart, he will pay five shillings for each yoke of animals.

The crisis described as the crisis of the fourteenth century was heralded by the abandoning of the bad lands, of the marginal lands on which the wave of clearances created by the population boom had come to die. As early as the end of the thirteenth century, especially in England, lands incapable of reconstituting themselves, whose yields were lower than the economic minimum, were abandoned. Moorland and coppices regained possession. Medieval man was not driven back to the starting-point, but he could not enlarge his cultivated clearings as he wished. Nature put up a resistance and sometimes staged a successful reversal. This was true everywhere from England to Pomerania, where the sources in the fourteenth century speak to us of '*mansi* covered with sand borne by the wind and therefore left deserted or in any case uncultivated'. The exhaustion of the soil was the most serious problem for the medieval economy, which was essentially rural.

But when the monetary economy started to expand, it too rapidly collided with a natural limitation, in addition to other difficulties: the exhaustion of the mines. In spite of the fact that gold coins started to be struck once more in the thirteenth century, the important metal was silver. The end of the thirteenth century saw the decline of the traditional mines in Derbyshire, Devon, Poitou and the Massif Central, Hungary, and Saxony. Here too the stranglehold was primarily a technological one. Most of these old mines had reached the level where the danger of flooding had become serious or where the miner had become powerless before the water. Sometimes, too, the lodes had purely and simply become exhausted. Alphonse of Poitiers, brother of St Louis, anxious to collect precious metal in view of the Tunisian Crusade, complained to his steward of Rouergue in 1268 about 'so small a total of silver' produced by his mine at Orzeals. He ordered that all the technical equipment possible be set up there: watermills, windmills, or, if there were not enough horses or men, that the workforce be increased, but in vain. Of course, new mines took over in Bohemia, Moravia, Transylvania, Bosnia, and Serbia. Yet their production levels were not sufficient for the needs of Christian Europe at the end of the fifteenth century. Christian Europe suffered from a 'monetary famine', which the gold and above all the silver of the Americas in the following century would satisfy.

The final limitation was the exhaustion of the workforce. For centuries the medieval economy did not suffer from a shortage of manpower. Of course the runaway serf was actively pursued by his master, and the new religious orders of the twelfth century – with the Cistercians in the lead – tried to make up for the absence of serfs with the institution of the *conversi* or lay-brothers. But here people were trying to procure manpower as cheaply as possible. There was no real shortage of manpower. The number of beggars and the esteem in which they were held – Franciscans and Dominicans turned begging into a spiritual value – witness to the existence of an assisted and honoured unemployment. In the second half of the thirteenth century William de St Amour and Jean de Meung launched the first attacks against able-bodied beggars. The halt, and then the reversal, of the growth of population, made peasant manpower less numerous and more expensive; the emancipation of the serfs had already made it scarcer and more expensive. The demographic recession and the manpower crisis, which had both appeared several decades earlier, were turned into a catastrophe by the Black Death in 1348. Everywhere one hears nothing except complaints about the shortage of men, which meant the abandonment of newly cultivated lands. One source among many may be quoted, from Brandenburg in 1372: 'It is known that the plague and the mortality were so violent that they carried off most of the farmers, so much so that today they are very few and rare and most of the lands remain uncultivated and deserted'. In the final reckoning there was a shortage of the peasants themselves, underfed, their numbers thinned out by epidemics in the medieval economy. The demographic handicap was the ultimate restriction on a world on the edge of the limit.

To a large extent the intellectual insecurity in which men lived in the middle ages is explained by material insecurity. Lucien Febvre prayed that someone would write a history of the feeling of security, a fundamental aspiration of human societies. It remains to be done. The medieval west would figure in it largely negatively. Its inhabitants, in short, took refuge in the sole security of religion. There was security here below, thanks to the miracle. This might save the workman when he was a victim of an accident at work, like the masons who fell off the scaffolding and were supported miraculously by a saint in their fall or were resuscitated by a saint on the ground. Millers or peasants trapped by the millwheel might be saved from death by miraculous intervention. Among the land-clearers, there was the companion of Gaucher of Aureil, the holy hermit and wood-cutter in the Limousin in the eleventh century, who, when he was on the point of being crushed by the fall of a tree, found himself safe and sound under a miraculous hollow of the trunk made by God at the prayer of the blessed Gaucher. Miracles took the place of social security in the middle ages. Above all, there was security in the world to come, where heaven promised the elect a life finally free of fears, evil surprises, and death. And yet here, too, who could be sure of being saved? Fear of hell extended earthly insecurity.

XIII

Of course material culture in the middle ages did undergo a definite advance. Although we cannot attain the precision of modern, contemporary periods, both because we lack precise quantitative data and because the feudal economy does not lend itself easily to statistical methods, which were perfected to measure the evolution of economies which were certainly monetary if not capitalistic, it is possible to form a rough idea of the position of the medieval economy. We can make out a long phase of expansion which, to some extent, tallied with increased wellbeing.

We should cite the data for this growth, beginning with the growth of population. The population of the west doubled between the end of the tenth and the middle of the fourteenth centuries. Western Europe, according to J. C. Russell, is supposed to have gone from 22½ million inhabitants in about 950 to 54½ million on the eve of the Black Death in 1348, while Europe as a whole, according to M. K. Bennett, is supposed to have had 42 million inhabitants in about 1000 and 73 million in about 1300. The rise in population is supposed to have been particularly steep around 1200. The indices of growth calculated by Slicher Van Bath for 50-year periods are 109.5 for 1000–1050, 104.3 for 1050–1100, 104.2 for 1100–1150, 122 for 1150–1200, 113.1 for 1200–1250, 105.8 for 1250–1300. The population of France is supposed to have risen from 12 to 21 million between 1200 and 1340, that of Germany from 8 to 14 million, that of England from 2.2 to 4.5 million. This period of growth came between two periods of demographic recession when the population of Europe fell from about 67 million in about 200 AD to about 27 million around 700, and from the 73 million reached around 1300 to about 45 million around 1400. We may note that the maximum figure, for the start of the fourteenth century, is only a little greater than that from the period of Roman prosperity at the end of the second century. In demographic terms, the middle ages may be defined quantitatively as simply a catching-up process.

The same evolution took place in agricultural production, prices, and salaries. Numerical evaluation of the agricultural production of the medieval west is impossible, at any rate in the present state of historical knowledge. One single index can be followed in a fragmentary and rough fashion: the increase in yields which we have already spoken of. But can one compare, for wheat for example, the figure of 2.7 at Annapes in 810 with those of 4 in 1155-6 calculated by Georges Duby for two manors of the abbey of Cluny, of 5 mentioned by the *Anonymous Husbandry*, an English treatise on agronomy of the thirteenth century, and the average figure of 3.7 calculated by J. Titow for the manors of the bishop of Winchester between 1211 and 1299? And, as we have seen, the increase in the surface area under cultivation certainly contributed more to the increase in agricultural production than did the intensification of farming.

For prices, the index is more useful. We do not at present possess graphs of prices going back before 1160 for England or before 1200 for western Europe generally. If one takes the level of wheat prices during the period 1160–79 as the index 100, this index rises, according to Slicher Van Bath's calculations, which are based on the data of Lord Beveridge, to 139.3 (1180–99), 203 (1200–19), 196.1 (1220–39), 214.2 (1240–59), 262.9 (1260–79), 279.2 (1280–99), with a peak of 324.7 reached in the period 1300–19, caused by the great famine of 1315–16, and a relative (compared with the abnormal rise of the preceding period) falling-back to 289.7 (1320–39). This clearly shows Sir Michael Postan's 'true revolution of prices'. Wages indicate a similar advance. In England net earnings went from the index 100 for the period 1251–1300 to the index 105.1 for the period 1301–50 for agricultural workers and from 100 to 109.4 for woodcutters. Yet the rise in wages remained small and, although the number of wage-earners rose sharply, they were still only a minority of the working masses. This observation does not call into question the reality of a definite economic growth between the tenth and the fourteenth century, but it makes it clear that it is necessary to put the economic situation into the context of the evolution of economic and social structures, that is to say what are traditionally called, respectively, the shift from the natural to the monetary economy, and the evolution of the feudal income.

XIV

It is a century since Bruno Hildebrand divided the economic evolution of societies into three phases: *Naturalwirtschaft, Geldwirtschaft* and *Kreditwirtschaft* – the natural economy, the monetary economy, and the credit economy – and Alfons Dopsch, in his great 1930 book, *Economie-nature et économie-argent dans l'histoire mondiale* made medievalists use this terminology and at any rate face up to this problem. So it is a question of appreciating the role played by money in the economy. Should this role be insignificant one is dealing with a natural economy, where production, consumption, and exchanges occur without the intervention of money, with certain exceptions. On the other hand, if money is essential to the functioning of economic life, one is faced with a monetary economy. Which of these was true of the medieval west?

Let us first, following Henri Pirenne and Marc Bloch, remind ourselves of some necessary distinctions. Firstly, barter played a rather small part in medieval exchanges. By a natural economy one should understand for the medieval west an economy where exchanges, all exchanges, were reduced to a strict minimum. Thus a natural economy would be almost synonymous with a closed economy. The lord and the peasant found their needs satisfied in the framework of the manor, and in the case of the peasant, above all, in the compass of his home. Food was produced from the garden attached to the house and from the part of the yield from his smallholding which remained to him after he had paid his dues to the lord and the tithe owing to the church; clothes were made by women at home, and the basic tools – the quern or hand-mill, the distaff, and the loom – belonged to the family.

If, in the sources, dues are indicated in money, this does not mean that they were actually paid in money. Monetary evaluation was not tightly linked to payment in money. Money was only a term of reference, 'it served as a measure of value', it was an *apreciadura*, an evaluation, as a passage of the *Cantar de mio Cid* says on the subject of payment in kind. Of course, this survival of monetary terminology was not insignificant. This relic of the antique inheritance, as in so many other areas, is, in the end, only a witness to regression. One should no more take the mention of money in medieval texts 'as valid currency' than the pagan expressions remaining in medieval Christian literature. When the sea was called Neptune it was a linguistic mannerism. When a horse promised by the monks of St Père of Chartres in 1107 to a certain Milo de Lèves is represented in the charter by 20 *solidi* it is a case of defining the value of the horse which was the object of the transaction. It is merely that since monetary evaluations were not combated by the Church with the same zeal as expressions recalling pagan religion they have survived better. Marc Bloch noted a remarkable document from Passau in which the word 'price' is paradoxically employed to designate the natural equivalent of a sum evaluated in money.

In short, money clearly never disappeared from use in the medieval west. Not only did the Church and the feudal lords always have a certain supply of money at their disposal to cope with their spending on luxuries, but the peasant himself could not live entirely without buying some things with money, such as salt, which he did not produce, which he did not receive, and which he could only rarely buy by barter. Such things had to be bought with cash. But in the last-mentioned case it is probable that the peasants and more generally the poor acquired the few coins which they needed more through alms than through selling their produce. In times of shortage, precisely when the lack of cash came to be cruelly felt by the poor, distributions of money accompanied distributions of foodstuffs. At the time of the great famine in 1125 this was done by the count of Flanders, Charles the Good: 'In all the towns and villages where he passed, a crowd pressed round him every day and he gave them with his own hands food, money and clothes.' On 25 July at Bamberg, when the famine was coming to an end and a new and plentiful harvest was due, the bishop of Bamberg gave the poor 'a penny and a sickle, the work tool and the viaticum'.

It has been noted that the spread of the monetary economy was more extensive than it appears at first sight to have been if one takes into consideration two features which were very common in the medieval west: the use of treasures, luxury objects, pieces of the goldsmith's craft, as monetary reserves; and the existence of currencies other than metal coins. This is true. Charlemagne is supposed to have sold some of his most precious manuscripts to give aid to the poor. Here is another example, among hundreds of others, from 1197: a German monk met another walking along in a great hurry:

When I asked him where he was going, he answered me: 'To change money. Before the harvest we were obliged, to feed the poor, to kill our livestock and to pledge our chalices and our books. And lo, the Lord has just sent us a man who has given us a quantity of gold which will cover the two needs. So I am going to change the gold for silver to buy back what we pledged and to build up our herds again.'

But this form of hoarding which only yielded to need testifies to the weakness and inelasticity of the monetary circulation.

Similarly the existence of non-metallic currency, such as oxen, cows, pieces of cloth, and especially pepper, is an undeniable sign of archaism. It shows that an economy has with difficulty managed to pass from the natural level to the monetary level. In any case the nature of metallic money itself remained archaic for a long time. In effect money was appreciated because of its value, not as a symbol but as merchandise. It was not worth the theoretical value written on its face or its edge (which was very thin) but the real value of the precious metal which it contained. People weighed coins to find out how much they were worth. As Marc Bloch has said, 'a coin which one has to put in the scales looks very much like an ingot'. It was only just at the very end of the thirteenth century that French civil lawyers began to distinguish its intrinsic value – its weight in gold – from its extrinsic value, that is to say its transformation into a monetary symbol, an instrument of exchange. Moreover, at every phase of medieval monetary history, features which have often been interpreted as signs of a monetary renaissance witness far more to the limits of the monetary economy. In the early middle ages mints increased in number. Places which have since disappeared – this is particularly true of many mints in Visigothic Spain – and which definitely were only villages were seats of mints. But, as Marc Bloch justly observed, 'the great reason for there being so many scattered mints was that money did not circulate much'.

The monetary reform of Charlemagne, who instituted the monetary system of pounds, shillings, and pence (£1 = 20 shillings, 1 shilling = 12 pence) which survived until 1971 in Britain, meant in fact an adaptation to the regression of the monetary economy. Gold was no longer struck. The pound and the shilling were not real coins but simply accounting terms. The only coin actually struck was the silver penny, and it remained the only coin until the thirteenth century, that is to say a very small unit. It was the only one needed, but it also excluded, as far as even more modest exchanges were concerned, the existence of coins made of base alloys of smaller value. The reaction of the crusaders on the second crusade, when they entered Byzantine territory in 1147, is significant: 'Here we first encountered the copper money "staminae", and for one of these we unhappily gave five denarii, or rather we lost a mark on twelve solidi' (Odo of Deuil, 1948, p. 41).

Finally the monetary renaissance of the thirteenth century has made a deep impression on historians because of the return to striking gold coins: the *genovino* and the florin in 1252, St Louis' *écu*, and the Venetian ducat in 1284. But although this event was significant, it was still, in view of the small number of coins in circulation at the end of the thirteenth century, an economic index rather than an economic reality. The economic reality was the striking of the silver *grossus* or groat in Venice in 1201, in Florence in about 1235, in Flanders in 1260, in France in about 1265, at Montpellier in 1273, in England (fleetingly) in 1279, and in Bohemia in 1296. The progress of the monetary economy took place at that time at this middling level of exchange; this progress was real.

The Spanish example was perhaps peculiar, for the proximity of the Muslim economy (the emirs of Cordoba did not cease to strike gold coins, and, with the advance of the Reconquista, the Christian kings continued to strike them, at Toledo, for example, in 1175) introduced a contagious element into the Spanish economy. The work of Spanish and Argentinian medievalists (Claudio Sanchez-Albornoz, Luis Garcia de Valdeavellano, Reyna Pastor de Togneri) has, however, shown that the cycle of natural economy followed by monetary economy did in fact occur there, somewhat out of step with the rest of Christian Europe. The strong pull exerted by the Muslim centres of production in the south prolonged a phase of raised prices right up to the start of the eleventh century which coincided with the end of the period of the monetary economy. The eleventh century and the first half of the twelfth saw a fall in prices, indicative of a phase of natural economy, the preceding phase having accomplished the demonetarization of the Christian kingdoms. From the middle of the twelfth century, on the other hand, a phase of monetary economy evolved again.

Attitudes to money or more generally to silver also teach us indirectly about this economic evolution. Of course there was in Christian teaching a traditional distrust of money, but the scarcity of money in the early middle ages rather gave it a prestige which was strengthened by the fact that to strike money was a sign of power. In short, money had become a symbol of political and social power rather than of economic power. Rulers struck gold coins which did not have economic value but which were status symbols. Scenes of minting and minters figure prominently in iconography: we see them at St Martin de Boscherville, at Souvigny, and at Worms. Coins and minters shared the character, sacred and cursed at once, of smiths and more generally of metallurgists; in their case it was strengthened by the superior charm of precious metals. Robert Lopez has spoken of minters as an aristocracy of the early middle ages, but it was a magical aristocracy rather than an economic one. The rise of a monetary economy, on the other hand, provoked an explosion of hatred against money. It is true that nascent economic progress came into being to the profit of certain classes, and as a consequence it appeared as a new oppression. St Bernard inveighed against the cursed money. The great beneficiary of this evolution at its start was the Church, which, by the development of fees, collections, and ecclesiastical taxation, was soon able to appropriate a proportion of the money in circulation. It was denounced for its *avaritia* or cupidity. Gregory VII had declared: 'The Lord did not say: "My Name is Custom" .' The Goliards, in a satire, *The Holy Gospel according to the Silver Mark*, accused his successors of making the Lord say, 'My Name is Money.'

A shift in morality occurred. *Superbia*, pride, the feudal sin par excellence, until then generally considered to be the mother of all the vices, began to yield the first place to *avaritia* or desire for money. Another beneficiary of the economic evolution was what, for simplicity's sake, we shall call the burgess class, that is to say the upper class of the new social order in the towns; it was also denounced. Writers and artists in the service of the traditional ruling classes stigmatized it: the usurer weighed down by his purse which dragged him down into hell was exposed to the detestation and the horror of the faithful in carvings in churches. The slow replacement of the natural economy by the monetary economy was advanced enough at the end of the thirteenth century for serious social consequences to result.

XV

Although a portion of the dues from yields in kind was converted to money yields, the feudal income was relatively inflexible, and the revenue brought in from the monetized portion shrank owing to the rapid deterioration of the coinage. Thus part of the seigneurial class became impoverished just when the increase in spending to maintain social status made it need money more acutely. It was the first crisis of feudalism and the origin of the crisis of the fourteenth century.

Faced with this crisis in the seigneurial world, the peasant community divided. A minority who were able to make a profit from the sale of their surpluses became richer, rounded off their lands, and turned themselves into a privileged group, a kulak class. We come across them in English manorial documents and in literary sources. Thus in the *Roman de Renart*:

Dawn came, the sun rose, lighting up the roads white with snow, and behold Master Constant Desgranges, a wealthy farmer, who lived by the side of the pond, coming out of his house followed by his servants. . . . The farmer sounded his horn and called his hounds, and then ordered his horse to be got ready. Seeing this, Renart fled to his earth. . . . One day Renart had come to the outskirts of a farm which was near the woods and contained hens and cocks in large numbers, as well as ducks, drakes, and geese and ganders. It was the property of Master Constant Desnos, a farmer whose house was full of food of all sorts and an orchard where there were many fruit trees which gave cherries, apples and other fruits. There were in his house big capons, salted meat, and hams, and a great abundance of bacon. To prevent entry to his garden, he had surrounded it with strong oak stakes, bushes and thorns. Renart would have loved to leap inside very much. . . .

On the other hand, the rest of the peasant masses became increasingly impoverished. The rise in population did not only find expression in an extension of the cultivated areas and an improvement of yields on some lands. It more certainly led to a fragmentation of land-holdings, the result of which was that the lesser peasants had either to get into debt, or to hire themselves out to better-off peasants, thus accentuating their social dependence and their economic inferiority by depriving their own holding of some of their work. In peasant societies exploited by the lords or the richest people, where land was unproductive and there were too many mouths, debt was the great scourge. Peasants borrowed money from the urban money-lender – often a Jew – or from a richer peasant, usually cunning enough to avoid the usurer's code of behaviour, which was a hindrance only to the Jew.

We can see tenures getting smaller in the Boulonnais, for example, at Beuvrequen, on lands belonging to the abbey of St Bertin. In 1305, out of 60 holdings, 26 (or 43 per cent) had fewer than 2 hectares, 16 (or 27 per cent) had between 2 and 4, 12 (or 20 per cent) had between 4 and 8, and only 6 (that is to say 10 per cent) had more than 8. In England, at Weedon Beck, where, in 1248, only 20.9 per cent of the peasants had fewer than 6 hectares, the proportion had risen to 42.8 per cent in 1300. We can see peasants getting into debt to the Jews at Perpignan, for example, where notaries' registers around 1300 reveal that 65 per cent of the debtors of the town usurers were peasants; 40 per cent of them contracted their debts in autumn, at the time when marriages took place and when the lords' dues were paid, and 53 per cent bound themselves to pay back the debt in August and September, after the grain and wine harvests. Other creditors were Italian merchants and moneychangers. Lombards crop up as much in the Namurois, where documents show how almost an entire village got into debt between 1295 and 1311, as in the Alps, where at the start of the fourteenth century the usurers of Asti had pawnshops - *casane* - in almost all the villages of the territories of the House of Savoy.

Those who seem to have profited the most from the development of the monetary economy were the merchants. It is true that the rise of the towns of which they were the principal beneficiaries was bound up with the advance of the monetary economy and that the 'rise of the bourgeoisie' represents the appearance of a social class whose economic power relied more on money than on land. But how important was this class numerically before 1300 or 1350? How many small merchants were only small shopkeepers in every way comparable with the moneylenders in periods closer to us who as we well know have very little relation to capitalism? As for the minority which we find of great merchants or - not exactly the same thing - of the urban elite, which we might call the patrician class, what was the nature of its profits, of its economic behaviour, and how did it affect economic structures? The merchants were only marginally involved in agricultural production. Of course the usurers mentioned above, especially those in the Namurois, concealed an anticipated purchase of the harvests behind their pawnbroking, and they would then sell this in the market. But the proportion of agricultural products which were thus commercialized through the intervention of merchants and to their profit, although it was rising, remained low.

At the start of the fourteenth century the merchant was still essentially a seller of exceptional, rare, luxurious, exotic products, and it was the increasing demand for these products among the higher classes which effectively brought an increase in the number and importance of these traders. They were complementary, they brought in that small proportion of necessary extras which the manorial economy could not provide. In so far as they were 'epiphenomena' who did not disturb the structure of the economy and society to their foundations, understanding clerics excused and justified them. Thus Gilles le Muisit, abbot of St Martin of Tournai, wrote in his *Dit des Marchands*:

Nul pays ne se poet de li seus gouvrener, / Pourchou vont marchéant travaillier et pener / Chou qui faut ès pays, en tous règnes mener, / Se ne les doit-on mie sans raison fourmener.

*Chou que marchéant vont delà mer, dechà mer / Pour pourvir les pays, che les font
entr'amer.*

'No country can govern itself by itself alone, / That is why merchants go to work and
fatigue themselves / What is lacking to their country, to bring it to all kingdoms, / Thus
one must never misuse them without reason.
Because merchants go hither and thither on the sea / To provide for the countries,
that makes them beloved.'

In fact, rather than being complementary, merchants were marginal. The
essence of their transactions concentrated on expensive products of small
volume, such as spices, fine broadcloth, and silk. This is above all true of
the Italians, the pioneers of commerce. It seems likely that their principal
cunning had consisted simply of knowing that the stability of oriental prices
allowed them to calculate their profits in advance. For Ruggiero Romano was
surely right to see in this the essential cause of the merchant 'miracle' in
Christian Europe. It is also true, although to a lesser extent, of the Hanseatic
merchants, but it is probable, as M. P. Lesnikov among others has maintained,
that until the middle of the fourteenth century commerce in grains and even
in timber played only a secondary role in their trade, in which wax and furs
represented the big profits.

The very nature of mercantile profits from these luxury products, which
were often enormous, shows that these transactions occurred on the margin
of the basic economy. This is also clear from the structure of commercial
companies, where, in addition to societies of a durable type bound up with
a family, most associations of merchants formed themselves for a venture, a
voyage, or a period of time of 3, 4, or 5 years. There was no true continuity
in their enterprises, no long-term investment, not to mention the habit, long
adhered to, of squandering a large part, sometimes most, of their fortunes in
charitable bequests at their deaths. What the merchants, and even more the
urban patrician class, were seeking was: on the one hand manors which would
allow them, their families, and their servants to be protected from shortage,
which would give them the dignity due to a landowner and which, should
the occasion arise through the acquisition of a lordship, would let them rise
to the rank of the landed aristocracy; and on the other hand land and housing
in cities with profitable rents, loans to lords and rulers and sometimes to the
poor, and above all permanent sources of income.

Let us recall the economic and social evolution sketched above. The upper
classes were increasingly composed of *rentiers*, for the lords, too, were increasingly becoming, through the evolution of the feudal income, *'rentiers du sol'*,
as Marc Bloch put it, and less and less direct exploiters. In most countries,
the institution of a closed social hierarchy prevented the landed aristocracy

from involving itself in business, and what could at least have been invested in the land and thus have nourished agricultural progress disappeared in expenses to maintain status and to buy luxuries that were ever more onerous and more devouring.

It remains the case that the undeniable progress of the monetary economy had serious social repercussions. It began to shake the class status quo by increasing the number of wage-earners, especially in towns, but more and more in the countryside as well. Most often such progress enlarged the gap between classes or rather between the social categories existing within classes. We have seen this happening among the rural classes, the lords, and the peasants. An upper layer detached itself from the middling and lesser folk of the artisans and workmen.

But if money was very often the origin of their differences, the social hierarchy was from now on defined even more according to another value, a new value: work. The urban classes effectively won their places by the new force of their economic role. Against the seigneurial ideal based on the exploitation of the work of the peasants, they thus opposed their system of values based on work which had made them powerful. But, when they themselves had become a *rentier* class, the upper classes of the new urban social system imposed a new dividing line in social values, one which separated manual work from other forms of activities. This moreover corresponds to the development of the peasant classes, for a distinction was made between an elite which, by a curious evolution of terminology, was called in France the '*laboureurs*' or ploughmen (better-off peasants owning a team and their work gear) and the masses who had only their arms to use in their work, the '*manouvriers*' or, more aptly, the '*brassiers*'. In the urban classes, the new division isolated the 'mechanicals', the artisans and workmen, as yet not very numerous. Intellectuals and university graduates who were momentarily tempted to define themselves as workers, intellectual workers shoulder to shoulder with the other occupations in the urban workplace, hastened to join the elite which kept their hands unsullied. Even poor Rutebeuf exclaimed with pride 'I am not a manual worker.'

8

Christian Society
(Tenth to Thirteenth Centuries)

I

AROUND THE year 1000 AD, western sources depicted Christian society according to a new system which immediately enjoyed a great success: society was composed of a 'threefold people' – priests, warriors, and peasants. The three categories were distinct and complementary, each one having need of the other two. Together, the three worked in harmony to make up the fabric of society. This model apparently made its first appearance in the very free translation of Boethius' *Consolation* made by Alfred the Great of England in the late ninth century. The king had to have '*gebedmen, fyrdmen, weorcmen*', or 'men of prayer, men of war, men of work'. A century later, this tripartite plan reappears in the writings of Aelfric and Wulfstan. Then Bishop Adalbero of Laon, in a poem which he dedicated to the Capetian king Robert the Pious in about 1020, produced a more elaborate version:

The community of the faithful is a single body, but the condition of society is threefold in order. For human law distinguishes two classes. Nobles and serfs, indeed, are not governed by the same ordinance . . . . The former are the warriors and the protectors of the churches. They are the defenders of the people, of both great and small, in short, of everyone, and at the same time they ensure their own safety. The other class is that of the serfs. This luckless breed possesses nothing except at the cost of its own labour. Who could, reckoning with an abacus, add up the sum of the cares with which the peasants are occupied, of their journeys on foot, of their hard labours? The serfs provide money, clothes, and food, for the rest; no free man could exist without serfs. Is there a task to be done? Does anyone want to put himself out? We see kings and prelates make themselves the serfs of their serfs; the master, who claims to feed his serf, is fed by him. And the serf never sees an end to his tears and his sighs. God's house, which we think of as one, is thus divided into three; some pray, others fight, and yet others work. The three groups, which coexist, cannot bear to be separated; the services rendered by one are a precondition for the labours of the two others; each in his turn takes it upon himself to relieve the whole. Thus the threefold assembly is none the less united, and it is thus that law has been able to triumph, and that the world has been able to enjoy peace.

This crucial text contains some extraordinary phrases. The reality of feudal society is suddenly revealed in the formula 'the master, who claims to feed his serf, is fed by him'. And the existence of classes – and consequently of antagonism between them – although immediately disguised by the orthodox affirmation of social harmony, is admitted in the observation: 'God's house, which we think of as one, is thus divided into three.' What is important for us here is the characterization of the three classes of feudal society, which was to become classic: those who pray, those who fight, those who work: *oratores, bellatores, laboratores*.

It would be fascinating to follow the history of this theme, its changes, its connections with other motifs, for example with the three sons of Noah from biblical genealogy, or with the three sons of Rigr, from Germanic mythology. Out of dozens of texts, here is one in which the tripartite division has put on an animal guise. In the early twelfth century Eadmer of Canterbury, recording the teaching of Anselm of Canterbury, expanded this *exemplum* or sort of symbolic fable.

Exemplum of the sheep, the oxen and the dogs. The purpose of sheep is to provide milk and wool; that of oxen is to work the ground, and that of dogs is to defend sheep and oxen from wolves. If each type of animal performs its duty, God protects them . . . . Similarly he has set up orders which he has established in view of the various duties which must be fulfilled in this world. He has established some – clerks and monks – so that they may pray for the others and so that, full of gentleness, like sheep, they may give the others the milk of preaching to drink and may inspire in them a fervent love of God by the wool of good example. God has established the peasants to sustain their own lives and other people's, as the oxen do by their work. God has established yet others – the warriors – to show force in so far as it is needful, and to defend those who pray and those who till the land from enemies such as wolves.

But is a literary theme a good introduction to the study of medieval society? What relation does it bear to reality? Does it express the actual structure of social classes in the medieval west? Georges Dumézil has made the point that the division of society into three is characteristic of Indo-European societies, and thus the medieval west would be connected with, in particular, the Italic tradition of Jupiter, Mars, and Quirinus, with probably a Celtic intermediary. Others, who include Vasilii I. Abaev, think that the 'division into three by function' is 'a necessary stage of the evolution of all human ideology' or rather of all social ideology. The main point is, however, that this model emerged or re-emerged just when it seemed to suit the development of western European society. Between the eighth and the eleventh century the aristocracy organized itself into a military class, as we have seen, a typical member of this class being called a *miles* or knight. This seems to have been the case right up to the frontiers of Christian Europe, since a tombstone inscription recently found in Gniezno cathedral tells us about an eleventh-century *miles*. In the Carolingian period the clergy transformed themselves into a clerical caste, as Canon Delaruelle has shown, and the evolution of the liturgy and of religious architecture is an expression of this change. Choirs and cloisters were enclosed and restricted to the clergy of the chapter. External schools attached to monasteries were shut down. From now on the celibate priest celebrated Mass with his back turned to the faithful, who no longer came in procession to bear the 'oblations' to the celebrant. They were no longer able to hear the recitation of the canon of the mass which from now on was said in a low voice. The Host was no longer normal bread but unleavened bread, 'as if the mass had become foreign to daily life'. Finally, the condition of peasants tended to become more uniform and to sink to the lowest level, that of the serfs.

One has only to compare this schema with those of the early middle ages to appreciate the change. There are two images of society which occur most frequently between the fifth and the eleventh centuries. Sometimes it is a multiple, diversified model, listing a certain number of social and professional categories in which one can trace the relics of a Roman system of classification, distinguishing professional groups, legal categories, and social conditions. Thus Bishop Rather of Verona in the tenth century listed nineteen categories: civilians, soldiers, craftsmen, physicians, merchants, advocates, judges, witnesses, procurators, employers, mercenaries, councillors, lords, slaves (or serfs), masters, pupils, the rich, the middling, and beggars. This list more or less preserves the specialization of the professional and social categories which had been characteristic of Roman society, and which had perhaps survived to some extent in northern Italy.

More often, however, society was boiled down to two groups in confrontation – clergy and laity from one point of view, or strong and weak, rich and poor, if one was merely taking lay society into consideration, or free and unfree if one were viewing it from a legal standpoint. It is clear that this dualistic model corresponds to a simplification of social categories in western Europe in the early middle ages. Government, whether spiritual, political, or economic, was monopolized by a minority while the masses submitted. Less often, the middling or 'mediocre' make their appearance between the great and the small. This happened when people were careful to express nuances or when they fell back on a tripartite scheme because their minds automatically classsified everything into threes (just as in our schools where it comes naturally to divide essays into three parts). Ralph Glaber uses this pattern. But this division into three seems chiefly to be the result of a rhetorical mannerism: to what did it correspond in any concrete way?

The division of society by function, which makes its first appearance around the year 1000, was quite different. It was bound up with the functions of the priest, the warrior, and the farmer. It was characteristic of a certain phase of evolution in primitive societies, probably not only Indo-European ones. One could probably find affinities, if not continuity, between a source such as Eadmer of Canterbury's passage quoted above and the animal symbolism used for the tripartite division of functions in other societies, which would leave no doubt about the relationship between the way medieval people viewed society and the way in which it was viewed in other fairly primitive societies. E. Benveniste has emphasized how, in the agricultural lustration and the *suovetaurilia* of Graeco-Italic cults, one finds the pig corresponding to Tellus, the ram to Jupiter, and the bull to Mars. L. Gerschel has established the connection in the systems of divination and the thought of ancient Rome between the man, the horse, and the ox, as species, or the head, the four-horse chariot, and the heifer, as omens, with the three functional values of sovereignty, military prowess, and economic prosperity. Georges Dumézil has reminded us of the symbolic importance of the eagle of Jupiter, the shewolf of Mars, and the trout which symbolized the earth-goddesses and fertility. The sheep, oxen, and dogs of Eadmer are a medieval transformation of this custom of symbolizing a tripartite society by animals.

What is the meaning of the division into three functions? And, chiefly, what contacts did the three functions, or rather the three classes which represented them, maintain with each other? It is clear that the tripartite schema was a symbol of social harmony. Like the fable of Menenius Agrippa, *The Limbs and the Stomach*, it was a vivid way of defusing the class struggle and of mystifying the people. However, although it has been correctly observed that this schema aimed to keep the workers – the economic class, the producers – in a state of submission to the other two classes, it has not been sufficiently noticed that the schema, which was dreamed up by the clergy, aimed also at subjecting the warriors to the priests, and at making them the protectors of the Church and of religion. Thus it is an episode in the ancient rivalry between the magicians and the warriors, on a par with the Gregorian Reform and the conflict between Sacerdotium and Imperium. It is contemporary with the *chansons de geste*, which were the literary battleground of the conflict between the clerical and knightly classes, just as the *Iliad* is a witness to the conflict between the power of the magicians and the valour of the warriors, as Vasilii I. Abaev, working from the episode of the Trojan Horse, has cleverly

demonstrated. ~~Think of the distance which separates Roland and Lancelot.~~
What has been described as the Christianizing of the chivalric ideal is more
certainly the victory of the power of the priests over the strength of the warriors.
Roland, whatever has been said about him, has the ethics of his class. He thinks
about his lineage, his king, and his country. There is nothing in him of the
saint, except that he served as a model for the saint of his age – the eleventh
and twelfth centuries – the *miles Christi*. The whole of the Arthurian cycle,
on the other hand, culminates in the triumph of the 'first function' over the
second. Already in the work of Chrétien of Troyes a difficult balancing act
culminates, by way of the development of Percival, in the metamorphosis of
the knight, the quest of the Holy Grail, and the vision of Good Friday. The
prose Lancelot concludes the cycle. The epilogue with Arthur's death is a
twilight of the warriors. The symbolic implement of the military class, the
sword Excalibur, is finally thrown by the king into the lake and Lancelot
becomes truly a sort of saint. The power of the magicians, though in a rather
refined form, had absorbed the valour of the warriors.

On the other hand, one might wonder if the third category, that of the
workers, the *laboratores*, was entirely synonymous with the class of producers,
and if all the peasants represented the economic function. A whole series of
sources could be gathered together to show that between the end of the eighth
and the twelfth century the words related to the word *labor*, when used in
its economic sense (which in fact is rarely purely the case, since these terms
are almost always contaminated to some extent by the psychological idea of
weariness or distress) tally with a precise meaning, that of agricultural advance,
whether an increase in the area under cultivation or an improvement in
the yield. The Capitulary of the Saxons at the end of the eighth century
distinguishes *substantia* from *labor*, that is the patrimony or inheritance on
the one hand and the profits gained by working the land on the other. *Labor*
meant land clearance and its fruits. A gloss in a manuscript on one of the
canons of a Norwegian synod of 1164 defines *labores* as *novales*, that is to say
newly cleared lands or assarts. The *laborator* was the man whose productive
capacity was great enough for him to produce more than the others. As early
as 926 a charter of St Vincent of Mâcon refers to '*illi meliores qui sunt
laboratores*, 'those men of the better sort who are the *laboratores*'. Hence was
to be derived the French word '*laboureurs*', which, from the tenth century,
designated the upper level of the peasantry, the ones who owned at least a
yoke of oxen and their work-implements.

Thus the tripartite schema really portrayed only the upper classes: the clerical
class, the military class, and the upper layer of the productive class. Although
some writers, such as Adalbero of Laon, placed the entire peasant class in
the third order, and identified the *laboratores* with the serfs, the schema

included only the *melior pars*, the elites. We might moreover recall the way
in which this threefold society was transformed in the later middle ages. In
France it became the three estates: the clergy, the nobility, and the third estate.
However the third estate was not to be identified with the entire class of
commoners. It did not even represent all the bourgeoisie. It was composed
of the upper levels of the bourgeoisie, the 'notables'. The ambiguity which
had gone on since the middle ages over the nature of this third class, which
theoretically contained all those who did not figure in the first two classes,
and which in fact was limited to the richest or most learned section of the
remainder, was cleared up in the dispute which occurred in the French
Revolution between the men of '89 who wanted to halt the Revolution at the
victory of the elite of the Third Estate and those who wanted to turn it into
a triumph for the entire people.

In fact, in the society of what has been called the first feudal age, up to
about the middle of the twelfth century, the mass of manual workers quite
simply did not exist. An eleventh-century work, again of St Vincent of Mâcon,
contrasts the *'laboratores'* with the *'pauperiores qui manibus laborant'*, 'the poorer
people who work with their hands'. Marc Bloch noticed with surprise that
the lay and ecclesiastical lords of this period had precious metals turned into
pieces of craftsmanship which they then had melted down again in case of
need, as we have seen. They reckoned the work of the artist or craftsman as
of no economic value. It is a fact that this age was unaware of work or workers.
Only an error of vocabulary lets us translate *laboratores* simply as 'workers'.

Nonetheless it is the case that we have just been talking about social classes
and have been applying this term to the three categories of the tripartite schema,
even though traditionally they were seen as orders; orders were supposed to
correspond in the medieval period to functions, not to class distinctions. But,
first, this vocabulary is usually not exact. The term *ordo*, which is Carolingian
rather than specifically feudal, belongs to religious terminology and thus relates
generally to a religious vision of society, to clerics and to laymen, to the spiritual
and the temporal. Thus there could only be two orders, the clergy and the
people, *clerus* and *populus*, and the sources moreover usually say *'utraque ordo'*,
'each of the two orders'. Second, only modern jurists have wanted to establish,
without any semblance of justification, a distinction between a class which they
suppose to be defined economically, and an order which they suppose to be
defined legally. In fact, the orders were religious, but just like social classes
they were based on socioeconomic foundations. It is still true that the real
inclination of the originators and the users of the tripartite schema in the middle
ages (to make three classes of which it was composed into 'orders') was to
consecrate this social structure, to make it into an objective, eternal reality
created and willed by God, and thus to make a social revolution impossible.

II

Thus it was a profound change when, as had happened occasionally already in the eleventh century, *ordo* was replaced by *conditio* or condition, and, in about 1200, by 'estate'. This laicizing of the way in which society was viewed would be important in itself, but, even more importantly, it was accompanied by the destruction of the tripartite model which itself corresponded to a crucial development in medieval society. Clearly a critical moment in the history of the tripartite model in a society comes when a new class appears which has not hitherto had a place in the system. The solutions adopted by different societies, which Georges Dumézil has studied for Indo-European societies, are varied. Three of them do not disturb the traditional view of things much. The first solution manages to keep the new class on one side and to refuse it a place in the system. The second amalgamates and dissolves it into one of the three pre-existing classes. Even the more revolutionary third solution, which turns the three-part model into a four-part one, does not disturb things much. Usually the spoilsport class is the mercantile one. This marks the change from a closed to an open economy and the emergence of a powerful productive class which is not content to submit itself to the clerical and military classes. We see clearly how traditional medieval society experimented with these conservative solutions when we read in a fourteenth-century English sermon, 'God made the clerics, the knights and the ploughmen, but the devil made the burgesses and the usurers,' or when a thirteenth-century German poem says that from now on the fourth class, that of the usurers or *Wuocher*, governs the other three.

What is significant is that in the second half of the twelfth century and during the course of the thirteenth the tripartite model of society, even if it continued to be used as a literary and ideological theme for a long time to come, was being pulled apart. It yielded to a more complicated and more subtle model which resulted from, and reflected, a social upheaval. The tripartite society was succeeded by the society of 'estates', that is to say of socio-professional conditions. The number of these conditions varied according to the taste of the writers, but some features of the models are constant, notably the mixture of a religious classification based on clerical and family criteria with a division according to professional roles and social conditions.

Sometimes, moreover, just as the three sons of Noah had lent themselves to the representation of the tripartite model, other themes from Biblical or Christian symbolism were adapted to the new model of society. Honorius of Autun compared society to a church whose columns were the bishops, the stained-glass windows the masters, the vaults the kings, the roof-tiles the knights, and the paved floor the people who by their work fed and sustained

Christendom. In the thirteenth century the popular Saxon preacher Conrad, a Franciscan, more simply identified the altar with Christ, the towers with the pope and the bishops, the choir with the clerics, and the nave with the laity. At about the same time Berthold of Regensburg distinguished ten social classes corresponding to the ten angelic choirs. A German sermon collection of about 1220 listed as many as 28 estates: (1) the pope, (2) the cardinals, (3) the patriarchs, (4) the bishops, (5) the prelates, (6) the monks, (7) the crusaders, (8) the lay brothers, (9) the wandering monks, (10) the secular priests, (11) the lawyers and physicians, (12) the students, (13) the wandering students, (14) the nuns, (15) the emperor, (16) the kings, (17) the princes and counts, (18) the knights, (19) the nobles, (20) the squires, (21) the burgesses, (22) the merchants, (23) the retail shopkeepers, (24) the heralds, (25) the obedient peasants, (26) the rebellious peasants, (27) women . . . and (28) the preaching friars. In fact it is a double, parallel hierarchy of clergy and laity, the former headed by the pope and the latter by the emperor. Without yet mentioning estates, Stephen of Fougères, in his *Livre de manières*, written in about 1175, had already, in the first part of his poem, defined the duties of the kings, clergy, bishops, archbishops, cardinals, and knights, and in the second part the duties of the villeins, the citizens and burgesses, and of married and unmarried ladies.

The new schema is still that of a hierarchical society, moving from top to bottom, except in the Spanish *Libro de Alexandre* from the mid-thirteenth century where the survey of the estates starts with the 'labourers' and ends with the nobles. But the hierarchy involved is different from that of the tripartite society of the orders. Here the hierarchy is more horizontal than vertical, more human than divine. It does not involve the will of God, does not derive from divine law, and can be modified to some extent. Here again iconography makes the ideological and intellectual shift clear. The portrayal of orders imposed from above, though this was to persist and even be reinforced in the age of absolute monarchy, was replaced by a picture of the estates in single file. Admittedly the powerful, the pope, the emperor, bishops, and knights, led the dance, but in which direction? Not upwards but downwards, to death, for the triumphant society of the orders had yielded to the procession of estates swept along in the dance of death. Society was desacralized and at the same time fragmented and broken up. This was at once a reflection of the evolution of social organization and the result of a fairly conscious manoeuvre by the clergy, who, seeing the society of the orders escape from them, weakened the new society by dividing it, shattering it into fragments and leading it towards death. Did not the Black Death arrive in 1348 to show precisely that God's will was to destroy all 'estates'?

The destruction of the tripartite model of society was bound up with the growth of towns from the eleventh to the thirteenth century, which itself must be set in the context of a growing division of labour, as we have seen. The three-part schema broke up at the same time as did that of the seven liberal arts. This was also the moment when bridges were being built between the liberal and the mechanical arts, between the intellectual and technical disciplines. The city workshop was the crucible where the tripartite society was dissolved and the new image was prepared. Willynilly, the Church adapted to this. The most openminded theologians announced that each profession and each condition could be justified if it organized itself with a view to salvation. In the mid-twelfth century, Gerhoch of Reichersberg, in his *Liber de aedificio Dei*, spoke of 'this great factory, this great workshop, the universe', and states,

He who by baptism has renounced the devil, even if he does not become a clerk or a monk, is supposed to have renounced the world so that all those who make profession of the Christian faith, whether they be rich or poor, nobles or serfs, merchants or peasants, must reject what is hostile to that faith and follow what belongs to it. In fact each order [the vocabulary is still one which thinks in terms of orders] and more generally each profession finds in the catholic faith and in apostolic teaching a rule adapted to his condition; and if each order fights the good fight it will be thus to attain the crown [that is to say salvation].

Of course this recognition went with careful surveillance. The Church admitted that the estates existed, by assigning specific sins to them, class sins, like distinctive labels, and also inculcating a professional morality in them.

To begin with, this new society was the society of the devil. Hence the considerable vogue in clerical literature, from the twelfth century, for the theme of the 'daughters of the devil' who were married to the estates of society. On a flyleaf of a thirteenth-century Florentine manuscript, for example, we read: 'The devil has nine daughters whom he has married off:

simony	to the secular clerks
hypocrisy	to the monks
rapine	to the knights
sacrilege	to the peasants
feint	to the sergeants
fraud	to the merchants
usury	to the burgesses
worldly pomp	to the matrons

and luxury which he did not want to marry to anyone but whom he offers to all as a common whore.'

An entire homiletic literature offering sermons *ad status* – addressed to each estate – flourished. The mendicant orders devoted prime time to this in their preaching in the thirteenth century. Humbert of Romans, the Dominican cardinal, codified them in the middle of the thirteenth century. The high point in this recognition of the estates came when they were enthroned in confession and penance. Thirteenth-century confessors' manuals which defined sins and cases of conscience ended by cataloguing sins according to social class. Each estate had its own vices and sins. Moral and spiritual life was adapted to the framework of society, and the society to which it was adapted was that of the estates. In the late thirteenth century, John of Freiburg, in his *Confessionale* which was a résumé of his great *Summa Confessorum* for the use of confessors who were 'simpler and less expert', classed sins under fourteen headings, each of which is an estate: (1) bishops and prelates, (2) clerks and benefice-holders, (3) parish priests, vicars, and confessors, (4) monks, (5) judges, (6) advocates and proctors, (7) physicians, (8) university doctors and masters, (9) princes and other nobles, (10) husbands and wives, (11) merchants and burgesses, (12) artisans and workmen, (13) peasants, (14) *laboratores*.

In this fragmented society, spiritual leaders preserved a nostalgia for unity in spite of everything. For long on the defensive, the Catholic flock, poor and despised by the rest of the world (which, from Cordoba to Constantinople, Cairo, Baghdad, and Peking was unaware of it, or else thought it beneath notice) could only reinforce itself by sticking together. Christian society had to form a body, a *corpus*. This ideal was affirmed by Carolingian theoreticians and by the papacy in the age of the crusades from the time of Urban II onwards. When unity seemed to be swept away by diversity, John of Salisbury, around 1160, was still trying, in his *Policraticus*, to rescue the unity of Christendom by comparing lay Christian society with a human body whose limbs and organs were made up of different professional categories. The sovereign was the head, the counsellors the heart, the judges and provincial administrators the eyes, ears, and tongue, the warriors the hands, the financial officials the stomach and intestines, and the peasants the feet. In medieval Christendom, a world of single combat, society was chiefly the arena of a struggle between unity and diversity, just as in a more general sense it was the arena of a duel between good and evil. Medieval Christianity with its totalitarian system for a long time identified good with unity and evil with diversity. Nonetheless, in the small points of everyday life a dialectic grew up between theory and practice, and affirmations of unity very often came to terms with an inevitable tolerance of diversity.

III

If Christianity was the body, what was the head? In fact Christianity was bicephalous: its two heads were the pope and the emperor. Medieval history is more concerned with their disagreements and conflicts than with their agreement, which was perhaps only realized, and then only in an ephemeral way, by Otto III and Silvester II around the year 1000. For the remainder of the period, the relations between the two heads of Christianity displayed the competition at the top of the two dominant but rival orders, the clerical and the lay hierarchy – priests and warriors, magical power and military might. Furthermore, the duel between Sacerdotium and Imperium did not always appear in an unmediated form. Other protagonists were involved.

On the side of Sacerdotium the situation can be explained fairly quickly. Once it had been accepted that it was impossible to make the patriarch of Constantinople and oriental Christianity admit Roman supremacy (this was underlined by the schism of 1054) the pope's leadership was hardly ever contested by the Church in the west. Here and there a bishop might rebel or an emperor sometimes raise up an anti-pope – there were about ten in the twelfth century – but the pope was certainly the head of religious society, even if he only affirmed his supremacy step by step and only let it become reality little by little. Gregory VII achieved a decisive step in this respect with his *Dictatus Papae* of 1075 where he declared, among other things: 'Only the Roman pontiff is justly called universal . . . . He is the only one whose name should be pronounced in all churches . . . . He who is not with the Roman church should not be considered a catholic.' In the course of the twelfth century the pope, from being the 'vicar of St Peter' became the 'vicar of Christ', and by the process of canonization controlled the consecration of new saints. During the thirteenth and fourteenth centuries, especially through advances in papal taxation, he made the Church into a true monarchy. It was only at the end of the fourteenth and the start of the fifteenth century that his supremacy was seriously threatened by the councils of the church, and in the end these were quelled as well.

Beside him, or opposite him, the emperor was far from being so unopposedly the head of lay society. First, there were periods with no emperor. These were longer than the short vacancies of the papal see; the longest papal vacancy, which was rather exceptional, was the 34-month one which occurred between the death of Clement IV in November 1268 and the election of Gregory X in September 1271. There was no emperor in the west from 476 to 800 and there was, practically speaking, none from 899, or at any rate from 924, until 962. Again, there was no emperor during the Great Interregnum between the death of Frederick II (1250) and the election of Rudolf of Habsburg in 1273. A double election in 1198 meant that for some years there were two kings, Otto IV and Philip of Swabia, and then from 1212 to 1218 Otto IV and Frederick II were both rulers together, in opposition to each other. Equally it should not be forgotten that a fairly long time often elapsed between the election in Germany, which made the elected candidate merely 'king of the Romans', and the coronation in Rome, prior to which the emperor as such did not exist. Frederick Barbarossa, crowned king of the Romans at Aachen on 9 March 1152, was only crowned emperor at Rome on 18 June 1155. Frederick II was made king at Aachen on 25 July 1215 and emperor at Rome on 22 November 1220.

More importantly, the emperor's hegemony over Christendom was more theoretical than real. It was often disputed in Germany, it was denied in Italy, and it was generally ignored by the most powerful rulers elsewhere. From the Ottonian period onwards the kings of France held themselves to be in no way subject to the emperor. From the early twelfth century English and Spanish canonists as well as French ones denied that their kings were subject to the emperor or to imperial laws. Pope Innocent III recognized in 1202 that, *de facto*, the king of France had no superior in temporal affairs. A canonist claimed in 1208 that 'every king has in his own kingdom the same powers as the emperor in the empire' – '*unusquisque enim tantum iuris habet in regno suo quantum imperator in imperio*'. The *Etablissements* of St Louis announced, '*Li rois ne tient de nului fors de Dieu et de lui*' – 'the king holds from no one save from God and himself'. In short, the theory that 'the king is emperor in his kingdom' was coming into being. Moreover, people had been observing since the tenth century what Robert Folz called the 'fragmentation of the idea of empire'.

The title of emperor started to be used a little more widely. Significantly it appeared in two lands which had escaped the domination of the Carolingian emperors, the British Isles and the Iberian peninsula, and in both cases it shows a claim to supremacy over a unified area – the Anglo-Saxon kingdoms and the Iberian Christian kingdoms. The imperial dream lasted barely a century in Britain. Aethelstan was the first to have himself referred to as emperor, in 930; Edgar declared himself to be an emperor in 970 ('I, Edgar, by the grace of God, august emperor of all Albion'), and, on the final occasion, Cnut, who died in 1035, declared, 'I, Cnut, emperor, who, by the favour of Christ, have taken to myself the kingdom of the Angles in the island,' and his biographer summed up, 'When he had reduced five kingdoms, Denmark, England, Wales, Scotland, and Norway, he became emperor.'

In Spain, the imperial chimera lasted longer. Ordoño II in 917 referred to his father, Alfonso III, as emperor, and the title continued to be used in chronicles and several diplomas of the tenth century. Meanwhile, curiously enough, the bishops of Compostela adopted the title *apostolicus* which was normally reserved for the bishop of Rome, the pope. From the time of Ferdinand I (1037-65), who united León to Castile, the imperial title became customary. From 1077 the formula became fixed in two forms: 'by the grace of God emperor of all Spain' or 'emperor of all the nations of Spain'. The 'Spanish empire' had its apogee under Alfonso VII who had himself crowned emperor at León in 1135. After him the Castilian monarchy was divided. Spain was broken up into the *'cinco reinos'* and the title of emperor of Spain disappeared only to make a brief reappearance for Ferdinand III in 1248, after the capture of Seville from the Muslims. Thus, although it could be partial, the idea of empire was always connected to the idea of unity, however fragmentary.

Parallel to this, the German emperors limited their claims increasingly to the German Holy Roman Empire in a strict sense, to Germany and its territorial extension in Italy. This was in spite of certain declarations by their chancery or by their flatterers – in 1199 Walther von der Vogelweide invited 'his emperor', Philip of Swabia, to put on the crown decorated with the white opal, the guiding star of all the princes. Chiefly it was restricted to Germany, especially after the emperor began to be elected by a college of princes. Already Frederick Barbarossa, who had taken the title of emperor before his coronation in Rome on 18 June 1155, had named the princes who had chosen him as 'fellow-workers in the glory of the emperor and the empire'. There was a double triumph for this electoral college in 1198 because instead of electing Henry VI's son, the future Frederick II, they elected Henry's brother Philip of Swabia, and soon afterwards a rival, Otto. They had created not one but two emperors. From now on this emperor was always the German emperor or the emperor of Germany under the title of the emperor of the Holy Roman German empire. The idea of universal empire assumed a dazzling final form under Frederick II, whose legal claims to world supremacy were crowned with an eschatological vision. While his enemies portrayed him as the Antichrist, or the herald of Antichrist, he presented himself as the Emperor of the End of Time, the saviour who was to lead the world into the golden age. He was the *immutator mirabilis*, a new Adam, a new Augustus, and soon almost a second Christ. In 1239 he extolled his birthplace, the town of Iesi in the Italian Marches, as his own Bethlehem. In reality, the behaviour of the emperors was always much more prudent; they contented themselves with an honorary pre-eminence and a moral authority which conferred on them a sort of patronage over other kingdoms: *auctoritas ad quam totius orbis spectat patrocinium* – 'an authority to which pertains the protection over the whole world', as Otto of Freising, Frederick Barbarossa's uncle, put it.

Thus, if medieval Christianity had two heads, these were not so much the pope and the emperor as the pope and the king (or king-emperor), or better, as the contemporary formula put it, Sacerdotium and Imperium, the spiritual and the temporal powers, the priest and the warrior. The imperial ideology probably retained fervent supporters even after it had been undermined.

Dante, the most passionate supporter of medieval Christendom, who craved for its unity, beseeched and implored the emperor to fulfil his role, his duty to be the supreme and universal leader, and abused him for not doing so. However the real dispute was between the *sacerdos* and the *rex*. How did each try to resolve this dispute in his favour? Each tried to unite the two powers in his person, the pope in becoming emperor, the king in becoming priest. Each tried to realize the unity of the *rex-sacerdos* in himself. In Byzantium, the basileus had succeeded in having himself regarded as a sacred figure and in being the religious leader at the same time as the political one. This is what is known as caesaropapism. Charlemagne seems to have tried to unite in his person the double dignity of emperor and priest. At the time of his coronation in 800, the laying on of hands recalled the gesture in a priestly ordination, and suggested that from now on Charles was invested with 'a royal priesthood'. He was a new David, a new Solomon, a new Josiah. However, Heinrich Fichtenau has shown that where he is called *rex et sacerdos*, it was the priest's ability to preach, not his charismatic functions, which were attributed to him, as Alcuin makes clear. No source describes him as a new Melchisedek, the only priest-king in the Old Testament in the strictest sense. Even so, kings and emperors were to pursue their attempt to have themselves recognized as having a religious character, sacred if not priestly, throughout the middle ages.

The chief means which they could use to further this policy was unction and coronation, religious ceremonies which made them the Lord's anointed, the king crowned by God, *rex a Deo coronatus*. Anointing was a sacrament. It was accompanied by liturgical acclamations or *laudes regiae*. Ernst Kantorowicz rightly discerned in these a solemn recognition on the part of the Church that the new sovereign was being added to the heavenly hierarchy. Sung after the litanies of the saints, they showed 'the union between the two worlds even more than their symmetry'. They proclaimed 'the cosmic harmony of Heaven, Church and State'. Unction was a form of ordination. The emperor Henry III announced in 1046 to Wazo, bishop of Liège, 'I too, who have received the right to exercise authority over all, have been anointed with holy oil.' One of Henry IV's propagandists in his conflict with Gregory VII, Wido of Osnabrück, wrote in 1084-5: 'The king must be set apart from the mass of laymen, for since he is anointed with consecrated oil, he partakes of the priestly ministry.' In the preamble to a diploma of 1143, Louis VII of France remarked:

We know that in accordance with the prescriptions of the Old Testament, and, in our day, with the law of the Church, only kings and priests are consecrated by anointing with holy chrism. It is fitting that those who, alone among everyone, are placed at the head of God's people, united amongst themselves by holy unction, should obtain for their subjects temporal as well as spiritual goods, and that kings and priests should obtain these for each other.

The ritual of this mixture of sacring and ordination was fixed in the *ordines* such as 'the order of the consecration and coronation of the kings of France' to be found in a manuscript from Châlons-sur-Marne, dating from about 1280, now preserved in the Bibliothèque Nationale in Paris.* Its precious miniatures show us some of the most significant moments of this religious ceremony. Here were asserted, on the one hand, the role of the military leader (the investiture with spurs and sword), and, on the other, the quasi-sacerdotal figure, priestly above all through unction, but also because he was invested with ring, sceptre, and crown. These pictures show the king being received at the door of Rheims Cathedral, the abbot of St Rémi of Rheims bearing the phial of holy oil or *sainte ampoule*, the king pronouncing his promise, the king prostrating himself while the litanies were being sung, the king receiving his silk shoes from the grand chamberlain and his gold spurs from the duke of Burgundy, the king anointed with holy oil on his forehead and on his hands (he was also anointed on his chest, on his back and shoulders), the king listening to the mass, the king dressed in a purple tunic, the king receiving the sword, the ring, then the sceptre, and finally the crown, and then, after the queen had been crowned, taking communion. The detail of this ceremony has been described according to this *ordo* by M. de Pange in his *Roi très chrétien*.

P. E. Schramm has thrown light on the religious symbols which bestowed all their meaning on imperial and royal insignia. The imperial crown, in the form of a diadem consisting of eight embossed gold plates and an arch rising over the crown of the head picked out with eight small semicircular plates, used the number eight, the symbol of eternal life. Like the octagon in the imperial chapel at Aachen, the imperial crown was the image of the heavenly Jerusalem with its walls covered with gold and precious stones. The *ordo* proclaimed the crown to be a 'sign of glory', and the crown announced the reign of Christ through the cross (a sign of triumph), through the single white opal, nicknamed the 'orphan' or *orphanus*, which was a sign of pre-eminence, and through the pictures of Christ, David, Solomon, and Hezekiah. The ring and the long staff or *virga* were copies of episcopal insignia. The emperor was also invested with the Holy Lance or lance of St Maurice which was borne before him and which was supposed to contain a nail from Christ's cross. We may recall that the kings of France and England had the power to touch for the king's evil, or scrofula, and to cure those who were affected. Finally, the fact that kings preferred charismatic power to military force is maintained by

*BN MS latin 1246

the Carmelite Jean Golein, in his *Traité du sacre* written in 1374 at the request of Charles V of France. The king

is supposed to keep homage to God which he has done him for his kingdom. He holds his kingdom from God and not at all by his sword alone, as the ancient writers said, but from God, just as he bears witness on his gold coins in so far as he says 'Christus vincit, Christus regnat, Christus imperat'. He never ever says 'the sword rules and conquers', but says 'Jesus conquers, Jesus reigns, Jesus commands'.

Thus, once they became Christian, the barbarian kings tried to recapture the power of the sorcerer-kings. This power had been held by the pagan Frankish kings, the *reges criniti*, the long-haired kings of a short-haired people. These kings had a magical head of hair which was the source of marvellous power; they were 'as great as Samson'.

Parallel to this the papacy began to attempt to take over the imperial function, particularly from the eighth century onwards with the forged Donation of Constantine. According to the text of the Donation the emperor announced that he would abandon the city of Rome to the pope and for this reason would transfer himself to Constantinople. He authorized the pope to wear the diadem and papal insignia and allotted senatorial trappings to the Roman clergy. 'We have also decreed that our venerable Father Silvester, supreme pontiff, as well as all his successors, should wear the diadem, that is to say the crown of very pure gold and of precious stones which we have removed from our head and granted to him.'

Silvester is supposed to have refused the diadem and accepted only a high white mitre, the *phrygium*, which itself was royal insignia of oriental origin. The *phrygium* evolved rapidly into a crown, and a Roman *ordo* of the ninth century already called it a *regnum*. When it reappeared in the mid-eleventh century, 'it had changed shape and significance', and had become the tiara. The circlet at the bottom was turned into a diadem adorned with precious stones. A crown with flowerets replaced it in the twelfth century, a second crown was superimposed in the thirteenth century and a third probably under the Avignon popes. It had become the *triregnum*. Already Innocent III had explained at the start of the thirteenth century that the pope wore the mitre '*in signum pontificii*', as a sign of the pontificate, of the supreme priesthood, and the *regnum*, '*in signum Imperii*', as a sign of the Empire. A *pontifex-rex* now answered the challenge of a *rex-sacerdos*. The pope did not wear the tiara while he was exercising his sacerdotal functions but in the ceremonies where he appeared as a sovereign. From the time of Paschal II, in 1099, the popes were crowned on their accession. After Gregory VII their 'enthronement' at the Lateran was accompanied by 'immantation' or the donning of the imperial red mantle or *cappa rubea*, possession of which, in the case of rivalry between two popes, conferred legitimacy. The pope without the mantle became the anti-pope. From the time of Urban II the Roman clergy was called the Curia, which at once evoked the ancient Roman senate and a feudal court.

Thus not only did the papacy detach itself, and begin to detach the Church, from a certain subservience to the lay feudal order, but also – and this is an essential aspect of the Gregorian reform – it proclaimed itself to be the head of the lay as well as of the religious hierarchy. From there it strove to make the subordination of imperial and royal power to its own power obvious and effective. We know the unending litigation and the immense quantity of literature arising out of, for example, the Investiture Contest, which itself was only one aspect or one episode in the great conflict between Sacerdotium and Imperium, or rather, as we have seen, between the two orders. We may recall that Innocent III increased the number of states owing allegiance to the Holy See. Let us now pause and consider certain symbols around which the argument hardened, because they were the most significant: the two swords and the sun and moon. These were theories and visual images at the same time, as was almost always the case in the medieval west.

Yet who helped the kings more than the Church did? Leo III had made Charlemagne and to a large degree the Benedictines of Fleury (St Benoît-sur-Loire) and of St Denis made the Capetians. The Church made use of the ambiguous nature of kingship (of which more later), which was the head of the feudal hierarchy but also of another hierarchy, that of the State, of a public power which transcended the feudal order. The Church favoured the former against its rival, military force, and the clergy assisted the king in mastering the warrior. Naturally this was with the intention of making the monarchs their instrument and of assigning to the kings the essential role of defender of the Church, both the actual Church of the priestly order and the ideal Church of the poor. The role which the medieval Church allotted to kingship was that of the secular arm, which carried out the commands of the priestly order, and polluted itself in the place of the Church by using physical force and violence and spilling the blood of which the Church washed its hands. A whole collection of books written by clerics defined this royal function. These were the numerous *Mirrors of Princes*; they flowered chiefly in the ninth century when bishops operated the imperial puppets after the humiliation and submission of Louis the Pious, and in the thirteenth century, when Louis IX strove to be the model king on both a moral and spiritual plane.

The Council of Paris in 829 defined the duties of kings in terms that were taken up and developed two years later by Jonas, bishop of Orléans in his *De institutione regia*. This was to remain the model for *Mirrors of Princes* throughout the middle ages. At the Council of Paris the bishops announced

The royal ministry consists especially in governing and ruling the people of God in fairness and justice and in seeing to the provision of peace and concord. Above all the king must be the defender of churches, of the servants of the God, of widows, orphans, and all other poor and needy people. He must also show himself to be as far as possible zealous and awe-inspiring so that no injustice may occur, and if it does, so that he may allow no one to guard a hope of not being discovered in the audacious act of wrongdoing, but so that all might know that nothing may remain unpunished.

In exchange, the Church endowed royal power with a sacral character. Thus it was necessary that all subjects should submit faithfully and with blind obedience to the royal power because 'he who resists this power resists the order willed by God'. Furthermore, it was in favour of the emperor and the king rather than of the feudal lord that the clergy established a parallel between heaven and earth and made the king into the personification of God on earth. Iconography tended to let God in majesty be merged with the king on his throne. Hugh of Fleury, in the *Tractatus de regia potestate et sacerdotali dignitate* which he dedicated to Henry I of England, went so far as to compare the king with God the Father and a bishop merely with Christ. 'One alone reigns in the kingdom of heaven, he who hurls the thunderbolts. It is natural for there to be only one following him who reigns on earth, one only who is to be an example to all men.' Alcuin spoke in similar terms and what he said for the emperor held good for a king from the point where the latter became 'emperor in his own kingdom'. But let the king step aside from this programme, let him cease to be submissive, and the Church immediately reminded him of his unworthiness and denied to him the priestly character that he was endeavouring to acquire.

Philip I of France was excommunicated for marrying Bertrade de Montfort. According to Orderic Vitalis, he was struck by God with shameful sicknesses, and according to Guibert of Nogent he lost his thaumaturgical powers. Gregory VII reminded the emperor that since he did not know how to drive out demons he was certainly inferior to the exorcists. Honorius of Autun stated that the king was a layman.

In fact, the king can only be either a layman or a cleric. If he is not a layman, he is a cleric. But if he is a cleric, he must be a doorkeeper, reader, or exorcist, or an acolyte, subdeacon, deacon or priest. If he has none of these grades, then he is not a clerk. If he is neither a layman nor a clerk, he must be a monk. But his wife and his sword prevent him from being taken for a monk.

Here we can grasp the reasons for the relentlessness with which Gregory VII and his successors imposed celibacy and the renunciation of fighting on the clergy. It was not a moral preoccupation. It was a question of separating the class of priests from that of the fighters, lumped together with the other isolated and humbled laymen, by keeping the sacerdotal order free of the defilement of blood and sperm, which were unclean liquids affected by taboos.

When the archbishop Thomas Becket was assassinated by knights, possibly at the instigation of Henry II of England, the priestly order broke out against the knightly order. The extraordinary propaganda spread by the Church throughout all Christendom in favour of the martyr, to whom churches, altars, ceremonies, statues, and frescos were dedicated, was a manifestation of the struggle between the two orders. John of Salisbury, an associate of the murdered prelate, made use of Thomas' martyrdom to carry to its extremes the doctrine of the limitation of royal power. This doctrine had been prudently affirmed by the Church from the first moment when it had, for its own purposes, exalted royal power. The bad king – the one who did not obey the Church – became a tyrant. He lost his dignity. The bishops of the Council of Paris in 829 had declared: 'If the king governs with piety, justice and mercy, he merits his kingly title. If he lacks these qualities, he is not a king but a tyrant.' It was the immovable teaching of the medieval Church, and Thomas Aquinas supported it with solid theological grounds. But the medieval Church was never very precise either in theory or practice about the practical consequences to be drawn from condemning a bad king who had become a tyrant. Excommunications, interdictions, and depositions occurred. John of Salisbury was alone or almost alone in going to the extreme limit of the doctrine and preaching tyrannicide in the cases where no other solution seemed to exist. Thus the Becket affair showed that the duel between the two orders found its logical conclusion in a settling of accounts.

However, in theory the Church's weapons were more spiritual. The popes responded to imperial and royal pretensions with the image of the two swords which, since the time of the Fathers of the Church, had symbolized spiritual and temporal power. Alcuin had claimed them for Charlemagne. St Bernard constructed a complex doctrine which concluded in spite of everything by restoring the two swords to the pope. It was Peter to whom the two swords had been entrusted. The priest made use of the spiritual sword and the knight the temporal one, but only for the Church, and at the nod (*nutu*) of the priest, the emperor contenting himself with transmitting the order. The canonists of the late twelfth and the thirteenth centuries did not hesitate any longer. Since the pope had become the vicar of Christ, and Christ was alone the keeper of the two swords, the pope alone – Christ's lieutenant – controlled them here below.

The same thing happened with the simile of the sun and the moon. The Roman emperor had identified himself with the sun and certain medieval emperors tried to revive this comparison. The papacy under Gregory VII, and even more under Innocent III, cut this endeavour short. It borrowed the image of the sun and moon from Genesis:

And God said, Let there be lights in the firmament of heaven to divide the day from the night; and let them be for signs, and for seasons, and for days, and for years. And let them be for lights in the firmament of the heaven to give light upon the earth. And it was so. And God made two great lights; the greater light to rule the day, and the lesser light to rule the night: he made the stars also. And God set them in the firmament of the heaven to give light upon the earth. And to rule over the day and over the night. . . .

For the Church the greater light, the sun, was the pope, while the lesser light, the moon, was the emperor or king. The moon has no light of its own, but only a light which it borrows from the sun. The emperor was not only the lesser light but also the leader of the world of the night, in contrast to the world of the day, which was ruled and symbolized by the pope. If we realize what day and night meant to men in the middle ages, we can understand that the lay hierarchy from the Church's point of view was only a society of suspect forces, the shadowy half of the body of society.

If the pope prevented the emperor and the other monarchs from appropriating the role of a priest, he failed to seize temporal power. The two swords remained in separate hands, and when the emperor slipped into the background in the middle of the thirteenth century, it was Philip the Fair who decisively checked the pretensions of Boniface VIII. Yet almost everywhere in Christendom the temporal sword was already firmly in the hands of the lay rulers. It only remained to the two dominant powers to forget their rivalry and think only of their solidarity and jointly establish their ascendancy over society. In modern times the alliance of throne and altar, sabre and aspergillum, despite minor vicissitudes and antagonisms such as pragmatic sanctions and concordats, Gallicanism, Josephism, and the Napoleonic tyrany, was to continue this medieval complicity between Sacerdotium and Imperium, the sacerdotal and the warrior forces, between the *oratores* and the *bellatores*, in the exploitation of the *laboratores*. As the bishop of Paris, Maurice of Sully, said in 1170, in the vulgar tongue, so as to be better understood; 'Good people, render your earthly lord what you owe him. You must understand and accept that you owe your earthly lord your dues, tallages, forfeits, services, cartage and military service. Render it all, entire, in the place and at the time desired.'

IV

The dreams of unity were always disappointed. Adalbero of Laon remarked 'God's house, which was thought to be one, is thus divided in three' at the start of the eleventh century, the very century when the unattainable unity of Christendom effectively broke up. The crusades would not succeed in creating this unity or in recreating it, but would contribute a little more to its fragmentation. Social fragmentation would be accompanied by political rupture once the rival leaderships of pope and emperor were asserted. In 1077 Canossa represented the collapse of the brief period of harmony which had united Otto III and Silvester II in the year 1000. Unity was prevented even more by national divisions, or, rather, by increasing linguistic differences. Of course, we know, as famous historical examples and some present-day exceptions (some happy, other traumatic) tell us, that national frontiers are not identical with linguistic ones. Yet who would deny that difference of language causes separation more than unity? The inhabitants of medieval Christian Europe were acutely conscious of the fact. The clergy wrote lamentations which said that the diversity of languages was one of the consequences of original sin. They associated this evil with Babylon, mother of all the vices. Rangerius of Lucca stated in the early twelfth century, 'Just as once Babylon, by multiplying the languages, added new and worse evils to the old ones, so the multiplication of peoples multiplies the harvest of crimes.' And the common people were saddened to realize that other people spoke differently. For example, the thirteenth-century German peasants in the story of Meier Helmbrecht did not recognize their prodigal son when he returned home pretending to speak several languages.

'My dear children,' he said in Low German, 'may God make you always blessed'. His sister ran up to him and hugged him, whereupon he said to her, 'Gracia vester!' The children then ran up and the old parents came up behind, and both of them welcomed him with boundless joy. He said to his father, 'Deu sal!' and to his mother, Bohemian-fashion, 'Dobra ytra!' The man and his wife looked at each other, and the mistress of the house said, 'Husband, we are mistaken, this is not our child. This is a Bohemian or a Wend.' The father said, 'He's a Frenchman! He's not our son (may God preserve him), and yet he looks like him.' So then Gotelint, the sister, said, 'It's not your child. He spoke to me in Latin, so he must be a clerk.' 'Faith,' said the servant, 'if I judge from what he said, he was born in Saxony or Brabant. He spoke in Low German, so he must be a Saxon.' The father said simply, 'If you are my son Helmbrecht, I shall be won over to you if you pronounce one word according to our custom and in the manner of our ancestors, so that I may understand you. You are always saying 'Deu sal', and I don't understand one word of what you are saying. Honour your mother and myself – we have always deserved this. Speak one word in German and I will rub down your horse, I myself, not the servant . . . .'

Medieval men always put their ideas into pictures, and they made use of the Tower of Babel as a symbol for representing the misfortune of linguistic diversity. In imitation of oriental iconography, they usually made it an image of terror and catastrophe. The full impact of the image on medieval minds has been shown by Arno Borst in the collection of his marvellously erudite body of work. The distressing image of the Tower of Babel began to acquire resonance in the western European imagination from around the year 1000. The oldest representation in western Europe can be found in a manuscript of Caedmon from the end of the tenth or the early eleventh century. In an *interrogatio* from the early eleventh century we come across the following questions and answers: 'How many languages are there in the world? Answer: 62. Question: Why are there no more and no fewer? Answer: Because of the three sons of Noah, Shem, Ham and Japheth. Shem had 27 sons, Ham 30, and Japheth 15, which add up to 62 altogether.' The clergy in the middle ages and even in our own day tried to drive away the shadow of Babel by using Latin. Latin is supposed to have effected the unity of medieval civilization and thus of European civilization, or so Ernst Robert Curtius has brilliantly argued. But what Latin? It was a dead Latin, from which its true heirs, the vulgar languages, were detaching themselves. It was sterilized slightly more by each succeeding renaissance, beginning with the Carolingian renaissance. Kitchen Latin, the humanists called it; but, on the contrary, it was a deodorized, flavourless Latin. It was the language of a caste, it was clerical Latin, and it was an instrument for dominating the masses rather than for international communication. It was a true example of a sacred language which isolated the social group which had the privilege not of understanding it – which was not very important – but of speaking it, whether well or badly. The naïve lamented the fact that the common people turned the essential prayers into gibberish, as in Walter de Coincy's *Ave Maria du vilain*. Even more they deplored the fact that in this respect the priests might be crassly ignorant. In 1199 Gerald of Wales reported a series of howlers uttered by English clergy. Eudes Rigaud, archbishop of Rouen from 1248 to 1269, reported other cases from among the priests of his diocese. The Latin of the medieval church was tending to turn into the incomprehensible language of the *Fratres Arvales* in ancient Rome. Even among university graduates, Latin had difficulty in maintaining itself. It was necessary for college statutes to forbid students and masters to abandon Latin for the vulgar tongue.

The living reality of the medieval west was the progressive triumph of the vulgar tongues and the increase in the number of interpreters, translations, and dictionaries. Of course, there was no shortage of nostalgia-sufferers who dreamed of a return to a single language which would be a token of purity and of a rediscovered golden age. Joachim of Fiore branded the Tower of Babel as a symbol of the pride of men possessed by Satan. When the eternal Gospel reigns on the earth made new and the regenerated Church is 'the only mistress of the nations' – *sola domina gentium* – her reign will be combined with the rule of Latin: 'the Roman Church, that is to say all Latinity – *Romana ecclesia, hoc est tota Latinitas*'. The Christian exclusiveness of those demanding a single language was reminiscent of the linguistic xenophobia of the Greeks. Everyone who did not speak Latin was a barbarian who did not speak properly, or who did not have a tongue, or who made animal noises. Writers even in vulgar languages were so smitten with '*clergie*' that they made the word Latin synonymous with the word language. In the writings of William IX of Aquitaine and of Chrétien of Troyes the birds sing 'in their Latin'.

The retreat of Latin before the vulgar languages did not take place without linguistic nationalism creeping in. Here a nation in the making asserted itself by defending its language. Jakob Swinka, archbishop of Gniezno at the end of the thirteenth century, complained to the Curia about the German Franciscans who did not understand Polish, and ordered that sermons should be preached in Polish, '*ad conservationem et promocionem lingue Polonice*' – 'for the defence and furthering of the Polish language'. That a nation tended to identify itself with a language is exemplified by medieval France, which was only with difficulty welded together out of northern France, the *langue d'oil*, .and southern France, the *langue d'oc*. Already in 920, at an encounter between Charles the Simple and Henry the Fowler at Worms, young German and French knights met in a bloody skirmish, according to Richer, because they were 'angered by the other side's different language'. According to Hildegard of Bingen, Adam and Eve spoke German, but others claimed that French had been first. In the middle of the thirteenth century, in Italy, the anonymous author of a poem written in French on the Antichrist stated: 'The French language / is such that he who learns it first / can never thenceforth talk otherwise / or learn another tongue.' And Bruno Latini wrote his *Trésor* in French 'because this speech is more delectable and more widespread among the people'.

After the barbarian nations had settled in all their variety in the shattered unity of the Roman Empire, and nationality had encroached on or taken the place of the 'territoriality' spoken of in the laws, some clerics created a literary genre which gave every nation a national virtue and vice. In the rise of national feeling after the eleventh century antagonism seemed to carry the day, for from now on only the vices were linked with the various 'nations' as national attributes. This can be seen in the universities where students and masters, who were grouped in 'nations' (which were as yet, however, far from corresponding to any single nation in territorial or political sense) saw themselves described by Jacques de Vitry thus: 'the drunken English with tails (in the Hundred Years' War, the English were to be called the '*Anglais caudés*' or tailed English), the arrogant and effeminate French, the brutal and lewd Germans, the conceited and boastful Normans, the treacherous, reckless Poitevins, the vulgar, stupid Burgundians, the faithless, fickle Bretons, the avaricious, vicious, and cowardly Lombards, the seditious and scandal-mongering Romans, the tyrannical, cruel Sicilians, the bloodthirsty, fire-raising Brabantine brigands, the prodigal, gluttonous Flemings, as soft as butter and idle.' Thus each linguistic group was married off to a vice just as the groups in society had each been married to a daughter of the devil. A divided society seemed condemned to shame and misfortune. However, just as some farseeing minds justified a division into socio-professional groups, so others defended the making of a division along linguistic and nationalistic lines. They took refuge behind a passage of Augustine, 'African, Syrian, Greek, Hebrew and all the other different languages make up the variety of the dress of this queen, Christian teaching. But just as the different pieces of clothing join to make a single garment, so all the languages join together in a single faith. May there be variety in the dress but no rent.' Stephen of Hungary said in 1030: 'The guests who come from different lands bring different languages, customs, tools, and weapons, and all this diversity is an adornment to the kingdom, an embellishment to the court and an object of fear to enemies outside, for a kingdom which has only one language and one custom is weak and fragile.' And just as Gerhoch of Reichersberg had declared in the twelfth century that no profession was useless, and that all professions could lead to salvation, so Thomas Aquinas in the thirteenth century asserted that all languages are able to lead men to the truth. '*Quaecumque sint illae linguae seu nationes, possunt erudiri de divina sapientia et virtute*'. Here one senses that totalitarian society had had a setback and that it was ready to spill over into pluralism and tolerance.

V

Medieval law did not give its sanction to fragmentation without resistance. The orderly system of unanimity was imposed for a long time. A maxim bequeathed by Roman law which passed into canon law governed medieval legal practice: *Quod omnes tangit ab omnibus comprobari debet* – 'What touches all must be approved by all.' The fracturing of unity was a scandal. The great canon lawyer Huguccio in the thirteenth century states that the man who did not join the majority was *turpis* or shameful, and that 'in a body, a college, an administration, discord and diversity are shameful'. It is obvious that this unanimity had nothing democratic about it, for when rulers and lawyers were forced to do without it they replaced it with the notion and the practice of the qualitative majority, the *maior et sanior pars*, the greater and wiser part, where *sanior* defines *maior* and gives it a qualitative, not a quantitative, sense.

The theologians and canon lawyers of the thirteenth century who realized sadly that 'human nature is prone to discord' - '*natura humana prona est ad dissentiendum*' - emphasized that this was a question of the corruption of nature resulting from Original Sin. The medieval mind was ceaselessly creating communities or groups, what were then called *universitates*, a term which designated any sort of corporation or college, and not only the sort of corporation we now call a university. Obsessed by the idea of the group, the medieval mind could even envisage it as composed of a minimum number of persons. Starting from a definition in the *Digest*: 'Ten men form a people, ten sheep a flock, but only four or five pigs are needed to constitute a herd,' the canon lawyers in the twelfth and thirteenth centuries gravely discussed whether a group could exist if it contained as few as two or three persons only. The important thing was that the individual should not be left alone. The loner could do only wrong. The great sin was to stand out. If we try to approach men in medieval western Europe as individuals we quickly realize not only that, as in every society, each individual belonged to several groups or communities, but also that in the middle ages they seemed to merge into such groups rather than to assert themselves within them.

If pride was then thought of as 'the mother of all vices' it was because pride is 'exaggerated individualism'. Salvation lay only in and through the community; self-esteem was sin and perdition. Thus the medieval individual was trapped within networks of obedience, submission, and solidarity which ended up overlapping each other and contradicting each other to the point where he was allowed to free himself and assert his independence only by being forced to make a choice. The most typical one was that of the vassal of several lords who could be forced to choose between them if they found themselves on opposite sides in a dispute. But in general, and over a long period, these allegiances were harmonized with each other and were fitted into a hierarchy, with the result that the individual was even more closely attached. In fact, of all these bonds, the strongest was the feudal bond.

It is significant that for a long time medieval individuals were not portrayed with their own physical features. Personalities were not described or depicted in literature or art with their own characteristics. Each was reduced to a physical type corresponding to his rank and social category. Nobles had blond or red hair. Golden hair or flaxen hair, often curly, together with blue or grey eyes, must have been additions made by nordic warriors to the canon of medieval beauty. Even when, by chance, a great personality escaped this convention for describing physical details, such as Charlemagne, whom Einhard rightly described as being 7 feet tall - as was proved when his skeleton was measured after his tomb was opened in 1861 and found to be 1.92 metres - his intellectual personality was stifled under commonplaces. The emperor was endowed by his chronicler with all the Aristotelian and Stoic qualities which were proper to his rank. It is not at all surprising that autobiography was rare, and itself was often conventional, and, as Georg Misch has shown in his *Histoire de l'autobiographie*, we have to wait until the late eleventh century for Otloh of St Emmeram to write the first personal autobiography. It was still in the form of a *Libellus de suis tentationibus, varia fortuna et scriptis* which tried to present moral lessons through the example of the author; even a personality as independent as Abelard's, in his *Historia Calamitatum mearum* (History of my Calamities) was to do just the same. Coming between the two, in 1115, the *De vita sua* of Abbot Guibert de Nogent, although it flows more freely, was only an imitation of Augustine's *Confessions*.

Medieval man had no sense of freedom as it is conceived of today. Freedom to him was a privilege and the word was more readily used in the plural. Freedom meant a guaranteed status: it was, according to Gerd Tellenbach's definition, 'one's legitimate place before God and men'. It meant belonging to society. There was no liberty without community. It could only exist in a relationship of dependence, with a superior guaranteeing to a subordinate that he would respect his rights. The free man was the man who had a powerful protector. When the clergy demanded the 'freedom of the Church' at the time of the Gregorian reform what they meant by this was removing themselves from the domination of secular lords so as to be subject directly only to the highest lord, God.

VI

In medieval western Europe the individual belonged first and foremost to his family. The family was a large, patriarchal or tribal one, directed by the head of the family. It stifled the individual, forcing him to submit to the collective ownership of property, collective responsibility, and collective action. The importance of the family group at the level of the lordly class is well known; the knight had to accept the circumstances, duties, and ethics of his lineage. Lineage was a community of blood-ties made up of 'kin' and '*amis charnels*', that is to say relatives by marriage, but it was not a relic of some vast primitive family. It was a stage in the organization of the loosely knit family group, the *Sippe*, which was a feature of Germanic societies of the early middle ages. The members of the lineage were bound by the solidarity of the lineage, which was displayed chiefly on the battlefield and in affairs of honour. In the *Couronnement de Louis*, William of Orange begs Our Lady, 'Come to my aid / so that I do not commit an act of cowardice / which might be held against my lineage'. At Roncevaux Roland refused for a long time to sound the olifant to call Charlemagne to his aid, for fear that his kinsmen might be dishonoured. Above all, family solidarity was displayed in acts of private vengeance, in the feud. In Burgundy in Ralph Glaber's time an inexpiable hatred set two families against each other.

The struggle had lasted for many years, when one day during the wine harvest the two sides started to fight on land which was part of the very property concerned. In this fight many on each side lost their lives. From the house with which we are concerned, eleven sons and grandsons died. And in the course of time the quarrel persisted, the hatred became more bitter, and innumerable woes continued to affect the family, many of whose members were killed over a period of 30 years and more.

Vendetta was practised, recognized and extolled for a long time in medieval western Europe.

The support which one had the right to expect from a kinsman led to the common assertion that true riches lay in having many relatives. William of Orange lamented at the deathbed of his nephew Vivien, 'Alas! I have lost all the seed of my lineage.'

Lineage seems to correspond to the evolutionary stage known as the agnatic family, the basis and purpose of which are to conserve a common patrimony. What was original about the feudal agnatic family was that the military role and the personal relations inherent in allegiance to a superior were as important for the masculine half of the lineage as was the family's economic role. The mixture of interests and feelings aroused, moreover, unusually violent tensions within the feudal family. The lineage felt the appeal of drama even more than that of keeping faith. Rivalry was especially prevalent among brothers, since the eldest was not automatically assured of authority; this could pass to whichever of the brothers could make the others recognize his ability to command. However, such recognition was often unwilling and often disputed. Royal feudal families were full of fraternal rivalry and hatred which were further exacerbated by the lure of the crown: hence the struggles between the sons of William the Conqueror – Robert Curthose, William Rufus, and Henry I – or in fourteenth-century Castile between Peter the Cruel and Henry of Trastamara, who to make matters worse were only half-brothers.

Feudal lineages by their very nature begat young Cains. They also fathered disrespectful sons. The narrow timespan between generations, the limited life-expectancy and the need for the lord as military leader to establish his authority in battle once he was old enough to justify his rank, all exasperated the impatience of young feudal warriors. Hence sons rebelled against their fathers. The younger Henry, Richard, and Geoffrey of Brittany all rebelled against Henry II of England. In a later period Louis XI of France, by

Figures 21, 22, 23 Battles of Arsouf (1191), Bouvines (1214), Courtrai (1302)

In medieval battles, order and cohesion were decisive for success. Communal organization was essential. At Arsouf (21) on 7 September 1191, the crusading army under Richard I of England was marching in an orderly fashion along the shore, followed and protected by the Christian fleet, when the Muslim army under Saladin attacked it opposite the forest of Arsouf. The king was able to turn his column immediately into a mass several ranks deep, which made vigorous charges against the Muslims, who were routed. The cohesion of the different units or 'battles' grouping compatriots together played a key role in the victory. The Templars, who fought 'like the sons of a single father' and some families fighting as groups, such as that of Jacques of Avesnes, particularly distinguished themselves. The crusaders kept their ranks so close together that, according to the chronicler, if one had thrown an apple at the Christian army it would not have fallen on the ground but would have been certain to hit a horse or a man. At Bouvines (22) on 27 July 1214 the army of the king of France, Philip Augustus, beat the united armies of the Emperor Otto, Ferrand Count of Flanders, and of Reginald of Boulogne, thanks to a series of mistakes made by the imperial side, which were well exploited by the leader of the French king's army, Bishop Guérin. Guérin extended the front line of his troops (1200–1300 knights and 5000 infantry) to avoid the wings being overrun, but he did not spread them out as much as did his enemies, who deployed 1300–1500 knights and 7500 infantry, who were less cohesive, over about 10 km. When they had obtained a success they followed it up too quickly; the Germans under Otto plunged into the French infantry and got as far as Philip Augustus, whose horse was killed, and so Guérin was able to split up the allies' left wing and defeat it, and then their centre and right wing in succession. The cohesion of the French formations or *'batailles'* was decisive. An analysis of the description of the battle by the chronicler Guillaume le Breton yields mention of five single combats (three of them by a knight against an enemy unit) as against fifteen combats between units. This does treat the myth of medieval battles being composed of individual duels as it deserves. At Courtrai (23) on 11 July 1302 occurred a revolutionary victory of the infantry of the Flemish communes over the flower of French chivalry. The feudal armies misjudged the infantrymen: they estimated that ten heavily armoured knights were worth a hundred infantry. The French, numbering 2500 nobles and about 4000 crossbowmen and infantry, thus had a large lead, qualitatively speaking, over the 8000 Flemish infantry (mostly from Bruges), who were supported by about 500 nobles. However the Flemings overcame their trepidation. They were supported by the two princes and the nobles who placed themselves at their head and by the Franciscans who blessed the troops and heard confessions, and by the layer of soldiers in the first two ranks who were armed with pikes and *goedenday*. Furthermore they were able to choose a site which helped them. With their backs to the river Leie they could not flee and were forced to conquer or die. Two ditches which separated them from the French cavalry prevented the latter from launching their charges from a distance. The mêlée and the carnage which followed were appalling. Half the French knights, more than 1000, were killed and there was a huge amount of booty, including the 500 gilded spurs which gave the battle its traditional name (Battle of the Golden Spurs). The

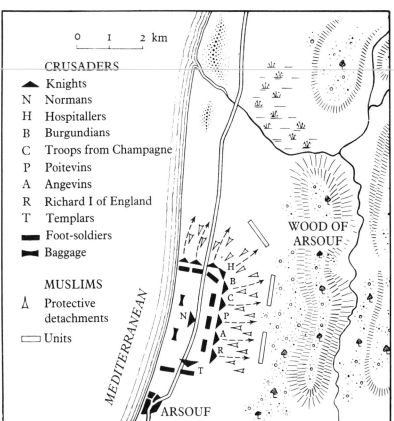

CRUSADERS

▲ Knights
N Normans
H Hospitallers
B Burgundians
C Troops from Champagne
P Poitevins
A Angevins
R Richard I of England
T Templars
▬ Foot-soldiers
▬ Baggage

MUSLIMS

Λ Protective detachments
▭ Units

WOOD OF ARSOUF

MEDITERRANEAN

ARSOUF

21 Battle of Arsouf (after Verbruggen, *De Krijgskunst in West-Europe*)

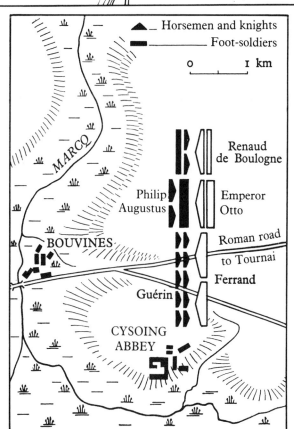

▲___ Horsemen and knights
▬___ Foot-soldiers

MARCQ

BOUVINES

Renaud de Boulogne

Philip Augustus

Emperor Otto

Roman road to Tournai

Ferrand

Guérin

CYSOING ABBEY

22 Battle of Bouvines (after Verbruggen, *ibid.*)

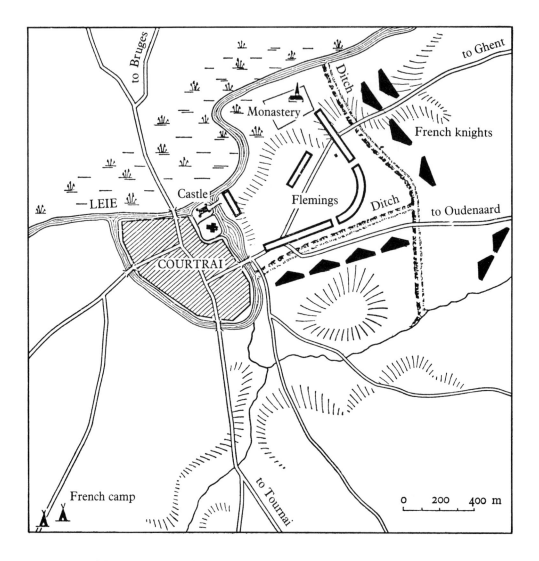

23 Battle of Courtrai
(after Verbruggen, *ibid.*)

Flemings hung them up in the church of Notre-Dame at Courtrai; the French knights took them back again after their revenge at Roosebecke in 1382. The fleeing knights were so terrified that when they returned to Tournai in the evening they could not eat. The victory of the '*ongles bleus*' was contemporary with the victories by Scottish and Swiss infantrymen (the former at Bannockburn in 1314, the latter at Morgarten in 1315 and at Vottem in 1346). Troops from the lower classes were able to organize themselves at the point when the decline of the feudal lords began.

rebelling against his father Charles VII, showed that he, too, was a feudal heir. Moreover, the need to gain money and a reputation combined to make the young lord, when he came of age, distance himself from his father and turn himself into a knight-errant while waiting for his inheritance. Tensions were also bred by multiple marriages and by the existence of numerous bastards, for illegitimacy, which was shameful among lesser people, brought no opprobrium among the great. Such tensions, which might have been expressly designed to give writers inspiration for dramatic action, can be found in epic literature. The *chansons de geste* are full of family drama. In Huon it is Charlot, Charlemagne's natural son, and also Huon's own brother, the traitor Gerard, who usurp his inheritance.

As is normal in an agnatic family, the bond linking uncle and nephew was especially important – more precisely the *avunculus* or mother's brother with her son, the nephew. Again, the *chansons de geste* depict a large number of pairs of uncles and nephews – Charlemagne and Roland, William of Orange and Vivien, Raoul de Cambrai and Gautier. Nepotism figured widely in medieval society; its ecclesiastical form was merely a special case owing to the force of circumstances. The agnatic rather than patriarchal type of family also occurred in the peasant class, where it was more closely connected with farming and with the inheritance of land. It grouped together all those who lived in the same house and devoted themselves to getting profit from the same land. We do not know much, however, about the peasant family, although it does constitute the basic economic and social unit of modern societies comparable with that of medieval western Europe. Even though it was a real community it had no means of expressing itself in law. It was, in fact, what in the France of the Ancien Régime was called the 'communauté taisible' or 'untalked-of community', and the very adjective 'taisible', 'what one keeps quiet about', almost a secret, clearly shows that the law was reluctant to recognize its existence.

VII

It is difficult to grasp the place which was held by women and children in the heart of this primordial unit, the family, and also to assess the evolution which occurred in their conditions. That women were inferiors in the family group is beyond question. In this warfaring, virile society, basic subsistence was always threatened. Consequently, fertility was more of a curse (hence the interpretation of Original Sin as being to do with sexual intercourse and procreation) than a blessing, and women were not held in honour. It is likely that Christianity had done little to improve their material or moral position.

Had not a woman been chiefly responsible for the Fall? Of all the forms taken by diabolic temptation, women were the worst incarnation of evil. '*Vir est caput mulieris* – The man is the head of the woman' said St Paul (Ephesians 5.23), and it became an item of Christian belief and teaching after him. Many have liked to believe that the cult of the Virgin, which triumphed in the twelfth and thirteenth centuries, was a turning-point in Christian spirituality, underlining the redemption of sinful woman by Mary, the new Eve. This turning point may also be observed in the cult of Mary Magdalen which started to grow from the twelfth century, as has been shown from the history of Vézelay in Burgundy as a religious centre. However, when Christianity agreed that women had made the grade, their rehabilitation occurred not at the beginning but at the end of a period in which the position of women in society was relatively high. The part played by women in medieval heretical movements, especially Catharism, or near-heretical movements such as that of the Béguines, is a sign of their dissatisfaction with the place which was allotted to them.

However, the contempt with which they were treated should be qualified. For one thing, women, even if they were not as useful as men in medieval society, nevertheless played (procreation apart) a significant part as far as the economy was concerned. In the peasant class women were almost equivalent to if not as good as men at work. When Helmbrecht tried to persuade his sister Gotelint to flee the home of her peasant father to marry an outlaw, who would let her live like a lady, he told her, 'If you marry a peasant, no woman will ever be more wretched than you. He will make you spin, break, strip and beat flax and pull up beets.' In the upper classes women, even though they had more refined pursuits, nevertheless were economically active to an important degree. They ran the women's quarters, where by fancy skills such as the weaving of fine materials, embroidery, and tapestry, they supplied a large proportion of the clothes needed by the lord and his companions. In more prosaic terms, they were the textile workers of the seigneurial class. The two sexes were customarily distinguished as the 'sword side' and the 'distaff side' not only in colloquial but also in legal terminology. In literature, the poetic genre associated with women, which Pierre le Gentil in fact named the '*chanson de femme*', was traditionally known as the '*chanson de toile*' (weaving song) because it was sung in the women's quarters, in the women's workshop where the spinning took place. When, between the ninth and eleventh centuries, the upper layer of the economically productive class, the *laboratores* of the age, managed to rise socially, the women who belonged to this layer benefited from this rise too. It is noticeable that, throughout the middle ages, although the birth of girls did not arouse great joy, girls were not, as in other misogynistic societies, penalized by infanticide, as far as we can conjecture.

The penitentials, which list a long series of barbarous and ferocious practices, are in general silent on this subject. Furthermore, in the upper classes of society, women, or at least some of them, always enjoyed a certain status. Once again, literature has caught some reflection of the brilliance shed by these great ladies. Bertha, Sibile, Guibourg, Kriemhild, and Brunhild, with their different characters and destinies, gentle or cruel, unfortunate or happy, form a group of first-class heroines. They are, as it were, the earthly understudies of the female religious figures who blossomed in Romanesque and Gothic art: solemn, ceremonial Madonnas who first became more human, then started to sway at the hips and became mannerized, or the wise and foolish virgins who held lengthy debates on vice and virtue, or the disquieted and disquieting Eves who seem to be moved by a medieval Manichaeanism to enquire, 'Did heaven form this constellation of wonders to be a serpent's dwelling?' In courtly literature, of course, the ladies who inspired or wrote poetry, real-life heroines such as Eleanor of Aquitaine, Marie de Champagne, or Marie de France, just as much as the fictional Iseult, Guinevere, or the *Princesse lointaine*, played a more important part; they invented modern love. But this is another story, which will be mentioned later.

It has often been claimed that the crusades, which left women on their own in western Europe, meant that their powers and rights increased. David Herlihy quite recently maintained that the condition of women, especially in the upper level of the seigneurial class and in southern France and Italy, had improved at two stages, in the Carolingian period and at the time of the crusades and the Reconquista. The poetry of the troubadours is supposed to reflect the growth in status of the women left behind. However, if we put our credence in St Bernard when he is conjuring up a Europe deprived of its menfolk, or Marcabru when he makes a châtelaine sigh because all her lovers are off on the second crusade, we are taking the longings of a fanatical propagandist of the crusade and the fiction of an imaginative poet to be universal realities. Anyway, one does not get the impression from reading the works of the troubadours that the world of courtly poetry is a universe of lonely women, to say the very least. And a study of legal documents proves that, in matters concerning the management of the property of married couples at any rate, the position of women grew worse between the twelfth and thirteenth centuries.

Children were a different case. Indeed, were there any children in the medieval west? If we look at works of art, children do not appear in them. In a later age angels were habitually portrayed as children and even as *putti*, those ambivalent mixtures of angels and cupids, but in the middle ages angels, whatever their sex, were always adults. Even when statues of the Virgin began to show her as a perfect woman, as beautiful as she was gentle and clearly feminine – evoking a real, doubtless often a loved model, whom the artist was trying to immortalize – the infant Jesus remained a horrid little dwarf, in whom clearly neither the artist, nor the commissioners of the work, nor for that matter the public, were interested. We must wait till the end of the middle ages for the spread of an iconographic theme which can be felt to display a new interest in children. It is an interest which, in a period of high infant mortality, was chiefly an anxious one. The theme was the massacre of the Innocents, which was echoed in devotion by the vogue for the feast of Holy Innocents. Foundling hospitals, placed under the patronage of the Innocents, are barely to be found before the fifteenth century. The utilitarian middle ages had no time to display pity or wonder towards children, and barely even noticed them. It has been said that in the middle ages there were no children, only small adults. Furthermore the child often did not have a grandfather, the figure involved in bringing up children in traditional societies, to form its character, since life-expectancy was too short in the middle ages for many children to have known their grandfather. Barely were they out of the women's quarters, where childhood was not treated as a matter of serious concern, when they were thrown into the toil of farming or military apprenticeship. Here again the terminology of the *chansons de geste* is enlightening. *Les Enfances Vivien*, or *Les Enfances du Cid* show the young precocious adolescent hero as already a young man – as is natural in primitive societies. The child was to make its appearance with the domestic family in which only a small group of direct descendants and ancestors lived together; this domestic family emerged and multiplied in the urban milieu, with the formation of the burgess class. The child was a product of the town and the burgess class which by contrast pushed down women and stifled them. Women were tied to the hearth while the child was freed and all of a sudden filled the houses, schools, and streets.

VIII

Trapped inside a family which imposed on him the slavery of collective ownership and community life, the individual was also, except in the towns, swallowed up inside another community, the territorial lordship on which he lived. Of course the difference between the noble vassal and the peasant, whatever might be the latter's condition, was considerable. But at different levels, glamorously or unglamorously, they both belonged to the lordship, or rather to the lord, whose dependants they were. Both of them were the 'men' of the lord, the former in a 'noble' sense, the latter in a humiliating one; the terms which often accompany the word 'man' moreover specify the gap which existed between their conditions. For example the phrase 'man of mouth and hands' for the vassal evokes an intimacy, communion, or contract which puts the vassal, although an inferior, into the same class as his lord, whereas the phrase '*homme de pôté*' or *homo potestatis* for the peasant means the man who depends on or is in the power of his lord. Yet in exchange for their only protection and the economic benefit of dependence, a fief for the one, a tenure for the other, the two had to render the lord a number of duties – aids, services, and rents – and both had to bow to his authority, which manifested itself nowhere more clearly than in that of the administration of justice.

Of all the functions annexed by feudal lords at the expense of the public power, there was none which was harder for the lord's dependants to bear than the judicial function. Probably the vassal was summoned more often to sit on the 'right' side of the tribunal as a judge at the side of, or even in place of, his lord, than on the 'wrong' side, but he also had to submit to the lord's verdicts in misdemeanours, if the lord only had the right to dispense lesser justice, and in serious cases too, if the lord had the right to hear these. In this state of affairs the prison, gallows, and pillory, the sinister extensions of the lord's court, were symbols of oppression rather than of justice. The forward march of royal justice probably did not only mean an improvement in justice but more importantly helped to emancipate individuals who saw their rights better protected in the larger community of the realm than in the smaller, and for that reason alone more constricting, if not more oppressive, community of the manor. Yet this advance was slow. St Louis, one of the sovereigns most careful both in combating injustice and in making royal power respected, was extremely anxious to respect private seigneurial jurisdictions. William of St Pathus narrates a significant story about this. The king, surrounded by a great crowd of people, was listening to a sermon being given by a Dominican, Friar Lambert, in the graveyard of the church at Vitry. Nearby a gathering of people in a tavern was making such a noise that it was impossible to hear what the preacher was saying. 'The blessed king asked to whom the jurisdiction in this place belonged and he was told that it belonged to him. So he ordered some of his sergeants to make the people who were disturbing God's word stop doing so, which was done.' The sovereign's biographer concludes, 'It is believed that the blessed king asked whose the local jurisdiction was because he was afraid that if it had belonged to someone else and not to him he might have encroached on someone else's jurisdiction.'

Just as a clever vassal could juggle to his advantage with the many, sometimes contradictory, duties which he owed as a faithful follower, so the cunning villein could escape without loss from the tangled operation of rival jurisdictions. However the masses usually found them an occasion for additional oppressions.

It is still true that the individual was a resourceful man. The oppression caused by the many layers of collectivism in the middle ages thus gave the word 'individual' a shifty sound: the individual was a man who could only escape from the group by committing some misdeed. He was prey for the lawkeepers, if not for the gallows. The individual was the automatic suspect. Most of these communities certainly claimed loyalty from their members and charged them with responsibilities; theoretically these were a payment for protection, but the burden of the price paid was heavy, while the protection was not always effective or obvious. In theory it was to provide for the needs of the poor that the Church levied tithes from the members of the parish (yet another community). Yet the tithe went more often to enrich the clergy, especially the higher clergy. Whether this was true or not, most parishioners believed it, and tithe was one of the taxes most hated by medieval people.

IX

Benefits and subjection seem to have achieved a better balance with each other in the heart of other, outwardly more egalitarian, communities: village and town communities. The village communities often put up a successful resistance to seigneurial exactions. They were essentially economic in purpose. They shared out, managed, and defended those pastures and the areas of forest which formed the common land. The upkeep of these was vital for most peasant families, who could not subsist without the essential contribution they could find there for feeding their pigs or their goats or for replenishing their woodpiles. However, the village community was not egalitarian. Its affairs were controlled and conducted by a few heads of families for their own profit. Often they were rich; sometimes they were the lowly descendants of families which had originally been more eminent. Rodney Hilton and Sir Michael Postan have shown that in many English villages in the thirteenth century there was a group of better-off villagers who advanced money both for individual loans (in such cases they were acting the part of usurers which the Jews could not, or could no longer, play in rural England) and for the numerous, often large, sums owed by the village as a whole: fines, legal expenses, and communal dues. These were the warrantors or guarantors, a group which was almost always made up of the same names for a given period, who appear in the village charters. They also often formed the guild or the confraternity of the village, for the village community itself was usually not the heir of a primitive rural community, but a relatively recent social formation. It was contemporary with the very movements which, as a result of the growth from the tenth to the thirteenth centuries, created completely new institutions in the countryside as well as in the town. It is perhaps in Italy that one can observe most clearly that these were two parallel aspects of the same phenomenon, although it was experienced throughout western Europe. In the twelfth century communal insurrections broke out, at the same time as in the towns, in the countryside in Ponthieu and in the area around Laon. Here the peasants set up federations of communes, based on a federation of villages and hamlets. Since the work of, notably, R. Caggese, P. Sella, F. Schneider, and G. P. Bognetti, it has been well known that in Italy the birth of rural communities went together with that of urban communes. More importantly, they have stressed the fundamental role played in both cases by the economic and ideological relationships which grew up between groups of neighbours. These *viciniae* or *vicinantiae* were the kernels of communities in the feudal epoch. The institution and the concept were fundamental. Opposed to them were, as we shall see, the institutions and concepts connected with foreigners. Good came from neighbours, evil from foreigners. Yet when they became organized communities the *viciniae* developed a class structure, and a group of *boni homines*, good or worthy men, appeared at their head. They were the notables from whom were recruited the consuls or officials or functionaries of the community.

Similarly in the towns the guilds and confraternities which ensured the economic, physical, and spiritual protection of their members were not, as often imagined, egalitarian institutions. It is true that they fought fraud, bad workmanship, and bogus imitations relatively effectively by controlling the work process, and by controlling production and the market they eliminated competition to the point of being, as Gunnar Mickwitz has argued, protectionist cartels. However, they allowed the 'natural' mechanisms of supply and demand to function under the cover of the 'just price' or *iustum pretium*. As John Baldwin has clearly proved by analysing the economic theories of scholastic theologians, this 'just price' is nothing other than the market price (*pretium in mercato*). The corporate system might be protectionist on a local level, but it favoured free trade in the wider context within which the town was situated. In fact the system favoured social inequalities, which grew just as much out of this *laissez-faire* on a higher level as out of the protectionism which functioned for the benefit of a minority at a lower level. The corporations were hierarchies and although the apprentice was a potential master, the workman was an inferior without great hope of promotion. More especially, the guilds excluded two social categories, whose existence really gave the lie to the harmonious economic and social planning which the system was theoretically destined to create.

One of these categories, at the top of society, was a rich minority who mostly maintained their economic power by the exercise of political power, directly or through an intermediary. They were *jurés*, *scabini*, and consuls. They escaped the iron collar of the guilds and acted as they pleased, as Armando Sapori has shown for the great Italian merchants. Sometimes they grouped themselves in guilds such as Florence's Arte di Calamala, which dominated economic life, and had a serious impact on political life. Sometimes they purely and simply ignored the shackles of corporate institutions and their statutes. They were chiefly merchants dealing in long-distance imports or exports, the *mercatores* or 'givers of work' who controlled an entire commodity in a locality, from the production of the raw material to the sale of the finished product. An exceptional document edited by Georges Espinas allows us to make the acquaintance of one of them, Sire Jehan Boinebroke, merchant-draper of Douai in the late thirteenth century. The Church demanded of the faithful, especially merchants, that at least at their deaths they should restore by their wills the sums which they had received unjustly by usury or any sort of exaction, so as to be sure of salvation. The formula thus turned up as a matter of course in the last wishes of the dead, but it was rarely effective. In the case of Jehan Boinebroke it was. His heirs invited his victims to come and reimburse or compensate themselves. The text of some of these claims has come down to us. From them emerges the terrible portrait of a man who must have been less an isolated case than a representative of an entire social class. He bought wool and dyestuffs at a low price; he paid 'little, very little or nothing at all' to his inferiors, the peasants and small workmen. Very often he paid them in kind, by what we would now call the truck system. He controlled them financially through usury and through employment and lodging, for he housed his employees as an extra form of pressure. Finally he could crush them by his political power, for he was *échevin* or *scabinus* (a sort of magistrate) at least nine times. Holding this office in 1280, he savagely crushed a strike by the Douai weavers. His hold over his victims was such (for it was not merely the ascendancy of a man who was perhaps exceptionally wicked, but that of a class) that those who dared to come and make a claim did so trembling, still terrorized by the memory of that tyrant who was clearly the urban equivalent of the feudal despot.

At the bottom the masses remained without protection: more of them later.

It is still true that even if rural and urban communities oppressed, rather than freed, the individual, they were founded on a principle which made the feudal world tremble. 'Commune, a detestable name,' exclaimed the ecclesiastical chronicler Guibert de Nogent in a famous phrase in the early twelfth century. What was revolutionary about the origins of the urban movement and its rural pendant – the formation of the rural communities – was that the oath which linked the members of the primitive urban society was an egalitarian oath, in contrast to the contract of vassalage, which bound the inferior to a superior. It substituted a society organized on horizontal lines for (and in opposition to) the vertical feudal hierarchy. The *vicinia*, the group of neighbours, who had originally been brought together simply because their houses stood next to each other, turned itself into a fraternity (*fraternitas*). The word and the reality which it defined had a particular success in Spain, with its flourishing *hermandades*, and in Germany, where the sworn fraternity, *Schwurbruderschaft*, gathered to itself all the emotive force of the old Germanic brotherhood. It demanded from the burgesses an obligation of fidelity, or *Treue*. At Soest in north-west Germany, in the mid-twelfth century, the burgess who had injured the person or the property of a *concivis*, or fellow-citizen, had to renounce his right to be a burgess. The fraternity finally turned itself into a community based on an oath – the *coniuratio* or *communio*. This was the German *Eidgenossenschaft* and the French and the Italian commune. It united equals to the point where, even if economic inequality (for example in matters of urban taxation) could not be eliminated, it had to coexist with formulae and practices which safeguarded a theoretical equality between all the citizens. Thus at Neuss in south-west Saxony in 1259 it was laid down that if it was necessary to raise a tax for the need of the commune, the poor and the rich would swear equally (*equo modo*) to pay according to their means.

X

Even if medieval towns were not the threat to feudalism or the antifeudal exception that they have often been described as being, it is none the less true that they were above all an unusual phenomenon. As far as men in the period of urban growth were concerned, they were new things in the scandalous sense which was given to this adjective in the middle ages. For the men from the fields, the forest, and the moors, the town was at once an object of attraction and repulsion. Like metal, money, and women, it was a temptation. Yet the medieval town was not, at first sight, a frighteningly large monster. By the start of the fourteenth century, very few towns exceeded the 100,000 mark, and then only slightly. Venice and Milan both did. Paris, the biggest town in northern Europe, whose size has sometimes been overestimated to as much as 200,000 inhabitants, probably at that time had no more than 80,000. Bruges, Ghent, Toulouse, London, Hamburg, Lübeck, and all the other cities of the same size, the first-class cities, numbered from 20,000 to 40,000 inhabitants.

Moreover, as has often been justly pointed out, the medieval town was completely intermingled with the countryside. Townsfolk led a semirural life within the walls, which gave protection to vines, gardens, indeed even meadows and ploughed fields, livestock, and dung. And yet the contrast between town and country was stronger in the middle ages than in most societies and civilizations. Town walls were a frontier, the strongest known in this period. The ramparts, with their towers and gates, separated two worlds. The towns asserted their singularity and individuality by ostentatiously displaying the walls which protected them on their seals. Whether it was viewed as Jerusalem, the throne of righteousness, or as Babylon, the seat of evil, the town was always a symbol of the extraordinary in the medieval west. The distinction between townsman and peasant was one of the sharpest dividing lines in medieval society.

Presumably early medieval towns had retained their Roman glamour in the eyes of prefeudal or feudal society. Towns were centres of political or religious power, the residences of the king or the count and of the bishop. They were the only places with great buildings, made of brick or stone, they were the places where the most important treasures were stored, and they were the localities whose capture, pillage, or possession brought riches and fame. Has it been sufficiently remarked that towns were a focus of attraction to the heroes of *chansons de geste*? In the *Chanson de Roland*, in contrast with hostile nature - rocks, mountains, or even flat country - the towns, for example Saragossa and Aachen, 'the finest seat in France' were beacons. Constantinople was a seductive vision because it was a City with a capital C. The habitual epithets for towns were 'proud', 'arrogant', or 'noble'. Thus Paris was 'the noble city' in *Mainet* and in *Berthe au grand pied*, who found the end of her trials there. Oberon, whom one would believe to be associated solely with the forests where his spells were spun, retained nostalgia for his birthplace, 'Monimur, his city'. The whole cycle of William of Orange revolves around towns: Orange, Nîmes, Vienne and, again, Paris. However, the *Moniage Guillaume* did not try to idealize Paris. 'France then was not very populous; it was barely cultivated, and one did not see there all the rich manors, castles, and rich towns which spread over her surface nowadays. Paris at that time was very small.' Nonetheless William had come to relieve the siege of King Louis, and his first sight of the town at the end of his journey was a revelation, an emotional moment. 'When William opened his eyes morning had broken and he could see Paris beyond the meadows.' And William left a memorial to the Parisians of today in the form of the name of his enemy, the Saxon pagan Ysoré, whom he slew in single combat and buried on the spot, in a place which became the Tombe Isoré, or Tombe Issoire. Narbonne, captured by Aimeri, was especially splendid:

Between two high crags, on the edge of a bay, he saw a fortified Saracen town standing on a height. It was well enclosed by walls and posts, and no one had ever seen a more solid town laid out. They saw leaves shaken by the wind in the plantations of yews and laburnums; no one could enjoy a finer sight. The town had twenty towers made of shining limestone. Another tower, in the middle, drew their glances. No man in this world, however good a storyteller he might be, would be able to describe to you in less time than a summer day the labours which the pagans had undertaken to build this tower. The battlements were entirely sealed with lead; the defenders were about a bowshot from the enemy. At the top of the keep stood a ball made of fine gold from Outremer. Within this the Saracens had enclosed a carbuncle which blazed and shone with a light like that of the sun at dawn. The king gazed at the town and desired it in his heart. . . .

Between the tenth and the thirteenth century the face of western towns changed. Henri Pirenne's work on their leap forward will always be a landmark. One function of towns came to be of prime importance, reviving the old cities and creating new ones. This was the economic and commercial role of the towns, and soon their artisanal role as well. The town became a centre of what feudal lords detested: shameful economic activity. Towns were cursed.

In 1128 the small town of Deutz, just across the Rhine from Cologne, burnt down. The abbot of the monastery of St Heribert there, the famous Rupert of Deutz, a theologian who was strongly attached to traditions, immediately saw in this the anger of God inflicting punishment on the place because it was involved in the development of Cologne and had turned itself into a trading centre, a haunt of unspeakable merchants and workmen. Thence, by way of the Bible, Rupert outlined an anti-urban history of mankind. Cain had been the inventer of towns and had constructed the first of them, and he had been imitated by all evil people, all the tyrants and enemies of God. On the other hand the patriarchs, and the righteous generally, those who feared God, had lived in tents in the desert. To settle in towns was to choose the world and indeed the growth of towns encouraged a new outlook on life: the result of fixing people in one spot, and of the development of property and of the instinct for property. In particular, towns encouraged the choice of the active life.

What also favoured the spread of an urban outlook was the birth of a city patriotism. Without doubt, as we shall see, the towns were the scene of a bitter struggle between the classes, and the ruling classes were the instigators and the principal beneficiaries of this urban spirit. Besides, as Armando Sapori has emphasized, the great merchants themselves, at least in the thirteenth century, were prepared to pay for this with their own money and their own lives. In 1260, when a fierce war broke out between Siena and Florence, one of the chief Sienese merchant-bankers, Salimbene dei Salimbeni, gave the commune 118,000 florins, closed his shops, and himself hurried off to war.

The rural lordship could only inspire in the mass of the peasants who lived there a sense of the oppression of which they were the victims, and the castle, even if it sometimes offered them refuge and protection, cast only a hated shadow over them. By contrast, the city skyline with its great buildings, even though they were an instrument and a symbol of the domination of the rich in the towns, inspired city-dwellers with feelings in which admiration and pride were often overwhelmingly dominant. Urban society had succeeded to a certain degree in creating common values in all inhabitants – aesthetic, cultural, and spiritual values. Dante's '*Il bel San Giovanni*' was an object of veneration and pride to all Florentines. This urban pride was first and foremost an achievement of the most urbanized areas – Flanders, Germany, northern and central Italy. Let us look at some evidence from three Italian cities. Milan's marvels were described by Fra Bonvesin dalla Riva in 1288 in his *De magnalibus urbis Mediolani* – 'The town is in the shape of a circle and its wonderful round form is a sign of its perfection.' Genoa's 'beauties' were praised in the vernacular by an anonymous poet at the end of the thirteenth century: '*Zenoa è citae piuna / de gente e de ogni ben fornia / Murao ha bello e adorno / chi la circonda tuto intorno*' – 'Genoa is a city full of people and well supplied in everything. She has fine ornate walls which surround her all around.' Lastly Chiaro Davanzati glorified Florence in 1267, before Dante did; '*Ah dolze e gaia terra fiorentina / fontana di valore e di piagenza . . . .*' – 'Ah sweet and gay land of Florence, fountain of worth and of pleasure . . . .'

But what the role and the destiny of these islands of urbanism in the land mass of western Europe? Their prosperity could in the end only be fed from the land. Even the towns which had most enriched themselves by trade – Ghent, Bruges, Genoa, Milan, Florence, Siena, and also Venice, which still had to struggle against the problems posed by its geographical situation, had to base their activity and power on their rural hinterland, or what Italian towns called their '*contado*' or 'countryside', from which Italian peasants obtained their name of *contadini*.

Relations between towns and the rural areas which they controlled were complex. At first sight cities were highly attractive to the population in the countryside. The peasant who left his village could above all find liberty there. Either he automatically became free by moving into the town, since servitude was unknown on town soil, or else the town, when it obtained control of the surrounding countryside, was eager to free the serfs. Hence the famous German phrase '*Stadtluft macht frei nach Jahr und Tag*' – 'Town air frees after a year and a day', that is after the new citizen had stayed this length of time in the town. Yet the town also exploited the land around it, behaving like a lord towards it. The urban lordship exercised its right of jurisdiction over the area in its control and above all exploited it economically. It bought its produce (grain, wool, and dairy products for sustenance, industrial production, and commerce) at low prices and forced it to buy its own produce. This included things which it supplied merely as an intermediary, for example salt, which became effectively a tax, since the town obliged villagers to buy it in quantities which it laid down, with a tax on the price. The urban armies were soon mostly formed of recruited peasants. Bruges for example got its soldiers from the countryside around – the '*Franc de Bruges*'. The towns built up a cheap rural workforce which they controlled entirely. Quite soon they were afraid of their peasants. Just as the lords in the open countryside barricaded themselves inside their castles, the towns, once night had fallen, pulled up their drawbridges, pulled chains in front of their doors, and garrisoned their walls with sentries. These were chiefly on the lookout for the nearest and likeliest enemy, the peasant from round about. At the end of the middle ages, university graduates and lawyers, who themselves were a product of the town, even worked out a legal system to crush the peasants.

Finally, even the towns which succeeded in becoming nation-states in the middle ages, the republic of Venice, the grand duchy of Tuscany, and the free Hanseatic towns, continued to flourish after the middle ages only against the trend of history. Little by little they became anachronisms. The lands where the towns continued longest to form the economical, political, and cultural backbone, Italy and Germany, were the last to establish their political unity, in the nineteenth century. Medieval urban society had no historic future ahead of it.

XI

The Church's dream of an ideal society which would be at least harmonious even if not united ran up against the bitter reality of social clashes and struggles. The quasi-monopoly which clerics had over literature, at least until the thirteenth century, disguised the intensity of the class struggle in the middle ages and sometimes gives the impression that only a few wicked laymen, lords or peasants, tried every now and then to disturb the social order by attacking the clergy or the Church's possessions. Nonetheless, ecclesiastical authors said enough on the subject for us to be able to uncover the longlasting nature of these antagonisms, which sometimes erupted in sudden violent explosions.

The best known source of conflict was the hostility of the burgesses to the nobles. This was spectacular. The urban setting resounded with it; the echo has been preserved for us in writings such as the narratives of chroniclers, and the charters, statutes, and treaties by which the sudden changes were often ratified. The fairly frequent cases in which urban revolts broke out against bishops as lords of towns, which are narrated with horror by clerical authors, have provided us with exciting accounts which show that, with the rise of new classes, a new system of values was emerging which no longer respected the sacred character of prelates. Events in Cologne in 1074 were recorded by the monk Lampert of Hersfeld.

The archbishop spent the period of Easter at Cologne with his friend, the bishop of Münster, whom he had invited to celebrate the feast with him. When the bishop of

Münster wished to return home, the archbishop ordered his sergeants to find him a suitable boat. By searching they discovered a good boat which belonged to a rich merchant of the city and claimed it for the archbishop's use. The merchant's men who were in charge of the boat resisted, but the archbishop's men threatened to ill-treat them if they did not obey immediately. The merchant's men hurried off to find their master, told him what had happened, and asked him what they should do. The merchant had a bold, vigorous son. He was related to the chief families of the town and was very popular because of his personality. He quickly assembled his men and as many young men of the town as he could, rushed towards the boat, ordered the archbishop's men to get out and drove them out by force . . . . The supporters of the two sides took arms and it seemed that a great battle was being prepared in the town. News of the struggle reached the archbishop, who immediately sent men to quell the revolt, and, since he was very angry, he threatened the young men who had rebelled with a harsh punishment at the next session of his court. The archbishop had all the virtues and he had often proved his excellence in all aspects of life, both temporal and ecclesiastical, but he had one fault. When he lost his temper, he could not control his tongue and he cursed every man without distinction with the most violent expressions. Finally the rebellion seemed to die down, but the young man, who was in a great rage and intoxicated by his success at the beginning, did not cease to cause as much trouble as he could. He went throughout the town making speeches to the people concerning the archbishop's bad government, and accused him of imposing unjust burdens on the people, of depriving innocent people of their goods and of insulting honest citizens. . . . It was not difficult for him to arouse the populace . . . Moreover everyone thought that the people of Worms had accomplished a great exploit in driving out their bishop who had ruled them too severely. And since they were more numerous and richer than the people of Worms and they had weapons, they did not like it that others might think that they were not as brave as the people of Worms and they thought that it was shameful to be subject like women to the power of the archbishop who was governing them like a tyrant . . . .

In Laon in 1111 we know, from the famous account of Guibert de Nogent, that the rebellion of the citizens ended with the butchering of Bishop Gaudri and the mutilation of his corpse. One rebel cut off a finger to seize the ring.

Ecclesiastical chroniclers faced with these urban rebellions were more astonished than indignant. The characters of some bishops probably seemed to them to explain, if not to justify, the anger of the burgesses and of the people. Yet when the latter rebelled against the feudal order, against the society approved of by the Church, and against a world which, since it had become Christian, seemed to have nothing to do save to wait for the transfer from the earthly to the heavenly city (this was the theme of Otto of Freising in his *History of Two Cities*), ecclesiastical historiography admitted that it could not understand it.

Thus at Le Mans in 1070 the inhabitants rebelled against William the Conqueror, who was busy making sure of his conquest of England, and the bishop took refuge with him.

Then the people [wrote the episcopal chronicler] formed an association which they called a commune, they united themselves by an oath and forced the lords from the surrounding countryside to swear allegiance to their commune. Emboldened by this conspiracy, they began to commit innumerable crimes, condemning many people without discrimination and without cause, blinding some for the most trivial of reasons, and horrible to say, hanging others for trivial faults. They even burnt down the castles in the region during Lent, and, what was worse, during Holy Week. And they did all this without reason.

XII

However, the chief battlefront of social tensions lay in the countryside. Struggle between lords and peasants was endemic and sometimes it erupted in attacks of extreme violence. Revolts in towns between the eleventh and the thirteenth century were led by burgesses who wished to ensure political power for themselves which would guarantee the free exercise of their professional activities and thus their financial prosperity, and which would bring them a status related to their economic power. In the country, by contrast, peasant risings aimed not only to improve the position of peasants by fixing, reducing, or abolishing the services and dues which weighed on them heavily, but were often simply an expression of their struggle for existence. The majority of peasants consisted of the masses who subsisted on the very edge of the starvation level, at risk from famine and epidemic. What was later in France to be called the Jacquerie could draw on an extraordinary strength of despair. In towns too, as we have seen in Cologne in 1074, the new social classes were motivated by hatred and the desire to take their revenge for the contempt in which they were held by ecclesiastical and lay lords, but this emotional motivation was very much stronger in the countryside, in proportion to the immense contempt which the lords had for their villeins. In spite of the improvements to their lot which the peasants gained in the eleventh and twelfth centuries, many lords did not, even at the end of the thirteenth century, recognize that their tenants had any property other than their naked bodies, for of course there was that essential difference between their condition and that of the slave in the ancient world. The abbot of Burton on Trent in Staffordshire, whose monastery had confiscated from its peasants all their livestock (800 head of cattle, sheep, and pigs), reminded them of this after they and their wives and children had followed the king from one of his residences to another to obtain a writ ordering the abbot to restore their animals. The abbot announced to them that they possessed nothing except their bellies – '*nihil praeter ventrem*'. He forgot that, owing to him, these bellies were often empty. In 1336, the Cistercian abbot of Vale Royal in Cheshire made his peasants admit by oath on the Bible that they 'were villeins, they and their sons after them, for all eternity. . . . ' The peasant was a savage beast, as sources rivalled each other in repeating. According to G. G. Coulton, the peasant was 'the medieval Caliban'. His natural destination was hell. He needed to be extraordinarily cunning to get to heaven – by using trickery as it were. This was the theme of the *fabliau Du vilain qui gagna le paradis par le plaid*, that is to say by pleading in court.

Here is Rigaut in the *geste* of Garin le Lorrain: 'He saw Rigaut, the son of the villein Hervis, advancing towards him. He was a strong-limbed youth with big arms, and a square back and shoulders, and his eyes were a hand's breadth apart; in 60 countries you would not have found a coarser, less attractive face. His hair was shaggy, his cheeks grimy and tanned; they had not been washed for six months, and the only water which had ever moistened them was rainwater.' Here is how another young peasant appeared in the forest where Aucassin was riding along. 'He had a great mop of a head as black as smut with eyes set a palm's width apart, broad cheeks, an enormous flat nose with cavernous nostrils, thick lips redder than underdone meat and great ugly, yellow teeth' (Matarasso, 1971, p. 45).

Similar hostility was shown concerning the moral state of the peasant. The feudal age derived the word villainy, meaning moral ugliness, from the word villein. The people who were fiercest in their attacks against the peasants were the Goliards, those clerks who were themselves pretty much beyond the pale, who suffered from intensified class prejudices. Hence the Goliardic poem *The Declension of the Peasant*:

Nominative singular	*hic vilanus*	this villein
Genitive	*huius rustici*	of this rustic
Dative	*huic tferfero*	to this devil
Accusative	*hunc furem*	this thief
Vocative	*o latro!*	o robber!
Ablative	*ab hoc depredatore*	by this plunderer
Nominative plural	*hi maledicti*	these accursed ones
Genitive	*horum tristium*	of these wretches
Dative	*his mendacibus*	to these liars
Accusative	*hos nequissimos*	these wicked people
Vocative	*o pessimi!*	o evil ones!
Ablative	*ab his infidelibus*	by these infidels

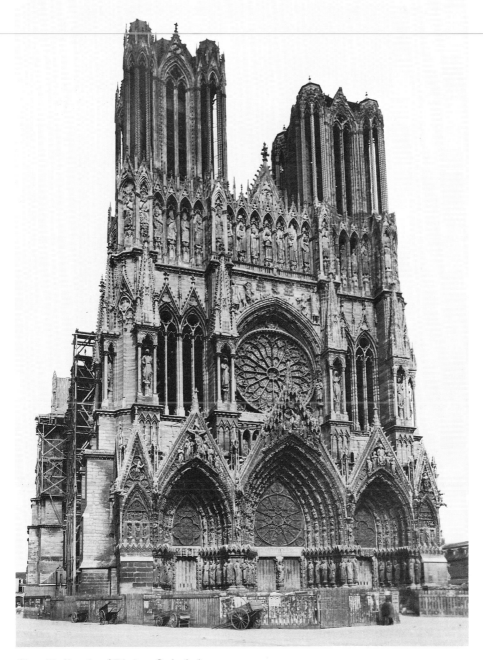

Plate 17 Facade of Rheims Cathedral

The work of four master masons and several sculpture workshops, this was built between 1210 and 1260.

(Photograph reproduced by courtesy of Photographie Lauros-Giraudon.)

Plate 18 Working in wood: shipbuilders

Working in wood and shipbuilding were important medieval crafts and sometimes (as at Venice, where the Arsenal early on became a major enterprise) rose to the status of industries. The biblical scene which allowed the portrayal of shipbuilding was the construction of Noah's Ark. Tools and craftsmen hold a place of honour on this sculpted door jamb (restored in modern times) in the Upper Chapel of the Sainte Chapelle in Paris (1246–8).

(Paris, Sainte Chapelle. Photograph reproduced by courtesy of Photographie Lauros-Giraudon.)

Plate 19 An episode in the history of a nation: the baptism of Clovis

No event was more important for the kings of France than the baptism of Clovis, who established the triumph of the Frankish kings (to whom the Capetians claimed to be linked). Thus the scene was depicted frequently. In this miniature from a manuscript of the life of St Denis, drawn in the abbey of St Denis' scriptorium in about 1250, all the essential elements are represented: God in the form of the Holy Spirit as a dove bringing the sainte ampoule (or vial of holy oil) with which St Remigius consecrates the king who is then also crowned.

(Paris, Bibliothèque Nationale, nouv. acq. fr. 1098, fo. 50.)

Plate 20 Remodelled towns: Boynes

Boynes (France, dept Loiret, arr. and canton Pithiviers), a settlement on the borderline between a village and a town, goes back to before the twelfth century; it has a surviving twelfth-century building with a Romanesque crypt. However, its decisive growth occurred in the thirteenth century, when the present-day church was built and also the high town walls, whose square plan influenced the axis of the street plan.

(Reproduced by kind permission of © IGN – Paris 1988.)

Plate 21 A medieval town: the stronghold of Carcassonne

Acquired by the king of France in 1229 after the Albigensian Crusade, Carcassonne became the seat of a royal seneschalry, and, like other towns, was fortified in the reigns of Louis IX (1226–70) and Philip III (1270–85). It was fortified with particular care, because of the danger of attack by the heretics, the inhabitants of Languedoc, the Spanish, the English, and, in the fourteenth century, the Great Companies.

(Reproduced by kind permission of Caisse Nationale des Monuments Historiques et des Sites: © Arch. Phot. Paris/S.P.A.D.E.M.)

Plate 22 Medieval cartography: the world in the thirteenth century

A characteristic example of medieval cartography. The map is circular, with the three continents shown in a T-pattern around the Mediterranean in the middle. Jerusalem, the 'navel of the world', occupies the centre, and the earthly paradise the upper edge, with the region where Gog and Magog are shut up to the left. A curious collection of towns is depicted, the fruit of the Christian historical and geographical mentality. In Europe are shown Rome, Athens, Constantinople and Paris (the map was made at St Denis). In Africa there is an unnamed town in North Africa, and Alexandria and 'Babylon' (Cairo) in Egypt. In Asia are Jerusalem, Nazareth, Damascus, Antioch, Troy, Mecca, Babylon and Nineveh. This map is an illustration to a manuscript of the Chronicles of St Denis written at the end of the reign of Louis IX, at the King's request, in French, by the monk Primatus, who offered the book to Philip III in about 1275. Charles V owned the manuscript and had it copied.

(Paris, Bibliothèque St Geneviève. Photograph reproduced by courtesy of Photographie Lauros-Giraudon.)

Plate 23 A medieval hero: Charlemagne

Of all the figures from the past, the one who had the greatest popularity in all Christian Europe, especially in Germany and France, was Charlemagne. This miniature, in a manuscript of the Chronicles of St Denis completed in about 1275 (see caption to plate 22), illustrates the start of the Roncesvaux episode. Charlemagne is pictured sending the traitor Ganelon to the two Saracen kings of Spain, Marsile and Baligand. Tales circulating during the Reconquista developed the episode at Roncesvaux.

(Paris, Bibliothèque St Geneviève, Ms 771. Photograph reproduced by courtesy of Photographie Lauros-Giraudon.)

Plate 24 Seal of Gravelines

This thirteenth-century seal represents the patron saint of the town, St Willibrord of Echternach, apostle of Belgium, Holland and Luxembourg in the eighth century. The saint, dressed as a mitred bishop, bearing a crozier and raising his hand in benediction, is performing the symbolic 'passage' or crossing in a boat.

(Paris, Photographie Lauros-Giraudon.)

Plate 25 Popular games and rustics: blindman's buff

This miniature is to be found in a collection of songs called *Le chansonnier de Paris,* written in a workshop in Paris between 1280 and 1315. It provides valuable evidence of fashionable songs and polyphonic settings, whose interest is heightened by the illustrations. These are inspired by three main influences – religious, courtly and rustic. The songs are in French and Latin; the miniatures do not always correspond to the text. One religious song in Latin has a picture of the Trinity above it and beneath it a representation of young people participating in the popular game of blindman's buff.

(Montpellier, Bibliothèque de la Faculté de Médecine, Ms. 196, fo. 88.)

Plate 26 A leper

A leper shaking his rattle at the gate of a town – together with a blind man and cripple. This miniature comes from an early fourteenth-century copy of a French translation of the Mirror of History by the Dominican Vincent of Beauvais – a summary of universal history in moral anecdotes from the Creation to St Louis (Louis IX).

(Paris, Bibliothèque de l'Arsenal, Ms 5080, fo. 373. Photograph reproduced by courtesy of Photographie Lauros-Giraudon.)

Plate 27 Aristocratic pastimes: a game of chess

Chess became an indoor battle comparable to tournaments. On this lid of an ivory mirror case made in France early in the fourteenth century, we see a chess game between the *chanson de geste* hero Huon of Bordeaux and Yvarin, the daughter of the Saracen admiral. They were playing for the damsel's hand in marriage or Huon's head.

(Paris, Musée du Louvre. Photograph reproduced by courtesy of Photographie Lauros-Giraudon.)

Plate 28 Profane history of the ancient world and typological symbolism

From the middle of the twelfth century, at a point when the church had to fight against Catharism, which completely or partially rejected the Old Testament, a hitherto unobtrusive form of symbolism came into its own, one which related the events preceding Christ's Incarnation (the 'types') with their opposite numbers in the New Testament (the 'antitypes'). An early example of this typological symbolism is to be found in the St Bertin cross pedestal illustrated above (plate 10). From the early fourteenth century two works which expounded all sacred history by means of this method were widely diffused: these were the *Biblia pauperum* or *Bible of the Poor* and the *Speculum humanae salvationis* or *Mirror of Human Salvation*. In the *Mirror*, each event of the New Testament is announced by three 'types'. Since sacred history did not always provide enough prefigurations, the *Mirror* fell back on the profane history of antiquity. These details of a miniature from a manuscript of the *Speculum humanae salvationis*, in a copy belonging to the abbey of Kremsmünster made in about 1336 from a manuscript from the abbey of Weissenau, represent two types of the Virgin: the daughter of Jephtha and Semiramis, whose hanging garden is connected with the theme of the enclosed garden which is a symbol of virginity. (Vienna, Österreichische Nationalbibliothek, cod. SN 2612, fo. 8v.)

Plate 29 Feeding the townsfolk: a seller of salt-meat

The miniatures of this early fifteenth-century manuscript of the medical treatise of the Spanish Arab Albucasis (tenth century) were probably painted in Italy, but the copy went soon after to Bohemia because it bears notes in a cursive hand in Czech. The miniatures show the preparation and sale of various products whose advantages and disadvantages for the health are described in the text. The middle ages made great use of salt, the main means of preserving food and an important trade commodity.

(Paris, Bibliothèque Nationale, nouv. acq. lat. 1673, fo. 39. Photograph reproduced by courtesy of Photographie Bulloz.)

S non essent regiltrantes et futuris ministrantes que viderunt et que audiunt. et illa que euemunt in diuersis temporibus et in suis etatibus p libros et per scripturas vbi po nuit magnas curas. pauca si rentur de factis in temporibus transactis. Idarco sunt comme dandi et q plurimum laudan Di qui faciunt regiftrare nota bilia. et quare? quia sepe legen tibus et studere uolentibus tant solamen et gaudium. quia per bonum studium legunt. videt. medicantur. et super visis le cantur quando noua reperiunt

que non viderunt nec saunt per scripturas edocemur si nos bene recordemur. que sunt bona vt amenius quia ue maltu vt iuremus. Ergo tu sane co dute ama scripturas. et studc. et non amabis vicia. In quib? sunt opprobria. Laudandum est multum scire scripturas et sic finire. Nam sunt faenae plu res. de lucranus non aures. Ca parum profunnt. et ammam nificiunt. Si studes in prim tuus aro eris faenie si vis. Est quoq philosophia lauda bilis faentia. Illam faentes laudantur et a amctis bono

rantur.

Plate 30 Calamities: the Black Death

The great plague which had disappeared from the west since the early middle ages reappeared in 1348, brought by a ship coming from the east. Almost all of Christian Europe was affected, and later recurrences, which became weaker, more widely spaced apart and more localized, lasted until the early eighteenth century. The Black Death must have killed about a third of the population of western Europe in 1348–50. The scenes of horror which it caused were impressed on the minds of the survivors. Towns barely managed to bury their dead. Many priests, monks and nuns fled. Those who remained to assist the sick and the dead were looked up to as examples. This miniature shows the burial of plague-victims at Tournai in 1348. It illustrates a manuscript of the *Annales* of Gilles le Muisis, abbot of St Martin, Tournai, who himself very probably died of the plague.

(Brussels, Bibliothèque royale, MS 13076–13077, fo. 24v.)

Plate 31 Ceremonies: the princely baptism of the Dauphin Charles (VI)

Princely ceremonies introduced another order into society, the monarchical order, at the affective level. The whole of the populace was bidden to participate in the events of the private lives of their rulers, which took on the importance of national events and assisted national cohesion. Here we see the baptismal procession of the future Charles VI. The queen, who had given birth only three days before, carries the baby, surrounded by the great princes of the court and preceded by torch-bearers. It is the hour of prime (6 a.m.) on 6 December 1368. The passage illustrated by this miniature in the *Grandes Chroniques de France* (composed for Charles V between 1375 and 1379) emphasizes the pomp lavished on this ceremony – crowd barriers set up the night before for the people, princesses 'finely adorned with crowns and jewels . . .'.

(Paris, Bibliothèque Nationale, MS fr. 2813, fo. 446. Photograph reproduced by courtesy of Photographie Lauros-Giraudon.)

Plate 32 Monarchical society at the end of the middle ages

In 1450, Charles VII had practically reconquered France and established royal authority. In that year the constable in Richemont, who had rallied Brittany (he is here wearing its arms) to the king, commissioned this manuscript of the Tree of Battles, on the occasion of the surrender of Cherbourg. In the picture the king on his throne is presiding over the three estates of society. At the top, the clergy surround the pope, who is superimposing his authority on the king's. In the centre is the sovereign with the Dauphin, the future Louis XI, at his right, and Richemont on his left, surrounded by the military aristocracy. Beneath is the third estate, burgesses on the left and merchants and peasants to the right. The purse, the sign of wealth but as yet not of rank, was the merchants' symbol.

(Paris, Bibliothèque de l'Arsenal, Ms 2695, fo. 6.)

Plate 33 The west and the sea: a Venetian ship at the end of the fifteenth century

By the fifteenth century, western European commercial expansion was asserting itself from the Baltic to the Mediterranean. In spite of the Turks, Venetian galleys dominated much of the trade of eastern Europe. This engraving, from Durazzo, shows a Venetian ship around 1470-80. (Paris, Musée du Louvre, no. 1710, from the Edmond de Rothschild collection. Photograph reproduced by courtesy of Photographie Bulloz.)

Plate 34 Humanistic morality and technology: Temperance and her clock

The humanistic theme of the virtues abounds in Italian art of the fourteenth and fifteenth centuries. It was Italians who introduced it into France in the tomb of Charles VIII at St-Denis, and tombs at Dol (Ille et Vilaine) and Ferrières (Loiret). But portraying the virtues became common after Michel Colombe and Jean Perréal, in the early years of the sixteenth century, built the magnificent tomb of the last duke of Brittany, Francis II, and his wife, Marguerite de Foix. The four medieval virtues stand at the four corners of the tomb. Temperance holds a clock, a symbol of the new measurement of time which defined an intellectual and mental universe which had broken with that of the middle ages. 'Humanistic pride triumphed over the old Christian modesty' (Emile Male).

(Nantes Cathedral. Photograph reproduced by courtesy of Photographie Lauros-Giraudon.)

The peasants who work for us all [wrote Geoffrey of Tours] who wear themselves
out in all weathers, throughout all the seasons, and who offer themselves up to servile
tasks, scorned by their masters, are ceaselessly overwhelmed, and this in order to provide
enough for other people's lives, clothing and frivolities . . . . They are persecuted by
fire, rapine and the sword; they are thrown into prisons, into chains; then they are
forced to ransom themselves, or else they are killed violently, tortured to death by hunger,
or they are offered up to all sorts of tortures . . . '

At the time of the Peasants' Revolt of 1381, the English peasants, according
to Froissart, cried out, 'We are men made in the semblance of Christ, and
yet we are treated like savage beasts.' An unusual poem of the first half of
the thirteenth century, *Le conte des vilains de Verson*, recounts the rebellion
of the peasants of the village of Verson-sur-Odon, near Caen, against their
lord, the abbot of Mont Saint Michel. The villeins' uprising was quelled by
the reply, 'Go and make them pay / they should acquit themselves well for
this / go and take their horses / Take their cows and calves / Because the villeins
are too disloyal.' As Frantisek Graus rightly said, the peasants 'were not only
exploited by feudal society, they were also ridiculed in art and literature', and
the Franciscan Berthold of Regensburg observed in the thirteenth century that
there had almost never been a peasant saint (whereas, for example, Innocent
III had canonized a merchant, Homobonus of Cremona, in 1199).

In such circumstances it cannot be surprising if an enduring impatience or
perpetual discontent lay at the back of the peasants' view of the world. 'The
peasants are always angry,' ran a Goliardic poem from Bohemia, 'and their
heart is never content.' So there is nothing surprising if this anger sometimes
exploded in outbursts. The monk who told the story of the conflict between
the abbot of Vale Royal and the peasants of Darnall and Over in 1336 was
indignant to see them behave like mad dogs - *rabicanes*. William of Jumièges
and Wace, in the *Roman de Rou* (the tale of Rollo, Duke of Normandy), describe
the rebellion of the Norman peasants in 977:

> The peasants and the villeins
> Those of the woodland and those of the open country
> Twenty, thirty, a hundred at a time
> Held many assemblies;
> They went about spreading the motto . . .
> 'Our enemy is our master'
> They talked in secret about this
> And several of them swore among themselves
> That never by their will
> Would they have a lord or an advocate . . .
> By these sayings and words

And by others even madder
They showed their consent
And they swore to each other on oath
That they would keep together
And would defend themselves together
And they elected, I know not where or when,
The most cunning and the best speakers
Who were to travel through the country
And who would receive oaths. . . .

'As soon as the duke was informed of this, he immediately sent Count Ralph with a great number of knights to repress the savagery in the countryside . . . ' And here is the seigneurial repression:

Ralph was so carried away
That he was incapable of judgement:
He made them sad and sore
He pulled out the teeth of many
And had others impaled
Had their eyes torn out or their fists cut off
He had their knees roasted
Even if they should die as a result.
Others were burnt alive
Or plunged into boiling lead
Thus he settled with them.
They were hideous to look at.
They could not been seen in that place from then on
Without being well recognized.
The commune was reduced to nothing
And the villeins behaved themselves;
They withdrew and climbed down
From what they had undertaken.

Iconography often represented the struggle of the peasant against the knight fairly openly in representations of David and Goliath. The way the two figures are dressed is evidence of the artists' intention.

However, the usual form taken by the struggle of the peasants against the lords was the muted guerilla war of pilfering from the lord's lands, poaching in his forests, and setting his ricks on fire; or it was passive resistance such as botching the labour service, or else refusing to deliver dues in kind or to pay taxes; or, finally, it could even sometimes be desertion or flight. In 1117 the abbot of the monastery of Marmoutier in Alsace put a stop to labour services by his serfs and replaced them by dues in money. He took this decision as a result of 'the carelessness, uselessness, slackness and laziness of those who performed services'.

In his treatise on *Housebondrie* written in the middle of the thirteenth century, Walter of Henley, always anxious to increase agricultural renders by all means, gave dozens of recommendations for the surveillance of peasants at work. Pictures show us the lord's overseers armed with sticks spying on the labourers. Although Walter of Henley admitted that the strength of the horse at work was greater than that of the ox, he judged with some disillusionment that it was useless for the lord to run to the considerable expense of buying a horse, since 'the spite of the labourers prevents the plough drawn by the horse from going faster than one pulled by oxen'.

Peasants' hostility to technical progress was even more striking. It cannot be explained, as can the machine-breaking by workers at the start of the industrial revolution, by the unemployment caused by technology. Peasants were hostile because the use of machines in the middle ages entailed a monopoly of the machine for the profit of the lord, who made men use the machine under obligation for his own profit, as an extra burden. Rebellions by peasants against manorial mills were common. Inversely, there were often cases where lords, especially abbots, had their peasants' handmills destroyed to force them to bring their grain to the abbot's mill and pay the mill tax. Already in 1207, the monks of Jumièges had the last handmills on one of their estates broken. A famous struggle over watermills broke out in England between the monks of St Albans and their peasants. When the abbot, Richard II of St Albans, finally triumphed in 1331, he treated the confiscated millstones as trophies and paved the floor of his parlour with them.

Amongst the insidious forms taken by the class struggle, a special place should be made for the immumerable battles which were fought out over weights and measures. Deciding the capacity of, and owning, the measuring standards which fixed the amount of work and the dues owed was an essential means of economic domination. Witold Kula has magisterially opened up our understanding of the social history of weights and measures. Appropriated by one side and contested by the other, the weights and measures, which were kept in the manor or in the castle, in the abbey, or in the town hall (when they belonged to burgesses), were constantly fought over. The many sources which mention the punishments inflicted on those peasants or artisans who used false measures (a crime which was likened to that of altering demesne boundaries) attract our attention to this form of class struggle. Just as the multiplication of jurisdictions favoured the high-handedness of the lords, the number and the variability (which were entirely at the lord's mercy) of the measures were a means of seigneurial oppression. When the English kings tried in the fourteenth century to impose a royal standard for the principal measures, they exempted feudal dues and rents for which the measuring standards were left to the lord's discretion. A reading of *fabliaux*, of legal and moral treatises, and of legal documents gives the impression that the middle ages was a paradise for tricksters and the great age of fraud. The way in which the ruling classes controlled measurements explains this, and the Church, which turned fraud into a serious sin, could not check these signs of class struggle.

XIII

Confrontation between classes, which was a basic feature of life in the countryside, soon reappeared in the towns. It was no longer the struggle of victorious burgesses against the lords, but the struggle of the lesser people against the rich burgesses. From the end of the twelfth to the fourteenth century a new dividing line effectively emerged in the towns, setting the poor against the rich, the weak against the strong, the common people against the burgesses, the *popolo minuto* against the *popolo grasso*. It was caused by the creation of that ruling urban class which was called the patriciate, made up of the group of families who accumulated wealth and real estate in the town. They managed to dominate economic and political life by taking over municipal responsibilities, which means that a mass of the newly oppressed rose up against them.

From the end of the twelfth century one can observe people called the *meliores burgenses* or *maiores oppidani*, who were quick to assert their dominance. From 1165 at Soest in Westphalia we find mentioned 'men of the better sort under whose authority the town prospered and in whom the essence of justice and affairs resides' – the '*meliores . . . quorum auctoritate pretaxata villa nunc pollebat et in quibus summa iuris et rerum consistebat*'. In Magdeburg in 1188 an urban statute laid down that 'it was forbidden in the assembly of the burgesses for the dolts to proffer suggestions contrary to the established order and to go against the will of the *meliores* in anything at all'. Thus rich and poor were set against each other in the towns. In French-speaking towns where it was traditional to describe occupations as being 'based on labour or on commodities', labour and trade were distinguished from each other. Manual workers soon arose against men whom they for their part called idlers. From the end of the thirteenth century strikes and riots against 'the rich men' increased in number, and in the fourteenth century, as a result of the crisis, they inspired the common people in the towns to rise up in violent rebellion.

In spite of the Manichaean taste of the middle ages for simplifying all conflicts into a confrontation between two sides, the good and the bad, it should not be thought that class struggle was limited to these duels between lords and peasants or burgesses and people. The reality was more complicated; one of the principal reasons for the constant failures of the weak in the face of the strong, apart from their economic and military powerlessness, was the internal divisions which made them even more impotent. We have already seen how social distinctions had grown up within the peasant classes. As early as the Norman revolt of 997 Wace noted that though the poorer peasants could not escape the tortures we have heard him describe, the richer ones escaped by buying their physical safety through having their goods confiscated.

Among the lower classes in the towns one should at least distinguish between the *popolo minuto* or the artisans and the journeymen of the guilds, and the masses of wage-earning manual workers who enjoyed no corporate protection: unskilled labourers were exposed to the luck of the labour market. A group of workers formed every day in the square where hiring took place (in Paris this happened in the Place de Grève), where the employers or their agents came to find labour; the proletariat was ceaselessly menaced by unemployment. At the end of the thirteenth century it was the men who had become the lowest class, the *laboratores*, whom John of Freiburg put in the final place in his summarized confessors' manual. Through them we can observe how, as Bronislaw Geremek has clearly shown for Paris, in the period from the thirteenth to the fifteenth centuries, work and workmen had become a commodity.

XIV

Exploitation of female labour certainly was one of the worst forms of oppression by the employers. Here is the lament of the silk-workers whom Chrétien of Troyes put into the song of Yvain (circa 1180). It is the *Song of the Shirt* of the middle ages:

We shall spend our days weaving cloths of silk, without ever being better clad. We shall always be poor and naked, and shall always suffer from hunger and thirst, for we shall never be able to earn enough to procure for ourselves any better food. Our bread supply is very scarce – a little in the morning and less at night, for none of us can gain by her handiwork more than fourpence a day for her daily bread. And with this we cannot provide ourselves with sufficient food and clothes. For though there is not one of us who does not earn as much as twenty sous a week, yet we cannot live without hardship . . . . So while we are reduced to such poverty, he, for whom we work, is rich with the product of our toil. We sit up many nights, as well as every day, to earn the more, for they threaten to do us injury, when we seek some rest, so we do not dare to rest ourselves. (Chrétien of Troyes, 1914, p. 249)

Women were also at the centre of an apparently less dramatic conflict. They were the object of rivalry between men from different social groups. These frivolous games between men and women were, however, one of the bitterest forms taken by class struggle. The contempt women could show for men of a particular social class was one of the most painful wounds the latter could receive. It is somewhat surprising to see clergy join in the conflict, but in fact the rector or the monk, lewd, and weighed down with prosperity, was one of the most common characters in the *fabliaux*. In fact it is above all the Goliard, the cleric on the edge of the ecclesiastical hierarchy, who voiced his claims in the matter. The disputation between the clerk and the knight was a commonplace in medieval literature. The clerk (who was always the author of the work) usually cast himself in the lead role, and thus gave himself a clear advantage over the warrior in women's hearts. In the poem *Le concile de Remiremont* the nuns, after a long debate, decreed the excommunication of those who preferred knights to clerks. The contempt which the clergy felt for peasants can also be seen in this Goliardic poem from Bohemia: '*Filia, vis rusticum / Nigrum et turpissimum? / Nolo, mater cara . . .*' – 'My daughter, do you want a peasant / Black and vile? / I do not want him, mother dear'. Finally, lyric poetry often proclaimed the love of knights for shepherdesses in *pastourelles*. In reality these adventures were not always fortunate. The poet Theobald, Count of Champagne, admitted, in verse, that two peasants put him to flight when he was getting ready to have it off with a shepherdess.

XV

Class struggle in medieval western Europe was paralleled by fierce rivalries within classes, as we know. Conflicts between feudatories and the continuation of clan warfare, the private wars springing out of the Germanic feud, the medieval seigneurial vendetta, fill history and literature. Furthermore, these violent group enmities, these 'lasting hatreds', these 'old grudges well preserved' were class privileges. At the end of the thirteenth century, Philippe de Beaumanoir observed that 'people other than gentlemen cannot wage war'. There were wars of the Lorrainers against the men of Bordeaux in the *Geste de Raoul de Cambrai*, the fights of the Cid's friends and kinsmen against the family of the *Infantes* of Carrión, the interminable vengeances concerning the *Infantes* of Lara, the ceaselessly recurring attacks of the Colonna and the Orsini who were allied with the Gaetani, in which a Gaetani pope, Boniface VIII, was involved, and, of course, clan warfare in the North of Europe, from Scotland to Scandinavia. Confrontations between feudal families fill medieval history, in the lists at tournaments, in the open country or at the sieges of castles.

In spite of its claims, however, the seigneurial class did not have a monopoly of these conflicts. In the heart of city society burgess families gave themselves up to ruthless struggles for the leadership of the patrician class or for the control of the town; sometimes they acted alone, and sometimes they organized factions. It is not surprising that these rivalries between citizens and between burgesses occurred especially in Italy, where towns had evolved early on. In 1216, in Florence, a series of vendettas set two groups of families, two *consorterie*, those of the Fifanti-Amidei and of the Buondelmonte, against each other. It arose from a broken-off marriage, an insult which was all the crueller for the Fifanti-Amidei since the Buondelmonte bridegroom failed to turn up on the day when the whole of the bride's *consorteria* were waiting for him in wedding clothes on the Ponte Vecchio. For this the villain was murdered when he turned up at the cathedral some time later to marry someone else. Grafting itself on to the struggle between two candidates for the Empire, Otto of Brunswick and Frederick of Staufen, which degenerated into the struggle between the emperor and the pope, the rivalry between the two Florentine families turned into the conflict between the Guelfs and the Ghibellines.

Less frequent perhaps, but still memorable, was the individual attitude of a few members of the upper classes who led the struggle on the side of the lower class rebels and often provided them with the educated leaders which they lacked. Sometimes they did this out of interest, sometimes out of idealism, or else, in the case of poor clerks, when they realized that they felt a stronger solidarity with the poor than with the clergy. These 'class traitors' came from the clergy or the burgess class, rarely from the nobility. In 1327 the '10,000' villeins and poor citizens who marched against the monks of Bury St Edmunds were led by two priests who bore the rebels' banners. Then there was the mysterious figure of Henry of Dinant, a tribune of Liège in the years 1253–5, a patrician who led the populace in the attack on the patrician class. Fernand Vercauteren, following the chroniclers of the thirteenth century, saw in him an ambitious man who used the people and his own discontent to reach the top, in short a Catiline. Yet we only know these popular leaders through their enemies. Jean of Outremeuse tells us of Henry of Dinant that he 'made the people rise against their lord and against the clerks and people put much trust in him . . . he was a man of high birth, wise and sly, but he was so false and treacherous and covetous, that the envy which he had for everyone made him worthless'. We should distrust those judgements which characteristically label the rebels as 'envious'. *Invidia*, envy, was, according to the moralists (clerics) and the confessors' manuals, the great sin of the peasants and the poor. Such a diagnosis, made by the spokesmen of the powerful, often masks what was only a revolt by the oppressed moved by justifiable indignation. All the great leaders of the great revolts of the fourteenth century, such as Jacques and Philippe van Artevelde and Etienne Marcel, were described as envious.

XVI

Beyond these individual cases one might ask whether the two powers of the Church and the monarchy did not automatically escape the class struggle, since they kept themselves outside it and sought to pacify it. The Christian ideal called on the Church to maintain an equal balance between rich and poor, between peasants and lords; indeed the Church was even supposed to give support to the poor to offset their weakness. It was supposed to ensure that social harmony would reign. It had given its blessing to such harmony in the tripartite model of society. Admittedly as far as charity went, in the battle against famine, the Church's action was of considerable importance; it is also true that its rivalry with the knightly class sometimes made it act in support of peasants or citizens against their common adversary. In particular, the Church had inspired the movements known as the Peace of God or the Truce of God which brought benefit to all the victims of feudal violence. Yet the claims so often made by the Church that it arbitrated impartially between the weak and the strong fail to hide that in fact it most often chose to side with the oppressors. Since the Church was active in the world and formed a privileged social group which by the grace of God it had turned into an order, that is to say a caste, it was naturally inclined to lean towards the side where it already in fact found itself.

Bishop Warin of Beauvais proposed the following peace oath, which he wished all lords to swear to King Robert the Pious:

I shall not take away any ox or cow or any other beast of burden; I shall not seize peasant men or women or merchants; I shall not take any of their money and I shall not force them to ransom themselves. I do not want them to lose their property because of the wars their lords fight, and I shall not whip them to take away their subsistence. From the Kalends of March to All Saints I shall not seize horse, mare or foal in the pastures. I shall not destroy the mills and I shall not steal the flour which is there, unless they are situated on my land or if I am on compaign; I shall give no thief protection.

In reading this it should not be forgotten that his oath applied to many abbots and bishops.

The monks of St Laud of Angers stated in the arenga to a charter: 'God himself willed that, among men, some should be lords and others serfs, in such a way that the lords should be obliged to venerate and love God, and that the serfs should be obliged to love and venerate their lord, according to the Apostle's saying: Servants, be obedient to them that are your masters according to the flesh, with fear and trembling. . . . And, ye masters, do the same things unto them, forbearing threatening: knowing that your Master also is in heaven.' They must have realized that to justify social inequality was to admit the inevitable class conflict which was the result. It is noteworthy that peasants were particularly hostile to ecclesiastical lords; presumably their anger must have been especially aroused by the gap between the ideal professed by these clerics and their behaviour. Certainly, since monasteries kept better archives and accounts, ecclesiastical lords obtained more effectively by law, supported by their charters and rent-rolls, the exactions which lay lords more often seized by force.

It does indeed seem that we should admit the justice of the self-criticism uttered by that anonymous ecclesiastical dignitary (sometimes erroneously identified with St Bernard) who exclaimed in the twelfth century:

No, I cannot say it without shedding tears: we, the Church leaders, are more timid than the coarse disciples of Christ in the age of the early Church. We deny or suppress the truth out of fear of the worldly. We deny Christ, the truth itself! When the plunderer pounces on the poor man we refuse to render assistance to this poor man. When a lord harasses a ward or a widow, we do not go against him: Christ is on the cross and we hold our peace!

The way in which the monarchy thought about and reacted to these problems has some analogy with the behaviour of the Church. Indeed, both often lent each other mutual support in a common struggle in which the battle cries against individual tyrannies were the defence of the general interest and the protection of the weak against the powerful. Kings made the maximum use of all the weapons provided for them by the feudal system. They got all the lords to do them liege homage; they refused to do homage for lands which they themselves held in fee in order to affirm that they were not merely at the top of the entire feudal hierarchy but absolutely above it; they ensured that their right of protection over many ecclesiastical establishments (their 'advocacy' or 'patronage') was recognized. French kings thrust themselves into the largest possible number of contracts of '*pariage*', by which they became the joint lords of lordships situated outside the royal domain and in areas where royal influence was weak. For their own benefit, kings strengthened the ideal of fidelity which was the essence of feudal morality and psychology. Yet at the same time kings sought everywhere to remove themselves from the control of lords. By making succession to the Crown hereditary, they enlarged the royal domain, imposed their officials everywhere, and attempted to replace feudal military service, aids, and jurisdictions with a national army, state taxation, and centralized justice. It is significant that the peasants tried to place themselves under royal protection, though admittedly it was more distant than that of the lords. It is also true that the lower classes, especially the peasantry, often placed their hopes in the person of the king who, they hoped, would deliver them from seigneurial tyranny. St Louis recounted to Joinville with emotion the attitude of the people towards him at the time of a baronial revolt during his minority:

And the saintly king told me that when he was at Montlhéry, neither he nor his mother dared to return to Paris until the inhabitants of Paris came armed to look for them. And he told me that from Montlhéry to Paris the roads were full of people, armed and unarmed, and that all of them acclaimed him and prayed to Our Lord to give him a long and good life and to defend and guard him from his enemies.

This royal myth was longlived. Until final explosions such as those of 1642-9 in England or 1792-3 in France, it was to survive all the occasions when the monarchy, on being faced with a serious danger of social subversion, showed that it too would join its natural side, that of the feudal lords, whose interests and prejudices it shared. Under Philip Augustus the peasants of the village of Vernon revolted against their lord, which was the chapter of Notre Dame in Paris, and refused to pay it *taille*. They sent a delegation to the king who gave judgement in favour of the canons and snapped at the peasants' delegation: 'May the chapter be cursed if it does not throw you into a latrine (*in unam latrinam*)'.

Yet the king sometimes felt himself to be lonely when faced with the classes of society. Far from controlling them, he felt himself to be threatened by every one of them. Since he was outside feudal society he was afraid of being annihilated by it. Such, according to the chronicle of John of Worcester, was the nightmare of Henry I of England. When the king was in Normandy in 1130 he had a triple vision. First he saw a mob of peasants besiege his bed with their work tools, grinding their teeth and disturbing him by telling him their complaints. Then a multitude of knights wearing hauberks and with helmets on their heads and armed with spears, lances, and arrows threatened to kill him. Finally a gathering of archbishops, bishops, abbots, deans, and priors besieged his bed, with their croziers raised against him. 'And here', wailed the chronicler, 'is what frightens a king clad in purple, whose word, according to the saying of Solomon, should strike terror as does the roaring of a lion.' This was the very lion ridiculed by Renart the Fox, in the *Roman de Renart*, and with it all kingly majesty. The kings were always to some extent outsiders in the medieval world.

XVII

In medieval Europe there were also other communities in addition to those we have just described, communities which overlapped more or less with the social classes, and they were particularly favoured by the Church which saw in them a means of diluting and weakening class conflict. Such were the confraternities. Their origins are not well known and their links with the guilds are obscure; whereas the latter were essentially professional the former were chiefly devotional. Yet in the fourteenth century it seems very probable that confraternities belonged, if not to professional groups, at least to particular social classes; the confraternities of barbers, apothecaries, and surgeons, for example, which were usually under the patronage of the Holy Sepulchre, were separate from the superior confraternities of the physicians or the 'long-robed surgeons' who were placed under the protection of Saints Cosmas and Damian.

Again, there were the groups of widows and virgins whom the Church held in special esteem. A spiritual work which was very fashionable in the twelfth and thirteenth centuries, the *Mirror of Virgins* or *Speculum virginum*, compared the fruits of virginity, widowhood, and marriage. A miniature in this work shows the comparison: married women only reaped 30-fold what they had sown whereas widows reaped what they had sown 60-fold and virgins 100-fold. But rather than forming groups which took no account of class, the virgins tended chiefly to be identified with the nuns, and the widows with the mass of the very poor, in an age where being deprived of a husband and breadwinner pushed most women who could not or would not remarry into extreme hardship.

Classes formed of different age-groups must have been livelier; not those which the clergy created in the theoretic and literary categories of the seven ages of life, but those well integrated into the real-life customs of military and peasant societies characteristic of traditional civilizations. Among these classes formed of different age-groups, one in particular was indeed organized and effective: the class of the young men, which, in primitive societies, is that of the adolescents who underwent initiation rites together. And indeed young men in the middle ages did undergo an apprenticeship, but here too social structures appeared which set this stratification within the framework of another system. The young men of the knightly class and those of the peasant class formed two quite distinct groups. For the former the apprenticeship was a training in arms and feudal warfare which ended with an initiation ceremony, that is, being dubbed knight, by which one entered into the knightly class. Among the latter the young people of the village were entrusted with rites intended to ensure the community's economic prosperity, in the form of the Chthonian cycle of spring festivals, from St George's Day (23 April) to St John's Day (24 June). These rites often consisted of long rides on horseback, or they were performed on horseback (we can see them in pictures of the labours of the months, for the months of April and May) and they culminated in the ordeal of leaping over the bonfires lit on St John the Baptist's Day. Here too, the town was often responsible for breaking these traditions and the personal links on which they were based. Yet relics of these rites survived, such as the initiation of the young schoolboys and students (the *béjaunes*, bejants, fledgelings) which was intended to make them lose their wild peasant nature. (Might there have been a connection between the word Jacques used to mean 'peasant' in France at the end of the middle ages and the name Zak or Jak used for newly matriculated students in Poland?) The young apprentices had their initiation in the course of working as a journeyman and more especially of the Grand Tour which they had to accomplish. Young lawyers received their initiation by joining the body of clerks attached to the courts of justice.

On the other hand it appears that the elderly as a class (the elders of traditional societies) did not play an important part in the world of medieval Christendom. It was a society where people died young, a society of knights and peasants who were only useful when they were in the prime of life. The clergy was led by bishops and popes, who, even if we overlook the scandal of the adolescents elected in the tenth century (John XI was made pope in 931 at 21 and John XII in 954 at 16), were often elected young; Innocent III was about 25 at his election in 1198. Medieval society was ignorant of gerontocracy. At the most it might perhaps have turned sentimental at the thought of grand old men with white beards, like the elders in Revelations and the prophets whom we see at church doors, or like the imitation of Charlemagne – the old emperor with the hoary beard – in literature. It was also how medieval society imagined and portrayed hermits, medieval patriarchs with an impressive lifespan.

XVIII

We must also think about the importance of social links which were forged in many places where people came together, and which were fairly closely linked with the structure of social classes and the different walks of life. The first of these meeting-places was the one which was controlled by the clergy: it was the church which was a centre of parish life. The church in the middle ages was not only a place of communal spiritual life (which was especially important since here ideas and emotions took shape around the themes of the Church's propaganda) but an assembly place. Meetings were held here, conversations, games, and markets were held here, and the church bells rang to summon people to assemble in case of danger, especially fire. For a long time, in spite of efforts by the clergy and church councils to reduce its role to that of God's house, it was a social centre with numerous functions, comparable to a Muslim mosque.

Just as the parish was a social microcosm organized by the Church, so the household inside a castle was a cell of society shaped by feudal lords. Here the young sons of vassals were assembled to serve the lord and undergo their military training, even, where necessary, acting as hostages, together with the lord's own family and household, and with a whole collection of entertainers who were intended to satisfy the need felt by great lords for amusement and pomp. Minstrels, trouvères, and troubadors held an ambiguous position. They were obliged to sing the praises and the chief merits of their employers. They were absolutely dependent on the wages and favours bestowed by these masters. They often wished to become lords in their own turn, and sometimes succeeded in doing so, like the Minnesänger who became knights and received armorial bearings. The famous Heidelberg manuscript whose miniatures show the Minnesänger and their coats of arms testifies to how men could be promoted by the noble art of lyric poetry. Just as often, however, they were handicapped by their position as artists dependent on the whims of a fighting man. They were intellectuals aroused by ideas which sometimes ran counter to those held by the great lords, and they were ready to make themselves critics of their masters. Literary and artistic offshoots from the castle milieu often testify in a somewhat disguised form to opposition to feudal society.

Common people had other meeting places. In the country the meeting place was the mill where the peasants had to bring their grain and stand in queues to wait for the flour. It may easily be imagined that they often discussed agricultural innovations there, and that, after these innovations had become widespread, the peasants hatched their rebellions at the mill. Two pieces of information prove how important mills were as meeting places for peasants. Statutes of religious orders in the twelfth century envisaged that monks would go there to collect alms. Furthermore, prostitutes hung around the approaches to mills in such numbers that St Bernard, who was always ready to set morality above economic interest, incited monks to destroy these haunts of vice.

In towns the burgesses had their covered markets and guild-halls such as that of the Parisian guild of the *Marchands de l'eau*. This group included the most important merchants of the city and their hall was suitably named the *Parloir aux Bourgeois* or Burgesses' Parlour. The great social centre in the town, as in the village, was the tavern. Since this was usually a 'manorial' tavern, one which belonged to the lord and which sold wine or ale which were generally made or taxed by him, the lord encouraged people to go there. The parish priest on the other hand poured forth tirades about these centres of vice where gambling and drunkenness went unchecked and which competed with parish meetings, sermons, and church services (we may recall the tavern which made so much noise that St Louis could not hear the Dominican preacher). Not only did the tavern gather together the men of the village or of the town ward (another form of community within the town, and one which was to assume great importance in the late middle ages, like the street where men of the same geographical origins or of the same profession bunched together), but also the tavern keeper often acted as a banker and lodged strangers, for the tavern was often also an inn, and hence an important nodal point in the network of relations. News telling of events far away, legends and myths all circulated from the tavern. Conversations held there formed men's views of the world. And since drink inflamed the wits, the tavern made a major contribution in giving medieval society its impassioned tone and those moments of drunkenness which made the violence within ferment and explode.

It has sometimes been maintained that religious faith gave some social rebellions a solidarity and an ideology which were lacking in their material claims. Heresy is thought to have been the supreme form of revolutionary movement. It is beyond question that heresies in the middle ages were chiefly adopted, more or less consciously, by social groups which were discontented with their lot. Even in the case of the nobility of southern France which actively participated on the side of the heretics in the first stage of the Albigensian crusade, historians have been able to stress how serious were its complaints against the Church. By increasing the number of degrees of consanguinity within which marriage was impossible, the Church had encouraged the fragmentation of the lay aristocracy's estates which thus fell all the more easily into its hands. Above all, it is certain that many heretical movements, by condemning earthly society and especially the Church, concealed a very powerful revolutionary ferment. This is the case with Catharism, with the more diffuse ideology of Joachimism, and with the various millenarian heresies whose subversive aspects have already been described. Yet the heresies gathered together heterogeneous social groupings, and the class differences within them weakened the effectiveness of the movement. Within Catharism – at least in the form it took in the Languedoc – one can distinguish an aristocratic phase when the nobility led affairs, a burgess phase where merchants, notaries, and town notables controlled the movement after it had been abandoned by the nobility following the crusade and the Treaty of Paris, and finally, at the end of the thirteenth century, survivals which were more openly lower class in appearance. By now village craftsmen and Pyrenean mountain dwellers and shepherds carried on the struggle almost alone. Above all the strictly religious preoccupations of the heresies in the end robbed these movements of their social content. Their revolutionary programme degenerated into millenarian anarchy which deprived men of all hope in earthly solutions. The nihilism which attacked work in particular, for work was more harshly condemned by many heretics than by anyone else – the Cathar *perfecti* were not supposed to work – paralysed the social effectiveness of rebellions conducted under a religious banner. Heresies were the most acute form of ideological alienation.

XIX

However, heresies were dangerous for the Church and for the feudal order. The heretics were therefore persecuted and condemned to social exclusion, which was increasingly clearly defined at the Church's instigation during the twelfth and thirteenth centuries. Under the influence of the canon lawyers, at the same time as the establishment of the Inquisition, heresy began to be defined as a crime of 'lèse-majesté'. Huguccio, the most important decretist at this decisive moment, defined it as an attack on 'the public wellbeing of the Church' and to the good order of Christian society in his *Summa* of about 1188.

Along with heretics, Jews (the Fourth Lateran Council in 1215 forced them to wear a distinctive badge) and lepers (leper hospitals multiplied after the Third Lateran Council in 1179) were put on the index, confined, and tracked down. Yet this was also a time when certain groups of outcasts were finally received into Christian society. The early middle ages had seen an increase in the number of suspect livelihoods. Increasing barbarism had allowed primitive taboos to reappear. There was a blood taboo which operated against butchers, hangmen, surgeons, and even soldiers; there was a taboo about dirt or impurity which affected fullers, dyers, cooks, and cloth-bleachers. In the early thirteenth century Jean de Garlande mentioned the aversion felt by women for the textile workers with their 'blue nails', who, with the butchers, were to play a leading part in the revolts of the fourteenth century. There was a money taboo which, as we have seen, is to be explained by the outlook of a society in which a natural economy predominates. The Germanic invaders added to this the contempt of the warrior for the workers, and Christianity added its distrust of worldly activities. These were at all events forbidden to clerics, and were therefore laden with a weight of disgrace which fell on the laymen who carried them out.

Yet economic and social evolution brought with it a division of labour and the promotion of distinct professions, and Martha was justified with respect to Mary, that is, the active life was justified; it forms an honourable counterpoint to the contemplative life on the doorways of Gothic cathedrals. Under such pressure the number of illicit or despised occupations was reduced almost to zero. The Franciscan Berthold of Regensburg in the thirteenth century put all the 'estates of the world' into the 'family of Christ' except the Jews, strolling jongleurs, and vagabonds who formed the 'family of the devil'.

All the same, this Christendom which had absorbed into itself the new society born of the growth of the eleventh and twelfth centuries, and which had now reached its 'frontier', was only the more ruthless to those who did not wish to adapt to the established order and to those whom the Church did not wish to admit to it. Furthermore its attitude towards the excluded remained ambiguous. The Church seemed to detest and admire them simultaneously; it was afraid of them, but the fear was mixed with a sense of fascination. It kept them at a distance, but fixed the distance so that it would be close enough for the outcasts to be within reach. What it called its charity towards them was like the attitude of a cat playing with a mouse. Thus leper hospitals had to be sited 'a stone's throw from the town' so that 'fraternal charity' could be exercised towards the lepers. Medieval society needed these pariahs, who were exiled because they were dangerous, and who yet had to be visible, because it eased its conscience by the cares which it expended on them. Even better, it could project on to and fix in them, magically, all the evils which it was banishing away from itself. Lepers, for example, lived both inside and outside the world, like the ones to whom Mark delivered up the guilty Iseult in Béroul's frightening narration from which the tender and courteous Thomas recoiled:

Then a hundred lepers, deformed, with shrivelled, whitish flesh, ran up on their crutches with a clattering of rattles, and pushed together in front of the pyre. Under their swollen eyelids their red eyes enjoyed the spectacle. Yvain, the most hideous of the sick people, cried out to the king in a shrill voice: 'Sire, you wish to throw your wife into that brazier; it's good justice but too short. That great fire will burn her quickly and that great wind will scatter her ashes quickly. And when the flame dies down soon after her agony will be over. Do you want me to suggest a much worse punishment to you so that she will live but in great dishonour and always hoping for death? Do you wish it, O king?' The king replied, 'Yes, life for her, but with great dishonour and worse than death. Whoever will teach me such a torture, I shall love him the better for it.' 'Sire, I shall briefly tell you what I think. See, I have here 100 companions. Give us Iseult, and let us have her in common. The sickness arouses our lust. Give her to your lepers. No lady will ever have had a worse end. Look, our rags are stuck to our oozing sores. She who in your presence took pleasure in rich stuffs lined with vair, in jewels and in rooms decorated with marble, she who enjoyed fine wines, honour and joy, when she sees the court of her lepers, when she is forced to enter our slums and sleep with us, then Iseult the Beautiful, the Fair, will recognize her sin and will regret this fine fire of thorns!' The king listened to him, stood up and remained motionless for a long time. Then he ran towards the queen and grasped her by the hand. She cried, 'For pity, Sire, burn me rather than that, burn me.' The king picked her up, Yvain took hold of her, and the 100 sick people crowded around him. On hearing them shout and yelp all hearts melted with pity, but Yvain was joyful. Iseult went away; Yvain took her away. Outside the city, the hideous procession made its way downhill. . . .

Carried away by its new idealization of work, Christian Europe even drove away the idle, both those who wanted to be and those who were forced to be. It threw on to the streets all sorts of infirm, sick, and unemployed people who were swallowed up in the great army of vagabonds. It treated all these wretches, whom it identified with Christ, just as it treated Christ, who was fascinating but terrifying to them. It is symptomatic that the man who really wanted to live like Christ, Francis of Assisi, not only mixed with outcasts but wanted only to be one of them. A poor man, a stranger, a jongleur – God's jongleur as he called himself – it was thus that he presented himself. How could he fail to cause scandal? The pious St Louis, on the other hand, once he had said his prayers, left his poor and his lepers and coldly legislated in his *Etablissements*, 'If some people have nothing and are in a town without earning (that is to say without working) and are fond of frequenting taverns, let the magistrates arrest them and ask them what they live on. And let them throw them out of the town.' It is the same mixture of attraction and fear that men had earlier felt for the smith, an admired yet sinister figure, whom Sigurd killed after he had received his sword from him.

With the Jews, Christians maintained a dialogue throughout the middle ages, which they interrupted with persecutions and massacres. The Jewish usurer, or rather irreplaceable moneylender, was hateful, but necessary and useful. Jews and Christians held debates, especially about the Bible. Public debates and private meetings between priests and rabbis occurred constantly. At the end of the eleventh century, Gilbert Crispin, abbot of Westminster, described in a bestseller his theological disputation with a Jew from Mainz. In the middle of the twelfth century Andrew of St Victor consulted rabbis because he was anxious to revive biblical exegesis. St Louis narrated to Joinville a discussion between clerics and Jews at the abbey of Cluny. Admittedly, he disapproved of such meetings. ' "So I tell you," said the king, "that no one, unless he is an expert theologian, should venture to argue with these people. But a layman, whenever he hears the Christian religion abused, should not attempt to defend its tenets, except with his sword, and that he should thrust into the scoundrel's belly, and as far as it will enter" ' (Joinville, 1971, p. 175).

Some kings, abbots, popes and above all German emperors protected the Jews. Yet from the end of the eleventh century antisemitism unleashed itself in the west. People have blamed this movement on the crusades, and it is not impossible that the crusading spirit gave antisemitism an additional, emotive verve, although, if one believes Ralph Glaber, the earliest pogroms seem to have happened in about 1000. It is true that they became far more numerous at the time of the First Crusade. Thus, reported the *Annales Saxonici*, at Worms and Mainz,

> the enemy of the human race did not hesitate to sow tares among the grain, to raise up false prophets, to mix false brothers and loose women in the army of Christ. By their hypocrisy, their lies and their impious suborning they perturbed the Lord's army . . . . They thought it right to avenge Christ on the pagans and the Jews. That was why they killed 900 Jews in the town of Mainz, without sparing women or children. . . . It was piteous to see the large and numerous heaps of corpses which were taken out of the town of Mainz on waggons.

At about the time of the Second Crusade in 1146 appeared the first accusation of ritual murder (the case of William of Norwich, who died in 1144), that is to say the murder of a Christian child whose blood was supposedly mixed into unleavened bread, and of the profanation of the host, a crime that was all the more serious in the Church's eyes because it was regarded as deicide. Thenceforth there was to be no lack of false accusations to give the Christians scapegoats in times of discontent or calamity. At the time of the Black Death in 1348 the Jews were accused in many places of having poisoned the wells, and they were massacred. Yet the chief reason for the fact that the Jews were kept apart was the evolution of the economy and the creation of the two worlds of town and countryside. The Jews could not be admitted to the social systems – the feudal system and the communes – that resulted. No one could do homage to a Jew or swear an oath to a Jew. The Jews thus found themselves little by little excluded from possessing or even being granted land, and also from the professions, including trade. Nothing remained to them except the borderline or illicit forms of commerce or usury. However it was not until the Council of Trent and the Counter-Reformation that the Church instituted and encouraged the ghetto. It was in the period of the great recession of the seventeenth century and of absolute monarchy that the *'grand renfermement'* or great enclosing set in, whose definitive history, at least in so far as the mad are concerned, has been written by Michel Foucault.

The middle ages were ambivalent in their treatment of the mad, too. Sometimes they were regarded as being almost inspired, and the lord's jester or the king's fool became a counsellor. The village idiot, in this peasant society, became the community's mascot. In the *Jeu de la Feuillée* the dervish, the mad young peasant, points the moral of the story. We can even see a certain attempt to distinguish different categories of madness: the 'furious' and the 'frenetics' who were sick people whom one could try to look after, or rather to shut up in special hospitals, one of the first of which was the Bethlehem or Bedlam hospital in London founded in the late thirteenth century; the 'melancholics' whose illness too was perhaps physical, linked with bad humours, but who had more need of the priest than of the doctor, and finally the great crowd of the possessed whom only exorcism could free of their fearsome legion of demons.

Many of these possessed were easily confused with wizards. Yet our middle ages were not the great period of witchcraft that the period from the fourteenth to the eighteenth century was to be. Between heretics and the possessed, wizards seem to have found it hard to find a place. They were the heirs, steadily declining in number it appears, of the pagan wizards and country fortune-tellers who had been pursued by the penitentials of the early middle ages as part of rural evangelization. Moreover it was from these penitentials that Regino of Prüm in his canon of circa 900 and Burchard of Worms in his *Decretum* of circa 1010 got their inspiration. Here we find ghouls or lamias, who are the vampires, and werewolves. These were called *Werenwulf* in German, said Burchard, which emphasizes the popular character of these beliefs and of the people who adhered to them. It was a wilderness-world in which the Church had only a limited ascendancy; and the Church remained cautious in its incursions. Did it not accept that a werewolf had come to watch over the head of the Anglo-Saxon king, St Edmund, who had been decapitated by the Vikings?

Yet from the thirteenth century the State, thanks to the rebirth of Roman law, started to hunt down witches. It is not surprising to see those kings who were most keen on state control throw themselves into this most energetically. The popes, who considered wizards, like heretics, to be guilty of *lèse-majesté* and disturbers of the Christian order, were among the first to have them persecuted. As early as 1270 a manual for Inquisitors, the *Summa de officio inquisitionis*, devoted a special chapter to the seers and idolators guilty of organizing 'demon worship'. Some tried, however, to make distinctions. The legal expert Oldradus da Ponte di Lodi wondered if telling fortunes and administering love potions were heretical acts. He decided that they were more a case of superstition than of heresy. Whatever the Church's diagnosis, however, from now on wizards and witches who did not recant were to be burnt at the stake.

Frederick II persecuted wizards, following Azzo of Bologna, who in his *Summa super Codicem* of around 1220 announced that *malefici* were liable to capital punishment, and the Doge Jacopo Tiepolo issued a statute against them. Yet the ruler who was most enthusiastic to eliminate them and who was most steadfast in accusing his enemies of witchcraft was Philip the Fair. His reign saw a certain number of cases where modern *raison d'état* appeared in the most monstrous forms: the softening up of the accused, the extraction of confessions by all means, and above all the technique of accusing suspects of all possible crimes, all mixed together: rebellion against the sovereign, impiety, witchcraft, debauchery, and most particularly sodomy.

The history of medieval homosexuality, however, has not yet been written – neither the practice nor the theory. In the eleventh and twelfth centuries poets can be observed singing the praises of young boys in the manner of antiquity, and monastic sources occasionally drop hints that the male clerical milieu cannot have been insensible to Socratic love. Chiefly, however, we see that with the inheritance of Jewish sexual taboos, and in complete opposition to the Graeco-Roman ethic, sodomy was ceaselessly denounced as the most abominable of all crimes. By way of Aristotelian philosophy, somewhat curiously invoked in this regard, unnatural vice was placed at the head of the hierarchy of vices. Yet, just as in the case of bastards who were despised when they were of low birth but treated like legitimate children in royal families, homosexuals who were highly born (such as the English kings William Rufus and Edward II) were not troubled about this in the slightest degree. On the other hand it is likely that the limited extent of homosexuality is to be explained less by the severity of canon law, which considered sodomy to be a capital crime, than by the fact that the structure of the family failed to produce conditions which might favour the formation of Oedipus complexes. Perhaps this is solely a false impression, created because the Church censored allusions to such behaviour. At any rate sodomy was one of the principal crimes attributed to the Templars, who were the most famous victims of the most famous trial mounted by Philip the Fair and his counsellors. A reading of the proceedings in the Templar trial shows that the king of France and his entourage in the early fourteenth century had perfected a system of judicial repression which could stand any comparison with the most notorious show trials of our age. Similar trials were mounted against others, notably the bishop of Troyes, Guichard, who was accused of having tried to kill the queen by voodoo on a wax statue with the help of a witch, and against other personalities at the court of Philip the Fair. Pope Boniface VIII was accused of having discreetly disposed of his unfortunate predecessor Celestine V.

This was also the period when lepers started to be locked up, but the predicament of leprosy, for reasons which were no doubt biological, differed from that of sorcery. Although it did not disappear, leprosy retreated considerably in western Europe from the fourteenth century. Its apogee was the twelfth and thirteenth centuries, when leper hospitals were founded in large numbers. Their memory is preserved in place names; for example, in France, the '*maladreries*', the suburbs named La Madeleine, and the names of hamlets and villages invoking the term *mésel*, a synonym for leper, and so on. In 1227 Louis VIII bequeathed in his will 100 *sous* to each of 2000 leper hospitals in the kingdom of France. The Third Lateran Council in 1179, in authorizing the construction of chapels and cemeteries inside hospitals, helped to make them into closed worlds which the lepers could only leave if they made a space before them by making a noise with a rattle which they had to shake, just as the Jews made good Christians scatter by wearing their badges. Yet the ritual of the 'separation' of lepers, which became generalized in the sixteenth and seventeenth centuries as a ceremony where the bishop, with symbolic gestures, cut the leper off from society and made him dead to the world (sometimes he had to descend into a tomb) was, as yet, rare in the middle ages. This separation did not even exist from the point of view of the law; legally the leper retained the rights of a healthy man, except in Normandy and the Beauvaisis.

However, lepers were affected by a large number of prohibitions, and they too were treated as scapegoats in times of calamity. After the great famine of 1315-18 Jews and lepers were persecuted throughout all France and suspected of having poisoned wells and springs. Philip V, a worthy son of Philip the Fair, had cases brought against lepers throughout the country, and, after they had been tortured into making confessions, many were burnt. High-born lepers, however, were no more inconvenienced than were noble bastards or pederasts. They could continue to perform their offices and live among healthy people, as in the cases of Baldwin IV, king of Jerusalem, Ralph, count of Vermandois, and Richard II, that terrible abbot of St Albans who had his parlour paved with the millstones that he had seized from his peasants.

Other social outcasts were the sick in general, and above all the crippled and the maimed. In a world where sickness and infirmity were considered to be exterior signs of sin, those who were afflicted with them were cursed by God and thus by man too. The Church took some of them in on a temporary basis, for the sick were usually allowed to stay only a very short time in hospital, and it fed some of them sporadically, on feastdays. The others had to fall back on begging and tramping the roads as their only resource. Being poor, sick, and a tramp were almost synonymous in the middle ages, and hospitals were often sited at bridges or mountain passes over which wanderers had to go. Guy de Chauliac, describing the attitude of Christians to the Black Death in 1348, narrates that in certain places people accused the Jews of causing the disaster and massacred them and that in other places it was the poor and the maimed (*pauperes et truncati*) who were blamed and they were driven out.

The Church refused to ordain cripples as priests. Even in 1346, for example, Jean de Hubant, who founded the College of Ave Maria in Paris, laid down that adolescents who had 'a physical deformity' should not have scholarships there.

The outcast *par excellence* in medieval society was, however, the stranger. As a primitive, closed society, medieval Christianity rejected the intruder who did not belong to any known community; he was a bringer of the unknown and of disquiet. St Louis devoted his attention to this theme in the chapter entitled *D'homme étrange* in his *Etablissements* and he defined him as the 'man unknown in the land'. Actors, jongleurs, and foreigners were put in the same category in a law made at Goslar in 1219. A foreigner was a man who was not faithful to someone, who was not someone's man, who had not sworn obedience and who was, in feudal society, 'oathless'.

So medieval Christianity established fixed points for some of its eyesores. Towns and, in the countryside, the areas round castles showed off their places and instruments of punishment: the gallows on the highroad just outside the town or just below the castle, the pillory in the market place, in the courtyard or in front of the church, and, above all, the prison, possession of which was the sign of supreme judicial power, of high justice, of the highest social rank. There is nothing astonishing about the fact that medieval artists were particularly fond of drawing prisons when they were illustrating scenes from the Bible or from the lives of saints and martyrs. They were an ever-present reality, a threat, and a nightmare in the medieval world.

Medieval society released on to the streets all the people it could not tie up or shut away. Sick people and vagabonds, mixed up with pilgrims and merchants, wandered singly, in small groups, even in processions. The strongest and the most fanatical went off to swell the gangs of robbers hidden in the woods. Thus the story of Helmbrecht, the young German peasant of the thirteenth century who wanted to escape from his social condition, is a useful summary of social history. ' I saw, and this is certainly true, a peasant's son who had curly blond hair which fell in full length over his shoulders. He gathered it up into a cap, which was adorned with pictures. I doubt if anyone has seen so many birds on a cap; parrots and doves, they were all embroidered on it.'

Helmbrecht announced to his father, 'I wish to see for myself what being at court is like. Your corn sacks will never ride on my neck again. I shall never load dung on to your cart again either. May God curse me if I ever harness your oxen and sow your oats. In truth, it does not go with my long blond hair, with my curly locks, or with my nicely fitting clothes, or my artistic bonnet and the silk doves which ladies sewed on it. Never again shall I help you farm.' In vain his father reminded him of the moral of medieval society, 'Seldom does he succeed who fights against his rank. Your rank is the plough.'

However, Helmbrecht wanted to live like a lord, and the life of the lord meant the exhilaration of riding fast horses (the cars of the middle ages) and the oppression of the peasants. 'I want to hear the cattle low when I drive them across the fields. If I stay so long, it is because I have no horse. That I do not gallop away with the others and drag the serfs by their hair through the hedges truly pains me.' Months passed and the prodigal son returned to dazzle his parents. But he had become a brigand, not a lord. 'Long ago when I was a boy,' his father told him, 'your grandfather Helmbrecht – my father – sent me to the court with cheese and eggs, as farmers do today. There I saw the knights and I observed all that they did.' And the old farmer recalled what he, the bedazzled young countryman, had seen from a corner of the courtyard of the castle. He saw the inhabitants of the castle at their revels: tournaments, dancing, fiddlers, and jugglers. However, he knew that a lord's life was not for him nor for his son. The young brigand departed once more, enticing away his sister, whom he married off, peasant-fashion, without benefit of clergy, to one of his companions of fortune. From now on he was called Slintezgeu or Devour-Land. His brother-in-law was Lemberslint or Devour-Lambs, and the rest of the gang were called Slickenwider (Swallow-ram), Hellesac (Hell's sack), Rütelschrîn (Force-Chest), Küefraz (Eat-Cow), and Müschenkelch (Cup-Crusher). Here they are torturing and stealing from the peasants: 'I take one man's eye out; I hang another in the smoke; I tie this one on to an antheap; I pull the hair out of another's beard with pincers; I flay one; I beat up that one's limbs; I hang up this one by his heels. Thus what the peasants have is mine.' Helmbrecht's end, as we might suppose, was unfortunate. 'What must happen happens. God does not fail to punish the one who does what he should not do.' God chose two instruments to punish Helmbrecht. The first of these was the lord's bailiff.

They were not allowed any lawyer. . . . The constable had nine of the thieves hanged, and spared the life of only one of them, Helmbrecht (Devour-Land). The hangman put out his eyes and cut off one of his hands and one of his feet . . . . Helmbrecht, the blind robber, was given a stick and a boy guided him to his father's house, but his father refused to take him in; he drove him away, without wishing to relieve his distress . . . . 'Hey! lad! take away the blind man . . . . Vile blackguard, get away out of the door right now . . . .' Yet his mother slipped a loaf into his hand, as if to a child. Thus the blind robber departed. When he was walking through the countryside, accompanied by his guide, no peasant failed to shout at him: 'Ha ha! Helmbrecht the robber! If you had stayed on the farm like me you would not be being led around blind.'

The other instrument of God was the peasants from whom Helmbrecht had stolen, and who would not forgive a man of their own class crimes which they were obliged to allow in their lord:

They made the wretch confess to his sins; then one of them picked up a pinch of earth from the ground and gave it to the poor sinner as a viaticum against hell, and they hanged him from a tree . . . . On all the roads and the paths cart traffic had stopped, but now all can travel in safety, since Helmbrecht was hanged . . . . What if Helmbrecht perhaps still has some young followers? They too will become little Helmbrechts. I can give you no peace from them, until they swing too.

9

Mentalities, Sensibilities, and Attitudes

I

THE MENTALITIES and sensibilities of medieval men were dominated by sense of insecurity which determined the basis of their attitudes. It was a material and moral insecurity, for which, according to the Church, there was only one remedy, as we have seen: to rely on the solidarity of the group, of the communities of which one formed a part, and to avoid breaching this solidarity by ambition or derogation. It was a fundamental insecurity which boiled down to a fear of the life to come. This was assured to no one, and good works and good conduct never guaranteed it absolutely. The risks of damnation, with the help of the devil, were so great and the chances of salvation so slim that fear inevitably prevailed over hope. The Franciscan preacher Berthold of Regensburg in the thirteenth century gave the chances of damnation as 100,000 to 1, and the usual image for calculating the proportion of the chosen and the damned was that of the little group of Noah and his companions as opposed to the huge number of mankind wiped out by the Flood. Indeed, for the men of the middle ages natural calamities were the image and the measure of spiritual realities, and the historian can justifiably say that the yield of the moral life seemed as small to medieval mankind as the yield from agriculture. So mentalities, sensibilities, and attitudes were prescribed predominantly by the need for reassurance.

II

Chiefly they needed to rely on the past, on their predecessors. In the same way that the Old Testament prefigured and laid the foundations for the New, the ancients provided a justification for the moderns. Nothing that could be proposed was certain, except what had been vouchsafed for in the past. Some of the sureties were especially favoured and referred to as 'authorities'. Obviously it was in theology, the highest branch of learning, that the use of authorities found its greatest glory, and, since it was the basis of spiritual and intellectual life, it was subjected to strict regulation. The supreme authority was Scripture, and, with it, the Fathers of the Church. However, this general authority tended to take the form of quotations. In practice these became 'authentic' opinions and, in the end, the 'authorities' themselves. Since these authorities were often difficult and obscure, they were explained by glosses which themselves had to come from an 'authentic author'. Very often the glosses replaced the original text. Of all the florilegia which conveyed the results of intellectual activity in the middle ages, the anthologies of glosses were consulted and ransacked the most. Learning was a mosaic of quotations or 'flowers' which, in the twelfth century, were called 'sentences' (*sententiae* or opinions). The collections or *summae* of sentences were collections of authorities. Robert of Melun was already protesting in the middle of the twelfth century against according credit to glosses in these sentences, but in vain. Père Chenu acknowledged that the *Sentences* of the inferior thinker Peter Lombard, which was to be the theology textbook in universities in the thirteenth century, was a collection of glosses 'whose source can only be discovered with difficulty', and furthermore that, even in the *Summa Theologica* of Thomas Aquinas 'one can see a largish number of texts acting as authorities which can only be identified through the distortions of the *glossae*.'

Of course the men who used authorities stretched their meanings to the point where they barely impeded personal opinions. Alain of Lille, in a saying which was to become proverbial, stated 'the authority has a wax nose which can be pushed in all directions'. Of course the medieval intellectuals were also to welcome unexpected authors, such as pagan and Arab philosophers, as authorities. Again, it was Alain of Lille who asserted that one had to fall back on the authorities of the 'gentile' philosophers to shame Christian ones. In the twelfth century, Arab writers were so fashionable that Adelard of Bath slyly remarked that he had attributed many of his own thoughts to the Arabs so that they would be more willingly accepted by his readers. This, it should be stressed, ought to make us prudent when we consider the influence of the Arabs on medieval Christian thought, which has been exaggerated by some. References to Arab thinkers were often only a sacrifice to fashion, original thought being masked for the sake of publicity. References to the past, however, were almost obligatory in the middle ages. Innovation was a sin. The Church made a point of condemning *novitates* or novelties. This happened with both technical and intellectual progress. Inventions were immoral. The most serious thing was that the respectable 'argument from tradition', which can be understood to be valuable when it was a matter 'of an agreement of witnesses unanimously coming to give their evidence over the centuries' was often made the object of a disputable practice. 'Here, most of the time,' wrote Père Chenu, 'one author is cited, one text is used, with no regard to time and place, without worrying about the body of evidence to be established.'

The weight of ancient authorities did not oppress the intellectual domain alone; it made itself felt in all sectors of life. Indeed it is the mark of a traditional, peasant society where truth is the secret handed down from generation to generation, bequeathed by a 'sage' to the one whom he has judged worthy of this trust, and spread by hearsay much more than by writing. A monk made a note on a manuscript of Adhemar of Chabannes of the continuity which formed the basis of the value of a learning transmitted by tradition: 'Theodore the monk and Abbot Hadrian taught Aldhelm the art of grammar. Aldhelm instructed Bede, Bede (through the intermediary of Egbert) instructed Alcuin, the latter instructed Rabanus and Smaragdus, the latter Theodulf; after him came Heiric, Hucbald, and Remigius, the latter with numerous pupils.'

Moral life was also ruled by authorities. Medieval ethics were taught and preached with stereotyped anecdotes which illustrated a lesson and which were ceaselessly repeated by moralists and preachers. These collections of *exempla* are made up of a monotonous sequence of medieval moral tales. At a first reading, they can be amusing; but when they turn up hundreds of times elsewhere, they show how repetition was used as a method. Repetition was the expression, in the intellectual and spiritual life, of the desire to abolish time and change and of the force of inertia which seems to have absorbed a large part of the mental energy of medieval men. Here is one *exemplum* out of many, whose formation has been revealed by Astrik Gabriel: the anecdote of the fickle student, of the 'son of inconstancy' who commits the great sin of wanting to change his status. The *exemplum* appears in the *De Disciplina Scolarium*, a treatise written between 1230 and 1240 by an English cleric, who, of course, begins by attributing it to one of the most incontestable authorities, Boethius himself. Then, with or without embellishments, with different variants, the story of this student, who makes his way through the clerical life, trade, farming, knighthood, law, marriage, and astronomy (a pretext for satirizing the 'worldly estates') recurs everywhere. Thus, intriguingly, it crops up in certain fourteenth-century French translations of Boethius' *Consolation of Philosophy* into which it was inserted by the translators, who believed that Boethius was the author of the *exemplum*. It also occurs in the numerous *fabliaux* dedicated to the estates of the world and, again, in various commentaries, some on Boethius, and some on the *De disciplina scolarium*. The palm was finally won back by the English Dominican Nicholas Trivet (who died around 1328), who quoted the story in the two commentaries which he wrote, one on each of these two works. In addition he betrays what is perhaps the foundation of the story by quoting the popular proverb 'a rolling stone gathers no moss', *non fit hirsutus lapis per loca volutus*. With proverbs we reach the basic level of folk-culture. We are still waiting for the fundamental study of proverbs which would give us access to the very storehouse of the medieval mind. In this traditional peasant society, the proverb played an important role. But how far was it the learned elaboration of earthy wisdom, or the popular echo of propaganda put out by the ruling classes?

As one would expect, the past exerted its full weight at the level of the basic framework of medieval society, the feudal class-structure. The foundation of feudal law and practice was formed by custom. In legal terms, to quote the classic definition of François Olivier-Martin, it is 'a juridical usage born of the repetition of public, peaceful acts, which have encountered no resistance over a long period of time'. One word in this – 'peaceful' – might make us hesitate, for custom was only law established by a force which was able to silence dissent over a long period. We may calculate how revolutionary was the impact of Pope Gregory VII's famous saying, 'The Lord did not say "My name is Custom".' However, custom ruled society long after Gregory's time. It was anchored in time before mind. It was what went back furthest in the collective memory. Legal proof in the feudal epoch was existence 'from all eternity'. In a conflict between the cathedral chapter of Notre Dame, Paris, and its serfs at Orly in 1252, we see, for example, how the parties proceeded to prove their rights. When the peasants claimed that they did not have to pay the *taille* to the chapter, the canons responded by instituting an inquest of knowledgeable people, who were questioned *de fama*, that is about what tradition said. Thus one of the oldest men in the area, Simon, bailiff (*maire*) of Corbreuse, who was more than 70 years old, 'old and sick', was questioned. He replied that according to the *fama*, the chapter could impose the *taille* on its men and that it had done so 'since time immemorial' *a tempore a quo non exstat memoria*. Another witness, the archdeacon John, a former canon, stated that he had seen in the chapter 'ancient rolls', in which it was written that the canons had the right to tallage the men of Orly. He also stated that he had heard even older men say that the usage existed 'since times far past' *a longe retroactis temporibus*, and that the chapter put its faith in these rolls 'as it should be given to the antiquity of the writing', *sicut adhibetur ancientie scripture*. Even nobility was chiefly a guarantee of an honourable family standing from a long way back. This, even more than the social recruitment of the higher clergy, explains to a great extent the number of noblemen among the saints and the fact that nobility was attributed to many saints who in reality did not possess it. Similarly the tree of Jesse proved the antiquity of the royal line in Mary's family and thus in Christ's earthly family. It was a survival of a medieval spirit which made a naïve archbishop of Paris under the restoration of the monarchy in the early nineteenth century say, 'Not only was Our Lord the son of God but equally he belonged to an excellent family.'

III

There was proof by miracle as well as proof by authority (that is to say by proven antiquity). What made medieval minds agree to believe in something was not what could be observed and proved by a natural law or by a regularly repeated mechanism; on the contrary, it was the extraordinary, the supernatural, or at any rate the abnormal. Science itself was more willing to take as its subject the exceptional, the *mirabilia*, and prodigies. Earthquakes, comets, and eclipses were the subjects worthy of admiration and study. Medieval art and science tackled man by way of a detour among strange monsters.

Of course, proof by miracle chiefly defined beings who were themselves extraordinary, the saints. Popular belief here tallied with Church doctrine. When, from the end of the twelfth century, the papacy began to reserve to itself the canonization of saints (hitherto they had most often been proclaimed by the *vox populi*), it made miracles one of the obligatory conditions which the candidate had to fulfil at his canonization. At the start of the fourteenth century, when canonization processes were regulated, the dossiers on each case had obligatorily to include special chapters narrating the candidate's miracles, the *capitula miraculorum*. However, miracles were not limited to the ones which God worked through the intermediary of the saints. They could occur in anyone's life, or rather at the critical moments in the lives of all those who, for one reason or another, had deserved to benefit from these supernatural interventions. Of course, the favoured beneficiaries of these manifestations were the heroes. In the *geste* of *Girard de Vienne* it was an angel who brought the duel between Roland and Oliver to an end. In the *Chanson de Roland* God halted the sun; in the *Pèlerinage de Charlemagne* he gave the valiant knights the superhuman power to allow them to carry out the exploits which they had rashly boasted they could perform in the 'gabs'. However, even the simplest people could be favoured with a miracle, and, what was more, the greatest sinners, if they had been devout. Faithfulness (modelled on that of the vassal) towards God, the Virgin or a saint, could save men more effectively than an exemplary life. A famous work of the early thirteenth century, Walter de Coincy's *Miracles of the Virgin*, shows us the compassion of Mary towards her faithful. For three days she supported in her hands a thief who had been hanged for his misdeeds, because he had never forgotten to pray to her before going off to steal. She resuscitated a monk who was drowned when coming back from visiting his mistress, but who was saying his matins at the moment when he fell into the water. She secretly delivered a pregnant abbess who had pledged her particular devotion.

The outstanding proof of truth by miracle was conferred by the judgement of God in the ordeal. 'God stands by the side of right' was the high-sounding saying which justified one of the most barbarous customs of the middle ages. Admittedly, so that chances should not be too unequal on the terrestrial plane, the weak, especially women, were authorized to have themselves replaced by a champion - there were professional ones, condemned as the worst mercenaries by the moralists - who would undergo the trial in their place. Here again a completely formal notion of righteousness justified the ordeal. Thus in the *geste* of *Ami* and *Amile,* the two friends who resembled each other like twins, Ami took the place of the guilty Amile in a judicial combat, for he himself was innocent of the fault of which his companion was accused, and he triumphed over his adversary. In the Holy Land, according to the *Chanson de Jérusalem,* a clerk called Peter claimed that St Andrew had revealed to him the burying place of the Holy Lance, which had pierced Christ's side on the Cross. Excavations were started and a lance was found. To know if the lance was authentic, that is to say if the clerk had spoken the truth, he was submitted to the ordeal by fire. The clerk died of his wounds after five days. However, it was soon considered that he had undergone the ordeal victoriously and that the lance was authentic. His legs had been burnt because he had doubted the truth of his vision to begin with. And the ordeal of Iseult is well known. 'She approached the fire, pale and unsteady. All were silent: the iron was red. Then she plunged her naked arms into the embers, grasped the iron bar, walked nine paces carrying it, and then, having thrown it away, stretched out her arms in a cross with the palms open, and each saw that her flesh was sounder than a plum from a plum-tree. Then from all chests arose a great cry of praise towards God.'

Merely examining the etymology of the word 'symbol' helps us to understand the place held by symbolic thought not only in the theology, literature, and art of medieval western Europe, but in its intellectual equipment. *Symbolon,* to the Greeks, meant a sign of recognition, represented by the two halves of an object shared between two persons. The symbol was the sign of a contract. It was a reference to a lost unity; it brought to mind or summoned up a superior, hidden reality. Now, in medieval thinking, 'each material object was considered to be the representation of something which corresponded to it on a higher level, and thus it became its symbol'. Symbolism was universal, and thought was a perpetual discovery of hidden meanings, a constant 'hierophany'. For the hidden world was a sacred world, and symbolic thinking was only the elaborated, decanted form, at a learned level, of the magic thinking in which the popular mentality was bathed. Amulets, philtres, and magical formulae, widespread in both trade and use, were only the coarsest of these beliefs and these practices. Relics, sacraments, and prayers were the authorized equivalents of these as far as the masses were concerned. It was always a question of finding the keys which would force open the hidden world, the true and eternal world, the one in which men could be saved. Acts of devotion were symbolic acts by which men tried to make God recognize them and to oblige Him to keep the contract made with Him. The wording of charters of donation, in which the grantors mentioned their desire to save their souls by this means, made this magic trafficking plain. It turned God into the grantor's debtor and constrained Him to save the grantor. Similarly thought consisted in finding the keys which opened the doors of the world of ideas.

Thus medieval symbolism began at the level of words. To name something was already to have explained it. Or so Isidore of Seville had said, and, after him, etymology flourished in the middle ages as a fundamental science. To name things and realities was to know them and to take possession of them. In medicine, to diagnose was automatically to cure by pronouncing the name of the illness. When the bishop or the inquisitor could declare a suspect 'heretical', the main point had been achieved, and the enemy had been called to account and unmasked. The *res* and the *verba* did not oppose each other; each symbolized the other. Although language veiled reality for the intellectuals of the middle ages, it was also the key, the instrument matching this reality. 'Language,' said Alain of Lille 'is the faithful hand of the spirit.' For Dante, the word was an entire sign which uncovered reason and meaning – *rationale signum et sensuale*. One can therefore understand the importance of the argument concerning the exact nature of the relations between the *verba* and the *res*. From the eleventh century to the end of the middle ages almost all thinkers were ranged on one side or the other, so much so that traditional historians of philosophy have sometimes simplified the intellectual history of the middle ages into a confrontation of realists and nominalists, the Guelfs and Ghibellines of medieval thought. This was the conflict over the 'universals'.

The foundation of medieval pedagogy was the study of words and of language, the *trivium* of grammar, rhetoric, and dialectic, the first half of the course in the seven liberal arts. The basis of all education until at least the end of the twelfth century was grammar. Through it one arrived at all other branches of learning, especially at ethics, which superimposed itself on the liberal arts and to some extent topped them off. Grammar was a discipline of many values, 'polyvalent', as Canon Delhaye defined it, not only because it allowed men to deal with all subjects through commentaries on authors, but because it allowed men, thanks to the words, to arrive at the hidden meanings of which they were the keys. In his *Source of Philosophy, Fons Philosophiae*, Godfrey of St Victor in the twelfth century gave homage to grammar, which taught him letters, syllables, and 'literal' and 'tropic' discourse, tropic discourse being that which reveals the figurative, allegorical meaning. At Chartres the famous master Bernard of Chartres also based all his teaching on grammar. In any case they were only following or taking up a tradition going back to antiquity, which had been bequeathed to the middle ages by Augustine and Martianus Capella. In expounding the Scriptures according to the four types of meaning, some medieval exegetes, following St Paul, thought that the letter killed while the spirit gave life, but most saw in the *littera* an introduction to the *sensus*.

Nature was the great reservoir of symbols. The constituents of the different natural orders were the trees in this forest of symbols. Minerals, plants, and animals were all symbolic. Tradition liked to give some of them special treatment: among the minerals, the precious stones, which struck men's feelings for colour and which evoked the myths of riches; among the vegetables, the plants and flowers mentioned in the Bible; among the animals, the exotic, legendary, and monstrous beasts which flattered the medieval tastes for the extravagant. Lapidaries, lists of flowers, and bestiaries, in which these symbols were catalogued and explained, occupied an important place in the ideal library of the middle ages.

Stones and flowers not only had symbolic meanings but also beneficent or maleficent powers. Yellow or green stones, by a homeopathy of colours, cured jaundice and liver illnesses, while red stones cured haemorrhages and blood-flows. The red sard signified Christ spilling his blood on the cross for mankind, and the transparent beryl, pierced by the sun, represented the Christian enlightened by Christ. *Floraria* were close to being herbals. They introduced into medieval thought collections of simples, old wives' remedies, and the secrets of monastic herborists. The bunch of grapes was Christ who gave his blood for mankind in an image symbolized by the mystic wine-press. The Virgin was represented by the olive-tree, the lily, the lily-of-the-valley, the violet, and the rose. St Bernard stressed that the Virgin was symbolized as much by the white rose which signified her virginity as by the red rose which portrayed her charity. The centaury, whose stalk is four-sided, was a cure for the quartan ague, while the apple was the symbol of evil and the mandragora was aphrodisiac and demoniac. When someone gave it a tug it cried out, and whoever heard it died or went mad. In these two cases etymology gave enlightenment to medieval men: the apple was *malum* in Latin, which also meant evil, and the mandragora was a 'man-dragon' (mandrake in English).

The animal kingdom was chiefly composed of evil things. The ostrich which laid its eggs in the sand and forgot to sit on them was an illustration of the sinner who forgets his duties towards God. The goat was a symbol of lechery. The scorpion which stings with its tail was the incarnation of falsehood; in particular it was the incarnation of the Jewish people. The symbolism of the dog was pulled in two directions, between antique tradition which made it a representation of uncleanness, and the tendency of feudal society to rehabilitate it as a noble animal, the indispensable companion of the lord out hunting, and a symbol of fidelity, the highest of the feudal virtues. Mythical animals were all satanic, true images of the devil, such as the asp, the basilisk, the dragon, and the gryphon. The lion and the unicorn were ambiguous. They were symbols of strength and purity, but they could also be symbols of violence and hypocrisy. However, the unicorn became fashionable and was idealized at the end of the middle ages, immortalized in the sequence of tapestries of the *Dame à la Licorne*.

Medieval symbolism found a particularly large field of application in the very rich Christian liturgy, chiefly in fact in interpreting religious architecture. Honorius of Autun explained the meaning of the two principal types of church. Both cases, the round plan and the cross-shaped plan, were aiming at an image of perfection. It is easy to understand that the round church was the image of the perfection of the circle, but it must be realized that the cross-shaped plan did not only represent Christ's crucifixion, but rather was the *ad quadratum* form based on the square, designating the four points of the compass and epitomizing the universe. In both cases the church was a microcosm.

Amongst the most basic forms of medieval symbolism, the symbolism of numbers played an important role. It was a framework for thinking and was one of the guiding principles of architecture. Beauty came from proportion and harmony, whence the pre-eminence of music as a numerical science. 'To know music,' said Thomas of York, 'is to know the order of all things.' According to William of Passavant, bishop of Le Mans from 1145 to 1187, the architect was a 'composer'. Solomon had said to the Lord, *Omnia in mensura et numero et pondere disposuisti* (Wisdom, 11.21), 'You have disposed all things according to measure, number and weight'. Number was the measure of things. Like words, numbers adhered to realities. 'To create numbers,' said Thierry of Chartres, 'is to create things'. Art, which was an imitation of nature and of creation, had to take number as a guide. At Cluny, according to Kenneth John Conant, the monk Gunzo, who inspired the great church of Abbot Hugh which was begun in 1088 (Cluny III), was a celebrated musician, *psalmista praecipuus*. A miniature shows him seeing in a dream Saints Paul, Peter, and Stephen tracing out the plan of the future church for him with ropes. According to Conant, the symbolic number which is supposed to have been the sum of all the numerical symbolisms used in the construction of the church at Cluny was 153, the number of fish in the miraculous draught.

Guy Beaujouan has drawn our attention to unpublished treatises of the twelfth century which show that number symbolism enjoyed an even greater vogue in the Romanesque period than we think. Victorines and Cistercians distinguished themselves in this game, which they took seriously. In a treatise printed in the *Patrologia Latina*, Hugh of St Victor, expounding the symbolic numerical data according to the Scriptures, explained the significance of the disparities between numbers. Beginning with the seven days of Genesis (or rather of the six days when the Creator did his work, or the Hexaemeron), $7 > 6$ is rest after labour, $8 > 7$ is eternity after earthly life (the 8 recurs in the octagon of the chapel at Aachen, in San Vitale at Ravenna, in the Holy Sepulchre, and in the Heavenly Jerusalem, or, if we begin from 10 which is the image of perfection, $9 < 10$ is the lack of perfection and $11 > 10$ is excess. The Cistercian Odo of Morimond, who died in 1161, revived St Jerome's numerical speculation in his *Analytica Numerorum*. St Jerome, in his short work against Jovinian, a small treatise in favour of virginity, which was to enjoy a great vogue in the twelfth century, the 'antimatrimonial century' (perhaps as a remedy for the growth in population), explained the symbolism of the numbers 30, 60, and 100 applied to the three states of marriage, widowhood, and virginity.

To represent 30, the tips of the thumb and the index finger caress each other softly, which depicts marriage. To show 60, the thumb is bent over, and so to speak submissive to the index, which surrounds it, and this is the image of the widow whose continence suppresses the memory of past pleasures, or who is bent under her veil. Finally, to make 100, the fingers represent a virginal crown. Moving on from this, Odo of Morimond expounded the symbolism of the fingers. The little (or auricular) finger, which cleans the ears so that they can hear, symbolizes faith and good will, the ring-finger symbolizes penitence, the middle finger charity, the index finger demonstrative reason, and the thumb divinity. Obviously all this can only be understood if one reflects that people in the middle ages calculated with their fingers and that counting on the fingers was at the basis of these symbolic interpretations, just as proportions were determined by natural measurements, such as the length of the footstep or the forearm, the span of the fingers, the area which could be ploughed in a day, and so on. The loftiest speculations were linked to the humblest gestures. We realize from these examples that it is difficult to distinguish the role of the abstract and that of the concrete in the mental furniture of medieval men. Claude Lévi-Strauss rightly took exception to the 'so-called incapacity of primitive people to think in abstract terms'. On the contrary, the medieval mind was inclined to abstraction, or more precisely towards a vision of the world which relied on abstract connections. Thus the complexion was considered particularly beautiful because it was a mixture of white and red, excellent colours which symbolized purity and charity, as we have seen. Yet, conversely, one feels the concrete images to be on a level behind the abstract notions. Following Isidore of Seville, the medieval clerics thought that *pulcher* came from *pellis rubens*. A handsome man has a red skin because one feels the palpitation of the blood flowing underneath, a principle of nobility as of impurity, but in any case a basic principle. But how does one disentangle the concrete from the abstract in this taste for blood? It recurs in another word which means beautiful: *venustus*, which again was supposed to be derived from *venae* or veins.

In fact, this overlapping of the concrete and the abstract was the very foundation of the framework of medieval attitudes and feelings. A single passion, a single need made men sway between, on the one hand, desiring to find behind the concrete, which was perceptible, the abstract, which was more real and, on the other hand, trying to make this hidden reality appear in a form which could be perceived by the senses. Nor is it any more certain that the propensity for the abstract was more the prerogative of the learned, intellectual classes of the clergy, with the propensity towards the concrete occurring more among the uneducated groups, a sense for the abstract characterizing the *litterati* on one side and a sense for the concrete characterizing the *illitterati* on the other. One might be tempted to think that the medieval masses were rather inclined primarily to perceive an evil principle in the symbols of evil, and that the clergy then made them see this in the concrete forms of the devil and his incarnations. We are aware of the popular success of a heresy such as Catharism, a variety of Manichaeanism which replaced God and Satan with a good principle and an evil principle. In the same way the art of the early middle ages, through the aesthetic traditions which inspired it, whether they were indigenous or from the Steppes, showed that 'non-figurative' tendencies were more 'primitive' than the others.

IV

Given the taste for colour and the glamour of physical appearance, which were fundamental tendencies of medieval feeling, one may wonder what fascinated men in the middle ages more: perceptible attractions or abstract ideas, such as light energy or force, which were concealed behind the appearances. The medieval taste for bright colours is well known. It was a 'barbarous' taste, which favoured big jewels inserted into the boards of book-bindings, glowing gold objects, brightly painted sculpture, paintings covering the walls of churches and of the houses of the powerful, and the coloured magic of stained glass. The almost colourless middle ages which we admire today are the work of the destruction wrought by time and of the anachronistic taste of our contemporaries. However, behind this coloured phantasmagoria lay the fear of darkness and the quest for light which was salvation.

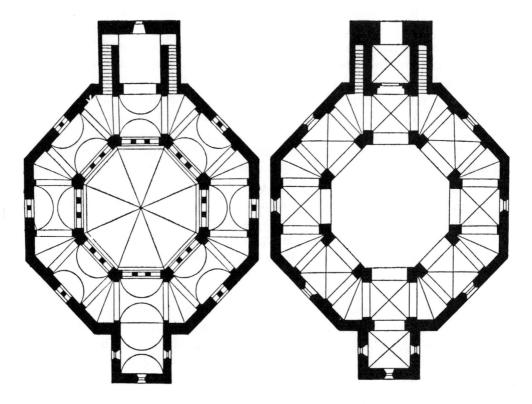

24 Ottmarsheim
(after Kautzsch)

Figures 24, 25 Church plans: the central plan and the basilican plan

These are the two most common types of church plan in the Christian west. The former derives from the Holy Sepulchre in Jerusalem and the latter from the Roman basilica. Each is based on oriental models and symbolic interpretations. The octagonal church at Ottmarsheim (24) in Alsace, which was consecrated by Pope Leo IX in 1049 in the course of a tour of consecrations, is modelled on the famous imperial chapel of Charlemagne in Aachen. The fashion set by this church, especially in German-speaking areas, increased the number of churches with a round plan, which, in the early middle ages, had chiefly been reliquary churches or *martyria*. Sant' Ambrogio, Milan (25), was built in about 1100 on the site of a ninth-century Carolingian basilica, which itself had replaced a fourth-century sanctuary. The new church kept the unusually large atrium and the tri-apsidal choir, which extended into a basilica with a nave and three aisles. The great innovation was the rib vaulting, which might suggest Gothic if the forms were not purely Romanesque in character, 'that is to say intended to emphasize the masses and strength of the walls, not to eliminate them' (A. Chastel).

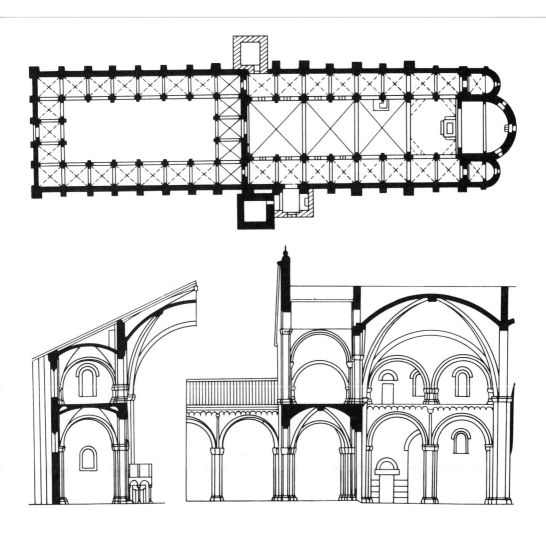

25 Sant'Ambrogio, Milan
(after Dehio and Bezold)

Technical and ethical advances seem to have directed themselves towards an ever-increasing domestication of light. The walls of Gothic churches were scooped out, letting floods of light enter, coloured by the stained glass windows. Window glass made a timid appearance in houses from the thirteenth century. Under Grosseteste, Witelo, and others, thirteenth-century science scrutinized light, put optics in the forefront of its preoccupations, and, on the technical level, gave tired or sick eyes the ability to focus with the invention of spectacles at the extreme end of the century. Scientists were particularly interested in the rainbow. It was coloured light, natural analysis, a whim of nature. It simultaneously satisfied traditional propensities and the new directions of the medieval scientific spirit. Behind all this, there was what has been called the 'medieval metaphysics of light', or as we might more generally and more modestly put it, the search for the security of light. Beauty was light. Light reassured. It was a sign of nobility. In this respect, the medieval saint is a good example. As André Vauchez wrote, 'the saint is a being of light': for example St Clare's ' . . . angelic face was brighter and more beautiful after prayer, it shone so much with joy. Truly the gracious and generous Lord filled his poor little bride so much with his rays that she spread divine light all around her.' On the death of St Edmund of Canterbury, 'a dew of light suddenly arose from him and his face was flushed a fine pink.' The *Elucidarium* stated that at the Last Judgement the saints would be resurrected with bodies of different colours according to whether they had been martyrs, confessors, or virgins. Think about the odour of sanctity, which of course was symbolic, but which was real for people in the middle ages. At Bologna, on the night of the 23-24 May 1233, on the occasion of the canonization of St Dominic, his coffin was opened to translate the body in the presence of a group of preaching friars and of a delegation of noblemen and burgesses. 'Anxious, pale, the brothers prayed, full of disquiet.' When the coffin had been unnailed all the onlookers were immersed in a wonderful odour.

Yet light was the object of the most ardent aspirations, charged with the highest symbols. Here are Cligès and Fénice as depicted by Chrétien of Troyes: 'The day outside was somewhat dark, but he and the maiden were both so fair that a ray shone forth from their beauty which illumined the palace, just as the morning sun shines clear and red' (Chrétien of Troyes, 1914, pp. 126-7). 'Among all bodies, physical light is whatever is the best, the most delectable, the most beautiful. . . . That which constitutes the perfection and beauty of corporeal things is light,' said Robert Grosseteste, and quoting Augustine he recalled that 'the name of beauty', once it is understood, makes us perceive 'the first light' directly. This first light is none other than God, the luminous and incandescent centre. Dante's *Paradiso* is a march towards the light.

William of Auvergne joined together number and colour to define what is beautiful. 'Visible beauty is defined either by the appearance and the position of the parts within the whole, or else by the colour, or else by these two characteristics put together, whether one juxtaposes them or one considers the harmonic relation which relates the one to the other.' Grosseteste, furthermore, made colour and proportion derive simultaneously from the fundamental light energy.

The beautiful was also the valuable. Of course one of the reasons why the powerful had precious objects collected was the economic function of treasure-hoards – as a reserve in case of need. However, aesthetic taste also had its part in this admiration for works of art and perhaps particularly for the raw materials. Medieval men admired the quality of the raw material more than the work of the artist. It is from this point of view that one should study church treasures or the presents which rulers and magnates offered to each other, or descriptions of great buildings and towns. The *Liber Pontificalis*, which describes the artistic undertakings of the popes in the early middle ages, is full of gold and glitter. An anonymous work of the mid-twelfth century on the *Mirabilia Romae*, the Wonders of Rome, speaks chiefly of gold, silver, bronze, ivory, and precious stones. Describing, or rather enumerating, the riches of Constantinople, the great attraction for the western Christians of the middle ages, is a commonplace in historical writings and romances. In the *Pèlerinage de Charlemagne*, what chiefly struck the westerners were the bell-towers, the eagles, the 'shining' bridges. Inside the palace in Constantinople, it was the tables and chairs of fine gold, the walls covered with rich paintings, the great hall whose vaulting was supported by a pillar of silver covered with inlaid enamel, surrounded by a hundred columns of marble inlaid with gold.

The beautiful was the colourful and brilliant, which was most often what was valuable. However, the beautiful was at the same time the good. The high value set on physical beauty was such that beauty was an obligatory attribute of sanctity. The Good God was first of all the Beautiful God, and the Gothic sculptors fulfilled the ideal of men of the middle ages. Medieval saints did not only possess the seven gifts of the soul (friendliness, wisdom, concord, honour, power, security, and joy) but also the seven gifts of the body – beauty, agility, force, liberty, health, pleasure, and longevity. This was true even of 'intellectual' saints. Thomas Aquinas is a case in point. A Dominican legendary tells us: 'When St Thomas used to walk in the countryside, the people who were busy in the fields there used to abandon their labours and hurry to meet him, admiring the imposing stature of his body and the beauty of his human features: they were drawn towards him much more by his beauty than by his sanctity.' In southern Italy he was called the *Bos Siciliae* or the ox of Sicily. So this intellectual was viewed by the people of his time principally as a hulk.

This cult of physical force was obviously to be found mainly among the members of the military aristocracy, the knights, for whom warfare was a passion. The bellicose ideal of medieval men of war was hymned by the troubadour Bertran de Born. Before he became a Cistercian monk, he had been the companion of Richard I of England, that paragon of a knight (Joinville, a century later, recorded admiringly: 'When any horse belonging to a Saracen shied at a bush its master would say to it: "D'you think that's King Richard of England?" And when the children of the Saracen women started to cry, their mothers would say to them: "Stop it, do! Or I'll go and fetch King Richard, and he'll kill you!"' (Joinville, 1971, p. 305).

Fair to me is the press of bucklers
with colours of vermilion and azure,
of standards and banners,
of different colours among each other
to put up tents, shelters, and rich pavilions,
to break lances, to pierce shields
and to split burnished helms; to give and receive blows.
And I have great pleasure
when I see ranged in the country
armed knights and horses
I am pleased when the scouts
make people and livestock flee;
I am pleased to see warriors
charge against them by force all together.
Above all it makes my heart happy
to see castles besieged,
baileys broken and thrown down,
to see the army on the edge
all around the walled ditches
and the lists with their stout, serried stakes.
I like it also when the lord
throws himself the first into the attack,
on his armed horse, without quivering
to embolden his men
with his valiant courage . . .
I tell you, nothing has savour for me,
neither eating, drinking or sleeping, as much as hearing someone cry: 'Forward!'
on both sides, and to hear horses
neigh, riderless, in the forest,
and to cry 'Help, Help!'
and to see fall into the ditches
great and small in the plain,

~~and to see the dead with, in their sides,~~
stumps of lances and their pennons.

> For a great war turns a mean lord into a generous one:
> thus I love to see the pomp of kings,
> let them need stakes, ropes and pommels
> and let the tents be put up to camp outside.
> Ah, let us meet by hundreds and by thousands,
> Let someone sing of our deeds after us!
> Trumpets, drums, banners and pennons
> flags and black and white horses
> we shall soon see; let it make for good living!
> Usurers will have their goods stolen from them,
> and on the roads convoys will no longer
> go peacefully by day, nor burgesses without a *fracas*,
> nor merchants who will come from France,
> but he will be rich who will pillage with a good will!

Joinville says at the outset of his hagiographical biography of St Louis that he will deal with the king's life in two parts. 'The first part tells how, on all occasions, King Louis governed his life according to the will of God and the laws of Holy Church, as also for the good of his realm. The second part speaks of his outstanding valour and his great feats of arms' (Joinville, 1971, p. 163). The military ideal was hand-to-hand fighting: 'Know that this was a fine deed of arms, for there was no shooting with the bow or the cross-bow, but men fought hand-to-hand with blows of maces and swords.' This is what men boasted of, to please women: 'The good count of Soissons, hard put to it as we were at that moment, still made a joke of it and said to me gaily: "Seneschal, let these dogs howl as they will. By God's bonnet" – that was his favourite oath – "we shall talk of this day yet, you and I, sitting at home with our ladies!"' (Joinville, 1971, p. 225).

The 'idols' of people of all conditions were the doers of exploits or *'prouesses'*, those great deeds of sportsmanship. Here is one of Tristan's exploits:

> Near the road by which they were travelling
> stood a chapel on a hill,
> on the corner of a crag,
> looking down on the sea, facing the blast.
> The part which is called the chancel
> was built on a little pinnacle.
> Beyond it, nothing at all: the cliff.
> This hill was all made of stone.
> If a squirrel had leapt from there,

He would have perished, without fail . . .
Tristan did not go slowly!
Behind the altar, he went to the window,
pulled it towards him with his right hand
and, through the opening, he leapt out . . .
Lords, a great wide stone
projected from the middle of this crag.
Tristan leapt from it very lightly.
The wind was puffed up inside his clothes
and kept him from falling heavily.
The Cornishmen still call
this stone 'Tristan's leap' . . .
Tristan leapt: the sand was soft . . .
The others waited for him before the church,
but in vain: Tristan had gone away!
God has done him a fine act of grace.
On the shore, with great leaps, he fled.
He clearly heard the fire which crackled!
He did not have the will to go back:
He could not run faster than he ran . . . '

We find the same impulse towards heroic acts among the clergy, especially among the monks. The Irish taught medieval religious high deeds of asceticism and the rapture of mortifications. The saints, who were the successors of the martyrs of the earliest times, were the 'athletes of Christ'. Their exploits too were chiefly physical ones. Art, too, sought to display prowess, through a finicky treatment of objects in detail or extravagance in building, which ever-increasingly opened out the walls to make windows or went higher or bigger. The Gothic artist worked towards the exploit. A frequently expressed habit of thinking embodied the warrior vision and dualistic simplicity together. This was thinking by way of the opposition between two adversaries. For men of the middle ages, the whole of one's moral life was a duel between good and evil, between the virtues and the vices, the soul and the body. Prudentius in his *Psychomachia* had made the vices and virtues fight each other. Both the work and the theme enjoyed a singular success in the middle ages. The virtues became knights and the vices became monsters.

V

All this exaltation was a quest. To escape from this empty, delusive and ungrateful world was what medieval society, high and low, ceaselessly attempted to do. To go and recover the hidden truth (*verità ascoza sotto bella menzogna*, Dante, *Convivio*, II, 1) on the other side of deceitful earthly reality was the major preoccupation of the men of the middle ages. Medieval art and literature were full of *integumenta* or veils, and intellectual or aesthetic progress in the middle ages was above all an unveiling.

Hence there was a constant recourse to those who could provide forgetfulness or create an escape. There were aphrodisiacs and stimulants, love-philtres, spices and potions to cause hallucinations for all tastes and for all purses. Village witches provided them for peasants and merchants, and physicians provided them for knights and rulers. Everyone was in search of visions and apparitions and they were often favoured with them. The Church, which disapproved of these magical methods, recommended other ones. According to it, every important action should be prepared for with prolonged fasts (usually lasting three days), with ascetic practices, and with prayers which created the necessary void for the arrival of inspiration and grace. The life of men in the middle ages was haunted by dreams. Dreams which warned, revealed, and instigated, they were the very weft of the life of the mind, as well as its stimuli. The innumerable dreams of biblical figures which sculpture and painting rivalled in depicting were perpetuated in every man and woman in medieval Christendom.

Whence come dreams? [asks the pupil in the *Elucidarium*] Sometimes from God, when it is a case of a revelation of what is to come, as when Joseph learned from the stars that he would be preferred to his brothers, or of a necessary warning, as when the other Joseph learned that he had to flee to Egypt. Sometimes they come from the devil, when it is a case of a shameful vision or of an incitation to evil, as when we read in the Passion of our Lord concerning the wife of Pilate. Sometimes they come from the man himself, when he pictures in a dream what he has seen, heard, or read, and receives from it fear if it concerns sad things and hope if it concerns cheerful ones.

All levels of society dreamed. The king of England, Henry I, saw in a dream the three estates of his people in revolt against him, the monk Gunzo received in a dream the numerical specifications for the rebuilding of the church of Cluny, Helmbrecht's father observed in a dream the stages of his son's tragic fate. There were suspect dreams, too, inspired by the devil. In the Life of St Marie d'Oignies by Jacques de Vitry, the devil appeared to the saint and said to her: 'My name is dream. In fact I appear to many people in dreams and above all to monks and religious, as Lucifer; they obey me, and under the impact of my consolations, they let themselves be exalted and go so far as to believe that they are worthy of having dealings with the angels and the divine powers.' Dreaming was knowledge. 'On the third night, Iseult dreamed that she was holding in her lap the head of a great boar which was staining her dress with blood, and she knew from this that she would never see her lover alive again.'

VI

In addition to these magical attitudes and feelings, other structures appeared and evolved, especially within and through the agency of the towns where developments were more rapid. Already noticeable in the twelfth century, these changes seem to have won the day in the thirteenth century. Of course we shall recall, with Claude Lévi-Strauss, that 'magical thought was not a beginning, a commencement, an outline, a part of a whole not yet realized; it formed a properly articulated system, independent, in this regard, of that other system which was to constitute science . . . '. In fact, however, the two systems did not merely cohabit in medieval society, often in the same men, but, in spite of resistance, tension, and incoherency, the new system permeated and progressively destroyed the old one. We should also observe that the outlook of the historian of civilizations in the face of these changes in mentalities and feelings is necessarily different from that of historians of philosophy and spirituality, who are searching for the stable foundation of a faith in these transformations. Even where their analyses are as luminous, as penetrating, and as sensitive to developments as are those of Père Chenu or Père de Lubac, which have deepened historical understanding, they are dependent on a *parti pris* (in the best sense of the phrase). One must distance oneself from this to try to cast a light on the intellectual history of the middle ages which is perhaps less 'affectionate', but which has the advantage, from being placed at a distance, of making certain proportions and relations emerge better. When, at the start of his fine work *La théologie au douzième siècle*, Père Chenu wrote, 'Our understanding of the twelfth century has been distorted by the rationalist prejudices of Enlightenment philosophy . . . we should firmly maintain against this philosophy and its adherents that symbolic methods of religious expression have at least as much importance and certainly more Christian efficaciousness than dialectical methods' (Chenu, 1957, p. xix). One should answer that 'Christian efficacy' cannot be the historian's term of reference. In spite of its excesses, its lack of understanding, its naïvetés, its errors, Enlightenment philosophy had the merit (though admittedly one must subtract the value-judgements which it incorporated) of pointing out that the 'symbolic methods of religious expression' already belonged to the past in the twelfth century, whereas the 'dialectic methods' represented the mental and intellectual mechanism of the future, while waiting to yield ground to other 'novelties'.

The first novelty in this area in the twelfth century, as we have seen, was the perfection of a new intellectual machinery by men who themselves were 'new', the masters of the urban schools which became the universities. This intellectual machinery constituted itself out of a physical tool, the book. We must not be deceived in this: the university book was quite different from the monastic book. This is not to say that the latter had not been a cultural tool. The great history of monastic culture – as depicted, for example, by Dom Jean Leclercq – suffices to bear witness to the role of the book in this cultural system. However, the monastic book, even including its spiritual and intellectual functions, was first and foremost a treasure. The university book was chiefly a tool. In spite of the efforts made in technique – cursive writing, which was less careful and faster; the great increase in the number of copies through the *pecia* system; the absence of miniatures, or having illustrations where they existed – mass produced books remained expensive until the arrival of printing. One may recall the sixth-century miracle of St Benedict saving the blade of a sickle from sinking. To this miracle corresponds one of St Dominic in the thirteenth century – a new age and new tools: 'One day when St Dominic was crossing a river on the outskirts of Toulouse, his books fell into the water. Then, three days later a fisherman, having cast his line in this place, thought that he had caught a heavy fish, and he pulled the saints' books out of the water, as intact as if they had been carefully kept in a cupboard.' It was not the case, however, that St Dominic succumbed to a new fetishism for the book, which not all university teachers were to avoid. He knew how to restrict the role of the book to its auxiliary function. The *Golden Legend* also bears witness to this: 'When he was asked which was the book which he had most studied, he replied, "The book of charity".'

It is symptomatic, however, that the mendicant orders themselves adapted with difficulty to this new role of the book. St Francis was very distrustful towards intellectual culture because he always considered it to be a treasure and because the economic value of books seemed to him to be in contradiction with the practice of poverty which he wanted for his brothers. A great figure in the order of the Preaching Friars in the thirteenth century, Cardinal Humbert of Romans, was indignant to see the book becoming utilitarian and no longer the object of attentive care. 'Just as the bones which are the relics of the saints are conserved with so much reverence that they are wrapped in silk and enclosed in gold and silver, it is damnable to see books which contain so much sanctity kept with so little care.'

In fact, the change in the function of the book was only a particular instance of a more general development, which diffused the use of the written word and above all recognized that it had a new value, as proof. The ordeal, which was banned by the Fourth Lateran Council in 1215, was gradually replaced by written evidence, which threw justice into confusion. In his *Coutumes de Beauvaisis* in the late thirteenth century, Philippe de Beaumanoir in listing categories of proof placed proof 'by letters' in second place after the direct knowledge of the case by the judge, ahead of proof 'by pledge of battle', that is to say by trial by combat, of which he remarked, 'of all the types of proof this is the most dangerous'. Furthermore, he stressed that in cases of proof by letters one should accord as little importance as possible to mortal witnesses – in opposition to what had been the case in the past, 'whence it figures that the letters are valid in themselves and this is in fact the case'. Here too one notices during this transition period the difficulty which people had in adapting to the new function of the written word. The archdeacon summoned to give evidence in the Orly case in 1252 spoke of the 'ancient rolls' which he had seen in the chapter's library more as proofs in themselves by function of their antiquity than by reason of their contents.

In fact, this was the time when customs were generally being written down, when charters were rapidly increasing in number, and when feudal law, like Roman law and canon law, was being embodied in treatises. The traditional society of hearsay and oral tradition was slowly becoming used to handle, if not to read, the written word, just as it had served an apprenticeship in handling money in economic life. In all areas equipment was being renewed. Just as in the case of the technical innovations in the economic field, novelties in the cultural domain did not occur without resistance for, besides the reserve of the traditionalist circles, here too there was opposition from the lower classes to the ruling classes appropriating the new skills which sometimes strengthened seigneurial exploitation. Sometimes the charter guaranteed the rights of the lord more than those of the peasants and it was to be as much detested as the mill or the manorial oven. From now on the destruction of archives and inventories (later known as *terriers*), was to be one of the essential gestures in revolts.

The desacralizing of the book was accompanied by a 'rationalization' of intellectual methods and of mental mechanisms. Not that it was a case of putting the object of the examination and the search in question. Critiques, which were increasingly numerous on the subject of relics, for example (such as the well-known treatise by Guibert de Nogent, who however was not very progressive, from the early twelfth century) did not put the efficacity of relics in question. They simply strove to set aside the false relics which were becoming more and more common because of the crusades and the development of the financial needs of churches. On a deeper level, the scholastic method did not put faith in question. On the contrary, it originated from the wish to illumine, discern, and understand this faith better. It was the development of the famous formula of St Anselm, *Fides quaerens intellectum*, faith itself seeking understanding. Even so, the methods implemented to this end represented a real transformation in mental attitudes. At the higher level of theology, Père Chenu has clearly shown all that the action of transforming itself into a 'science', as it did in the thirteenth century, signified for theology.

VII

It would be presumptuous to try to define the scholastic method in a few lines. In its origins it had evolved through the development from the *lectio* to the *questio* and from the *questio* to the *disputatio*. The scholastic method firstly generalized the old process of *questiones* and *responsiones*, of questions and answers, which was used mainly with respect to the Bible. But posing problems and putting authorities 'into questions' in the plural led to putting them 'into question' in the singular. Scholasticism in this early period was the foundation of a problematic. Later it evolved into a debate, a 'dispute', as recourse to reasoning became of increasing importance as against the argument purely from authority. Finally the dispute culminated in a *conclusio* given by the master. Of course this conclusion could suffer from the personal limitations of the man who pronounced it, and since the university masters had a tendency to set themselves up as authorities, the conclusion could be a source of intellectual tyranny. But these abuses were unimportant; what mattered was that the system forced the intellectual into a particular alignment. He could not be content with questioning, he had to commit himself. The result of the scholastic method was that the individual had to affirm himself in his intellectual responsibility.

How far some of them went beyond this moderate use of scholasticism it is hard to know. The condemnations of 1270 and 1277 seem to allude not only to the '*Averroists*', who, under the influence of masters such as Siger of Brabant, are supposed to have professed a doctrine of the 'double truth', which dangerously separated faith from reason, but also to real agnostics. It is difficult to find out their true opinions, or how many they were, or what their audience was. Indeed, any trace seems to have been wiped out by ecclesiastical censure, but that means merely that their influence was probably limited to rather narrow university circles. In thirteenth-century literature characters appear who are presented as altogether misbelieving or unbelieving. Here too it does not seem that the 'atheists' were more than isolated cases.

One can measure the refinement produced in intellectual equipment by the development of scholasticism in three areas. The first was the more subtle use of authorities, as perfected in Abelard's famous work, the *Sic et Non*, a true *Discours de la méthode* of the middle ages. Firstly the method involved trying to eliminate the apparent divergences between authorities. According to Père Chenu's summary, a check had to be made to see if this disagreement did not arise from the use of words in an unusual sense or with different meanings, from inauthentic works, or corrupt texts, from passages where the author was a simple reporter of someone else's opinions, or in which he was adapting himself to current ideas, from sentences where he was speaking not in a dogmatic way but by way of exhortation, counsel, or dispensation, or from the variety of senses of the word according to the different authors. Finally, if the disagreement seemed irreducible, one should follow the best qualified authority.

The *disputatio* helped minds to get used to the coexistence of different opinions, to recognize the legitimacy of diversity. Of course the ideal remained that of unity, concord, and harmony. Gratian proclaimed in his *Decretum* that he was seeking the *concordantia discordantium canonum*, the agreement between the discordant canons. He was a symphonist. Yet this symphony was born out of polyphony. 'If you look at the beauty and the magnificence of the universe,' wrote William of Auvergne, 'you will discover that the universe is like a very fine hymn and that the creatures, by their variety, sing in unison and make a harmony of a supreme beauty.'

Finally, men were decreasingly afraid of modernity. As early as the beginning of the twelfth century John Cotton was asserting in his *De Musica* that the modern musicians 'were more subtle and sagacious, for, according to the saying of Priscian, the younger one is, the more perspicacious one is'. In his mediocre *Sentences*, Peter Lombard inserted what his contemporaries referred to as 'profane novelties', *profanae novitates*, and William of Tocco, Thomas Aquinas' biographer, praised him for his innovations: 'Friar Thomas posed new problems in his lecture-courses, discovered new methods, and employed new systems of proofs'.

In the search for new proofs, the scholastics, or at least some of them, developed the use of observation and experimentation. The name most often cited is that of Roger Bacon, who seems to have been the first to have employed the term *scientia experimentalis*. He disdained the Parisian masters, who were too dogmatic, with the exception of Pierre de Maricourt, author of a *Treatise on the Magnet*, whom he called 'the master of the experiments'; he contrasted them with the masters of Oxford, who were instructed in the sciences of nature. In fact the Oxford masters were and remained chiefly mathematicians, and this reveals the difficulties which medieval intellectuals had in establishing organic relations between theory and practice. The reasons for this are numerous, but the social evolution of the university masters bore much of the responsibility for the semi-failure of these attempts. Scholasticism at its birth had tried to establish a link between the liberal and the mechanical arts, between science and technology. The university men, by placing themselves in the social classes which were ashamed of manual work, made this attempt miscarry. In some fields the divorce between theory and practice had serious consequences. Physicists preferred Aristotle to experiments, physicians and surgeons preferred Galen to dissections. It was the prejudices of the teachers, even more than the reluctance of the Church, which held up the practice of dissection and progress in anatomy, which had in fact had promising beginnings at Bologna and Montpellier around 1300. In their turn the humanists were to live out these inner contradictions.

VIII

However, while they were asserting their grip on nature and acquiring a growing assurance towards the world, the men of the twelfth and thirteenth centuries found new depths in themselves. Spiritual life was growing inwards. A pioneer front was opening up in men's consciences and scholastic questions were getting extended into cases of conscience. Traditionally the merit for this great reversal in psychology and sensibility has been given to Abelard, but it actually resulted from profound changes in what Alphonse Dupont called the 'collective mentality'. Man had sought the measure and the punishment or reward of his faults and his merits outside himself. The penitentials inflicted punishments on him which were equivalent to fines. When he had paid, he was reconciled with God, the Church, society, and himself. From now on regret and contrition (scrupulous souls went as far as remorse) were demanded from him, and he wanted them himself. Contrition absolved him. In the *fabliau* of the *Chevalier au barizel*, the wicked knight accepted the physical penance which consisted in filling the barrel by plunging it in the water, but as long as his heart felt no contrition the barrel remained empty. The day when he repented and shed a tear it was enough in itself to fill up the barrel. There was a lot of weeping in the middle ages, but the heroes of the *chansons de geste* had wept over the pain or the sadness which the world caused them, not those which they inspired in themselves. Gregory the Great in the late sixth century recommended tears as a sign of the reward of compunction. It was not really understood by the men of the middle ages until six centuries later.

Let us seek evidence of this refinement of sensibility, which from now on was to pay more attention to the intention than to the act, by looking at the story of an old woman in Acre at the time of King Louis' Crusade.

As they were on their way from the lodgings to the Sultan's palace Brother Yves caught sight of an old woman going across the street, with a bowl full of flaming coals in her right hand and a flask filled with water in her left. 'What are you going to do with these?' he asked her. The old woman answered that with the fire she intended to burn up paradise and destroy it utterly, and with the water she would quench the fires of hell, so that it too would be gone for ever. 'Why do you want to do that?' asked Brother Yves. 'Because,' said she, 'I don't want anyone ever to do good in the hope of gaining paradise, or from fear of hell; but solely for the love of God, who deserves so much from us, and Who will do for us all the good He can'. (Joinville, 1971, p. 274)

Just as the penitents changed, the saints changed. In addition to the traditional outward signs of sanctity, poverty and charity were increasingly demanded of them. Moral influence and apostleship counted for more than thaumaturgical or ascetic feats. The twelfth century had deepened their ideal in the mystical life. Etienne Gilson could talk about St Bernard's 'Christian socraticism', but according to André Vauchez,

The traditional saint of the twelfth century was someone who abstained, who refused, and whose sanctity presented a somewhat 'grating' aspect. The thirteenth-century saint was no less exacting towards himself than his predecessor had been, but he seems less tense to us, more smiling and in short more open and positive in his virtues. Francis' poverty was not only a refusal to possess and acquire. It was a new attitude towards the world. . . .

The saint no longer needed to be physically beautiful.

One day [say the *Little Flowers of St Francis*] when they had arrived in a village very hungry, they went to beg for bread for the love of God, according to the rule; and St Francis went into one quarter and Brother Masseo into another. But because St Francis was a man of too despicable an appearance and short of stature and because for this reason he passed for a vile little poor man among those who did not know him, he only received a few mouthfuls of dry bread; but people gave Brother Masseo, because he was a tall man of fine bearing, plenty of big, good fragments and some whole loaves.

The pessimistic Romanesque twelfth century had taken pleasure in the bestiary. The Gothic thirteenth century, which was trying its hand at happiness, turned towards flowers and men. It was more allegorical than symbolic. It was in human form that the abstractions, good and evil, of the *Roman de la Rose* (Avarice, Vieillesse, Bel Accueil, Danger, Raison, Faux-Semblant, Nature) were represented. Gothic was still full of phantasy, but it conformed more to the bizarre than to the monstrous. Above all, it became moral. Iconography became a lesson. The active and the contemplative lives and the virtues and vices in human form, placed in order, decorated the doorways of cathedrals and furnished preachers with the illustration of their moral teachings. Admittedly, clerics had always assigned art an edifying role. 'Painting has three ends,' said Honorius of Autun. The first of these was a catechetic aim, for painting was 'the literature of the laymen'; the two other aims were the aesthetic and the historical. Already in 1025 the Council of Arras was asserting, 'The illiterate contemplate in paintings what they cannot see through writing.' But the main intention was to impress and even to frighten. From now on everything was *moralisé* or illustrated: bibles, psalters, and illustrated herbals transformed scripture and religious education into moral anecdotes. *Exempla* flourished. This development had disadvantages, too. Sensibility became insipid and religion often became childish. At the level of the vulgarizers, of Vincent of Beauvais, for example, the Gothic age appears to lack vigour. Furthermore, the more mawkish moralizing tyranny was not accepted more readily than the other tyrannies had been. The ordinances of St Louis at the end of his reign on blasphemy and gambling aroused a grieved censure even among his entourage.

IX

Yet in this period there was one feeling whose transmutation appears resolutely modern. This was love. In the more properly feudal age, with its virile, warrior society, the refinement of feelings between two beings had seemed to be confined to friendship between men; the *geste* of *Ami et Amile* being the consummate expression of this. Then courtly love came along. In a valuable book, Denis de Rougemont used it as a pretext for brilliant digressions about the west, marriage, and war, rather than elucidating the phenomenon in his own time. Writing after the appearance of a huge literature on the subject (doubtless with more to come), René Nelli has tackled the problem with knowledge, profundity, and passion. Even at the learned level, the origin of courtly love remains obscure. What does it owe to Muslim poetry and civilization? What links did it have with Catharism? Was it the heresy which Alexander Denommy saw it as? (He identified courtly love, perhaps too quickly, with Andreas Capellanus' treatise *De arte honeste amandi*, written in about 1185; in 1277 Etienne Tempier, with his habitual simplism, drew a few shocking propositions from this treatise to condemn them, mixed up with Thomism, Averroism, and several other doctrines, among the most advanced of the time, of which he disapproved.) On the level of interpreting courtly love, discussion is still continuing. Whereas many used to insist on the 'feudal' character of this concept of love, apparently inspired by the relations between a lord and his vassal, with the lord here being a lady, in an act of revenge by the fair sex, others, whom I am happier to follow, saw in it a form of revolt against the sexual morality of the same feudal world.

It is evident that courtly love was antimatrimonial, and marriage was, indeed, the favourite area for producing a conflict which aimed at revolutionizing not only morals but also feelings. There was certainly a real novelty in laying claim to the autonomy of feeling and in maintaining that other relations could exist between the sexes than those of instinct, force, interest, and conformity. Why should it be astonishing that it was the nobility of southern France which was the terrain on which this battle was joined? The southern French nobility was equivocal in all its circumstances. Its contradictions became striking in its attitude towards Catharism, which, however, it embraced for other reasons. It was a more cultivated nobility with finer sensibilities than the barbarous feudal lords in the north of France, but it was losing steam faced with a world where all the technical innovations were being born and diffused in the north, and thus it was uncertain. Yet was courtly love really Provençal love? Was not the finest courtly love story that of Tristan and Iseult, who belong to the *'matière de Bretagne'*?

It is still the case that, apart from this protest and this revolt, courtly love was able to find a marvellous balance between the soul and the body, heart and mind, sex and sentiment. Beyond the tawdriness of the vocabulary and ritual which make it a phenomenon of its time, beyond the mannerism and the abuse of courtly scholasticism, and, of course, the silliness of modern troubadours, it remains the imperishable gift which, out of all the mortal forms which it created, a civilization has bequeathed to human sensibility. To quote from it would be ridiculous: one must read it:

Lords, do you wish to hear a fine tale of love and of death?

and then, in addition:

In joy I have my hope, / in a fine heart and a firm will.

X

Perhaps the most important of the changes revealed to us by medieval art are the arrival of realism or naturalism, and the emergence of a new way of looking at the world, a new system of values. From now on the eye halted at the physical appearance, and the perceptible world, instead of being merely a symbol of the hidden reality, acquired value in itself and was an object of immediate delight. In Gothic art the flowers are real flowers, human features are individual features, the proportions are those of physical measurements and not of symbolic meanings. Of course, this desacralizing of the universe was an impoverishment in one way, but it also spelled freedom. In any case, as early as the Romanesque period, artists had often had aesthetic preoccupations closer to heart than ideological imperatives. One should not push the symbolic interpretation of medieval art too far. Very often artists were guided purely by a sense for beautiful forms and their chief worry was technical exigencies. Ecclesiastical patrons imposed a theme, and the men who were to carry it out found their freedom within the framework traced out for them. Medieval symbolism sometimes only exists in the mind of modern commentators, pseudo-learned men clouded by a conception of the middle ages which is partly mythical. In spite of the weight of ecclesiastical propaganda, many people probably succeeded in escaping from the stifling magical atmosphere in which they were surrounded. It is significant that many medieval works of art are sufficient in themselves without our having to possess the keys to their symbolic meaning. Most of the works of art (should one say the finest ones?) of the middle ages are able to move us purely by their forms, like the charming sirens who make us wish to forget that they represent evil. Feeling emerged slowly in the Gothic age from the forest of symbols into which it had been plunged by the early middle ages. If one looks at the miniatures which adorn Herrad of Landsberg's *Hortus Deliciarum* of the mid-twelfth century (copies, alas, of the originals, which were destroyed in 1870), one is dealing with a reaper, a ploughman, and a puppeteer. The artist has visibly set himself to represent scenes, people, and tools for themselves. Only rarely do details (a tiny angel, relegated to a corner of a miniature) remind us that the subject is the Gospel parable of the good grain and the tares, or man condemned to work after the Fall, or Solomon viewing the universe like a marionette theatre and crying out 'Vanity of vanities, all is vanity'. On the contrary, everything in the work of art tells us that the artist takes the perceptible world seriously, indeed, that he takes pleasure in it. The withering away of symbolism, or at any rate the fading away of symbolism before perceptible reality, shows a deep change in sensibility. Man, reassured, contemplates the world as God did after Creation, and finds that it is good. Gothic art is confidence.

XI

Before they arrived there, medieval men had to struggle (and the conflict was not over in the thirteenth century) against a widespread impression of insecurity. Their great uneasiness came from the fact that beings and things were not in reality what they appeared to be. What the middle ages most disliked was lying. The description of God's nature was 'he who never lies'. Wicked people were liars. 'You are a liar, Ferrando de Carrion,' Pero Bermuez accused the Infante, and the Cid's other companion, Martin Antolinez, told the other Infante to his face, 'Shut your mouth, liar, mouth without truth.' The whole of society was made of liars. The vassals were traitors, felons who disavowed their lords, imitators of Ganelon, and thence, of the great traitor who was the prototype of all traitors, Judas. Merchants were defrauders who thought of nothing save deceiving and stealing. Monks were hypocrites, like the Franciscan in the *Roman de la Rose*, Faux-Semblant. Medieval vocabulary was extraordinarily rich in words for designating innumerable types of lie and infinite varieties of liars. Even the prophets could be pseudo-prophets, and their miracles false miracles, works of the devil. Medieval man's grip on reality was so weak that he had to use trickery to prevail. We might imagine that this warlike society stormed everything by attack. This is the supreme illusion. Techniques were so mediocre that the defenders almost always prevailed over the offence. Even in the military domain, the castles and walls were almost impregnable. When an attacker forced an entry, it was almost always by a ruse. The total number of the goods placed at the disposal of medieval mankind was so insufficient that in order to live one had to make shift. He who had neither strength nor trickery was condemned almost certainly to perish. Who was sure and who was he who was sure? Out of all the huge oeuvre of St Augustine, the middle ages ensured a future for the treatise *De mendacio*, 'On Lying'.

XII

But what could one do in the face of vanishing realities other than clutch at appearances? For all that the Church urged medieval people to disregard and despise them and to seek the true, hidden, riches, medieval society was a society of outward show in its behaviour and its attitudes. The chief form of outward show was the body, which had to be humbled. Gregory the Great referred to it as 'this abominable garment of the soul'. 'When man dies, he is cured of the leprosy of the body,' said St Louis to Joinville. The monks, the model of medieval mankind, never ceased to humble the body by means of ascetic practices; monastic rules limited baths and care for one's appearance, which were an effeminate luxury. To the hermits, filth was a virtue. Baptism was supposed to wash a Christian once and for all in a literal as well as in a metaphorical sense. After work, nakedness was a punishment for sin; Adam and Eve after the Fall and Noah after his drunkenness displayed their immodest and sinful nakedness. In any case, nakedness was a sign of heresy and godlessness, and in every heretic there was, effectively, a son of Adam. It is odd to notice that here too St Francis of Assisi, who often bordered on heresy, was inclined to go against the grain and turn nakedness into a virtue. Poverty was nakedness, and it crossed over into actions, symbolic but real ones; in an unusual episode in the *Little Flowers of St Francis* we see St Francis and Friar Rufinus preaching stark naked from the pulpit at Assisi.

However, the warrior ideal exalted the body as much as the Christian ideal disparaged it. The young heroes in the *chansons de geste* had white skins and blond, curly hair. They were athletes.

> He had a broad back and a body in proportion
> Broad shoulders and a wide chest, he was strongly built
> Big, powerful arms and huge wrists,
> A long and graceful neck.

The whole of a knight's life consisted of exalting the physical: hunting, war, and tournaments were his passions. Charlemagne took pleasure in bathing naked with his companions in the pool at the palace in Aachen. Even as a corpse the body was the object of care and attention. Saints' bodies were venerated and their translation ratified canonization. St Clare of Montefalco, who died in 1308, appeared to a nun and told her 'My *body* must be canonized.' Medieval people, whose sight – an intellectual sense – developed only belatedly (we may recall that spectacles were only invented late in the thirteenth century), chiefly employed the most physical of the senses, the sense of touch. They were all doubting Thomases. To preserve the bodies of great people when they died, mercury was instilled into the nose; then the natural orifices were sealed with wadding soaked in sweet-smelling substances which were thought to prevent corruption, and the face was embalmed. When the body had to be transported over a distance, the intestines were cut out and buried separately, and the body was filled with myrrh, aloes, and other aromatic substances, and then sewn up. Religion promised the resurrection of the body.

To judge from the penitential literature, the number of bastards, the resistance of the clergy to the obligation of celibacy, and the allusions and even specific references in the fabliaux, medieval people's sex lives were little preoccupied with the exhortations of the Church.

Hygiene made progress and the towns must have played a pioneer role here, too. In 1292 at least 26 bath-houses existed in Paris. Hot baths were, moreover, places of pleasure, even of dissolute behaviour. Here is a description of the baths at Erfurt in the thirteenth century:

You will find the baths of this town very pleasant. If you need to wash and you
like your comforts, you can enter with confidence. You will have an agreeable
welcome. A pretty young girl will massage you absolutely in all good faith with her
soft hands. An expert barber will shave you, without letting the smallest drop of
sweat fall on your face. When you are tired from the bath you will find a bed to
rest on. Then a pretty woman of virginal appearance, who will not displease you,
will tidy your hair skilfully with a comb. Who would not kiss her, if he wishes
to and she puts up no resistance? When you are asked for payment, a single penny
will be enough. . . . !

Monastic writings, besides, provided their own contribution to the care of
the body. An unusual Alsatian manuscript of 1154 contains a manual on
dietetics written by a nun of Schwarzenthann and illustrated by Sintram, a
regular canon at Murbach. It is a calendar which indicates the regime to be
followed for each month. In the early thirteenth century, a *Guide to Health*
written at Salerno had a widespread circulation.

Medieval society was, as we have seen, obsessed by food. The mass of
the peasantry had to be content with little. Broth was the basis of its meals,
and often the main accompaniment was vegetables or fruits which had
been gathered. However, during the twelfth and thirteenth centuries the
companagium, or bread eaten as an accompaniment, became widespread among
all social classes, and it was at this point in the west that bread truly took
on an almost mythical significance, which was sanctioned by religion. The
peasant class did have one great feast: in December they killed their pigs and
the produce from this provided food for the feasts at the end of the year and
for the meals through the long winters. The pig-killing was enthroned in art
in pictures of the labours of the months.

Meals gave the ruling classes their chief opportunity to show their superiority
in this essential area of appearances. Ostentatious eating was the main luxury.
The produce unavailable to others was laid out: game from the seigneurial
forests, precious ingredients – spices – bought at a high price, and the unusual
dishes prepared by the cooks. Feasting scenes figure prominently in the
chansons de geste. The description of the departure of William of Orange's
expedition against the Saracens in *Le charroi de Nîmes* is instructive.

They took 300 pack-horses with them. I shall tell you what the first 100 carried: golden
chalices, missals and psalters, copes, crucifixes and censers; when they arrived in the
ravaged country they would give homage first of all to God. I can also tell you what
the next hundred carried: vessels of pure gold, missals and breviaries, and crucifixes
and fine linen; when they arrived in the pagan land, they would serve Jesus, the pure
spirit. I can tell you also what the last 100 were carrying: pots and frying-pans, cauldrons
and trivets, twisted hooks, tongs and andirons. When they came to the ravaged land,

they would be well able to prepare food, they would serve William the warrior, and with him all his knights.

Thus the chivalric ostentation, which was gastronomic, matched the ecclesiastical ostentation, which consisted of liturgical treasures. But the great lords of the Church were not slow to take part in abundant eating. Roger Dion has shown the important role played by abbeys and bishops in creating the medieval vineyard. 'Most of our bishops,' wrote the Chartrian William of Conches indignantly in the twelfth century, 'ransack the world to find tailors or cooks capable of making cunningly seasoned sauces. . . . As for those who devote themselves to learning, they flee from them as from lepers. . . . ' The lord's table was also an opportunity to display and to determine etiquette. The Welsh epics, the Mabinogion, reflect these customs, which had been perfected by French lords. Thus we find in *Pwyll, Prince of Dyved*: 'After they had washed, they seated themselves at table . . . the room was made ready and they seated themselves at table: Heveydd Hen sat on one side of Pwyll, Rhiannon on the other, and after them, each according to his rank.' In the depiction of vices, gluttony (*gula*) was the prerogative of the lords. However, gastronomy was to develop with the urban bourgeoisie. The earliest cookery books appeared in the middle of the thirteenth century in Denmark, and in the fourteenth and fifteenth centuries they occurred in increasing numbers in France and Italy, and then in Germany.

Finally, the body provided medieval society with one of its principal means of expression. We have already observed how people counted on their fingers. Medieval civilization was one of gestures. All the essential contracts and oaths in medieval society were accompanied by gestures and were made manifest by them. The vassal put his hands between those of his lord and spread them on the Bible; he broke a straw or threw down a glove as an act of defiance. Gestures had meaning and committed people. They were even more important in the liturgy. Signs of the cross were gestures of faith; joined hands, raised hands, hands outstretched in a cross, veiled hands were gestures of prayer. Beating one's breast was a gesture of penitence. The laying on of hands and signs of the cross were gestures of benediction. Censing was a gesture of exorcism. The ministration of sacraments culminated in a few gestures. The celebration of mass was a series of gestures. The pre-eminent literary genre of feudal society was the *chanson de geste*: the words *gesta* and *gestus* are related to each other.

The fact that gestures meant so much was of crucial importance for medieval art. Gestures gave it life, made it expressive, and gave it a sense of line and movement. Churches were gestures in stone, and God's hand emerged from the clouds to guide medieval society.

XIII

Clothing was of even greater social significance. It designated each social class and amounted to a uniform. To wear the clothes of a social condition other than one's own was to commit the serious sin of ambition or of derogation. The *pannosus*, the beggar dressed in rags, was despised. This was the term contemptuously used of St Yves, in the early fourteenth century, by those who despised him. The *leitmotiv* of *Meier Helmbrecht*, the story of the ambitious man who ends up as an outcast, is the embroidered bonnet, like the ones worn by lords, which Helmbrecht wears out of vanity. Monastic rules carefully laid down what clothing was to be worn, more out of respect for order than out of anxiety to prevent ostentation. It was necessary to wait for the eremitical orders of the eleventh and twelfth centuries, notably the Cistercians, to see monks adopt white, undyed garments as a sign of reform. The white monks set themselves up against the black monks, the Benedictines. The mendicant orders were to go further and wear frieze, an unbleached fabric. These were the grey monks. Each new social class was eager to give itself a costume. Guilds did this, first and foremost the guild of masters and scholars or university. Special attention was paid to accessories such as hats and gloves which determined rank more precisely. University doctors wore long gloves of chamois leather and birettas. Knights reserved spurs for themselves. Although it may seem curious to us, medieval armour was too functional to constitute a true uniform, but knights, in creating the nobility, added armorial bearings to their helmets, their mail coats, their shields, and swords. The coat of arms was born.

Ostentation in dress was flaunted by the rich. It was manifested partly in the quality and the quantity of material – heavy, ample, and finely woven stuffs, and silks embroidered with gold. Dyes also played a part. They changed with the fashion – cloth of scarlet, linked with red dyes, whether vegetable ones such as madder or animal ones such as cochineal, gave way in the thirteenth century to perse, the range of blues and greens which was encouraged by the developing cultivation of woad (but the madder-dealers in Germany had devils painted in blue to discredit this new fashion, to fight off the competition). Then there were furs, which the Hanse went as far as Novgorod to look for, and the Genoese as far as the Crimea. For women there were jewels.

In the late thirteenth century sumptuary laws appeared, particularly in Italy and France. They were doubtless connected with the economic crisis then entering on the scene; more certainly they were connected with the changes in society which were producing parvenus, who wanted to eclipse the long-established families by their flashy display. The sumptuary laws helped to maintain social order by enforcing differences in dress. St Louis, who wanted to reconcile the preservation of the social order with religious ideals, avoided excessive luxury and also excessive simplicity in clothing and advised his entourage to do the same. At Whitsun one year in Corbeil, Joinville and Master Robert de Sorbon had an argument:

You certainly deserve a reprimand for being more richly dressed than the king, since you are wearing a fur-trimmed mantle of fine green cloth, and he wears no such thing.' 'Master Robert,' I answered, 'I am, if you'll allow me to say so, doing nothing worthy of blame in wearing green cloth and fur, for I inherited the right to such dress from my father and mother. But you, on the other hand, are much to blame, for though both your parents were commoners, you have abandoned their style of dress, and are now wearing finer woollen cloth than the king himself.' Moral of King Louis: 'You ought to dress well, and in a manner suited to your condition, so that your wives will love you all the more and your men have more respect for you. For, as a wise philosopher has said, our clothing and our armour ought to be of such a kind that men of mature experience will not say that we have spent too much on them, nor younger men say that we have spent too little'. (Joinville, 1971, p. 171)

Women's clothing grew longer and shorter according to the rhythm of economic prosperity and crisis. It grew longer in the middle of the twelfth century, to the great indignation of moralists, who found this fashion profligate and indecent, and grew shorter again in the middle of the fourteenth century. By contrast, linen clothing became more important in the thirteenth and fourteenth centuries with the growing increase in hygiene and in the cultivation of flax. Shirts came to be generally worn. Drawers appeared. Like gastronomy, the triumph of underwear was linked to the rise of the bourgeoisie.

XIV

Houses were the final way in which social differences were manifested. The peasant house was built of cob or timber; if stone was used it was only for the foundations. Usually it was no larger than a single room and had no chimney other than a hole in the roof. It was poorly furnished and equipped. The peasant did not feel tied to his house; its poverty contributed to the mobility of the medieval peasant. Towns still continued to be chiefly built of wood, and fell easily victim to fires. Fire was a great scourge in the middle ages. Rouen burnt six times between 1200 and 1225. The Church had no difficulty in persuading medieval people that they were pilgrims on this earth. Even when they stayed in one place, they rarely had the time to become attached to their houses.

This was not the case with the rich. The castle was a sign of security, power, and status. Keeps were built in large numbers in the eleventh century; anxiety for protection was overriding. Then living comforts became important. Castles were still well defended, but they allowed more room for accommodation and developed living quarters within their walls. Still, life remained concentrated in the great hall. Furniture was limited; tables were usually collapsible and once the meal was over they were put away. The basic item of furniture was the chest or coffer where clothes and tableware were stored. Metal vessels were the supreme luxury. They shone brightly and were also an economic reserve. Since the lord's life remained an itinerant one, it was necessary for him to be able to carry his baggage away with him easily. Joinville on crusade burdened himself with almost nothing save jewels and relics. Another luxury was the tapestries which were also of practical use. When they were hung up they acted as a screen and divided bedrooms. They were carried from castle to castle. They reminded this warrior race of its principal form of habitation, the tent.

Perhaps the great ladies, however, acted as patrons and strove for more elegance in interior decoration. According to Baudri de Bourgueil, the bedroom of Adela of Blois, the daughter of William the Conqueror, had its walls decorated with tapestries depicting the scenes from the Old Testament and Ovid's *Metamorphoses* and with embroideries showing the conquest of England. On the ceiling there were paintings showing the heavens with the milky way, the constellations, the signs of the zodiac, the sun, the moon, and the planets. The floor was a mosaic which displayed a map of the world with monsters and animals. The bed had a canopy supported by eight statues: philosophy and the liberal arts.

The signs of status and wealth were stone, and the towers which crowned the castle. The rich burgesses built in a similar style in the towns in imitation – '*maison forte et belle*', as people said. However, the burgess became attached to his house and furnished it. Here too he set his mark on the evolution of taste and invented comfort. Since it was the symbol of the power of an individual or of a family, the castle was often razed when its owner was conquered. In the same way the rich exile from the town saw his house destroyed or burnt – the *abattis* or *arsis* of the house.

XV

Once the basic essentials of subsistence and, for the powerful, the no less important requirements of one's standing had been satisfied, little remained for the people of the middle ages. Careless of wellbeing, they sacrificed everything, when it was in their power to do so, on outward show. Their only profound and disinterested joys were feasts and games, although among the nobility feasts were also opportunities for ostentation and advertisement.

The castle, the church, and the town acted as theatrical backdrops. It is symptomatic that the middle ages had no specialized building for the theatre. Wherever there was a centre of social life, scenes and representations were improvised. In the church, religious ceremonies were holidays, and theatre in the strict sense emerged from the liturgical drama. In the castle there was a succession of banquets, tournaments, and acts by minstrels, jugglers, dancers, and bear-leaders. In the town, trestles were put up in the squares and the '*jeux de la feuillée*' were put on. All classes of society turned family holidays into ruinous celebrations. Marriages left peasants impoverished for years and lords impoverished for months. Games had a particular fascination for this alienated society. Slaves of nature, people devoted themselves to gambling; dice were rolled on all tables. Society was imprisoned in rigid social structures, but it turned the social structure itself into a game. Chess was bequeathed to the medieval west by the east as a royal game in the eleventh century; the westerners feudalized it by humbling the power of the king, and transformed it into a mirror of society after the Dominican Jacopo da Cessole, in the thirteenth century, had taught them to 'moralize' the game. Society projected and sublimated its professional preoccupations in symbolical and magical games. Tournaments and military sports expressed the essence of knightly life, and popular festivals the being of peasant communities. The Church had to put up with being travestied in the Feast of Fools. Above all music, singing, and dancing carried all classes of society away. The whole of medieval society acted itself. Monks and clerics abandoned themselves to the tones of the Gregorian chant, lords to profane modulations (the *Klangspielereien* of the jongleurs and the Minnesänger), and the peasants to the onomatopoeic verse of the charivari. Again, it is Augustine who has defined this medieval joy; it was jubilation, 'cries of joy without words'. Thus, in spite of calamities, violence, and dangers the men of the middle ages found forgetfulness, security, and release in the music which surrounded their civilization. They rejoiced.

Bibliography

Note by the translator

This bibliography has been completely recast to suit the needs of an English-speaking readership; works in other languages have been cited in translations where possible. As in the original bibliography, references to works dealing with the period before 1000 are few and no references to works dealing solely with the period after 1300 are given. However, the plan of the original bibliography has been abandoned to allow a smaller number of subsections and the inclusion of a selection of primary sources in translation.

Sources in translation

Abelard: *The Letters of Abelard and Heloise*, tr. B. Radice (Harmondsworth, 1974).
Ammianus Marcellinus, *Works*, tr. J. C. Rolfe, 3 vols (rev. edn, London, 1952).
Andreas Capellanus: *Andreas Capellanus on Love*, ed. P. G. Walsh (London, 1982).
Anna Comnena: *The Alexiad of Anna Comnena*, tr. E. R. A. Sewter (Harmondsworth, 1969).
Aucassin and Nicolette and Other Tales, tr. P. Matarasso (Harmondsworth, 1971).
Benedict: *The Rule of St Benedict in Latin and English*, ed. and tr. J. McCann (London, 1976).
Bernard of Clairvaux: *Treatises I* ('Apologia to Abbot William' and 'On precept and Dispensation'), tr. M. Casey (Spencer, Mass., 1970).
Bernard of Clairvaux: *Five Books on Consideration*, tr. J. D. Anderson and E. T. Kennan (Kalamazoo, 1976).
Boethius, *The Consolation of Philosophy*, tr. V. E. Watts (Harmondsworth, 1969).
Chrétien of Troyes: *Arthurian Romances*, tr. W. W. Comfort with notes by D. D. R. Owen (London, 1914, revised 1975).
The Cid: *The Poem of the Cid*, tr. L. B. Simpson, 6th edn (Berkeley, 1970).
De diversis ordinibus: Libellus de diversis ordinibus et professionibus qui sunt in aecclesia, ed. and tr. G. Constable and B. Smith (Oxford, 1972).

Fulk of Chartres, *A History of the Expedition to Jerusalem, 1095-1127*, tr. F. R. Ryan with notes by H. S. Fink (New York, 1973).

Galbert of Bruges, *The Murder of Charles the Good*, tr. J. B. Ross (repr. Toronto, 1982).

Gregory of Tours, *The History of the Franks*, tr. L. Thorpe (Harmondsworth, 1974).

Guibert of Nogent: *Self and Society in Medieval France. The Memoirs of Guibert of Nogent, 1064-1125*, tr. J. F. Benton (New York, 1970).

Helmbrecht: *Peasant Life in Old German Epics: Meier Helmbrecht and Der arme Heinrich*, tr. C. H. Bell (New York, 1931).

Hildegard of Bingen, *Scivias*, tr. B. Hozeski (Santa Fé, New Mexico, 1986).

James I of Aragon: *The Chronicle of James I of Aragon*, tr. J. Forster, 2 vols (London, 1888).

Joinville: Joinville and Villehardouin, *Chronicles of the Crusades*, tr. M. R. B. Shaw (Harmondsworth, 1971).

Jordanes, *The Gothic History of Jordanes*, tr. C. C. Mierow, 2nd edn (Princeton, 1915).

Mabinogion, tr. J. Gantz (Harmondsworth, 1976).

Marco Polo: *The Travels of Marco Polo*, tr. R. Latham (Harmondsworth, 1958).

Odo of Deuil, *De profectione Ludovici VII in orientem*, ed. and tr. V. G. Berry (New York, 1948).

Otto of Freising: *The Deeds of Frederick Barbarossa by Otto of Freising and his Continuator Rahewin*, tr. C. C. Mierow (New York, 1953).

Otto of Freising: *The Two Cities*, tr. C. C. Mierow (New York, 1928).

Paton: *The Greek Anthology*, 5 vols (London, 1906-8).

Roland: *The Song of Roland*, tr. H. S. Robertson (London, 1972).

Suger: *Abbot Suger on the Abbey Church of St Denis and its Art Treasures*, tr. E. Panofsky, 2nd edn (Princeton, 1969).

Theophilus: *De diversis artibus / The Various Arts*, tr. C. R. Dodwell (London, 1961).

H. J. Waddell, ed. *Medieval Latin Lyrics*, 5th edn (London, 1948).

William of St Thierry, *The Golden Epistle*, tr. T. Berkeley (Kalamazoo, 1976).

General works

H. Beumann, *Karl der Grosse, Lebenswerk und Nachleben*, 4 vols (Düsseldorf, 1965-7).

A. Borst, *Lebensformen im Mittelalter* (Frankfurt am Main, 1973).

C. N. L. Brooke, *The Central Middle Ages, 962-1154* (London, 1964).

R. H. C. Davis, *A History of Medieval Europe* (London, 1957).

L. Génicot, *Contours of the Middle Ages* (London, 1967).

A. H. M. Jones, *The Later Roman Empire, 284-602*, 3 vols (Oxford, 1964).

R. Lopez et al., *Western and World Civilizations* (Boston, 1975).

R. McKitterick, *The Frankish Kingdoms under the Carolingians, 751-987* (London, 1983).

J. H. Mundy, *Europe in the High Middle Ages (1150-1309)* (London, 1973).

S. Reynolds, *Kingdoms and Communities in Western Europe, 900-1300* (Oxford, 1984).

P. Riché, *Les carolingiens* (Paris, 1983).

R. W. Southern, *The Making of the Middle Ages* (London, 1953).

J. M. Wallace-Hadrill, *The Barbarian West 400-1000*, 3rd edn (London, 1967).

France

J. Baldwin, *The Government of Philip Augustus: Foundations of French Royal Power in the Middle Ages* (Berkeley, 1986).

E. Bournazel, *Le gouvernement capétien au XIIe siècle, 1108–1180* (Paris, 1975).

G. Duby, *Histoire de France*, vol I, Le moyen age (987–1460) (Paris, 1987).

J. Dunbabin, *France in the Making, 843–1180* (Oxford, 1985).

J. Favier, *Le temps des principautés* (Paris, 1984).

E. Hallam, *Capetian France, 987–1328* (London, 1980).

E. James, *The Origins of France from Clovis to the Capetians, 500–1000* (London, 1982).

J. F. Lemarignier, *La France médiévale: institutions et société* (Paris, 1971).

J. F. Lemarignier, *Le gouvernement royal aux premiers temps capétiens, 987–1108* (Paris, 1965).

F. Lot and R. Fawtier, *Histoire des institutions françaises au moyen âge*, 3 vols (Paris, 1957–62).

J. R. Strayer, *The Reign of Philip the Fair* (Princeton, 1980).

K. F. Werner, *Les origines* (Paris, 1984).

Germany and the Low Countries

H. Fuhrmann, *Germany in the High Middle Ages, c.1050–1200* (Cambridge, 1986).

F. L. Ganshof, *La Flandre sous les premiers comtes* (Brussels, 1949).

Gebhardt, *Handbuch der deutschen Geschichte*, 9th edn, by H. Grundmann, vol. I: *Frühzeit und Mittelalter* (Stuttgart, 1970).

L. Génicot *et al.*, *Histoire de Belgique* (Tournai, 1961).

J. Leuschner, *Germany in the Later Middle Ages* (Amsterdam, 1980).

K. Leyser, *Rule and Conflict in a Medieval Society* (London, 1979).

K. Leyser, *Medieval Germany and her Neighbours, 900–1250* (London, 1982).

The British Isles

G. W. S. Barrow, *The Kingdom of the Scots* (London, 1973).

G. W. S. Barrow, *Kingship and Unity: Scotland 1000–1306* (London, 1981).

M. Chibnall, *Anglo-Norman England 1066–1166* (Oxford, 1986).

M. T. Clanchy, *England and its Rulers 1066–1272* (Oxford, 1983).

R. R. Davies, *Conquest, Coexistence and Change: Wales 1063–1415* (Oxford, 1987).

A. A. M. Duncan, *Scotland, the Making of the Kingdom* (Edinburgh, 1975).

J. Le Patourel, *The Norman Empire* (Oxford, 1976).

K. Nicholls, *Gaelic and Gaelicised Ireland in the Middle Ages* (Dublin, 1972).

A. J. Otway-Ruthven, *A History of Medieval Ireland* (London, 1968).

A. L. Poole, *From Domesday Book to Magna Carta, 1087–1216* (Oxford, 1957).

F. M. Powicke, *The Thirteenth Century 1216–1307*, 2nd edn (Oxford, 1962).

F. M. Stenton, *Anglo-Saxon England*, 3rd edn (Oxford, 1971).
W. L. Warren, *Henry II* (London, 1973).

Italy

Einaudi: *Storia d'Italia Einaudi*, vols I and II (Turin, 1972–4), and *Annali*, vol. I (Turin, 1978).
K. Hyde, *Society and Politics in Medieval Italy: the Evolution of the Civic Life 1000–1350* (London, 1973).
P. Jones, *Economia e società nell'Italia medievale* (Turin, 1980).
J. Larner, *Italy in the Age of Dante and Petrarch, 1216–1380* (London, 1980).
C. J. Wickham, *Early Medieval Italy: Central Power and Local Society 400–1000* (London, 1981).

Spain

R. Collins, *Early Medieval Spain, Unity and Diversity 400–1000* (London, 1983).
R. Collins, *The Basques* (Oxford, 1986).
A. Mackay, *Spain in the Middle Ages: from Frontier to Empire 1000–1500* (London, 1977).
R. Menendez Pidal, *The Cid and His Spain* (London, 1934).
R. Pastor de Togneri, *Conflictos sociales y estancamiento economico en la España medieval* (Buenos Aires, 1973).
C. Sánchez-Albornoz, *España. Un enigma historíco*, 2 vols (Buenos Aires, 1957).
W. M. Watt, *A History of Islamic Spain* (Edinburgh, 1965).

Scandinavia and Eastern Europe

G. Barraclough, ed. *Eastern and Western Europe in the Middle Ages* (London, 1970) [includes essays by F. Graus, K. Bosl, F. Seibt, M. M. Postan, and A. Gieysztor].
F. Carsten, 'Slavs in North-eastern Germany', *Economic History Review*, 14 (1944).
E. Christiansen, *The Northern Crusades* (London, 1980).
N. Davies, *God's Playground: A History of Poland*, vol. I, *The Origins to 1795* (Oxford, 1981).
L. Musset, *Les peuples scandinaves au moyen âge* (Paris, 1951).
P. Sawyer, *The Age of the Vikings*, 2nd edn (London, 1971).
F. D. Scott, *Sweden: The Nation's History* (Minneapolis, 1977).
A. P. Vlasto, *The Entry of the Slavs into Christendom* (Cambridge, 1970).

Political ideology

M. Bloch, *The Royal Touch* (London, 1973).
R. Folz, *The Concept of Empire in Western Europe from the Fifth to the Fourteenth Century* (London, 1959).

R. Folz, *Les saints rois du moyen age en Occident* (VIe–XIIIe siècles) (Brussels, 1984).

E. Kantorowicz, *The King's Two Bodies* (Princeton, 1957).

A. W. Lewis, *Royal Succession in Capetian France. Studies in Familial Order and the State* (Cambridge, Mass., 1981).

J. B. Morrall, *Political Thought in Medieval Times*, 2nd edn (New York, 1962).

J. Nelson, *Politics and Ritual in Early Medieval Europe* (London, 1986).

G. Post, *Studies in Medieval Legal Thought, Public Law and the State, 1100-1322* (Princeton, 1964).

S. Roberts, *Order and Dispute: an Introduction to Legal Anthropology* (Harmondsworth, 1979).

P. E. Schramm, *Herrschaftszeichen und Staatssymbolik*, 3 vols (Stuttgart, 1954).

W. Ullmann, *Principles of Government and Politics in the Middle Ages* (London, 1961).

W. Ullmann, *Medieval Political Thought*, rev. edn (London, 1970).

M. Wilks, ed. *The World of John of Salisbury*, Studies in Church History, Subsidia 3 (Oxford, 1984).

Social and economic history

General

P. Ariès and G. Duby, eds, *Histoire de la vie privée*, vol. II: *De l'Europe féodale à la Renaissance* (Paris, 1985).

B. Arnold, *German Knighthood, 1050-1300* (Oxford, 1985).

J. W. Baldwin, *Masters, Princes, and Merchants: the Social Views of Peter the Chanter and his Circle*, 2 vols (Princeton, 1970).

R. J. Bartlett, *Trial by Fire and Water* (Oxford, 1986).

R.-H. Bautier, *The Economic Development of Medieval Europe* (London, 1971).

M. Bloch, *Feudal Society*, 2nd edn (London, 1962).

M. Bloch, *Land and Work in Mediaeval Europe* (selected papers) (London, 1967).

K. Bosl, *Die Gesellschaft in der Geschichte des Mittelalters*, 3rd edn (Göttingen, 1975).

R. Boutruche, *Seigneurie et féodalité*, 2 vols (Paris, 1968-70).

C. N. L. Brooke, *The Structure of Medieval Society* (London, 1971).

V. L. Bullough and J. Brundage, *Sexual Practices and the Medieval Church* (Buffalo, 1981).

J. Bumke, *The Concept of Knighthood in the Middle Ages* (New York, 1982).

The Cambridge Economic History of Europe, I: *The Agrarian Life of the Middle Ages* (2nd edn, Cambridge, 1966), II: *Trade and Industry in the Middle Ages* (Cambridge, 1952), III: *Economic Organisation and Policies in the Middle Ages* (Cambridge, 1963).

A. Burguière *et al.*, *Histoire de la famille*, vol. I. (Paris, 1986).

F. L. Cheyette, ed. *Lordship and Community in Medieval Europe* (London, 1968).

C. M. Cipolla, *The Economic History of World Population*, 5th edn (Harmondsworth, 1970).

C. M. Cipolla, ed. *The Fontana Economic History of Europe*, I, *The Middle Ages* (London, 1972).

P. Contamine, *War in the Middle Ages* (Oxford, 1984).

G. Duby, *La société aux XIe et XIIe siècles dans la région mâconnaise* (Paris, 1953).

G. Duby, *The Early Growth of the European Economy: Warriors and Peasants from the Seventh to the Twelfth Century* (London, 1974).

G. Duby, *The Knight, the Lady and the Priest: the Making of Modern Marriage in Medieval France* (London, 1984).

G. Duby, *The Three Orders: Feudal Society Imagined* (Chicago, 1980).

T. Evergates, *Feudal Society in the Baillage of Troyes under the Counts of Champagne, 1152-1284* (London, 1975).

F. L. Ganshof, *Feudalism*, 3rd English edn (London, 1964).

A. Gasiorowski, ed., *The Polish Nobility in the Middle Ages* (Wroclaw, 1984).

J. Gaudemet, *Le mariage en Occident: les moeurs et le droit* (Paris, 1987).

J. Goody, *The Development of the Family and Marriage in Europe* (Cambridge, 1983).

A. Gurevitch, *Categories of Medieval Culture* (London, 1985).

D. Herlihy, *Medieval Households* (Cambridge, Mass., 1985).

R. Hilton, *Class Conflict and the Crisis of Feudalism. Essays in Medieval Social History* (London, 1985).

M. Keen, *Chivalry* (New Haven, Connecticut and London, 1984).

J. Kirshner and S. F. Wemple, eds, *Women of the Medieval World: Essays in Honour of J. H. Mundy* (Oxford, 1985).

W. Kula, *Measures and Man* (Princeton, 1986).

J. Le Goff, *L'imaginaire médiéval* (Paris, 1985).

J. Le Goff, *Time, Work and Culture in the Middle Ages* (Chicago, 1980).

J. Le Goff, *Your Money or your Life. Economy and Religion in the Middle Ages* (New York, 1988).

J. P. Leguay, *La rue au moyen age* (Rennes, 1984).

J. T. Noonan, *Contraception: A History of its Treatment by the Catholic Theologians and Canonists*, rev. edn (Cambridge, Mass., 1986).

J. P. Poly and E. Bournazel, *La mutation féodale X^e-XIIe siècles* (Paris, 1980).

N. J. G. Pounds, *An Economic History of Medieval Europe* (London and New York, 1974).

T. Reuter, ed. *The Medieval Nobility* (Amsterdam, 1978).

J. C. Russell, *British Medieval Population* (Albuquerque, 1948).

J. C. Russell, *Late Ancient and Medieval Population* (Philadelphia, 1958).

S. Shahar, *The Fourth Estate: A History of Women in the Middle Ages* (London, 1983).

E. Warlop, *The Flemish Nobility before 1300*, 2 parts in 4 vols (Kortrijk, 1975-76).

P. Wolff, *Histoire générale du travail*, vol. II (Paris, 1960).

Rural

B. Andreolli, V. Fumagalli, and M. Montanari, *Le campagne italiane prima e dopo il mille* (Bologna, 1985).

H. S. Bennett, *Life on the English Manor. A Study of Peasant Condition 1150-1400* (Cambridge, 1937).

J. Chapelot and R. Fossier, *The Village and the House in the Middle Ages* (London, 1985).

F. Curschmann, *Hungersnöte im Mittelalter* (Leipzig, 1900).

H. Derby, *Domesday England* (Cambridge, 1977).

R. Dion, *Histoire de la vigne et du vin en France* (Paris, 1959).

G. Duby, *Rural Economy and Country Life in the Medieval West* (London, 1968).

R. Fossier, *La terre et les hommes en Picardie jusqu'à la fin du XIIIᵉ siècle*, 2 vols (Paris, 1968).

R. H. Hilton, *A Medieval Society: the West Midlands at the End of the Thirteenth Century* (London, 1966).

E. A. Kosminsky, *Studies in the Agrarian History of England in the Thirteenth Century* (Oxford, 1956).

R. Lennard, *Rural England, 1086-1135* (Oxford, 1959).

M. Montanari, *L'alimentazione contadina nell'alto Medioevo* (Naples, 1979).

M. Montanari, *Campagne medievali. Strutture produttive, rapporti di lavoro, sistemi alimentari* (Turin, 1984).

E. Perroy, *La terre et les paysans en France aux XIIᵉ et XIIIᵉ siècles* (Paris, 1973).

W. Rösener, *Bauern im Mittelalter* (Munich, 1985).

B. H. Slicher van Bath, *An Agrarian History of Western Europe* (London, 1963).

J. Z. Titow, *English Rural Society, 1200-1350* (London, 1969).

J. Z. Titow, *Winchester Yields. A Study in Medieval Agricultural Productivity* (Cambridge, 1972).

P. Toubert, *Les structures du Latium médiéval* (Rome, 1973).

Urban

M. Beresford, *New Towns of the Middle Ages. Town Plantation in England, Wales and Gascony* (London, 1967).

E. Ennen, *The Medieval Town* (Amsterdam, 1979).

P. Francastel, ed. *Les origines des villes polonaises* (Paris and The Hague, 1960).

B. Geremek, *The Margin of Society in Late Medieval Paris* (Cambridge, 1987).

J. Lestocquoy, *Les villes de Flandres et d'Italie sous le gouvernment des patriciens* (Paris, 1952).

A. Lombard-Jourdan, *Aux origines de Paris: la genèse de la Rive droite jusqu'en 1223* (Paris, 1985).

H. A. Miskimin, D. Herlihy and A. L. Udovitch, eds, *The Medieval City* (New Haven and London, 1977).

I. Origo, *The Merchant of Prato* (London, 1957).

H. Pirenne, *Medieval Cities, their Origins and the Revival of Trade* (Princeton, 1925).

C. Platt, *The English Medieval Town* (London, 1976).

S. Reynolds, *An Introduction to the History of English Medieval Towns* (Oxford, 1977).

F. Rörig, *The Medieval Town* (London, 1967).

D. Waley, *The Italian City Republics*, 2nd edn (New York, 1969).

Commerce and technology

D. Abulafia, *Italy, Sicily, and the Mediterranean, 1100-1400* (London, 1987).

D. Abulafia, *The Two Italies: Economic Relations between the Norman Kingdom of Sicily and the Northern Communes* (Cambridge, 1977).

J. W. Baldwin, *The Medieval Theories of the Just Price* (Philadelphia, 1959).

T. N. Bisson, *Conservation of Coinage: Monetary Expansion and its Restraint in France, Catalonia and Aragon, c.1000–c.1225* (Oxford, 1979).

C. M. Cipolla, *Money, Prices, and Civilization in the Mediterranean World* (Princeton, 1956).

J. Day, ed., *Etudes d'histoire monétaire* (Lille, 1984).

R. Delort, *La commerce des fourrures en Occident à la fin du moyen âge*, 2 vols (Rome, 1978).

R. de Roover, *Money, Banking, and Credit in Medieval Bruges* (Cambridge, Mass., 1948).

P. Dollinger, *The German Hansa* (London, 1970).

G. Espinas, *Les origines du capitalisme*, vol. I: *Sire Jehan Boinebroke* (Lille, 1933).

J. Gilchrist, *The Church and Economic Activity in the Middle Ages* (London and New York, 1969).

P. Grierson, *Monnaies du moyen âge* (Fribourg, 1976).

J. Le Goff, *Marchands et Banquiers du moyen âge*, 6th edn (Paris, 1980).

A. R. Lewis, *The Northern Seas: Shipping and Commerce in Northern Europe, AD 300–1100* (Princeton, 1958).

A. R. Lewis and T. J. Runyan, *European Naval and Maritime History 300–1500* (Bloomington, Indiana, 1985).

L. K. Little, *Religious Poverty and the Profit Economy in Medieval Europe* (London, 1978).

R. S. Lopez, *The Commercial Revolution of the Middle Ages, 950–1350* (Cambridge, 1976).

R. S. Lopez, *The Shape of Medieval Monetary History* (London, 1986).

J. Needham, *Clerks and Craftsmen in China and the West* (Cambridge, 1970).

E. Power, *The Wool Trade in English Medieval History* (Oxford, 1941).

A. Sapori, *Le marchand italien au moyen âge* (Paris, 1952).

C. Singer *et al.*, *A History of Technology*, vol. II (Oxford, 1956).

L. White Jr, *Medieval Technology and Social Change* (Oxford, 1962).

L. White, Jr, *The Expansion of Technology, 500–1500* (Oxford, 1969).

The crusades and western attitudes to Islam

P. M. Holt, *The Age of the Crusades: the Near East from the Eleventh Century to 1517* (London, 1986).

B. Z. Kedar, *Crusade and Mission. European Approaches towards the Muslims* (Princeton, 1984).

B. Z. Kedar *et al.*, eds, *Outremer: Studies in the History of the Crusading Kingdom of Jerusalem Presented to Joshua Prawer* (Jerusalem, 1982).

A. R. Lewis, *The Islamic World and the West, AD 622–1492* (New York, 1970).

B. Lewis, *The Arabs in History*, 5th edn (London, 1970).

B. Lewis, *The Muslim Discovery of Europe* (London, 1982).

H. E. Mayer, *The Crusades* (London, 1972).

J. Prawer, *Crusader Institutions* (Oxford, 1980).

J. Richard, *The Latin Kingdom of Jerusalem* (Amsterdam, 1979).

J. Riley-Smith, *The First Crusade and the Idea of Crusading* (London, 1986).

L. and J. Riley-Smith, *The Crusades: Idea and Reality, 1095–1274* (London, 1981).

S. Runciman, *A History of the Crusades*, 3 vols (Cambridge, 1951-54).

K. M. Setton, *A History of the Crusades*, 5 vols, in progress (Philadelphia, 1955–   ).

E. Siberry, *Criticism of Crusading* (Oxford, 1985).

R. W. Southern, *Western Views of Islam in the Middle Ages* (Cambridge, Mass., 1962).

Heretics, Jews and the excluded

A. Borst, *Die Katharer* (Stuttgart, 1953).

J. Boswell, *Christianity, Social Tolerance and Homosexuality* (Chicago and London, 1980).

S. N. Brody, *The Disease of the Soul: Leprosy in Medieval Literature* (Ithaca, 1974).

R. Chazan, *Medieval Jewry in Northern France* (Baltimore, 1973).

N. Cohn, *The Pursuit of the Millennium*, 2nd edn (London, 1970).

N. Golb, *Les juifs de Rouen au moyen âge. Portrait d'une culture oubliée* (Rouen, 1985).

H. Grundmann, *Ketzergeschichte des Mittelalters* (Göttingen, 1963).

B. Hamilton, *The Medieval Inquisition* (London, 1981).

J. Katz, *Exclusiveness and Tolerance. Studies in Jewish–Gentile Relations in Medieval and Modern Times* (Oxford, 1961).

M. Keen, *The Outlaws of Medieval Legend*, rev. edn (London, 1977).

G. Kisch, *The Jews in Medieval Germany. A Study of their Legal and Social Status* (New York, 1970).

M. D. Lambert, *Medieval Heresy* (London, 1977).

E. W. McDonnell, *The Beguines and Beghards in Medieval Culture* (New Brunswick, 1954).

G. Marcus, *Piety and Society. The Jewish Pietists of Medieval Germany* (Leyden, 1981).

P. Michaud-Quentin, *Universitas. Expressions du mouvement communautaire dans le moyen âge latin* (Paris, 1970).

M. Mollat et al., *Histoire des hôpitaux en France* (Toulouse, 1982).

R. I. Moore, *The Birth of Popular Heresy* (London, 1975).

R. I. Moore, *The Formation of a Persecuting Society* (Oxford, 1987).

R. I. Moore, *The Origins of European Dissent* (London, 1977).

C. Morris, *The Discovery of the Individual 1050–1200* (London, 1972).

J. H. Mundy, *The Repression of Catharism at Toulouse. The Royal Diploma of 1279* (Toronto, 1985).

R. B. Pugh, *Imprisonment in Medieval England* (Cambridge, 1968).

C. Thouzellier, *Catharisme et Valdéisme en Languedoc à la fin du XIIe et au début du XIIIe siècle*, 2nd edn (Louvain and Paris, 1969).

W. Ullmann, *The Individual and Society in the Middle Ages* (London, 1966).

E. Vodola, *Excommunication in the Middle Ages* (Berkeley and Los Angeles, 1986).

W. L. Wakefield and A. P. Evans, eds, *Heresies of the High Middle Ages: Selected Sources* (New York, 1969).

The Church (institutional history)

B. Bolton, *The Medieval Reformation* (London, 1983).

R. Brooke, *The Coming of the Friars* (London, 1975).

G. Constable, *Medieval Monasticism: A Select Bibliography* (Toronto, 1976).

H. E. J. Cowdrey, *The Cluniacs and the Gregorian Reform* (Oxford, 1970).

B. Hamilton, *Religion in the Medieval West* (London, 1986).

J. Herrin, *The Formation of Christendom* (Oxford, 1987).

W. A. Hinnebusch, *History of the Dominican Order* (New York, 1966).

N. Hunt, ed. *Cluniac Monasticism in the Central Middle Ages* (London, 1971).

D. Knowles and D. Obolensky, *The Middle Ages (The Christian Centuries, vol. II)* (London, 1969).

D. Knowles, *The Monastic Order in England*, 2nd edn (Cambridge, 1963).

D. Knowles and J. St Joseph, *Monastic Sites from the Air* (Cambridge, 1952).

C. H. Lawrence, *Medieval Monasticism* (London, 1984).

L. J. Lekai, *The Cistercians: Ideals and Reality* (Kent State, 1977).

H. Leyser, *Hermits and the New Monasticism* (London, 1984).

J. R. H. Moorman, *A History of the Franciscan Order* (Oxford, 1968).

R. W. Southern, *Western Society and the Church in the Middle Ages* (Harmondsworth, 1970).

Christian spirituality, miracles, and pilgrimages

D. D'Avray, *The Preaching of the Friars: Sermons Diffused from Paris before 1300* (Oxford, 1985).

R. Finucane, *Miracles and Pilgrims: Popular Beliefs in Medieval England* (London, 1973).

P. Geary, *Furta Sacra: the Theft of Relics in the Central Middle Ages* (Princeton, 1978).

E. H. Gilson, *The Mystical Theology of St Bernard* (London, 1940).

H. Grundmann, *Religiöse Bewegungen im Mittelalter*, 2nd edn (Darmstadt, 1961).

J. Leclercq *et al.*, *The Spirituality of the Middle Ages* (New York, 1968).

J. Le Goff, *The Birth of Purgatory* (London, 1984).

J. Longère, *La prédication médiévale* (Paris, 1983).

J. Sumption, *Pilgrimage: An Image of Medieval Religion* (London, 1974).

A. Vauchez, *Les laïcs au moyen age. Pratiques et expériences religieuses* (Paris, 1987).

A. Vauchez, *La spiritualité du moyen âge occidental: VIIIᵉ-XIIᵉ siècles* (Paris, 1975).

B. Ward, *Miracles and the Medieval Mind* (London, 1982).

Learning and science

R. L. Benson and G. Constable, eds, *Renaissance and Renewal in the Twelfth Century* (Oxford, 1982).

M. D. Chenu, *Nature, Man and Society in the Twelfth Century* (Chicago, 1957).

M. Clagett, *The Science of Mechanics in the Middle Ages* (Madison, 1956).

M. T. Clanchy, *From Memory to Written Record. England 1066-1307* (London, 1979).

A. M. Cobban, *The Medieval Universities: their Development and Organisation* (London, 1975).

A. C. Crombie, *Augustine to Galileo: The History of Science AD 400-1650* (London, 1952).

P. Duhem, *Medieval Cosmology: Theories of Infinity, Place, Time, Void and the Plurality of Worlds* (Chicago, 1985).

S. C. Ferruolo, *The Origins of the University. The Schools of Paris and their Critics, 1100-1215* (Stanford, 1985).

J. M. Gellrich, *The Idea of the Book in the Middle Ages. Language, Theory, Mythology and Fiction* (Ithaca, 1985).

E. Gilson, *History of Christian Philosophy in the Middle Ages* (London, 1955).

A. Gransden, *Historical Writing in England*, vol I, *c.550 to c.1307* (London, 1974).

F. Graus, *Lebendige Vergangenheit. Überlieferungen im Mittelalter und in den Vorstellungen vom Mittelalter* (Cologne and Vienna, 1975).

C. H. Haskins, *Studies in the History of Medieval Science*, 2nd edn (Cambridge, Mass., 1927).

D. Jacquart and C. Thomasset, *Sexualité et savoir médical au moyen âge* (Paris, 1985).

E. Jeauneau, *La philosophie médiévale* (Paris, 1963).

D. Knowles, *The Evolution of Medieval Thought* (London, 1962).

N. Kretzmann et al., eds, *The Cambridge History of Later Medieval Philosophy: From the Rediscovery of Aristotle to the Disintegration of Scholasticism, 1100-1600* (Cambridge, 1982).

M. L. W. Laistner, *Thought and Letters in Western Europe, 500-900*, 2nd edn (London, 1957).

B. Lawn, *The Salernitan Questions* (Oxford, 1963).

J. Leclercq, *The Love of Letters and the Desire for God* (New York, 1974).

J. Le Goff, *Les intellectuels au moyen âge* (Paris, 1957).

H. de Lubac, *Exégèse médiévale. Les quatre sens de l'Ecriture*, 4 vols (Paris, 1959-64).

J. Marenbon, *Early Medieval Philosophy (480-1150): An Introduction* (London, 1983).

A. Murray, *Reason and Society in the Middle Ages* (Oxford, 1978).

G. Paré et al., eds, *La renaissance du XIIe siècle: les écoles et l'enseignement* (Paris and Ottawa, 1933).

J. Pelikan, *The Growth of Medieval Theology (600-1300)* (Chicago, 1978).

H. Rashdall, *The Universities of Europe in the Middle Ages*, new edn by F. M. Powicke and A. B. Emden, 3 vols (London, 1936).

B. Smalley, *Historians in the Middle Ages* (London, 1974).

B. Smalley, *The Study of the Bible in the Middle Ages*, 3rd edn (Oxford, 1983).

R. Southern, *Robert Grosseteste* (Oxford, 1986).

B. Stock, *Myth and Science in the Twelfth Century* (Princeton, 1972).

L. Thorndike, *A History of Magic and Experimental Science*, 8 vols (New York, 1913-28).

J. Verger and J. Jolivet, *Bernard-Abélard ou le cloître et l'école* (Paris, 1982).

O. Weijers, *Terminologie des universités au XIIIe siècle* (Rome, 1987).

P. Wolff, *L'éveil intellectuel de l'Europe* (Paris, 1971).

Literature

R. Boase, *The Origin and Meaning of Courtly Love. A Critical Study of European Scholarship* (Manchester, 1977).

R. R. Bolgar, *The Classical Heritage and its Beneficiaries* (Cambridge, 1954).

P. Boyde, *Dante, Philomythes and Philosopher* (Cambridge, 1981).

E. R. Curtius, *European Literature and the Latin Middle Ages* (London, 1953).

P. Dronke, *The Medieval Lyric*, 2nd edn (London, 1978).

P. Dronke, *Poetic Individuality in the Middle Ages: New Departures in Poetry 1000-1150*, 2nd edn (London, 1986).

J. de Ghellinck, *L'essor de la littérature latine au XIIᵉ siècle*, 2 vols (Brussels, 1946).

C. V. Langlois, *La vie en France au moyen âge de la fin du XIIᵉ au milieu du XIVᵉ siècle*, 4 vols (Paris, 1926-28).

J. Leclercq, *Monks and Love in Twelfth-Century France* (Oxford, 1979).

M. D. Legge, *Anglo-Norman Literature and its Background* (Oxford, 1963).

C. S. Lewis, *The Allegory of Love* (Oxford, 1936).

C. S. Lewis, *The Discarded Image: An Introduction to Medieval and Renaissance Literature* (Cambridge, 1964).

R. S. Loomis, *Arthurian Literature in the Middle Ages* (Oxford, 1959).

E. Sears, *The Ages of Man. Medieval Interpretation of the Life Cycle* (Princeton, 1986).

H. J. Waddell, *The Wandering Scholars* (London, 1927).

Art

X. Barral and I. Altet, eds, *Artistes, artisans et production artistique au moyen age*, vol. I (Paris, 1986).

K. J. Conant, *Carolingian and Romanesque Architecture, 800-1200*, 3rd edn (Harmondsworth, 1973).

K. J. Conant, *Cluny. Les églises et la maison du chef d'ordre* (Cambridge, Mass., 1968).

J. Evans, *Art in Medieval France* (Oxford, 1948).

J. Evans, *Magical Jewels of the Middle Ages and the Renaissance* (Oxford, 1922).

P. Frankl, *Gothic Architecture* (Harmondsworth, 1962).

P. Frankl, *The Gothic, Literary Sources and Interpretations through Eight Centuries* (Princeton, 1960).

L. Grodecki, *Au seuil de l'art roman: l'architecture ottonienne* (Paris, 1958).

L. Grodecki, *The Stained Glass of French Churches* (London, 1948).

L. Grodecki *et al.* eds *Le siècle de l'An Mil* (Paris, 1973).

J. Harvey, *The Gothic World 1100-1600* (London, 1950).

G. Henderson, *Chartres* (Harmondsworth, 1968).

G. Henderson, *Gothic* (Harmondsworth, 1967).

H. Kraus, *Gold was the Mortar. The Economics of Cathedral Building* (London, 1979).

G. B. Ladner, *Ad Imaginem Dei. The Image of Man in Medieval Art* (Latrobe, Pennsylvania, 1965).

G. B. Ladner, *Images and Ideas in the Middle Ages* (Rome, 1983).

E. Panofsky, *Gothic Architecture and Scholasticism* (Latrobe, Pennsylvania, 1951).

W. Sauerländer, *La sculpture gothique en France, 1140-1270* (Paris, 1972).

O. von Simpson, *The Gothic Cathedral: Origins of Gothic Architecture and the Medieval Concept of Order* (New York, 1956).

G. Zarnecki, *Romanesque Art* (London, 1971).

G. Zarnecki, *Studies in Romanesque Sculpture* (London, 1979).

Index

Numerals in bold type refer to plate numbers; the plates may be found between pp. 172 and 173, and 300 and 301.